FRIEDA LAWRENCE

The Memoirs and Correspondence

*The D. H. Lawrences at their house
in Chapala, Mexico, 1923.*

FRIEDA LAWRENCE

The Memoirs
and Correspondence

EDITED BY *E. W. Tedlock, Jr.*

NEW YORK   *Alfred A. Knopf*

1 9 6 4

L. C. catalog card number: 64–12307

THIS IS A BORZOI BOOK,
PUBLISHED BY ALFRED A. KNOPF, INC.

FIRST AMERICAN EDITION

ACKNOWLEDGMENTS

To Barbara Barr and Montague Weekley, for the letters to them, for their kind interest and co-operation, and for the use of photographs; to Elsa Seaman, for her interest and hospitality; to Else Jaffe, for the letters to her, and for her graciousness and patience in answering queries; to Angelo Ravagli, for his kind co-operation in answering numerous queries, and for his confidence and encouragement; to Mrs. John Middleton Murry, for permission to use the letters of her late husband, and for making available Frieda's letters to him; to Witter Bynner, for the letters to him, for the use of photographs, and his talk of former days; to Sir Richard Rees, for the letters to him; to Dr. T. M. Pearce for the letters to him; to the Hon. Dorothy Brett for reading and commenting on portions of the memoir; to Harry T. Moore, for furnishing copies of the letters to himself, to S. S. Koteliansky, Lady Cynthia Asquith, Henry Savage, Mrs. Juliette Huxley, Rhys Davies, and Bertrand Russell; to David Garnett, for his kindness in reading and commenting on portions of the manuscript, and for putting me on the track of the letters to himself and his father, Edward Garnett; to Erna Fergusson, and to Marcella Matson, for helpful information on the 1937–1938 sojourn in Albuquerque and the early beginnings of the memoir; to Frederick R. Jeffrey, for his response to queries; to Rachel and Bill Hawk, to Betty Cottam, Bunny Goldtrap, George Meeter, and Mark Spilka, for letting me see letters to them; to Joe Glasco, for making available a letter from him to Frieda Lawrence's children; to William York Tindall, for making available Frieda's letter to him; to Laurence Pollinger, Ltd., agent for the D. H. Lawrence Estate; to the Viking Press; to Warren

Roberts of the Humanities Research Center of the University of Texas, for continued use of the manuscripts after they had gone there; to the New York Public Library and John D. Gordan, Curator of the Henry W. and Albert A. Berg Collection, for making available and giving permission to use the letters to Edward and David Garnett; to Marjorie G. Wynne, and to Donald Gallup, Curator of the Collection of American Literature, Yale University Library, for making available the letters to Dudley Nichols, Mabel Luhan, and Dorothy Brett; to The Dial Press, Inc., for permission to reprint the Foreword by Frieda Lawrence to *The First Lady Chatterley* by D. H. Lawrence, copyright © 1964 by The Dial Press, Inc.; to the Regents of the University of Wisconsin for permission to reprint from *D. H. Lawrence: A Composite Biography* by Edward Nehls, 1957, The University of Wisconsin Press; to Patrick Gregory of the editorial department of Alfred A. Knopf, Inc., for his co-operation and skillful help in revising the book for the American edition. To my colleague at the University, Hoyt Trowbridge, for reading the manuscript and for his helpful suggestions; to the Research Committee of the University, for grants of funds without which the manuscript could not have been completed.

E. W. Tedlock, Jr.
Albuquerque, 1964

PREFACE

The companion and wife of D. H. Lawrence from 1912 to his death in 1930, Frieda Lawrence Ravagli was a remarkable person in her own right. Before this climactic period of her life, there was a formative period of great interest and significance; and after it twenty-six active years, to her death on August 11, 1956. Other men besides Lawrence discovered in her a gift for life and love, a power rarely found to vitalize their existences, to make them whole, accompanied by a fighting spirit when she felt neglect, confinement, or bullying. None ever forgot, and some, as will be seen in this book, sent her their final tribute. Heretofore the world has had only glimpses of her through Lawrence's writing, memoirs focused on him, and her own *Not I But the Wind*, published in 1934, a rather hurried attempt to clarify her life with Lawrence, prompted by the spate of views from the outside that immediately followed his death. In 1935 she began in earnest to write what may be called her final testament to the value of life and the fullness of her own destiny. Through the years, at odd moments in an active existence, she worked out her understanding of the growth of her nature and affections; the often troubled, painful steps toward her encounter with Lawrence; once more their relationship from a larger, more comprehensive perspective; and the aftermath, inevitably somewhat anticlimactic, perhaps a decline, faithful in its championship of Lawrence, acknowledging old age, yet characteristically vital in achievement of a new life.

She continually reworked her treatment of the major episodes, and sometimes changed her plan. New crises, such as World War II, had to be faced. She kept on, preferring to be read after her death, leaving extensive manuscripts in various stages of organization, none complete and final. The text of these has been edited as nearly as possible according to her most clearly indicated plan. Though sometimes continuity is tenuous and passages are somewhat fragmentary, the memoir is a complete record of her adventure, and constitutes an important human and literary document. Like her speech, the writing is simple, candid, and forceful, rising to climaxes of intense feeling and characteristic wit. Through it run the elemental force and the fierce honesty with which she responded to everyday experience and the crises of her life. Clearly, she was much more than the robust *hausfrau* or sexually uninhibited woman some critics thought her. As a young girl she developed an unusual sympathy for men, centered in her grasp of the stresses and failures and potential victories entailed by their role in the world. It becomes clear that as a young wife she wanted to be much more than the Ibsenian doll, to read and to know and to share, even to participate in, the man's work. She was attracted to men with a sense of mission, men with strong ideas about the new direction life might take from the decadence and anarchy of the post-Victorian scene. Her sympathy for and attraction to such men, and her readiness to fight for them, are at the center of her relationship with Lawrence, and steadied her at those times when their mutual battle was at its fiercest and her temptation to defect at its strongest. The demands on her extraordinary vitality were great indeed, as an occasional outburst makes clear. No doubt, too, she could be difficult, even to the point of seeming uncontrollable. The portrait offered by this material is complex indeed.

Among her papers were other things of interest and value. As she responded to interpretation of Lawrence in articles and books, especially numerous from the mid-1940's, she wrote essays and letters to editors in clarification and vindication, and forewords to various books on Lawrence, and to *The First Lady Chatterley*. Most of these, along with a few essays on other people and subjects, have been collected here. There was also correspondence of a unique kind. Her letters in German to her family dating from girlhood through her English marriage to

Ernest Weekley are presented in translation, with his letters to her and her parents during the crisis of her departure with Lawrence. Other letters have been furnished by individuals and libraries. Letters to Edward and David Garnett supplement the picture of this troubled time and its aftermath. To Lawrence's death in 1930, her letters to mutual friends illuminate their life together—the pleasures and give-and-take; the worry over his health, mental in a sense as well as physical; and the fight between them, involving his friends' recognition of her dignity and significance as a person, and her contribution to his life and work. Continuity with this central phase of her life (through the twenty-five years remaining to her) is provided by letters to her old friend and New Mexico neighbor Witter Bynner, to Dorothy Brett and Mabel Luhan, and to others whose acquaintance had begun in Lawrence's lifetime. In letters to such new friends as Dudley Nichols, she was often concerned with clarifying Lawrence's meaning. And the later letters to her son Montague Weekley, and to her sister Else Jaffe, deeply involve the beginnings. Included also are excerpts from a good many of her letters to the scholars and critics who in increasing numbers came to inquire after Lawrence; her comments contain important facts and add significant perspective. The remarkable letters from Karl von Marbahr, an early love, and John Middleton Murry clarify the nature and intensity of her affections and, in Murry's case, the challenges to her loyalty to Lawrence.

Because of space limitations and the uneven nature of the material, it has not been feasible to attempt a complete collection of the correspondence. In the English edition (Heinemann, 1961), the editor's time and attention was largely taken up with the physical task of assembling and correcting a text of the memoirs from her papers, which were in a chaotic state; expanding the correspondence, in a very short time, from the nucleus the papers contained; and providing basic notes on the life. The preparation of the American edition has provided an opportunity for reconsideration, again governed by space limitations. Because of their significance, new letters now available have been introduced. Other letters have been dropped because of repetitiveness or concern with daily minutiae which are not of central interest. In the "Essays" section are now included her forewords to *D. H. Lawrence: A Composite Biography* and to *The First Lady Chatterley*. The annotations appear at appropriate points in the text. These notes have been greatly expanded; but not, it is hoped, to the point of distracting the reader from the words of this remarkable woman about the things that were important and dear to her.

E. W. Tedlock, Jr.
University of New Mexico
December, 1963

CONTENTS

"And the Fullness Thereof . . ."

Editor's Introduction	3
Introduction	7
Leaving for South America	22
A Contretemps	30
On the Road	34
From San Antonio to New Orleans	38
Christmas at Home	41
School	47
Childhood	52
Travelling On	56
Adolescence	62
More about Buenos Aires	70
Grown Up	73
English Marriage	77
Octavio	89
Andrew	103
[After Andrew's Death]	113
On the Boat Back	122
Coming Back	124
Last Chapter—Friends	128

Correspondence

To her sister Else, *February 4, 1890*	143
" *February 21, 1898*	143

xi

To her family, *December 15, 1899* 144
To her sister Else, *December 21, 1899* 145
"   *no date* 146
"   *July 4, 1900* 147
"   *[June 18, 1901?]* 148
"   *October 5, 1901* 149
"   *November 25, 1901* 150
"   *Monday* 151
"   *no date* 152
"   *Friday* 152
"   *March 3, 1902* 153
"   *no date* 155
To her mother, *no date* 156
To her mother, from Ernest Weekley, *September 13, 1902* 156
To her sister Else, from Ernest Weekley, *September 15, 1902* 157
To her father, from Ernest Weekley, *September 16, 1902* 158
To her mother, *no date* 159
To Edgar Jaffe, *May 20, 1907* 161
From Ernest Weekley, *May 10, 1912* 162
To her father, from Ernest Weekley, *May 11, 1912* 162
To her father, from Ernest Weekley, *May 12, 1912* 163
To her mother, from Ernest Weekley, *May 13, 1912* 164
From Maude Weekley, *May 14, [1912]* 165
From Lily Kipping, *no date* 166
To Edward Garnett, *[May 1912?]* 168
"   *[July 1912?]* 168
"   *[September 1912?]* 170
"   *postscript, no date* 171
To David Garnett, *[November 1912?]* 172
"   *[December 1912?]* 174
To Edward Garnett, *[January 1913?]* 175
To David Garnett, *[February 1913?]* 177
To Edward Garnett, *[March 1913?]* 178
To David Garnett, *[March 1913?]* 179

To Edward Garnett, [*April 1913?*]   181
"   [*May 1913?*]   182
"   [*June 1913?*]   184
To David Garnett, [*August 1913?*]   185
To Lady Cynthia Asquith, *October 23, 1913*   187
To Henry Savage, *December 1913*   188
To Lady Cynthia Asquith, [*December 21, 1913*]   189
To Edward Garnett, [*February 1914?*]   189
To Bertrand Russell, *1915*   191
"   *1915*   192
To Lady Cynthia Asquith, *1915*   193
To S. S. Koteliansky, *February 9, 1915*   195
"   *February 1915*   195
"   *1915*   196
To Lady Cynthia Asquith, *October 21, 1915*   197
To Bertrand Russell, *1916*   198
To S. S. Koteliansky, *February 13, 1916*   198
"   *1916*   199
To Lady Cynthia Asquith, *1916*   200
"   [*May 24, 1916*]   201
"   *1916*   202
To S. S. Koteliansky, *September 4, 1916*   203
"   *September 20, 1916*   203
"   *October 4, 1916*   204
"   *October 15, 1916*   205
"   *November 14, 1916*   206
"   *Before December 12, 1916*   207
To Lady Cynthia Asquith, [*December 1916*]   208
To S. S. Koteliansky, *February 6, 1917*   209
"   *June 1917*   211
"   [*September 11, 1917?*]   212
"   *February 12, 1918*   212
"   *February 19, 1918*   213
To Lady Cynthia Asquith, [*Early 1919?*]   214
To S. S. Koteliansky, *February 1919*   214
To Miss C. Lambert, *December 17, 1919*   215
To Miss Violet Monk, [*January 1, 1920?*]   215

To Miss C. Lambert, *March 1, 1920*   216
From her daughter Barbara, *Tuesday*   216
To Witter Bynner, *Sunday 1923*   220
To S. S. Koteliansky, *Wednesday 1923*   221
    "   *December 4, 1923*   222
To Witter Bynner, *no date*   224
To S. S. Koteliansky, *March 1926*   224
    "   *[Postmarked August 9, 1926]*   225
To her son Monty, *Sunday*   226
To Witter Bynner, *April 22*   227
    "   *no date*   228
    "   *Easter Monday*   229
To Mrs. Juliette Huxley, *Wednesday 1928*   230
To Rhys Davies, *December 25, 1928*   230
To Mabel Luhan, *April 5, 1929*   231
To Witter Bynner, *November 10, 1929*   232
To S. S. Koteliansky, *November 26, 1929*   233
    "   *January 26, 1930*   234
To Mabel Luhan, *no date*   234
To Witter Bynner, *March 12, 1930*   235
To Mabel Luhan, *no date*   236
To Witter Bynner, *no date*   236
To Edward Garnett, *Monday*   237
To Mabel Luhan, *April 1*   237
    "   *April 28, 1930*   238
To Witter Bynner, *July 23, 1930*   239
To Sir Richard Rees, *no date*   241
    "   *no date*   242
To Witter Bynner, *May 15, 1932*   243
    "   *no date*   244
To Sir Richard Rees, *June 6*   245
From Alice Dax, *January 23, 1935*   246
To Witter Bynner, *February 28, 1935*   249
To Mabel Luhan, *[1935?]*   250
To Dorothy Brett, *no date*   251
To Angelo Ravagli, *no date*   252
    "   *December 3, 1937*   254

Contents // xv

To Angelo Ravagli, *December 21, 1937* 256
" *January 17, 1938* 259
" *January 29, 1938* 260
" *February 16, 1938* 261
" *February 19, 1938* 263
" *March 5, 1938* 265
To Witter Bynner, *March 23, 1938* 267
" *March 28, 1938* 268
To Dudley Nichols, *October 8, 1938* 269
To Witter Bynner, *December 2, 1938* 270
" *no date* 271
To Montague Weekley, *May 6, 1939* 272
" *July 13, 1939* 272
To Witter Bynner, *July 25, 1939* 273
To Dudley Nichols, *no date* 274
To Montague Weekley, *August 22, 1939* 274
" *September 3, 1939* 275
To William York Tindall, *September 16, 1939* 277
To Montague Weekley, *October 29, 1939* 278
To Dudley Nichols, *November 4, 1939* 279
To Witter Bynner, *January 19, 1940* 279
To T. M. Pearce, *June 9, 1940* 280
To Witter Bynner, *December 9, 1940* 281
To T. M. Pearce, *[Postmarked March 18, 1941]* 282
To Witter Bynner, *December 12, 1941* 282
" *December 13, 1941* 283
" *January 19, 1942* 284
" *June 6, 1942* 285
" *September 10, 1942* 285
" *September 27, 1942* 286
" *January 3, 1943* 287
" *January 6, 1943* 288
To T. M. Pearce, *[March–April, 1944?]* 289
To Witter Bynner, *May 23, 1944* 290
To Dudley Nichols, *August 25, 1944* 291
" *no date* 291
To T. M. Pearce, *September 4, 1944* 292

To Edward Gilbert, *September 17, 1944*   294
From Karl von Marbahr, *no date*   296
To Witter Bynner, *November 15, 1944*   297
To E. W. Tedlock, Jr., *January 10, 1945*   298
To Dorothy Brett, *January 25, 1945*   299
   "   *March 21, 1945*   299
To Witter Bynner, *December 5, 1945*   300
From John Middleton Murry, *May 27, 1946*   301
To John Middleton Murry, *June 4, 1946*   303
From John Middleton Murry, *September 4, 1946*   304
To E. W. Tedlock, Jr., *October 9, 1946*   306
   "   *October 18, 1946*   307
   "   *December 15, 1946*   308
To Witter Bynner, *February 17, 1947*   308
To E. W. Tedlock, Jr., *January 29, 1948*   310
   "   *March 23, 1948*   311
   "   *April 4, 1948*   312
   "   *Monday*   313
To T. M. Pearce, *May 5, 1948*   313
To E. W. Tedlock, Jr., *September 11, 1948*   314
To Witter Bynner and Robert Hunt, *January 7, 1949*   315
To Witter Bynner, *February 14, 1949*   316
   "   *December 6, 1949*   316
   "   *January 8, 1950*   317
To Dudley Nichols, *January 11, 1950*   318
To Witter Bynner, *no date*   319
To Harry T. Moore, *May 27, 1950*   320
To Witter Bynner, *August 13, 1950*   321
   "   *no date*   322
To Lady Cynthia Asquith, *October 15, 1950*   323
To Harry T. Moore, *November 3, 1950*   323
To Montague Weekley, *November 10, 1950*   324
To Witter Bynner, *November 25, 1950*   325
   "   *January 20, 1951*   326
To Harry T. Moore, *January 24, 1951*   326
   "   *January 30, 1951*   328
   "   *February 18, 1951*   329

Contents // xvii

To T. M. Pearce, *June 11, 1951* 330
To Witter Bynner, *July 27, 1951* 331
" *[Late August, 1951]* 332
To Edward Gilbert, *October 13, 1951* 333
To Witter Bynner, *October 16, 1951* 334
To E. W. Tedlock, Jr., *November 2, 1951* 336
To Harry T. Moore, *November 15, 1951* 337
To Edward Gilbert, *November 25, 1951* 338
From John Middleton Murry, *December 9, 1951* 339
To John Middleton Murry, *December 19, 1951* 341
To Edward Gilbert, *no date* 342
" *no date* 343
" *no date* 344
To Dudley Nichols, *April 4, 1952* 345
To Montague Weekley, *May 9, 1952* 345
To John Middleton Murry, *July 1, 1952* 346
" *September 9, 1952* 347
To Harry T. Moore, *October 1, 1952* 348
To Montague Weekley, *December 8, 1952* 349
" *January 29, 1953* 350
From John Middleton Murry, *July 20, 1953* 352
To John Middleton Murry, *no date* 354
To Harry T. Moore, *July 21, 1953* 355
To John Middleton Murry, *August 2, 1953* 358
" *August 6, 1953* 360
" *August 29, 1953* 361
From John Middleton Murry, *September 24, 1953* 362
To John Middleton Murry, *no date* 365
From John Middleton Murry, *January 3, 1954* 366
To John Middleton Murry, *January 8, 1954* 367
To Harry T. Moore, *January 19, 1954* 368
To Montague Weekley, *January 27, 1954* 369
To E. W. Tedlock, Jr., *January 30, 1954* 370
To John Middleton Murry, *March 13, 1954* 371
To Else Jaffe, *March 15, 1954* 371
" *March 24, 1954* 372
To Richard Aldington, *March 29, 1954* 373

To Montague Weekley, *May 12, 1954* 375
To Else Jaffe, *May 18, 1954* 376
To John Middleton Murry, *May 1954* 377
" *July 16, 1954* 379
From John Middleton Murry, *August 13, 1954* 380
To Harry T. Moore, *September 20, 1954* 381
To Else Jaffe, *October 3, 1954* 382
To John Middleton Murry, *no date* 383
To Montague Weekley, *December 24, 1954* 384
To Harry T. Moore, *December 27, 1954* 386
To John Middleton Murry, *January 1955* 387
To Harry T. Moore, *January 14, 1955* 388
" *no date* 391
To Dudley Nichols, *February 15, 1955* 392
" *February 26, 1955* 392
To Else Jaffe, *February 26, 1955* 393
To John Middleton Murry, *April 15, 1955* 394
From John Middleton Murry, *April 21, 1955* 395
To Else Jaffe, *June 25, 1955* 397
To Barbara Barr, *October 3, 1955* 398
To Montague Weekley, *October* 399
From John Middleton Murry, *October 26, 1955* 400
To Else Jaffe, *November 8, 1955* 402
To John Middleton Murry, *November 16, 1955* 403
From John Middleton Murry, *November 27, 1955* 404
To John Middleton Murry, *December 10, 1955* 406
To Else Jaffe, *January 22, 1956* 407
To Witter Bynner, *February 13, 1956* 408
From John Middleton Murry, *May 10, 1956* 409
To John Middleton Murry, *May 18, 1956* 411
To F. R. Leavis, *[May 22, 1956?]* 412
To Barbara Barr, *July 21, 1956* 413
" *August 4, 1956* 414
To Witter Bynner, *August 10, 1956* 415
From Angelo Ravagli to Montague Weekley, Elsa Seaman, and Barbara Barr, *August 17, 1956* 415
From Joe Glasco to Barbara Barr, *August 16, 1956* 417

Essays

Katherine Mansfield Day by Day	425
Lunch with Mr. and Mrs. Bernard Shaw	428
Great Men, and Lies—People and Death	430
In Praise of Raymond Otis	433
Frieda Lawrence Likes Texas	435
D. H. Lawrence, the Failure	437
A Bit about D. H. Lawrence	440
A Small View of D. H. Lawrence	445
Bertrand Russell's Article on Lawrence	447
Foreword to *The First Lady Chatterley*	449
Foreword to *D. H. Lawrence: A Composite Biography*	457
Apropos of Harry T. Moore's Book, *The Intelligent Heart*	459

Appendix

FRAGMENTS OF "And the Fullness Thereof . . ."	467
Chronology	480
INDEX	*follows page* 481

ILLUSTRATIONS

The D. H. Lawrences at their house in Chapala, Mexico, 1923.
Taken by Witter Bynner (*in the possession of Witter Bynner*).
frontispiece

Frieda with Ernest Weekley and his parents. *facing page* 136
(*In the possession of Mrs. Barbara Barr*)

Frieda with her son, 1901. 137
(*In the possession of Montague Weekley*)

The Lawrences with John Middleton Murry at Selsfield
Terrace, 1914. 168
Taken by Katherine Mansfield (*in the possession of The Society of Authors*).

The Lawrences with Witter Bynner at Bynner's house in
Santa Fe, New Mexico, 1922. 169
Taken by Spud Johnson (*in the possession of Witter Bynner*).

Frieda in Mexico, 1923. 264
Taken by Witter Bynner (*in the possession of Witter Bynner*).

D. H. and Frieda Lawrence in Mexico, 1923. 265
(*In the possession of Witter Bynner*)

Frieda, a few years after Lawrence's death, at her resort in
the mountains, seventeen miles from Taos, New Mexico. 296
(*In the possession of Witter Bynner*)

Frieda and Angelo Ravagli, at their home at Taos, a few
weeks before her death in 1956. 297
(*In the possession of Mrs. Barbara Barr*)

"And the Fullness Thereof..."

———————————————————

Editor's Introduction

The title phrase is from Psalm 24, verse 1: "The earth is the Lord's, and the fullness thereof; the world, and they that dwell therein."

A great deal of material of an introductory nature was scattered among the papers. There was no indication of a final choice for an introduction. Eleven of these texts have been put together here, along with an invocation found in her diary, because of the concerns and the conception of her book revealed in them. The visit to San Felipe pueblo in the first section was probably made in February, 1938. She had come to Albuquerque from the Kiowa ranch near Taos late in 1937, and was living at the Central Park Auto Court while Angelo Ravagli visited his family in Italy. During an earlier separation in the winter of 1935, she had fallen ill and been taken to St. Joseph's Hospital in Albuquerque, where she remained under treatment from February 10 through March 20. Now it was thought that her health would be more secure in the warmer climate and more convenient situation. The time afforded by greater privacy she hoped to devote to her new book. One of the "wise young women" mentioned was Betty Cottam. The situation in the second section probably dates from the same time and involves the same friends. Her admiration for the pioneer spirit and for the Southwest is ironic in view of her subsequent failure to obtain citizenship, apparently because of the official objection to her relationship with Ravagli. When this objection was removed by their marriage in 1950, she had given up the idea of citizenship, because, Ravagli says, she felt she was too old.

These two sections, and the third and fourth, bore the title "Introduction." Her concern over World War II in the fourth section, and in the sections immediately following, should be read in the light of her German origin, the intimate associations with England of her youthful marriage to Ernest Weekley, the acute suffering of suspicion and surveillance in England with Lawrence during World War I, her love of the freedom of the American Southwest, and Ravagli's Italian origin and ties. The fifth section, untitled, may be related to a once projected chapter to be titled "Old Age." The sixth, also untitled, extends her reflections on the war. The seventh, headed "I," may represent an abandoned beginning of the memoirs. The eighth section is from one of the few manuscripts bearing the title "And the Fullness Thereof. . . ." The ninth, untitled, continues her reflections on the meaning of sex. The tenth, headed "I. Religion," may, like the seventh, represent a new beginning. The eleventh section is unique; essentially it is a letter, apparently to Karl von Marbahr, whom she had loved in her youth, and with whom she had now begun a correspondence. (See his letter under "Correspondence.") Of the personal memoir she promises him, a single chapter, "Childhood," was attached to this introductory passage. It has been placed in chronological sequence in the memoir. The last introductory section, dated in her diary some ten years after she began her book, expresses the intensely dedicated spirit of her struggle to complete her testament, without the resources of a professional writer, and at odd moments of a continuously active life. As in the memoir, "Paula" is Frieda.

Composition extended from 1935 to the last years of her life. On January 19, 1954, she wrote to Harry T. Moore: ". . . I am writing a bit, very slowly. I would rather have it published when I am dead." The major portion of the text is taken from the only typescript found among the papers— "Leaving for South America," "A Contretemps," "On the Road," "From San Antonio to New Orleans," "Christmas at Home," "Travelling On," "More about Buenos Aires," "Grown Up," an untitled chapter on the English marriage and the affair with "Octavio," and the chapter titled "Andrew," the last pages of which are missing. This incompleteness and the revisions within the typescript make even this advanced text essentially a book in progress. Accounts of other episodes of her life found in other manuscripts have been introduced into this text. At times this violates the point of view in the typescript, and strains the continuity, already somewhat tenuous because of the movements from present time to remembrance; but it has the advantage of presenting her account of the past in approximately chronological sequence. An account of insertions, substitutions, and occasionally a mingling of fragments is given in the notes on the chapters.

Her feelings about the book in 1937, and her plans, can be traced in the letters to Angelo Ravagli from December 3, 1937, through February 26, 1938. Her chapter plan was very like that of the typescript text: "I. The Ranch; II. Leaving the Ranch; III. Contretemps; IV. To San Antonio; V. On to New Orleans; VI. Christmas at Home; VII. Buenos Aires; VIII. Adolescence; IX. Rio de Janeiro." By December 21, 1937, this was as far as she had got, but she indicated what would come next: "Then there are those letters of Otto's and England and more Lawrence. It will be an interesting book of a woman's life." As for her earlier "NOT I BUT THE WIND . . ." she felt that the new book would be better. "It is good to write about our life together and all my past. I believe I can write simply and beautifully (I hope so!)."

The 1937–1938 text, as recalled by her typist, Marcella Matson, was straight autobiography, using the real names of people and places. The early text was also less polished, less correct. A few examples remained among the papers. A portion is included in the last chapter, where it supplied continuity. The method of revision involved complete and repeated rewriting rather than correction. The fictionalizing of names may have been prompted in part by the consideration that some of the people involved were still living; but it probably resulted also from shyness as she re-created her most intimate past.

The manuscript text at any stage of revision presented editorial problems. The elisions in can't and won't appear as ca'nt and wo'nt or without the apostrophe altogether. Dashes appear where commas or periods would normally be used. In the typescript text all this had been regularized, except of course where longhand revisions occurred. This correction has been extended to all the text used here. Spelling, too, has been regularized. In those few places where insertions and slight alterations were necessary for sense, brackets have been used. Short passages have occasionally been omitted, at the editor's discretion, to avoid causing unnecessary distress or difficulty.

Introduction

IT HAD RAINED in the night. It was early February. There was no dust on the road as they drove over the desert to San Felipe. The Sandia mountain edges stood out against the high cloudless sky like razor-blades. Paula was driving with three wise young women she dearly loved to the deer and buffalo dance at San Felipe. They crossed the Rio Grande and there was the *pueblo* low under a mesa that reached out into the desert. There were the tidy corrals, low roofs topped with firewood, and feed for the horses, pigs and sheep, and shaggy horses were wandering about. It was morning and no other cars and white people yet. They turned into the large, empty plaza surrounded by the low adobe houses. The Indian men and women and children were sitting on the adobe benches along the houses, and on the low roofs a colourful, solid mass of Indian people in blue and purple and magenta and scarlet shawls. No clever stage director could have achieved a more effective setting. In the plaza itself on the pink sand the four deer, four antelopes and four buffaloes were dancing. The hunt was up! They had heard the drums beating already, Paula and her friends. The men wore mountain lion skins over their backs, tails dangling behind, earth-red moccasins and gaiters and bright silk shirts and in their glistening, so very black hair the soft white fluff of eagles. It was a gay show. And they sang, with a deep, powerful vibrating sound, like drums their voices too. All danced on the soft pink earth. The rhythm began to beat in your veins like an infusion of some strange power. She stood behind the band of men drumming and singing unaware, untouched, their whole being turned into the dance and singing. "How brave and strong they

7

are," thought Paula, "singing away and dancing in the bright daylight, in the face of the world of today, of motors and trains and radios and movies and all the rest of it." For them these things did not exist. And what a relief it was! These were the hundred per cent Americans, the only ones! Over the houses opposite her Paula could see the soft rounded walls of the two small adobe church towers holding a bell each. The padres from Mexico had brought the Christian touch. And now two Koshares pranced into the plaza. They were Spaniards on horses. What a good performance it was! When the Indians had first seen Spaniards on horses, they had thought these were miraculous beings, horse and man in one. These Koshares wore big Spanish hats with plumes, the head and neck of the caparisoned horse could be pulled up in a most convincing fashion, and below the waist of the men in front and back the horse's body was built and only the two feet of each man gave the show away. The two caballeros turned and pranced, sabres held up in their right hand. How the Spaniards must have impressed the imagination of these Indians, who had never seen a horse, it was clear in this horsemanship of the Koshares, the imitation of a man on a horse was perfect. At midday Paula and her friends, hardly saying a word, absorbed and happy in the dance, sat by a heap of adobe bricks near the Rio Grande and ate their lunch, while the shaggy horses wandered near them. "I love this country, it has adopted me. I am more of a Columbus than Columbus ever was; he only discovered America, but I have made it my own," said Paula to her friends. "I love it like a pregnant woman who loves her unborn child. I shall become a bore with my love for it." Up this Rio Grande before her eyes the Spaniards had come from Mexico long ago as far as here and no further, and down the Rio Grande the North Americans had come and they had driven the Spaniards out back to Mexico. It was still a frontier. Now there were Indians and Mexicans called Spanish Americans and white Americans in the land. She loved the stark simplified country. Everything was itself. The earth was the earth and bare, and the sky was a great dome where the clouds had space to travel and meet, and the mountains rose solid and stern from the plains. No trimmings, no disguises, all things stood distinct and defined. "I have become American," thought Paula, "Europe has gone out of me, with its nations and its bogeys of war, the nations frightening each other." America had settled that problem long ago. Here Europeans of different nationalities lived side by side without wanting to annihilate each other in worked-up hatred. Difference of nations had kept the place alive. You only had to go to the next delicatessen shop. It was like a symbol for America. There were Italian spaghetti and English steak and German sausage and Russian caviar, French wines, all friendly side by side. It was the very contact of the different races settling in this vast country, adjusting themselves to it and each other, the variety that made America what it was. There was a tolerance not to be found anywhere else, almost incomprehensible to a European, and from the pioneer days a helpful neighbourliness born of necessity. The process of turning from a heterogeneous population into a homogeneous one was going on. At the best there was a wider, disinterested outlook on everything. Politics seemed only a game, but an expensive one. Why a man's vote should cost even a cent was a mystery. A man voted with his brains, if he had any, and with his hand. Why this should have anything to do with the money in his pocket seemed a mystery.

Paula remembered a passage in a book called *Coronado's Children:* "Yet the legends of the old world, that have persisted with most vitality and have called most powerfully to the imaginations of men, are legends of women. . . . The new world has been a world of men exploring unknown continents, subduing wildernesses and savage tribes, felling forests, butchering buffaloes, digging gold out of mountains and pumping oil out of hot earth."

Yes, in America the "eternal feminine" wasn't so eternal. The role was played out; on the Madonna and the scarlet woman the curtain had closed. Even in Europe the Madonna's smile had become strained, and the scarlet ones had lost their lustre and become dingy. The pioneer women in America were the new type of woman, sharing their men's adventures. It was like the corn dance at San Domingo where each woman danced behind her man, he meeting boldly the space in front of him, she guarding his rear. Now the era of pioneers was over, what would the next step be that America would take? Its men and women?

America, she knew, had metamorphosed her. She slowly grew to have an idea what America really was. Americans were as different from Europeans as chalk from cheese. Was it the bright sun and the vast spaces and the violence of natural phenomena that had changed people so much? Europeans were still medieval and dim inside like Gothic cathedrals with unknown fears and unclarified emotions. In America most emotions were burnt away and washed out. A man was no longer a soul but an entity of cells, and you looked at problems with an attempt to solve them out in the open. Right or wrong you tried anyhow. So far American writing had been still mostly distorted Europe. The soulfulness of Europe had given men colour and light and shadow, America would be completely different. It approached life from another angle. It was tougher, less vulnerable, less scared. It hadn't lost its sense of adventure, it went for things with a will.

At times Paula's enthusiasm for America boiled over at unheroic moments like making cinnamon toast and coffee in the kitchen for two friends who had appeared.

She had just read a proclamation by Frederick the Great's father to his Prussian subjects. "You belong to me body and soul," the proclamation declared. "You may pray to your maker on the sabbath, but otherwise you do as I tell you or else . . ." And yet the King took his human responsibility like a very stern parent. It was not as inhuman as the abstract state, where your *raison d'être* is to be the obedient tool of the state; there was still some human relation and responsibility. The idea of the state floats in a void like a lost soul for a place to settle. That's why the idea looks for other lands to conquer, because even in its own land it has not found a home. If a new state has truth in it it will stand on its own strength and draw people to it, they will flock to it like they did to America; few people now want to live in Russia. The state that is [not] basically feeble in its human truth and attraction doesn't have to be supported by bullying and propaganda. There are also individuals who run around attaching themselves to this creed or that, this person or that one; if they found their home in themselves, they would not have to run around, but others would come to them.

Only the great ones like the founders of religions, like a Buddha or a Confucius, a Christ, who lived their unfolding lives from deep human roots without forcing their will on others, put their seal on the lives of their fellow men forever. Dictators with their idea bully us by all means, fair or foul, into submission, and there is enough mule in us to finally kick them and their idea into limbo. They are doomed from the start. But here in America human beings had a chance. They came and struggled for existence, a new kind of existence, and the very toughness of the struggle had knit them together in mutual helpfulness. Willy-nilly you had to help your neighbour in the pioneer days when his house was on fire; you might need him some day soon yourself. Thus American democracy is not first and foremost an idea but an experience. Then the founders of the nation climaxed their young nation's experience in the triumphant words: "the pursuit of happiness." No other leader in all the world had ever conceived this. But here it was: be happy everybody, almost a command. Happy the children, happy the grown-ups and the old! What a country to live in!

The friends agreed, having had their coffee and cinnamon toast. "I guess we don't know how lucky we are," said the girl, handsome in a forthright, highstepping way. Yes, what a country to live in! For thousands of miles you travel in your car on splendid roads, no uniform stops you to interrogate you. You eat in a little town and you are told: "Come again, folks." You sleep in a tourist camp, you give your name and pay your nights, you come or leave at your own time, you arrive in a Rolls-Royce or a trembling ancient Ford, it's the same! In Europe you felt self-conscious. You ought to be something socially prominent. You would like to pretend you are a duke. But they'd find you out, they know. In America you may be a millionaire or an attorney general, you are just "another guy" for all that. Maybe when "our time is up" and we merge with the whole, it does not matter whether we were Buddha or Scott Fitzgerald. There is so much that we don't know, thank the Lord. Christ lived his sublimely logical life, more logical than a Gandhi's: "I love you, my fellow men, whatever you do." He was only crucified once and died in triumph in his last words: "Father forgive them," sticking to his guns that were love. Fitzgerald went at living full tilt, limitless, but he felt crucified more than once. Nobody can tell what living as a human being is all about, we can only try to find out or go along on the adventure. Time flows along so fast yet easily in America, it seems to make even the hard work seem more like a game, less effort here than in Europe. "Time is money," that is a stupid thing to assert; time is so much more, whatever it is. When our time is up, then we will know. When Homer wrote his *Iliad*, where did he write it? By the sea or on a terrace? Did he write it in the evening or in the morning? Did it take him a long time or did he recite it only? Shakespeare may have written wonderful words in a tavern, or at Anne Hathaway's cottage, anywhere at midnight, or at noon. I would like to sit down, as it were, with the great ones, when they said their say, and see in my mind's eye what the setting of their writing was. They are the ones who did not take living for granted, but tried to find out what it was all about, this unknown quantity: what is a human being, how does it click?

Paula's mother had told her and she had never forgotten: "You, you are an *Atavismus*." Now after a long life Paula knew this was true. She certainly was not modern. If primitive people felt a unity embracing the whole world, they were the fish, the cow, the stone, always part of the whole, the living universe of which you are part, alive or dead, then she was like them. This background of the universe behind her gave her her strength, her deep contentment. This was not mysticism, but a fact. Like hungry creatures we look for the living splendour of the world to feed us, and the splendour is there. We know a tree not only with our eyes but with this other sense of unity. You participate in the life of the tree. If you only see it with your eyes and only your

brain works, you get tired, and don't get a sense of the tree, but
when you are wholly aware, with all the faculties working, only
then will you be aware of the tree and it seems as if the tree were
aware of you too and it nourished your being. We know so much
and experience so little.

So help me God, I have got to write this book. One me doesn't
want to write it the least little bit. I want to go to the small house
and sow seeds. I have bought some morning glory seed and
alyssum and marigolds. I want to watch the two couples of birds
who are so busy to carry chicken feathers and straws, such long
straws, to their nests on the kitchen porch. And there is the bread
to make and the floor to polish and why, oh why must I write a
book? I hope it isn't because I want to show off, I hope it isn't
because I think I am so smart and know better than others, I
hope it isn't because I want to convert anybody to anything, I
have "learnt better" than that!

Yet I must write this book. Maybe it is because I am an old
woman now and would like to share the experiences of a lifetime
with my fellows. Life itself has changed so terrifically, its
outlook, its values, the very heart and soul of humanity has
changed in these last fifty years, so I will have to write my
book.

So Paula sat down solemnly with her copybook and pencil to
write. The whole world was ablaze with war. One's thoughts
had to jump one minute to India and then to Madagascar and
Stalingrad and Dieppe, and there was war on the ground and in
the air and the many hundreds of thousands of dead, young dead,
under earth. What had everybody thought of and worried about
before there was a war? You could not remember. People were
starving and dying of hunger and misery. But we are tough and
go on.

In Paula's world there was no war. Her small cabin was
peacefully tucked away on the mountainside. The autumn sun
was breaking through the mist, the clock ticked away the quiet

moments, and outside, the cows and horses, with their noses to the ground eating away, knew nothing of war. Occasionally a hen cackled triumphantly announcing her newly laid egg.

The trees stood wet and shiny after the night's rain, oblivious of the world of fighting men.

It would not be so very important if she wrote her book or not. There would always be trees and cows and all the beautiful nonhuman world. Human beings were really not so very important, the war had made that clear. It made one feel very frail, "come today and gone tomorrow." The individual seemed an evanescent nothing compared to the fate of nations and whole races. Yet, she wanted to write her book. She was old now and wanted to leave behind some result of her years of living and the satisfaction of it all.

Even if there was war all around the globe there was peace in this little world. Perhaps the meaning of it was a new thing, a new shape of man coming after this destruction of everything. People had become like canned salmon, instead of being the live skipping article. There was plenty of room, plenty, for an improved human soul to be brought forth.

You could not imagine quite what this new man and his soul would be like. He would be finer, more alert, not so encumbered with old, stale ideas and ideals in his head; he would be wholesomer, cleaner, not revelling in stupid dirty stories out of sheer boredom, he would not be so scared of his own and his neighbour's shadow. What a lovely creature he would be, this new man! We would change. Always a change was a terrible, hard event.

After Christianity came, men changed, and that was a hard struggle too! So the war was hopeful really, an end and a beginning.

Human beings were so heartily sick of themselves, they hated the whole human show; there was so much to blow up, the structure we ourselves had created that towered on top of us that we no longer could [breathe] was being knocked to smithereens. If only the new thing arose fresh and bright the catastrophe could be borne.

I am sixty-three and most of these years I have looked at the universe and I am still looking. It's a wonderful universe. I am on the best of terms with it. There isn't a thing wrong with it except humanity and that is very wrong. I think few humans would disagree with me. It seems as if humanity couldn't see straight or hear straight or think straight, but maybe that is because humanity does not see eye to eye with me.

If you are a woman, you have the privilege to think as you please, and you do, but also nobody cares a hoot what you do think.

Thinking of this war, it forces us to abandon our positions, our little shallow securities. We are not by any means those charming good fellows and sweet little women, we are demons and impersonal killers, we are elemental like murdering avalanches and icebergs that squeeze a ship to smithereens. When under pressure the lid of [the] human kettle blows up, the steam hisses and pours out. So, under pressure, instead of a pleasantly simmering kettle, there is a blow-up and a mess. In the French Revolution the kettle blew up under pressure of the aristocrats and in Russia under pressure of the Czars and in Germany under the pressure of after-the-war years.

What is the meaning of this war? Have we read history or the fates of nations and races with too narrow an understanding? What moves people to such upheavals? We don't really know. May it not be that the spirit of Europe conquered the pre-Columbus spirit of America and now America is taking its revenge and freeing itself of old Europe to become truly a new America? Shake off the old joke of Europe to be at long last itself? Today Sicily is invaded. They are fighting round Taormina that lives in my memory like a nearly forgotten dream. The outline of Etna, with its plume of smoke, the drawnout slope to the sea, the coastline, the Greek theatre, the radiance of almond blossom and peach, and now there is war. On the narrow mulepath behind our Villa Fontana Vecchia I can hear a Sicilian sing his "Comare Nina" early in the morning; maybe the villa is bombed and the stream where the women were washing the

linen and spreading it on the stones and sort of holding its hand
to help it dry and the mulberry bushes and the asphodels and the
little Greek temple in the garden, so glorious a world and now
war was destroying it! Would old Grazia, she must be very old
now, have a shelter to get into? There was the old cellar where
the olive oil and wine were kept, but it would not be bombproof.

Paula was old now, not so very old, but old. She felt very
much alive still—she could still change and go on and wonder.
Through the First World War she had been in England, but
that war had been child's play compared to this new one. Then
the wobbly zeppelins had come over London one at a time, and
they were terrifying enough, but now in all parts of the universe
hundreds of bombs were bursting in the air, and the sea was
alive with danger, and tanks rolled over the earth, and guns
blasted human beings to nothing and it was all unthinkable. In
her own quiet corner nobody could grasp it—and the misery and
pain and hatred all over the world while she lived her peaceful
life and had no connexion with the horror. She was a woman and
it was her privilege not to hate. She could not do it.

History after all was not the whole story of mankind. History
recorded mostly the mistakes and crimes of humanity. All
nations and all races have committed crimes against the brother-
hood of men. They are like Christ's adulteress: let him who is
blameless throw the first stone. The real story of peoples was the
living day by day, children growing up, food and marrying,
having friends and talking to your neighbours and sleeping and
having a new dress. Meanwhile our so-called civilization had
grown topheavy and it was tumbling. It is all too complicated. If
only things could be simplified and if we could remember the
fundamentals for all living things. We all need food and work
and companionship and shelter.

If human beings had built up a monstrously imperfect world,
they were also capable of mighty dreams for a new way.

It could all be so simple. Twelve men in twelve sections of the
world would be responsible for the distribution of products all
over the globe. They would just have to be honest, intelligent

men. Then, when all needs were supplied, the genuine fun of living would begin: the pursuit of happiness, the delicate adjustment of personal relationships. There would not be any need for politics, power or otherwise, each human being's natural individual power would come forth and flourish. It might be an experiment to take criminals and treat them like millionaires in grand houses and give them all they want, so that they could no longer have a grouch against society.

Freedom: "Man is born free," says J. J. Rousseau, "and everywhere we find him in chains." But what about it? If a baby is born, it is not free. Left to its freedom, there won't be any baby soon. If I sit in the desert with all the freedom in the world but have no water and no food, what is my freedom? Not worth a cent till a man comes along and gives me water and food. Freedom is an abstraction and a negative thing, because we need one another, we depend on each other, we don't do without each other. We are interwoven with the rest of the universe, denying this is disaster. It is not even love or generosity, it's common sense. If I am at war with a country that has coffee and I have no coffee, then I bite off my nose to spite my face. We need one another, all the people of this world hang together and now more than ever. . . .

And America knows this and has lived it. Here and only here races live side by side and here the problem of a united Europe and more than Europe has been solved. That is why this war in Europe is no longer interesting; America has grown beyond it. This is the meaning of America. It made America what she is, that all nations and races came here and threw their genius into the pot to make a good, strong soup. It was America's luck. The genius of all the world combined here to tussle with this fierce continent and now America is the hope of the entire world. She cannot help but be broadminded. In many Americans there is a new frail reaching out to a finer awareness, an honest-to-God goodness and fairness to all mankind.

Women would never make wars. Any sensible woman who has had a child and brought it up, would not want it killed knowing how much living effort goes to produce a fully grown man, or would not want to kill another woman's child however much she detested the woman, unless she were a criminal. If women understand their own female selves and don't try to be imitation men, they will hate war.

Long ago Electra says: "I am not here for hate, I came for love." Being women we are allowed to love everything. Our business is to make things flourish and flower around us. That is our only satisfaction.

In the beginning was a spark and the spark was God or the eternal or creation or any other name it bears for you.

It was not the "word" at all, that came much later . . . and it can have devilishness in it. . . .

Look at the words "capital and labour" and if the devil is not in them, I don't know where he is.

The two pretend they are opposed but they are only halves of the same show—a marriage rather like most marriages. Surely if there weren't bosses with enterprise to create lots of jobs where would labour be? But the men feel ill used because they are not the boss, but you can't have everybody being the boss. The boss is no more "free" to do as he likes [than] the men are, he is in the boat too. Now the boss may have champagne for dinner and have a swanky car and a million dollars in the bank and what of it? Maybe he has a flighty son who gives him a lot of worry, maybe he has a wife with a melancholy disposition and indigestion. On the other hand, his least paid worker is a jolly soul and [has] a wife that he is happy with and believes that water from a cool spring is fine stuff to drink. I would rather change places with the last man. There is the devil in that boat of capital and labour.

As for our "spark," we have forgotten about it. We don't care a hoot about it and yet nothing is so worthwhile, so essential, it is our life itself. Do we cherish it? No, not in the least.

All individual life starts with the spark of sex. That spark develops into a tree, a columbine, a cow, a human being. So sex, with the elements that nourish the growing spark, is almost the essence of living. When Freud made his great discovery of the unconscious and sex, it was very important. But when he found the "complexes" in the human individual he did not go far enough. The complexes were there all right, but they were not the root of the matter, but only a symptom. That human being had already broken its connexion with the bigger sex, that spark which connects us with all life. Then something went askew in his own small personal sex. That is where psychoanalysis has gone wrong. By probing into those complexes, the individual only intensifies those complexes, his little sex becomes more conscious and yet what he really needs and wants is to be incorporated into that bigger sex that is life. Our own little spark of sex is meaningless if it is not embedded in all the sex of the universe that links our being to everything. Animals had not eaten of the tree of knowledge, there was no good and evil problem for them. Paradise lost for men meant that state of a cat sitting in the sun at peace with the universe after having swallowed the canary. That cat feels no guilt. Maybe a wicked man could argue: "The Lord made me, the Lord made me wicked, it is his responsibility not mine."

When Christ said: "The sun shines on the just and the unjust," he made a profound statement of fact. Why do we assume that everybody must be good, when we are not? A man can say, "I choose to be good and have compassion if I am wise because it fulfils a need in me." But maybe we put up with tyrants because deep in our hearts we know that they are what they are, and we cannot in a way blame them. We assume, and what right have we to that assumption, that people must be good. We are outraged when they are not.

What was religion, what was belief? To Paula it was awareness, awareness of all that the universe holds and means. Belief was the secret and forever unknowable mystery that people called God or many gods or Buddha or Christ or the great spirit. It had many names. It did not matter what it was called, but it was there. It was the prime nourisher of every living entity, the umbilical cord that feeds us and connects us with the whole. Once the connexion is broken, we become loosely floating, meaningless atoms, our pivot gone. Animals and plants never lose it, only to man is given the choice of severing it or keeping it. A prowling devil seems to try his devilish hardest to make us lose our most precious possession, our faith, our good will, our wholesome and harmonious balance. "Whatever happens to me, good or ill, however people hurt me one way or another, I won't let my blood turn sour and my spirit grow resentful," Paula vowed to herself.

I want to hear from you [1] so much. I want to know where you are, what you are doing and how you are.

And you can't write to me and I can't write to you, there is this war like more than a Chinese wall between us. I dread to think of you. I hope you are not a soldier again in this war, you are too old and you were already pensioned and had your successful work as a movie director. And now with Hitler how difficult your position must be.

The last letter I had from you said among other things: "You are like the wild geese that fly overhead and honk their wild call and the tame geese on the ground hear them, would like to rise and fly with them, but they can't." And then again you said: "There are women of sixty to whom a man still wishes to bring roses."

And now I have not heard from you for more than three years. But it is always the same: I don't hear from you, I go on with my living all those years since I was seventeen and you were twenty-four and we never met again and I forget you. Then suddenly you are there and nearer than anything else in the world and I hear your unforgettable voice right in my ears. You are just you to me and without a name, though I love your beautiful old family name. I cannot talk to you, but I will write down all about myself and what happened to me, so when the war is over and we can write again I want you to read this because I know you care. You always have cared and you always

---

[1] In this version of the memoirs, the book was to be addressed to her old friend, Karl von Marbahr (see p. 296).

will. Now that I am old only now I know. I will tell you all about myself right from the beginning, as far as I can remember, and you will deal kindly with my offering. You understood me so well. I believe I had what few women have, a real destiny. Destinies are not mathematics and they don't come out like two and two make four. Our deepest selves are buried so very deep down and we don't let them come up to the surface. We think we know so much and we don't really and maybe about ourselves least of all.

Invocation (Diary, January 5, 1948)

You words that I want to use in this book be good to me, be like butterfly wings iridescent and light on the air and heavy as lead to sink into the soul and to warm the cockles of the heart and cold to cool the brain. I love you, words, now you love me too, that you help me to say what I want to say.

Leaving for South America

*"Paula" is Frieda Lawrence, and "Dario" is Angelo Rava-
gli. "Andrew" is D. H. Lawrence. Ravagli, a captain in the
Italian army, had met the Lawrences in Italy in 1925. A
friendship developed with him and his family: his wife,
Professor Yna-Serafina Astingo, who taught in a high
school at Savona, and the three children, Stefano, Magda-
Micaela, and Federico, who was Mrs. Lawrence's godson
and derived his name from hers. Lawrence died on
March 2, 1930. In the spring of 1931 Mrs. Lawrence and
Captain Ravagli reached a decision to live together at the
New Mexico ranch given to Mrs. Lawrence by Mabel
Luhan in 1924. The first stay was interrupted when he,
on six months' leave, was recalled to the Italian army.
They returned to the ranch in the spring of 1933. The
new house, just below the Lawrence cabin, was begun on
May 30, 1933. That autumn they left for South America
to visit Ravagli's sister and brother in Buenos Aires.*

*Of the building of the new house at the ranch Ravagli
wrote in his diary:*

*Today, 30 May 1933, we started to build the new
house in Kiowa Ranch—San Cristobal, New Mexico.*

*Under the first stone on the south corner we put a
glass bottle with a list of the names of Mrs. Frieda
Lawrence, Captain Angelo Ravagli, and one of the
workmen, with this note: "This house is wanted by
Frieda Lawrence, and Captain Angelo Ravagli in its
simple style and modest appearance to represent unity
of intent and construction, that comes from the finest*

22

sentiment of friendship." (The note was written in
Italian.) In the bottle we added Mrs. Frieda Law-
rence's and Captain Ravagli's photographs . . . some
coins of American, French and German money, plus a
piece of coral and two molars of Ravagli's teeth.

"Will you come to South America with me?" Dario asked,
leaning towards Paula. She was pleased at the eagerness in his
voice.

"Yes, I will come," she said.

They were sitting on the porch in the late afternoon, a bright
sun overhead, but snow on the ground.

Paula looked around. The summer autumn had gone. No
longer the humming birds were humming and hovering over the
fuchsia flowers, so intensely pink and magenta in this high
altitude. The birds' beaks were diving into the hearts of the
blossoms; then the bright, quick, dithering things, like butterflies, would chase each other.

The corn and alfalfa and oats had been cut and were stacked
in the corral. Thank goodness the animals would have enough to
eat through the many winter months. A few marigolds in the
garden limply lifted their heads above the snow. On the mountains, aspens still made a patch of gold in the whiteness. Far
across the desert, the Pecoris Peaks looked out of the clouds, cold
and blue and sparkling, lilac shadows moving across them. The
desert lay below, cream and pink. A shadow fell. A lump of snow
had melted and slipped from a pine tree. Fonso, the dog, jumped
and went to investigate.

"I love this place," Paula said.

Dario nodded. Dario had come to America with Paula two
years ago.

When Andrew, her husband, had died, Paula had been
knocked over by his death. The shock had blinded her into a new
awareness. No longer young, she had never seen anybody die.
From her childhood days, from the story of Good Friday she had
held an impression that death was dramatic, terrific, temple

curtains rent and darkness and the earth quaked, lightning and thunder. But what she saw was not like that. A last struggle, and then the quiet otherness of death. Still, and final. She had written to her mother,

> Dear Mother,
>
> In the next room lies our Andrew, still and dead.
>
> He looks so bold and unconquered. He suffered much the last days, but fought still. I was with him mostly day and night. It just gripped me to see him, but towards the end all went fast and there was peace in him. The H's were here at his death in true friendship. I have arranged all today with A., the grave in the cemetery, from where you see the sea. Tomorrow at four is the funeral. We had a nurse. His death was only beautiful. B. is deeply moved. I shall miss him so very much. Wednesday I go to B. then back here. I must find myself again.
>
> Your daughter,
> Paula

At last she could see him, the whole of him, the achievement of his life, the splendour of it. In a kind of ecstasy, she saw the unbroken wholeness of the man. She thought of him as he had written of Dido. "But what of him my unconscious had I could not tell you. Something, I am sure, and something that has come to me without my knowledge; something that flew away in the flames; something that flew away from that pillar of fire which was his body, day after day while he lived, flocking into nothingness to make a difference there. The reckoning of his money and his mortal assets may be discoverable in print. But what he is in the roomy space of somethingness, called nothingness, is all that matters to me." Here was no beaten-down Christ who had been crucified by his fellow men, or a Napoleon, dwindling away into meaninglessness on St. Helena. No, life had never conquered Andrew. He was himself right to the end. With flying colours he had lived, and so death had found him. Paula's chief feeling was exultation. She could imagine Andrew, a hero in the old days, being burnt on a funeral pyre and she throwing herself as a last tribute into the flames.

Dario had written to her: "Come and see me." She had gone, forlorn in a world in which Andrew no longer lived.

"I am not fit to be with people," she had lamented.

But Dario had given himself in comfort for her and let her weep her heart out, with a man's silent sympathy.

"He was so brave, so brave," she cried. "He suffered so." Her tears ran down, she sobbed out her grief.

From then on she had thought, "I want Dario to come to America with me, to that small wild place in the Rockies; and I will see what happens to him there." It would be an experiment that fascinated her. And now for two summers they had been on the ranch.

When Dario had first come, driving up from the desert, the ranch looked desolate and shabby; he had been dismayed. Always he had lived among people; his whole life seemed to have been people. He was horrified at the loneliness; not a soul for miles, and the place was so primitive.

One late autumn evening they were sitting by the big adobe fireplace with the burning logs in the little three-roomed cabin, two candles lit on the crude mantelpiece. There was no running water, no electric light in the cabin, the low ceiling of corrugated iron. Outside the silence of the pine trees and the loneliness of the stars. Paula liked it; the minimum of comfort seemed comfort to her. Having a bath in a tub in front of the fireplace or out in the irrigation ditch in the sun seemed more luxurious than the grandest bathroom. She liked the utter loneliness, the silence, the space; it gave her room to be herself.

But to Dario it seemed a comedown; he could not live like this. He admired all the modern conveniences of America. *"Viva l' America,"* he would exclaim when he saw a clever new dodge to open a tin can.

"I can't stand this loneliness," he had moaned that night.

Paula was frightened. She knew so little of Dario after all. At the best he seemed to have stepped across the centuries right out of the *Iliad*, an Achilles or Menelaus. Fresh as dawn in his reactions, the blood of his ancient race running unmixed and undiluted through his veins. But when she was dissatisfied she grumbled to herself about him. "He is so *terre à terre;* he has no intellect, no imagination." She argued with him; she tried to make him state his convictions. She bullied him, but it was no use. He seemed to fly out of her hands like a bird. She thought she was quite brilliant in her arguments, but slowly she came to the conclusion that maybe she was not so clever after all. The Lord had made Dario, and she had no business trying to make him over. He was as he was. But she was scared. Had she made a mistake bringing him here, pulling him out of his old surroundings? Wasn't he going to be happy? She had put a new hope into this life up here with Dario; and now he longed for his old activity, his old civilized Europe.

She was angry with him. Was he so fixed in his old ways? Couldn't he see what a wonderful opportunity it was for a man to get out of the old routine, the tightness of Europe; to realize his own powers in this vast country and find new ways to use them? Wasn't he unutterably grateful to this America for so much inner and outer space it gave you to be purely yourself? Europe had closed in on you, there was no getting away from old burdens. But here if you kept the laws, paid your debts, you were left alone. People might talk, but on the whole you did as you pleased. You could put your own meaning into this great emptiness, the trees only helped.

Underneath she felt a mysterious fluttering of an unknown, happy future trying to emerge. She would have to be patient, terribly patient. It would take time for him to forget and to wake up to new possibilities. There was a pure energy in Dario. Once set going it would achieve its ends.

He never talked much; hardly ever of himself. But that night he sat very still, his brown eyes bright, talking into himself.

"Ah," he said, "there is nothing like war. All other experiences are nothing compared to war. Once you have known war, everything else seems dull and insipid." In his eyes was the look that Paula had seen in the eyes of men of many nations, men who had been through the World War; as if at the back of their minds was fixed forever only one reality: the war. She felt helpless. She wanted these men to forget the war.

"War," Dario went on, "calls forth all and every faculty in a man, all his strength, all his intelligence and courage, above all courage. And the comradeship between men, it does not exist in civil life."

But when he told her his actual experiences, it seemed only confusion. Men wandering about aimlessly, not knowing what it was all about. The misery of being taken prisoner; hunger and thirst and dirt; being transported in cattle trucks. A few thousand men at a railway station, waiting naked while their clothes were being disinfected. He was talking about the First World War and when he was a prisoner of war in Germany. "Food was what we longed for, we had food on the brain. Mostly I longed for bread. When our rations were cut and handed out we counted the crumbs. We were so weak that we could hardly stand up. The Germans were very fair. Later, when the Red Cross parcels came, they scrupulously gave us each his parcel, not an ounce of food was taken and they did not have enough themselves. Then we tried to dig a tunnel to escape. We dug at night under the barracks with the knives we had and had a bucket on a rope to put the dirt in, and the dirt was distributed under the barracks. We dug for many nights. We had gone a long way, always with the danger that the tunnel might cave in, when one night at midnight there was a shout: '*Raus, Raus,*' and I saw bayonets gleaming. So we were caught and taken to the commandant of the camp. But before we could be punished the Armistice came, there was food at last. One of my co-officers held up a loaf of bread and said solemnly: 'Thank God for the bread of our land.' "

That was the men's world that women know nothing about.

Paula was silent to his story. She did not believe him. She did not want to. Had he not been disillusioned when he came home to his native country and found his own people suspicious of all the prisoners when they had suffered so much? If life was only war and death, why begin life at all? Why not murder all the newborn children and have done with it once and for all?

She found it hard that she could have no mental contact with him, she who had enjoyed the fierce arguments with Andrew and the brilliant talk with the clever men she had known. But this man did not want to hear what she had to say. Dario had an ancient inner-security that she could not touch with words. So finally she left him alone. And, in the end, it was peace to her. If he sang as he worked and was happy, she was at peace.

At last, one morning, Dario's energy had asserted itself. The spirit of the continent had done its work.

"I will build a house, a house fit to live in, not an old cow-shed like this one but a fit place for human beings to live in. Here the packrats are running overhead like elephants and the chipmunks will soon drive us out. Get a string and show me where you want your new house and how big you want it."

Paula ran to the string-bag in the kitchen, pulled out strings and tied them together and went outside to find the spot for a new house. They staked off a long piece of land in the place Paula had chosen. They felt like pioneers.

"I want a big kitchen to work in," said Paula.

"There must be a bathroom and running water," said Dario.

Then he set to work. Paula heard him singing and yelling at the Mexican workmen. Now he was happy. They levelled the earth for the house and a garden; logs were cut and the foundation laid with stone and cement. Under one corner stone, in the old European way, a bottle was buried and everybody had to put something into the bottle for luck.

"This will be a solid house," said Dario. "No packrats can come in here."

He schemed and planned gardens and new fields and a swimming-pool. He worked from dawn till night. The logs rose higher and higher. The walls were chinked and adobed; like buttons the ends of the big logs stuck out of the walls. There were two storeys and Dario had successfully worried out a water-system, the water coming down from the irrigation ditch higher up. The drinking water would still be carried from the lovely, ever-fresh spring in the canyon under the spruce and aspen. Albert the Swede, who was such a clever carpenter, came and said "Goddam" when Dario borrowed a tool from his tidy bench or stole a piece of wood.

And at last the house was finished. The curtains were up, a piano had arrived, and the water was running. Now Dario and Paula lived in the new house.

At first Paula regretted her old shack that she had loved; it held so many memories. In the new house she would get up at dawn, still filled with the silence of the night outside, the potent presence of the trees and the tinkling noise of the little stream. The moonlight had passed through her room.

She ran to the window. The sun was spreading; so far it was only a stripe on the desert; it widened down below. The mountain-tops were fading out of their rosiness; soon the sun would reach the ranch. What new flowers had opened their buds in the night? Had that big bronze dahlia quite come out? That red lily seemed to come forth a little crumpled. There were the horses, Ambrose looking very white in the green alfalfa field, the pintos near him; he was the boss. Their noses were on the ground. Anita was already mooing to be milked. She was born on the ranch. She had been a gay young heifer, but now she was a stately cow, a wonder of patience and goodness. Madonna-like, she bent her head towards her red calf and licked it all over, gently, with deep satisfaction, and the calf skipped round her in delight.

Paula went noiselessly down into the kitchen, not to wake Dario. She lit the fire with the pine cones and the wood that scented the kitchen. Soon the coffee-water boiled. She did not dare open the kitchen door yet because Fonso, the dog, and Mizzi, the cat, would burst in and Fonso would dance up to her in his "pim pete pim" way on his hind-legs. Mizzi would insist on getting into her bacon plate. The lambs must not hear her yet either or their "ma-ma" would not stop till she gave them each their bottle of milk.

The sun was on the ranch now. She heard Dario overhead, singing his old soldier songs while he dressed. The horses had trooped round to the saddlehouse. Epimenio must be near; he would soon come riding along; the horses were neighing their morning salute to his horse.

A Contretemps

*"Los Animos" is Taos, New Mexico. "Allambrosa" here
and in the next chapter is Alamosa, Colorado.*

They were driving in the car to New Orleans [to] leave it there
and take the boat to Buenos Aires. At the ranch you could not
just turn the front door key and be off; you had to think of many
things. The saddles had to be hung up from the rafters that the
packrats could not chew them; the water had to be drained and
Prestone put into the W.C.s because of the strong frost. The
pigs have been killed, the hams after being cured hang in the
larder. The coloured corn hangs in bunches from the kitchen
ceiling. The horses' shoes are taken off for the winter. Epimenio
says all the matches must be covered or the mice might nibble
them and set the house on fire. All the potted plants have been
taken to the neighbours.

Epimenio will come riding through the snow every morning
to feed the animals. They will be waiting for him, feeling lonely
every morning in a daze of cold like wintersleep, in their thick
winter coats almost as thick as sheep's wool.

The garage has a bar inside now; only the blue shutters have
to be closed. The bags are packed, and Dario and Paula are
ready to be off in the La Salle.

But there is a hitch. A little while ago a man had spoken to
Dario and Paula as they were getting into the car in the little
plaza of Los Animos. He was a fellow-countryman of Dario's, a
well-knit figure with an out-of-doors air about him. Only his eyes
were like pebbles, with no play of light in them. He came to the

ranch. He knew all about horses; he told them that the cedars on the ranch must have been there when Columbus came. He fixed the lightning conductor. Paula was glad Dario had found a friend; she had so many. B— . . . told them a story.

"When I first come to New York, very young, I go to a speakeasy with a cousin. We order some beer and we just going to drink it when a big man next to me spits into my glass and he says, 'Drink that, you damn dago.' 'Must I take this?' I say to my cousin, and I lift up the spittoon and I hit the stranger with it. He hit back and we fight, and I know no more till I am in hospital. The other man, he was in hospital too. But the judge, he let me free."

There was a charm about the man; he was always full of plans and schemes; he wanted to make a racecourse; he always was going to make lots of money. But in his schemes Paula noticed that he always thought of the profit they would bring; expenses he did not seem to consider.

Then Paula was giving a housewarming. B—'s little black ouzle of a wife had come to do the cooking. Paula did not like her; she seemed mean and yet wasteful in the kitchen. Paula had hated the housewarming; these people made an awful feeling about the place. She was thankful when they left.

Then Dario came to her and said, "Will you lend B— a thousand dollars? He wants it for some enterprise."

"I will," Paula said. She never guessed at the time what it would let her in for.

She gave B— the cheque and said to him, "It is a pleasure to lend an energetic man like you this money."

He bent low in a Sir Walter Raleigh fashion and thanked her.

Dario had gone for a few days with B— to see about his enterprise. Dario had lived with his officers and men, and the comradeship of men in a regiment had given him trust. But now he found, being with B—, that he was paying for everything, that B— was always expecting money that never came.

Dario had become suspicious; and finally B—'s so-called friends told Dario the most astounding stories about him. So

Dario told B— he would leave him, and he did. B— was furious. He must have built all sorts of rosy dreams on this acquaintance and saw his birds flying away from him.

So, one day, the sheriff appeared to arrest Dario. The accuser was B—. "For confidence trick and for trying to use him to provide Dario with women," the warrant read.

There were some old friends staying at the ranch, Danes, who were speechless. Only bonds would leave Dario his freedom. The good neighbours were bondsmen.

And Paula was to be arrested too. When B—'s wife had come to work at the ranch, she had given her a bag with some odd trinkets: a ring, a watch that did not go, rubbish.

"The boys are in and out of my house all day long; and this bag isn't safe in my house." Paula had wondered at the time, but put the bag away and forgot it. But when things had gone wrong with B—, she had taken the bag to the bank.

On the first of October B— was supposed to pay the thousand dollars back. He did not.

Then the sheriff came to arrest Paula at her lawyer's. She was to go to the Justice of the Peace. O, wild and woolly West! She went with the bag. On the way she met a friend. "I hear you are being arrested." "Yes," she said, "and all for lending a man a thousand dollars."

The B—s were there in the little office.

"You have a bag of trinkets that belong to these people," said the Justice of the Peace.

"Here it is," she said, angrily. "I lent these people a thousand dollars to help them; and that's what I get for it."

B— jumped up, and, pointing to his wife, said, "She did it. I have nothing against this lady, this Mrs. Elmer. I will give her a written statement. She must have all the freedom in the world." And he made a speech in her praise.

She turned and left.

But now, just as Dario and Paula were leaving, they got warning that B— had got out another warrant. So Dario ran for his bags. A friend would drive him across the border of the state into safety. It was dark already, a cold night; and Paula and

Dario took a frightened farewell under the pines. It seemed like Napoleon fleeing from Elba. Paula would join him the next day at Allambrosa. She watched anxiously after their departure. Could she see lights on the road? She listened for sounds all night.

Next morning, Epimenio helped her to close the house and she was off. Later on she met B— and he talked to her and told her how he had lost his truck and much business through her.

But here was a warning not to lend anybody a thousand dollars. They might come back at you like a boomerang.

On the Road

Paula is driven to Allambrosa in the La Salle by the Danish friends. The La Salle is the first car that Paula ever had and she loved it. She could sympathize with the man who had engraved on his diamond ring, not his mother's features, nor those of his wife or child, but his beloved car. The La Salle is solid and steady. A bit pompous, he likes his food, lots of it; but he also swallows the road like an Italian swallows spaghetti.

Now he is swallowing the Colorado road. They have wound their way over the foothills down to Sunshine Valley, the tragic. Fifty thousand people had been tempted to settle here with all their families and goods and chattels in the hope of prosperity and riches. Of them all there was nothing left but a few ruined houses and an unfinished irrigation ditch. How many failures in this big land for one millionaire!

Paula feels like traveling at the bottom of the sea. Out of the vast plain rise the mauve and delicate blue hills, like frozen waves. On the right are mountains, softly moulded like breasts, like the breasts of many breasted Artemis. And, floating away in front, more pale blue hills folded behind hills of still paler blue. Distance that only America knows.

In Allambrosa Paula and Dario meet. The inhabitants take a keen but short-lived interest in them.

Better be off now as they are still fleeing from justice. They drive over the high pass. It is cold and the snow is like crystals. I don't think Americans know how beautiful America is. Is it because the people that came from Europe had still only European eyes to see with; or were they too busy to fight for existence and making America one hundred per cent American?

Paula's heart went out to these vast, unconquered spaces. She thought of Tuscany where every inch of ground had been ploughed and planted for thousands of years, where stone wall above stone wall had been built by men's hands, often a little bit of ground just big enough to hold one fig tree or vine.

And here the earth, for miles and miles, with no sign of any human effort. They passed a lake lying high and exposed to the open sky, the rounded mountain tops reflected in it like human flesh with a rosy tinge.

They fly along in the La Salle. There is a dead rabbit in the road; two huge birds rise from it, slowly; their enormous wings lift. The mountains are left behind. It is all open road to the next town now. A terrific wind is blowing across the plain. Shivering cattle try to shelter behind a sandbank or a tousled haystack. With a swish of wings, a great flock of tiny birds rises just in front of the car, birds thick as a swarm of bees. Are they flying south, as they are, away from the cold? The wind is getting their ears and cheeks.

Few are the homesteads and townlets they pass. A gasoline station with its red pump now and then. A few houses along a wide road. On some of the houses is written: "Eats" or "Eat." They choose the most promising one. "Where are you folks from?" Once the question is answered, the conversation is exhausted. "Can I have some buttermilk?" asks Paula. "You betcha," is the amiable answer. Paula sits on her high stool by the counter near a shy cowboy in the fascinating cowboy boots with sloping heels, his hips incredibly slender; the hat he is wearing is immense. He looks like a mushroom. Another cowboy comes and sits by the first. "Hallo, Ed." On the newcomer's trouserleg is a large number thirteen. Paula would like to know what it means but dares not ask.

Dario is watching the lively slim girl who has evidently returned from a spree and is telling an elderly woman all about it behind the counter that is decorated with green and red paper flowers. On the walls are "texts." "If your wife can't cook don't abuse her—eat here and keep her for a pet." "Full credit extended to anyone over 80 years of age, accompanied by both parents."

"Don't ask for information—if we knew anything we wouldn't be here."

"Come again, folks."

Paula thought, "Dashing along the road in this huge country is a strange thing. You are on the wing like a bird; there is no before and no after. You just watch the road and the country you fly through. You are creatures in a car, unconnected, unattached. You may have committed murder in one town; by the time you arrive at the next, you have forgotten it. No mind, no memory, no interest beyond the car and the road."

Dario had been silently driving the La Salle. He was devoured with rage.

"If it hadn't been for me, you would never have lent that man the thousand dollars. Now they are lost."

"You pay for your experiences. It wasn't your fault. It's only money."

They came to the big Colorado town.

"I don't like towns," said Dario.

She laughed. He was not quite equal yet to driving in town traffic.

The big town seemed to be all outskirts. They had an ice-cream soda at Woolworth's. Paula buys some Christmas cards; she asks for motor goggles.

"No, honey," says the pretty blonde girl. "We are out of them."

Over a door is written "Kenwood Hotel." Paula dashes in while Dario struggles with the car. She climbs a steep, narrow stair. In a long corridor she detects a button and presses it. Nothing happens. She presses again. A frowzy woman appears.

"I want two single rooms for the night, please."

"How many of you?"

"Two."

"Can you afford a dollar a room?"

"Yes."

Like an old friend, across the road they see a Montgomery Ward store. The Montgomery Ward catalogue is the Bible of the West. Paula did not know a place for miles around where people did not order from Montgomery Ward's. The catalogue in spring and autumn is an event. "Have you seen the new Montgomery Ward?" people ask each other. It took hours to go through it. There was everything in it, and more.

The next morning early they go on. There is still a terrific wind. Large round bushes are blowing along the road, bouncing like footballs, and are caught in the wire fences.

They are in Kansas now. They are told that there has been no rain for three years in this region. It looks like it. All the farmers are "broke." The farmhouses they pass are derelict; the sheds are empty; the paint is gone; the doors and gates hang limp on broken hinges. Dead and uncut wheat lies in the flatly spreading fields.

The sun sinks and sets over a world with nothing in it at all. An immense afterglow covers the empty land, but not for long; it fades, and the stars come out in the night sky.

They stop at a tiny camp. It is very gay, all trimmed up for Christmas; it is like a gypsy caravan.

One more day along the road and then a few days' rest in San Antonio.

From San Antonio to New Orleans

Dead-tired, they arrive at San Antonio. So the Lord has mercy on them and leads them straight to a most comfortable camp.

What a blessing these camps are when they are good! Especially when you travel by car. And travelling by car is the ideal way. No train to catch, no being boxed in with strangers. You can stop when you want and have had enough. This "Angelo Courts" has fifty-two cabins round a grass plot, and each cabin a space for the car. Their cabin has two bright rooms, a kitchen, a showerbath, an icebox, electric iron, and a friendly, helpful manager. Right away it's a home.

In the nearby café where they eat, the radio is on. A soulful man's voice answers little Virginia's question whether there really is a Santa Claus. "Yes, little Virginia," says the squilchy voice, "there is a Santa Claus because what would life be without romance, beauty, and love?"

"Lord help us," says Paula.

They try to sleep. But the motion of the car on the long drive keeps them rocking still, and the wind has stirred up their nerves. But the air is balmy after the cold of the ranch, a caress to their windpipes; and a small, gentle moon looks through the window. Here she is not the great, frightening monster at the ranch, that climbs over the mountains.

In San Antonio, with its Alamo where heroic battles were fought, there still lingers something of the frontier town's romance. Paula and Dario drive to a zoo in a low-lying park outside the town.

In an enclosure of pink rock there are monkeys, lots of

monkeys, playing in their monkey way. Golden-brown ones with those indecent pink cushions on their rears, scratching so deftly and watching, alert with their narrow, quick eyes in the small crumpled faces, ears on the *qui vive*. In the cage near them is a large black chimpanzee, large as a small man. He holds the bars with his strong hands and watches the two children near the bars. He is so still, but intense, a bored expression on his face. "Nothing exciting on this earth; nothing worth bothering about."

Dario calls to him and he gets excited. Suddenly he springs on to the ring that hangs from a rope in the centre of his cage and swings round and round; he works himself up into a frenzy. Quicker and quicker he circles, and out of his very wide-open mouth comes, "Ou-ou-ou," like the sound from the black face of woe of all the ages. At last he takes a high jump and lands very near them and stares. Then, bored and sad like a little old man, he walks to the far corner, *"finita la commedia,"* folds his arms, sits down and closes his eyes.

For sheer beauty and splendour, the lioness has it. Creamy and soft and indifferent, she stares with strong, unseeing eyes beyond us. Her cage is so small for her and the lion. In the cage next to them another lioness roars to the lion.

On the way home, Dario, not being used to the town traffic, dashes across the red light. An elegant young policeman steps up.

"What's the big idea?" he drawls.[1]

"Oh, no big idea. You see, we are strangers."

He hesitates. "I ought to fine you people. All right, go on."

"Have I any big idea," Paula mused, "or haven't I?"

After a few days' rest, they leave their nice camp and go on to New Orleans where they will take the ship for Buenos Aires.

Off they start, early in the morning. It is misty still, but later on the sun will triumph.

---

[1] In several manuscript fragments among the papers, the policeman's "What's the big idea?" is used as an amusing point of departure for exploration of her intention in the book. —"Have I any big idea?"

"I think I can smell the sea from the Gulf of Mexico," says Dario.

The road is slippery, and suddenly and unexpectedly the car spins completely round on itself. A brake that was too tight. Now they have found their No. 90 road, going to New Orleans. Another problem solved, Oh, America! Even a complete dumbbell can easily get anywhere, following the road and hanging on to the number.

It is Christmas Eve. Now they are on the red soil of the South. It smells different here. It smells delicious, somehow soft and gentle. So far they had not smelled anything; it had been too cold. But now there are scents of moist trees and red earth. They meet nothing but Negroes along the road. "There was an old Negro and his name was Uncle Ned" and "Old Folks at Home" sing through Paula's head.

The sun has conquered the mist. "Nothing suggests Christmas in this gentle air," says Paula.

A lilac mist hangs softly over the leafless woods they pass, soft as pigeons' wings on the horizon; and the sky blooms out like love-in-the-mist.

"Look at the adorable carriage," cries Paula. Along comes a high, tiny carriage, a kind of old-fashioned cab, drawn by one brown horse, and a young couple in it, romantic as romance itself. They are coming out of church in this small town, Gonzales, but only whites.

"I suppose the black people have their own church."

Towards evening, along the road they can see Christmas trees alight in the small houses. They are tired. For hours they have been on the road. In the big, barnlike place where they eat, men come in already tipsy. "It's early to be drunk," says Paula, full of resentment.

At last they land at Beaumont to spend the night.

Christmas at Home

*This first of the returns to the past is concerned with her
early childhood in Germany and her relations with her
family. "Edna" is Else, the eldest of the three von Richthofen sisters, born October 8, 1874, in Chateal. After at-
tending finishing school at Freiburg and studying at a
teachers' college in Metz, she became one of the first
women students at Heidelberg, did her doctor's dissertation under the economist Max Weber, and on November 18, 1902, married one of her teachers, Dr. Edgar
Jaffe, professor of political economy. In 1910 they moved
to Munich, where he had accepted a post at the university. "Manya" is Johanna (Nusch), the youngest of the
sisters (later Frau Max Schreibershofer, and Frau Emil
Krug). Frieda and she attended a Catholic convent
school, half French, and a girls' high school in Metz.
When Frieda was seventeen and "Nusch" fifteen, they
were sent to a finishing school in the Black Forest, kept
by Moravian Brothers. The von Richthofen family traced
its descent from a commoner, Samuel Schmidt, the son
of a pastor, who was adopted by a nobleman in 1562.
Schmidt's grandson became a Bohemian knight in 1661
and took the name of von Richthofen. He was the sisters'
great-great-great-great grandfather. Most of the Richthofen men were diplomats. Emil, the uncle of Frieda's father, was ambassador to Sweden. Emil's son, Oswald
(1847–1906), was State Secretary of the Foreign Office
and Prussian Secretary of State. Frieda's visit to his
household in Berlin, when she was seventeen, is de-*

scribed in the chapter titled "Grown Up." Frieda's father, Friedrich, born in 1845, had begun a career in the army in 1862, had served in the Franco-Prussian War, and, during the childhood and adolescence described in this and other chapters of the memoirs, was an official in the civil service in Metz. Among Frieda's papers were several parts of a translation she had made of her father's war diary; these she had hoped to incorporate into her book, to show, she said in a letter to Harry T. Moore dated September 20, 1954, "what a decent war it was, to counteract the Hitler regime impression of Germany!" Else Jaffe said of the von Richthofen background, in a letter to the editor dated December 6, 1957:

> *. . . They were landowners in Silesia, gentry, as you would call them. But my father's father having lost somehow his possessions, my father had no foothold there—and drifted to the West of the Empire and to the newly conquered Lorraine. The only Richthofens he kept in touch with were his brother, a dried up military justice, and his cousin, later on Secretary of State, in whose house Frieda spent a winter. He liked to tease Frieda as, to my feeling, she overdid the importance of the Richthofens in a romantic way: they were no Cecils or Rohans, but, as I said, gentry, dating from the middle of the Sixteenth Century. Their really most important member was Ferdinand v. R., an explorer of China, a very learned man and a most perfect gentleman—but no near relation.*

Lying in her quiet hotel bedroom at the Lafayette, half asleep, Paula relived a childhood Christmas, as this Christmas Eve reminded her.

Already in October Edna, the eldest, had told Paula and Manya: "We must begin and save our weekly pocket money for the Seidels for Christmas."

Paula and Manya made long faces, it was hard to part with

the weekly fifty cents that you bought those liquorice shoestrings [with], and the little surprise packets with a whistle or a very tiny doll in them or a drum and some sweets.

But they submitted. There was Edna with her cameo face that was mostly so serious who, since she was quite small, had this passion for the poor, this social conscience. But Paula did not feel sorry for Frau Seidel, the washerwoman. Paula envied her, when she stood so firmly planted over the huge washtub, her arms to the elbows in the soft steaming suds, and then hanging up the flapping, snow-white washing in the kitchen yard. Frau Seidel looked so clean in her frock of heavy cotton and her strong boots and fair hair brushed neatly close to her head. She was so contented and peaceful. There were eight flaxen-haired Seidel children, roundfaced and clean as if they too went into the washtub and were scrubbed and rinsed.

When Paula read *A Tree Grows in Brooklyn*, it struck her that these very poor people's children had piano lessons and the brother bought the sister a pair of black lace panties for Christmas. Such ambitions for her children would never have entered Frau Seidel's head. America must change people in their desires.

"Do you like washing, Frau Seidel?" Paula had asked.

"Ah, child," she said, "it's got to be done."

The old toys were collected and mended, and the old dolls dressed in new clothes. That was Paula's job. She loved dolls.

So the winter came; on their children's room windows the iceflowers were thick, and you had to blow hard before there was a hole of clear glass that you could look through. And there, far away, was the one tall finger of the cathedral rising out of the mass of stone in a white, level world of snow. The hills on both sides were lower than in their summer attire. And then the hanging lamp was lit and the three girls waxed enthusiastic over the work for the Seidel Christmas.

"We will give them the monster." "I will make her a new dress." "And I can mend that small cart I hope."

The monster was an unbeloved doll, who was accused of all sorts of bad deeds and was scolded and kicked around.

The old family clothes were collected and mended, and the sixpences grew.

Paula was a wild, sunburnt child with straw-coloured hair standing out from her head and scratched knees from climbing trees and falling into ditches too wide for her to jump. [She] was the least good-looking of the sisters. Manya, the youngest, was lovely. She had a heart-shaped face, great brown eyes with a quiet wonder in them, all warm and cream and brown and red she was, her rounded movements full of charm, like a fairychild she seemed to Paula. Grown-ups—and what strange creatures grown-ups were—would come and exclaim over Manya's beauty. Paula was making faces at her. Then they would look at Paula and say nothing. Paula made more faces, and Manya began to giggle; so their mother shoved them both out of the room. "You insufferable brats," she would scold.

Christmas was coming nearer; the preparations were nearly finished. The little case that held the adhesive plaster for her father had embroidered on it: "I heal all wounds but those of love." The gift was nearly done. In the world of grown-ups much went on. The brown-gold drawing-room was locked and held mystery itself; parcels disappeared into it. The larder was festooned with sausages of all sorts and sizes. From the kitchen came a scent of hot honey and spices; the old thick hand-written cookery book lay on the kitchen table. In one of the outhouses lay a wild boar with large tusks and bristles and a wild smell; partridges were hanging from the ceiling, and hares. Her father had shot them. Though German, he had many friends among the French aristocracy in Lorraine. He had spoken French like a Frenchman. One of his friends was a Vicomte L— who was also a writer and had one of those charming small châteaux in Lorraine. Many actors came to stay with him. Among them, Sarah Bernhardt. Her father had returned from one of the shooting expeditions with the Vicomte. Later on, when Paula read Maupassant's *Contes de la Bécasse*, she thought, "Surely, my father's expeditions must have been like that."

From his visit her father was full of stories of Sarah: how she had given the village hairdresser a priceless ring because she liked the way he had done her hair.

"Oh, take me there, Papa," Paula had asked him.

But he would not. There was the world, and the half-world; and actors belonged to the half-world, and his daughters were ladies.

"Dear Papa," Paula thought, "what world would you think this daughter of yours belongs to now?"

A few days before Christmas came the *Marzipan* evening. On the round dining-room table under the hanging lamp lay a big board with the marzipan paste on it, made of ground almonds and icing sugar and rosewater. They all moulded small round loaves, and long ones; then they were burned across with a hot poker. They made apples with a clove for pip, and pears out of the paste. But her father made creatures—ducks and cats—with great skill.

At last Christmas Eve had come. Paula was almost sick with excitement. No Eleusinian mystery could have held more wonder than Christmas Eve. The girls were in their new white cloth dresses. Up in their room they had prepared the Seidel feast. In the kitchen the Seidel children were waiting, shining from an extra scrub. The small candles on the tree were quickly lit, the toys and gifts spread out on the white cloth of the table under it. Then the children trooped in. They were shy; so were Paula and Manya. They hovered by the door, but Edna manoeuvered them forward, and the Seidel children sang: *"Kinderlein Ihr Kommet,"* etc.

When the children had finally packed all their things into the enormous wash-basket and left, Manya and Paula flew down the garden path along the inside wall, the snow crunching under their feet. They listened to the joyful exclamations of the Seidel children coming along outside. They were no longer shy out here amongst themselves; and, hearing their joyful exclamations, Paula and Manya did not regret their departed sixpences any more.

People say there are no miracles. Paula saw so many. The love of parents seems a miracle. Before they are born, those brats are a burden and an anxiety, they howl at night and don't let you sleep. Later on they are noisy and destructive and expensive and a worry, and yet parents or most of them love them with an unwavering love. That is a miracle. How horrible it would be to be a state child, no place where you feel: "Here I belong, here I am wanted, even if I am a nuisance sometimes." Communism can never live long, it has no love in it. And that we need like water and air and food. When you do things for people to make them happy, you are happy yourself. Like warm garments this love envelops the child, and with horror we know that in Russia instead of parents, a cold abstract takes the place of this miracle.

Now the bell was ringing for their own feast. It was only the ordinary silver dinner-bell, but it had a different, special sound tonight. They all stood waiting in front of the double doors of the drawing-room. The brown-gold doors opened and there, up to the ceiling, streaming its light from many candles shimmering over silver and gold, stood the tree. Nothing but the tree in the world! Paula solemnly recited: "*Heilige Nacht, auf Engels Schwingen, nahst Du leise dich der Welt.*" "Holy night, on wings of angels, softly you to earth descend.")

Then the solemn first moment was over and everybody rushed to an individual table. So many presents! Books and dolls and toys, for Paula a much longed-for little sewing machine that really sewed! Lovely small pots and pans from Grandfather, for Manya a doll's house, with curtains and doors that opened and a father and mother and children and a lamp and flowerpots! Then the friends came with gifts, the old friends Baron K. and Dr. A. and Baron P., the bachelor. And the feast was ready. There were the hares that came every Christmas, and the special dessert, a coffee cream, and the fruit. It was a real feast. And then seeing the friends off, everybody made their imprint on the snow stretching out on their backs with their arms out!

That wonderful Christmas!

School

The text of this chapter is taken from a manuscript that is not part of the typescript, though it was together with it. The heading "Chapter III" had been struck out. The chapter seems to have come from a different version with a different time sequence, now lost. It has been placed here because its dream technique follows reasonably naturally the bedtime reflections of "Christmas at Home," and because it continues the story of Frieda's childhood.

That night Paula in her dreams was a child at home again. She was coming up the hill on to the high ground that centuries ago had been a Roman burial place. Now it was a parade ground.

In the distance the hills sloped down with the grapes ripening; between, the river gleamed its way and behind her rose the cathedral on its hill, a crouching, spreading cathedral with one tower, lifting its finger to heaven, the other finger was never built.

She was crying but mostly with rage. She held her school report crumpled in a hot hand. Her report was good, but why did they have to make this remark at the foot: "Paula's behaviour would be much improved, if she were a little more humble and reticent." Why should I be humble?

They thought her a nuisance, all those teachers. She did not like them either, except the old headmaster, who could make history [so] live for you that you were in those gone-by days that were past and so different. While the other teachers only

47

deadened your wits. She ran under the hot sun through the garden getting a whiff of the roses. Ah, she was home, on her own ground, always she ran home from school, she wanted so badly to be there again. The wistaria was clustering all round the house entrance.

She went straight to her father's study. He was writing at his desk. His bushy brows twitched as he saw her disturbed face.

On his desk lay the meteor and paperweight perfectly symmetrically dented, the big seal and red sealing wax, an onyx bowl and all sorts of objects that were somehow like her father. And by the big window bloomed the cacti and big leafy plants. On the wall behind him hung a row of guns between boarheads and chamoisheads and deer that he had shot.

Two dogs rose from what her mother scornfully called the dog-sofa, but she was too angry to take any notice of them.

"Here is my report," she said. She uncrumpled it from her hot hand and gave it to him.

He watched her roused face.

"It's a good report," he said, "but what about the remark at the end?"

"Why?" she shot out fiercely. "Why? They are such inferiors."

She remembered angrily the scene she had had with Miss Myers, one of the teachers, Miss Myers had been soulful over her.

"We would all love you, if you were only not so wild and independent, if you would only listen and do as we wish."

"I don't want you to love me, I don't love you. Your neck is too long and your legs are too short, and there is no love in your water-blue eyes," she thought, but was silent.

She could not bear it. Her father was watching her expressive face.

"That's no way for a small girl to talk," he remonstrated. "Do you think it's any fun to teach day in day out, year in year out?" Paula felt the first pang for Fräulein Myers's dreary existence.

He knew her so well, how almost fanatical she was in her

affections, but also in her dislikes, he loved her so much, his own flesh and blood.

But he felt it his duty to talk to her as a father should. She listened, but in her listening she dismissed his words and only heard the love underneath the words. Her heart came up again like a bird. Here she was at home.

They knew each other. Somewhere, she knew, he had been hurt; he also had suffered from inferiors, and she wanted to make up to him for it, in her helpless child's way.

She loved his thick, soft brown hair and the quick impatient movements, his clothes, that were so much part of him, his shining boots, even his ivory brushes and the snow white handkerchiefs with the crown in the corner. It all was him. And the poem he had written in her birthday album: comparing her to all the creatures, birds and bees, and she was to have all their virtues.

"Let's go to lunch."

Happily, she took his hand that was so alive in spite of the crooked forefinger that had never come straight again after having been shattered in the war.

"Polly-Putzli come along."

"Polly-Putzli" was the result of his reading Prescott's *Conquest of Mexico.*

Lunch was served under the cherry-trees, the cherries were ripe. There were the dark red cherries and the white and red ones, and then pale yellow ones, very sweet.

Her mother was there in her summer checked dress, buttoned down the front, vivid in her strength and integrity, and Manya, the young one, and Edna the eldest.

William, the manservant in white cotton gloves, was handing the soup round. William was woven into the family pattern, he was a gentle soul. His life was their life.

"Why must a man have his soup so boiling hot that he can't swallow it?" said her father testily, with a shake of his impatient hand.

"Wait then," came her mother's voice.

William adored his mistress and sided with her.

You always went to William when in trouble about broken windowpanes or if you wanted to hide from visitors. Paula was still chewing on Miss Myers's soulfulness. Paula had seen this very morning before her encounter with Miss Myers a poem written by Edna. Edna had a crush on Miss Myers. Now the devil tempted Paula and in a solemn voice she began to recite Edna's poem:

> "Thou art fair as the night,
> For also the night is fair."

Edna jumped as if she had been shot. She looked at Paula with deep reproach in her beautiful grey eyes.

The mother felt the tension.

"Now what is it, you two?"

Manya also looked disapproval. That Paula was always making trouble or getting into deep waters.

The father was eating his soup now. Paula in her young impudence felt how much better she would be able to handle her father than ever her mother did. He was beyond criticism.

"This isn't hair," he would tell her, stroking her head, "it's fluff like a young sparrow's."

That hurt her feelings, she was aware of her light hair sticking out in all directions.

She suffered tortures when he looked at her unpolished shoes or on her unfresh gloves with distaste.

Later Paula found all her beloved dolls hanging ignominiously upside down on the exercise bar. That was Edna's revenge.

Paula took the dolls and smoothed them down and, holding them consolingly in her arms, retired under the drawing-room sofa. There was nobody in the drawing-room on this warm summer afternoon, and she went to sleep with the dolls in her arms. When she woke up, she remembered it was Saturday afternoon, when her friends would come to play. Ada and Hans and Martin and Herbert and Felix and others.

On the table in the garden was a stack of bread and butter and a bowl of cherries and strawberries. You played hide-and-seek in the trenches the soldiers had dug and you also had to dodge the sentinel. There were huts and foxholes you raced about hot and dusty all afternoon. Manya would be dragged along too, though she was so small; Paula loved Manya, she was so lovely with her quiet velvety brown eyes and her heart-shaped face. Manya was sometimes overwhelmed by Paula's wild ways, but she had the firm belief that Paula would be able to do anything. . . .

Childhood

---

*This chapter, not in the typescript, originated as a new
beginning of the memoirs. The occasion was Mrs.
Lawrence's correspondence at the time of World War II
with Karl von Marbahr, whom she had loved in her
youth. An introductory passage addressed to him appears in the Introduction, where it is the next to the
last section. In contrast to the typescript, this chapter is
in the first person, but in tone and style they are essentially the same, and the chapter extends the account
of her childhood presented in the two preceding chapters.
The elision at the beginning represents a duplication of
the story of the teasing of Edna and her revenge through
the dolls.*

The first thing I can remember loving was Manya . . . whom
you remember as an adorable flapper. She was a quiet child,
sitting quietly, hugging her furry rabbit. She had a heart-
shaped little face with big brown eyes and the loveliest colouring
of red and brown and such pretty limbs. Her little arms and legs
of just the right firmness of flesh. I loved the perfection of her
and felt responsible for her. When the French nurse put her for
punishment in the cellar, I could not bear the thought of Manya
in the dark down there and I stood at the top of the kitchen
stairs and yelled with all my might. The whole household
came running and Manya had to be released. Manya had such
dignified ways, like a princess conferring favours. When she
politely thanked some friends for having been their guest, so

small a thing, I was impressed she had such natu
manners. She never said much, but her velvety eyes wat
and one day she said: "You know I don't really belong to
this family here. I belong there." Pointing with her sm;
to one of the fortifications of the town in the distance, on
"lunettes" crowned with a clump of trees. "My grandmother
lives there. I stay with her. She likes me. She gives me sweets. I
will bring you some."

Sure enough Manya presented me with some sweets soon
after this. But I knew what she had done. She had dipped some
lumps of sugar into some raspberry syrup. I thanked her for her
gift. I belonged so passionately to this home, the house, the
gardens, but if Manya imagined this other home, that was her
affair.

My next widening circle of love included the gardens. After
being pent up in the children's room through the winter, looking
through the windows and wiping the moisture off them with my
apron, spring came. The first event a crocus, then snowdrops
and the blue scylla—all frail and frightened it seemed to venture
forth. And then they came in a rush and splendid. The hyacinths,
the tulips and the parrot tulips, then the bushes burst out, lilac
and snowballs and red hawthorn bushes, and the fruit trees in
bloom. Then came the day when I stepped carefully behind my
father, who cut the first asparagus with the asparagus knife.
And the drama of the garden went on. The strawberries came,
there were white ones too. Then the cherries. Black, big ones,
yellow and red, and yellow. By then I was to be found mostly in
the trees, Manya looking up at me, always a bit astonished at this
wild sister of hers. Then the heat of summer came and the pears
and apples and plums and "mirabelles" ripened. The yellow
fruit lay on the ground and the wasps were hovering over them
and you were afraid to go near. I saw my father carefully catch
flies and throw them into the spiderwebs that were spun over the
vines and covered with dewdrops. The spider would dash from
under a grape leaf and weave round the fly. Then in the heat I
remember the first time my father took me swimming in the
clear river. He took me on his shoulders and dived from the

board. I remember the surprise of being under water, but I emerged and swam around like a tadpole. After that I could swim.

There was also Edna, our oldest sister. She was five years older than I. She was very serious and intellectual with a delicate cameo face. Her eyes were long and grey, with long lashes that slowly covered her eyes like wings. I don't believe she ever got the same intense joy out of our surroundings as I did. Her demands were for intellectual satisfaction.

There were no tragedies in our young lives, except minor ones. When our guinea pigs died of an unexpected early frost, we found them in their pen stiff and dead. "Well," we said, "if they died of cold maybe if we put them to warm in the oven, they will come alive again." We covered them on a tray with leaves and put them in the oven in the kitchen, but they did not come to life again, they remained dead.

Then Tom, a mongrel, who had appeared and stayed, was my special favourite. He had a broken rope round his neck when he first came, so he must have escaped from some miserable life. He was very good-natured and let us play with him and we pulled him around and rode him. But one day, he was having his midday-meal and I went near him to stroke him, when he turned and bit me over the eye, where I still have a tiny scar. I was very upset that Tom misunderstood my intentions, it must have been some fear on his part out of his former unhappy life.

Then I was going to school. With white, uncomfortable gloves my father took me to introduce me. This going out of my safety, my home, where I belonged, where I had a right to be was another step. I was a wild and restive child. My knees were always scratched, my face burnt with the sun and my hair stood up on my head. When guests came to the house they would exclaim over Manya: "What a lovely child," then look at me and say nothing. I would make a quick grimace at Manya and we would laugh and my mother would be angry. I remember when I was with you and a group of officers and one of them said to me as we passed a very pretty little girl: "You must have been a pretty child like this one." "Oh no, nothing of the sort,"

I answered. "Well," you drawled, "sometimes the plain children grow up to be pretty, but sometimes they don't." For a moment I was scared that you should think me a plain girl, till I saw the twinkle in your eye. It seems such a silly thing to remember but I do.

Grown-ups were queer objects, you couldn't understand them in the least, there was no clue. Your parents and the real friends and the servants, you felt towards them rather as the Greeks must have felt about their Olympus full of gods. I cannot think except with profound horror of children being brought up by the state, regimented, when the individual reaching out to all the surroundings was so real and the love of your parents was the soil you grew on. When you think what a nuisance, what hard work, what an anxiety most brats are, it is a miracle how the parents go along loving them and caring for them.

My parents were wonderful parents. Their own marriage was not so perfect. My father was alert, interested in doing things, impatient. My mother was slower in temperament, philosophical, and only much later on I loved her as she deserved. In my young impudence, when they argued, I often thought, "You don't handle him right, I would know better than you how to do it." He had hurt her in many ways bitterly, but never did she complain about him to us, he was a father. I thought him perfection on earth. And I also felt from a small child sorry for him as I felt instinctively sorry for all men. They had the responsibility of living for all other people, the burden of governments and religions and what went on in the big world, that I sensed. About this my father was not at ease. He had a side to him that was like Francis of Assisi, animals meant so much to him and our gardens were his creation and beautiful. But some time earlier in his life, he had lost his faith in himself, lost faith in everything. He was stuck in the old prejudices and taboos. Later on [he and] Edna, who was a born reformer, had long arguments, Edna with her inborn love for the underdog and my father saying: "The world does not change. There always were and there always will be underdogs. . . ."

Travelling On

Here the narrative returns to present time, Christmas Day, 1933, in Beaumont, Texas, and continues the journey to New Orleans, and thence to Buenos Aires and the visit to Ravagli's sister Luisa (Mrs. Ferruccio Castori) and his brother Giovacchino Ravagli. The reading of Goethe's Faust *and Frieda's distaste for it is a thematic episode that recurs in various manuscript fragments.*

The next day is Christmas Day. "Even the sparrows rest on Christmas Day," says Dario.

In the lounge of the hotel, in the bright daylight, a Christmas tree is burning. But, instead of flickering candle flames and the smell of wax, it has steady, dead electric coloured bulbs.

"No Christmas tree for me," says Paula.

The next day they drive on through Louisiana. The road is A-1. It seems like a very long bridge. At both sides are swamps that look endless. Trees grow in the water, palms with beautiful green fan-leaves. "I didn't know palms could grow in water." But from some of the taller trees long beards of grey hang down from the branches. The trees are not so happy.

Many cars that seem to come off a dust heap wobble along on spindly legs, lots of Negroes in them, grandmothers and young ones and babies. The older the car, the more people it contains.

For the first time, they pass cotton fields; from the distance they look like fields of white roses.

"Get me some of those cotton flowers, Dario, please."

They are lovely in their clean, fluffy cottonness, with five hard, brown leaves that hold them together. Why has nobody made the cotton flower the symbol of the South?

The country is no longer swampy. On the large sugar cane fields, the tall cane is being cut by many Negroes and loaded on to mule wagons. They pass a sugar factory and get a whiff of burned sugar. Negro huts stand along ditches off the road.

"I wish I could paint all those dingy huts a bright colour," says Paula.

This is Longfellow's Evangeline country, they are told at a petrol station.

It is evening; they will be at New Orleans tonight. There is a strong draft from the higher bank on the left. "I think the Mississippi is up there," Paula tells Dario. They climb up the bank. Higher than the road, swift and grey and very wide, the masses of water rush along. Paula shivers in the twilight. So much powerful water.

They must cross by ferry now into New Orleans. It is easy. They drive on to the ferry along with the other cars. After driving off the ferry they are in New Orleans.

Their hotel, "Ponchartrain," is very French. They have an excellent, delicate Louisiana-French meal: a fresh crab dish and cream cheese with cream over it.

Next day they must go to the emigration office. How hateful the torture of passports! The Argentine Consul insists on a police certificate. Neither Paula nor Dario has such a thing. She is reminded of the poor American sailor who is left behind in Europe without a passport. He is taken over the frontier in every country. Finally in Paris he is put into prison. Quite pleasantly, they tell him: "You ought to have some papers to show who you are."

"I know who I am without papers," says the sailor, as well he might.

It is a terrible story, "Traven's Deathship." Losing your soul is less dangerous than losing your passport. Dario goes to his young, smart Italian Consul who gives him a letter for the

Argentine Consul. Paula's British Vice-Consul telephones the Argentine one that the fact of her having a passport means that the British police have nothing against her. Then they must be vaccinated. So, instead of seeing New Orleans, they rush from one Consulate to another. But the young porter at the hotel informs her, "Napoleon died in New Orleans. He is buried here!"

At last they get on the boat. It is long and narrow, carries the mail and freight, and has only a few passengers. They watch the loading. Hundreds of barrels of tar and boxes of fireproof bricks; the long arms of the cranes swinging the boxes into the holds; Negroes and white men working fast. An immense tank is the last thing the crane picks up from the wharf and lets down on to the ship. It is dusk. A young man in uniform watches his young wife on shore till the last moment. The boat slides away on the big river. Seventeen days before they land again.

The new year has come in tempestuously. The sea is rough. Dario feels ill and does not want any food. There are only a few business men on board and two elderly women who are sitting glued to their chairs, knitting with black wool. There is the sprightly young business Jew who makes jokes and repeats Mae West's famous saying, "Come up and see me some time." There is one man Paula dislikes. He asks her, "Do you know any dirty stories?" Considering her feelings, her "No" is mild. But she has her revenge on him. She watches him bathe in his blue and white bathing suit.

"You, your tootsies are turned in, and you are heavy on your feet, and your body is the soft body of a child; and yet there are cynical lines on your face that is already so old."

Dario is disappointed that there are no nice young women for him to dance with.

Paula stays in her cabin mostly, like a nun in her cell, and embroiders: bright, fantastic flowers and tropical birds that never flew in any tropics. She had brought with her one of her mother's treasures, Goethe's *Faust*, bound in soft leather, to read.

Her mother would quote:

"Nach Golde drängt,
Am Golde hängt,
Doch alles! Ach, wir Armen!"

And here was Paula—oh, shades of her mother—finding *Faust* mere bunk! Poor little Gretchen! What business had she being a heroine? Because Faust, the elderly student, has a desire to go on a belated spree, as elderly students have a way of doing, egged on by the bold Mephisto, a tragedy, a terrible one, is the result. Impressed by the "gentleman" Faust, she, the little girl of the people, has fallen for him and is going to have a child. Now the horrors pile up, all because of this *faux pas*. The mother is poisoned, the brother stabbed, and Gretchen kills the baby and goes mad. How happy she would have been making little jackets for the baby and showing it off, like a good little mother, to the neighbours in a grand pelisse! She was done out of all that, poor thing.

So Gretchen is out of the picture, but Faust goes on to a *zweiter Teil*, a second part. That Faust goes off like that into all sorts of intellectual stuff after this first part, after all this tragedy, seemed to her quite unnatural. Paula had heard it praised as the most wonderful thing ever written. No, she couldn't see it. So people change from generation to generation. What is one generation's poetry is another one's bunk.

In the next cabin Dario was struggling with his English. He struggled mightily but went about it in such a mechanical, dumb way that Paula got exasperated helping him, so she left him to it.

Paula found a *Benvenuto Cellini* on the ship's bookshelves, with an introduction by an Englishwoman she had slightly known. The woman was the true London garden-suburb type. In her introduction, she was very shocked, very shocked indeed, at Benvenuto. Paula amused herself by imagining what would have happened if she could have put the garden-suburb lady back into Benvenuto's time and Benvenuto into the garden-suburb.

If only that bad gramophone were not going all the time!

Outside it got warmer; they would pass the Equator. But the sea was still rough, and one day the stairs on the outside of the ship had worked loose and were broken in two. One of the young engineers climbed down and mended it. The waves were dashing over him; he was rocking and hanging on by the skin of his teeth. It looked like a scene done for the movies. In front, the ship was diving its nose into the sea and rising high in the air. At night the sailors would move about with lanterns, looking like pirates.

After seventeen days of nothing but sea, they arrive at Rio de Janeiro. It looks like a dream place from the sea, with clear, bright blue bays where people bathe, all shades from white to deep brown.

"I want to live here on one of these bays with the palm trees, in a little white villa."

Green hills, very green, lie behind the bays. One of the hills is crowned with an enormous white Christ, his arms extended in blessing. They drive through an avenue of magnificent palms where the governor's palace stands. In front of the cathedral a row of soldiers is lined up in uniforms of comic opera. There is some ceremony on. The streets are full of the army. Dario gives them a critical, military scrutiny. "They look all right," he says.

In a funicular they run up the Azucar. Hanging in the air, they look down on palatial barracks where soldiers are playing football in the open space by the sea.

Driving up to San Paolo is a treat. The semi-tropical growth along the steep, climbing road, the flowers, are pure joy. There is a paper-white lily with a sweet scent, and a big, red, unknown flower; and Paula's heart gives a twinge as she sees the flowering plant that at the last bloomed in her dying husband's room.

They have climbed to the top. Cataracts have rushed down the mountainside. There are little lakes and moist places along the road that look as if snakes lived in them, lots of them; you would not like to put bare feet into that water. It is a kind of damp plateau, and they drive on for miles.

A straggling San Paolo begins. They arrive in the market place, a bustling, busy town with trams clanking. San Paolo is the Chicago of Brazil.

They have a very grand lunch. Four Germans eat near them;

Paula has not seen any Germans like them since before the war. They are restful and prosperous, and have that "we are the Lords of creation" look. You see it no more in Germany.

Finally they arrive at Buenos Aires. Paula feels nothing but heat—no *buenos aires* at all. The River Plata is not like *plata* either, but a slow, brown, muddy river. Dario had come here to visit his sister and his brother. Paula is staying with them too. They drive through dreary streets and arrive at a dreary house. They pass through ugly stone corridors and arrive at the door of Dario's sister's apartment. The sister stands waiting in a frenzy of excitement with her small child. She kisses Dario, and weeps and weeps.

Poor Gina and her husband are not happy in this dreary place. Paula tries to look out of her window: nothing but ugly walls; not even standing on her toes can she see the sky. Paula's heart aches for these people. They are not poor, but exiles; they do not live, but exist.

Gina sings like a thrush in the kitchen: a bird in a cage—not a gilt one either, but a bird in a cement box. She is so pretty, and looks like a madonna when her little girl goes to sleep on her lap. The husband is a strong, good fellow, but his face is city-white from working in an office. He is anti-Fascist and cannot go back to Italy. There are fierce arguments between Dario and him, Dario saying, "But look what Mussolini has made of Italy." But Ferruccio is firm in his condemnation.

At night they all try to get cool on the roof. There is nothing to be seen but more roofs and a hospital. On the next roof are many bird cages; and to her horror Paula sees the tiny doors of the cages open—left open to decoy the birds that fly overhead. Paula would love to go and open all the cages at night and let all the birds fly, but feels too depressed even for that adventure.

There is no privacy in the apartment; from the anteroom all the other rooms open out.

Adolescence

As an escape from the unpleasantness of the situation in Buenos Aires, Frieda turns to the past, continuing the story of her girlhood through her first serious love. Among the papers were numerous revisions of this episode. Most of the typescript version, titled "Boris," had been struck out. The text of a longer and more complete manuscript is given here. The Good Friday experience is another thematic episode that recurs in the manuscripts. It is repeated, in another context but with the same significance, in "Last Chapter—Friends."

Else Jaffe says of this period of Frieda's life: "Her first 'love,' the cousin, was Kurt von Richthofen, then an ensign at the Kriegschule at Metz, a boy of eighteen or nineteen; she must have been about sixteen. It ended dramatically, as he gave her, as a parting gift, a big box of macaroons which, to our disgust, she did not share but ate up all by herself, and felt very sick afterwards. . . . A more serious attachment was that to Lieutenant K. von Marbahr; it remained, of course, in the conventional limits of that time. I don't think they ever saw each other alone. When I was in Berlin as a student and he was stationed there, he sometimes met me just to talk about Frieda."

So Paula spends much time in her room and tries to write.

What a blessing her memories are!

Almost like somebody else she sees herself at fifteen getting ready to go to church on Good Friday.

Carefully she dresses. She puts on her pink and white thin flannel dress, the floppy Florentine hat with the black velvet ribbon hanging down the back. Round her neck is a thin gold chain from which hangs a black enamelled heart with small pearls on it that she has begged from her mother. Even white gloves.

A change has come over her. The wild child with scratched knees and hair sticking out all over its head has become vain and is comparatively civilized.

The reason is Olaf. Olaf is a distant cousin from Silesia and he has come as cadet to be a lieutenant soon and stays at the old military school, where Napoleon had been a hardworking young artillery-officer.

Olaf had come to her hospitable home, where as a member of the family all welcomed him. By the parents he was almost treated as a son. Edna talked ideas to him, social and political, and he gently teased little Manya. But with Paula it was different. She was aware of him as she had never been aware of anybody before.

He was so slender in his uniform, the sword almost slipping over the narrow hips. His head was sleek like a seal's and his wide mouth that laughed in such a comical way was full of splendid teeth. He was twenty-one. He and Paula played tennis together, there were excursions on the river and picnics, and the mysterious attraction grew between them, delicious to Paula and a little scaring. He told her stories of romantic lovers from families known all over Europe and then he would complain: "I am dumb, I am dumb, I don't get the hang of these tactics I am supposed to understand."

"I don't think you are dumb," Paula would protest.

All his Sundays he spent at her home, and when he went away in the evening Paula said to herself: "I am just like a glow-worm, I glow to myself all the time and that is because of Olaf."

He began to love the gardens with the flowers coming into bud and all the luxurious growths springing up as much as she did. "Come and look at the irises," she would tell him. There were

almost black ones, big ones and brown ones with a yellow edge
and very dark blue ones and small ones, almost like orchids. "Do
you know, Olaf, there are sixteen different varieties of iris all
about the gardens?" And she told him about her father's big
gardening book with plans of the gardens and every plant,
especially the espalier pear and apple trees, were there in the
book. Then he had to get the first strawberries with her; beside
the big red ones, there were also white ones, that she never saw
or tasted again; they had a pineapple flavour.

She met his company of cadets on horseback and of course
they all knew her and she blushed and he would bring some of
them to the house. Then, when she was in the town one of the
cadets would see her and soon Cousin Olaf would be at her elbow
as if stamped out of the ground and drive her home in a landau.
She felt grown-up and important; there she was, only a schoolgirl, and yet all of these young men, who seemed so manly and
splendid, were watching for her and waiting. She knew that
today at the garrison church Olaf would be there too.

She started out with her hymnbook in her gloved hand and
before long she met her friend, the "woman with the harp." She
was an elderly woman with a weatherbeaten skin and clean but
washed out clothes. There was a daughter with her, but Paula
was hardly aware of her, while the mother fascinated her; the
woman was so calm, with an underknowledge of layers and
layers of life that moved Paula. She loved her more than any
other one that came to the house. The harp was carried over one
shoulder like one wing of an angel. She would sing her songs on
the lawn and the raucous voice of the woman and her hands
pulling the harpstrings had a strange, disturbing effect. Her
songs: "I am a poor musician," and "I am twenty, O dear,
twenty," and "Fly to her house, little birds . . ." She would
listen with all her heart to the woman singing, and it was as if
that voice told her many, many strange and sad facts. Paula
became attached in an inarticulate way to her harping friend.
When she did not come for some time, Paula wished she would
appear. So she had been very distressed when her father said to
her, "You can't be so friendly with that woman, that girl of hers

is quite impossible." "He doesn't know how wonderful this woman is," Paula thought. She was unhappy that the woman with the harp was served a meal in the kitchen, but then Paula never could see social distinctions; some people you loved and some you didn't, that was all. Now on her way she met her friend with the harp and she kissed Paula's hand.

"Don't do that, please," Paula said in genuine distress, pulling away her hands, and very unhappy remembering her father's words. She wanted to invite the woman to stay with the family, but she couldn't. She went on her way, puzzling about all this.

She came to the garrison church, that was so different from the cathedral.

You entered the cathedral like the hollow skeleton of an enormous prehistoric animal. A stained-glass rose-window like a medieval sun threw dim coloured lights on the stone floor. There was the big altar in the distance, and little altars in the side chapels with clumps of candles flickering, and lingering incense filled the silent air. Olaf had told her that some of the cadets had their "rendezvous" behind the big altar with some of the town girls. Just before sunset especially Paula liked to go into the cathedral, the rose-window shone so mysteriously at that hour, then there were only a few silent women about.

But in the garrison church the light was harsh and grey. The church was filled with soldiers. Paula stood between some officers in shining high boots, their hands resting in front of them on the helmet and the sword. They stood firm and solid, heads held high.

From all around her and from the choir arose a mighty but hushed sound of soldiers' voices singing

> "O Head of blood and sorrow
> Of wounds and full of scorn. . . ."

The sound swelled and you were swamped in its powerful waves and then it sank and the parson had mounted the pulpit. Behind him the big crucifix was draped in black for Good Friday. The

parson looked like Martin Luther and read the gospel of Good
Friday with a powerful voice. "And it was about the sixth hour
and there was a darkness over all the earth until the ninth hour.
And the sun was darkened, and the veil of the temple was rent in
the midst. And when Jesus had cried with a loud voice, he said:
'Father, into thy hands I commend my spirit.' And having said
thus, he gave up the ghost."

She shivered, looking at the figure on the cross, with the bent
head, the slim body hanging from the nails that his fellow human
beings had driven through his hands and feet. Was this the end
and the meaning of a man's existence? Why had he not answered
to Pontius Pilate, who seemed a fair and just man, who was on
his side; he could have saved him. When you love people you
don't let them kill you. She looked at the colonel by her side,
what was he thinking of?

Paula could almost see that young Jesus, walking by the Lake
of Galilee, walking on light feet, his body relaxed, because he
was not burdened with any eagerness to buy or sell anything, or
ambition to impose himself on others. The sun would shine
wherever he was. The shores of the lake were covered with wild
flowers and in the lake now and then a fish would jump. He
would watch an olive tree and look at the lilies with a sacred joy
in all things on earth. No "man of sorrow" this young Jesus but
a gay man and a friendly one. He went into people's houses and
talked to them, he asked a handsome woman at a well for a drink
that she gladly gave him, he went to weddings. "People say of
me: 'What kind of fellow is this who eats and drinks with
sinners?' " He talked about the things he knew, of seeds and
birds, and the core of him was love, love that radiated from him
and compelled his disciples to follow him and his love. "Love thy
neighbour as thyself." That was new. Before him you had only
loved your own mortal self and went around in a cage of
yourself. What a release to get out of that cage and expand to
others! One poor man from a small town who clung to his vision
and gave to his disciples from his poet's and prophet's soul in full
measure. "I am the resurrection and the life." He himself was
the resurrection from the now dead Mosaic law. Not a resurrec-

tion after death, not a life hereafter, but here and now: new life.
Gandhi's non-resistance is nothing compared to Christ's positive
love. Jesus is the only being who paid back by his unique living
in infinite gratitude the privilege of being born into this world.
We are not grateful, not a bit. Only when we are going to die,
when the privilege is taken from us, then we may have an inkling
what it has meant. After those radiant years of youth and
wisdom—they were happy years, spent with his disciples,
helping his fellow men in every way—came the great test. "To
them that have shall be given and from them that have not shall
be taken away," and the have-nots were his furious enemies. But
nothing could deter him from his path. "You hate, my enemies,
but my way is to love and I will love, whatever happens." So his
enemies persecuted him and insulted him and murdered him.
The most sublime words ever spoken are these: "Father, forgive
them, they know not what they do." His love survived to the
bitter end in inevitable logic. But they knew what they were
doing, his enemies, they could not bear this splendour, they had
to destroy it. And what had been done with this glorious new
vision? Hellfire and inquisition and *"sois mon frère ou je te tue."*
Resplendent church fathers, the very opposite of that life that
had been lived by the Lake of Galilee. Like the miracle of Jesus
on one hand was the miracle of horror that had been done to his
meaning. All the dogma and doctrine were dead words to Paula.

She looked around for Olaf. He was standing at the church
door. Round the corner he had a landau waiting, she got in and
they drove home in splendour. She could not say much, Good
Friday had disturbed her so deeply. . . .

Easter Sunday came and was a feast, both parents were good
at feasts. The blue scyllas and snowdrops were out and a bush
called "Son before the Father" was flowering; the bush has this
name because the yellow flowers come before the leaves. It was a
gay day. Manya and Paula, though of course the day had long
gone by when they believed in the Easter hare, insisted that he
should come, with his chocolate eggs, and red sugar rabbits and
eggs of porcelain, filled with exquisite chocolates and sweets of
all sorts. The Easter hare had to hide them in the garden. They

hunted for the eggs in the grass and bushes and to their dismay some of the chocolate eggs had melted in the hot sun and were nothing but a brown mess.

Olaf and Paula had spent the day together, and when he was leaving she went along the garden path with him to the small gate at the end of the garden. It was a mild spring night, dark, no moon, but the stars were out and the lilacs and hyacinths gave their perfume to the air. They had talked and laughed, now they walked side by side silently. When they came to the gate, she held out her hand to say "good night" but he turned to her and gently, his lips, like butterfly wings, came down on her mouth. "Little one, sweet one," she heard him say to himself with clenched teeth. She went off like a firecracker and like a wild thing raced back the garden path to the house and her room. She threw off her clothes and got into bed and lay there in an unknown, unbelievable state of bliss.

Next morning after a deep sleep she woke and told herself: "The family thinks I am still a child, but now I am no longer so. They think it is just a joke but it isn't, this our friendship." All through the summer this happiness between her and Olaf went on. He came whenever he could, Sundays he would spend with them and even the servants treated him as one of the household. When he went with his detachment on a military expedition he sent her some special brand of candy. She put the box of candy under her bed and was not at all generous with it. But Manya was an understanding soul, she did not remonstrate, though at other times the sisters shared everything. The months flew by, Olaf loved the house and garden as much as Paula did. He would remember it all his life.

She knew him so well. He shared so openly with her all he had known and all he was: he was a sunny person. She had a glimpse of what a young man was like. He loved Paula with a first trusting love. Always, through the summer, she waited for the enchantment of the silent walk to the garden gate in the night, enveloped by the summer scents and the light of the stars. And silently he kissed her, the kiss that she had been waiting for, the miracle of his kiss! She knew that he hoped that later on they might marry. But with the fatality of youth she also knew this day would never come. The terrible day came when he was leaving. She waved to him, to the moving train, the train clanking to the faraway, and then and then slowly it was gone. She could not cry, her feet were heavy to move from the spot where she stood. Gone! No more Olaf to look at her and talk to her and tease her and love her! "If I were the moon," she wrote in her diary that night, "I know where I would shine." She was thankful that the family did not realize the depth of her first grief.

More about Buenos Aires

Frieda's reaction to the unhappy lives of Ravagli's brother and sister in the following unfictionalized fragment reveals her remarkable drive and her attitude toward life, and shows, as nowhere else, the strain that this sometimes led to in her relations.

So at last we have come to our last halt, Buenos Aires—have rescued the luggage. I can feel nothing but heat, no buenos aires at all. I am miserable, but I knew beforehand I wouldn't like it. Angelino's sister and husband and his brother I am staying with. They are so kind and decent but "under." I can't stand people that are under, I can't be with them. At last Angelino realises sadly, that even money means nothing, that only good will and a little faith between men makes life. He still feels the warm blood-connection with the body of mankind and now he knows it is broken and one must stand alone and apart. His sadness swamps me, he puts the burden of it on me, as always I have to bear the burden of hopelessness; the sister's husband is a bit of a hero, but a hopeless one. And the sister Gigina is unhappy and Angelino tries to cheer her up. He scolds her and is tender with her and in the long run it's no use, I know. I am resentful. I have given so much of myself, given and given, as if my giving again was without end, a bottomless pit, and what I gave to Lawrence he gave to the world, and Angelino does the same; what I give of hopeful life to Angelino, he

gives to others and I can whistle, whistle for more
life, I suppose. People take from me as if I were the
sun and not a human being at all. . . .

Dario and Gina talk about their little home town so far away.
Here it was once more translated into another nation, the story of
Sons and Lovers. Gina comes alive and they talk their home
dialect, calling their old neighbours by their funny nicknames.
The mother had been the pivot of the family—mother of nine
children, a husband who worked and occasionally drank too
much wine on a Saturday night. The mother sacrificing herself
to the family. The children adore her and rest in her. Then she
dies and the family goes to pieces. Gina has an almost too intense
love for her youngest sister. Now the sister is ill and so far away
Gina is almost sick with longing. She wails and moans and wants
to be with her sister. There is a deadly emotional strain in the
house. The husband is beside himself, the child cries, and Gina,
no longer the madonna, slaps it and yells at it.

"Stop being miserable," says Paula at last. "You can't do
anything. You will only make yourself and everybody else ill."

There is also Gina's brother; he comes and goes silently as a
ghost. He has become speechless by now.

Paula would like to see something of the Argentine, so Dario
and she take tickets. But the tickets are returned after two days.
The governor of the province they wanted to go to was murdered
and nobody can go there now.

It is carnival now and they go to see the display along the
River Plata at the Balneario, land that has been regained from
the river. There is an unpleasant dampness in the air, the large
trees look dank as if they suffered from too much moisture. They
sit on a bank and watch the cars go by under brightly lit arches.
There is no real fun. It is all showing-off. Pretty girls, with their
skirts spread out over the backs of cars, look like poppies and
roses. There are many poorish people walking, only their children dressed up. The children do not enjoy their fancy dress.
Only the mother must have had some satisfaction in dressing up

her child. There is no leading up to anything, no climax. Only some gauchos that are dancing give Paula a thrill.

One day, walking in the town, she stood still in surprise. She saw a bookshop and in it a display of nothing but her dead husband's books. It gave her a strange feeling. Here where Andrew had never been, they were selling thousands of his books. She thought of the narrow, frail figure of a man that he had been. Was the human spirit so strong that it could influence so many people in a foreign land?

She saw some beautiful paintings by Argentine artists: gauchos in the Pampas, with a new light and space; a very simple picture of a workman lying asleep, sound asleep in the heat of the day, a woman with a baby lying beside him.

Paula is panting to get away. Gina is heartbroken to see her beloved brother depart. He was a part of the old home, of her real life, and now he was going away. But Paula must go.

They must stay in Rio de Janeiro some time to wait for their boat. Paula has her dream of the little white villa, but she cannot have it; the time is too short. So they stay in a second-rate, rambling old hotel. It is not a happy place. The waiters seem dissatisfied, with a subtle underlying insolence. There is a barber's shop where a young, very painted girl seems to linger. The whole place has something unpleasant about it.

They bathe in the morning; on the streets the people walk in bathing gowns to the sea and swim. But there are so many people, and the bathing is no fun. They ride up to the white Christ. Paula looks at his large feet; she does not really like him. He is so self-conscious, a second thought.

In the evening they go to the Casino, a real temple, the temple of Mammon. It is very still inside in spite of many people. The rooms are beautiful, nobody talks, nobody flirts, only *faites votre jeu.*

Grown Up

See the notes on "Christmas at Home." Harry T. Moore in The Intelligent Heart *tells the following anecdote: "It was at one of those balls . . . when Nusch was in Berlin also, that the Kaiser asked who 'those two young ladies' were, and on being told, said, 'Ah, the Herr Under Secretary has very beautiful nieces!' "*

The Rio de Janeiro Casino reminded Paula of her stay in Berlin. Her uncle was then Colonial Secretary, later on Minister of Foreign Affairs. She was seventeen and her uncle had invited her to spend the winter with him; she was supposed to be grown up.

Her uncle seemed busy as a bee. When he showed her the room where he had worked under Bismarck as a young man, she waltzed around the desk.

"You have no respect for high politics, my child," he laughed.

She listened when he told her that he never believed in a united Germany, that he thought small courts were better adapted to the German character and had been centres of genuine culture. She listened when he told her that he would never be one of the Kaiser's intimates, that the Kaiser did not possess the simple virtues of loyalty and gratitude of his father and grandfather.

"How much ink we have spilled arranging a marriage for the crown prince," he said one day.

When young men came to him begging to go to the German colonies, he was upset and unhappy and tried to persuade them

73

not to go. "The climate will kill them; it has killed so many already."

Her uncle had been a long time in Cairo. In his absence, his wife had died of cholera; all the servants had deserted her, only the faithful Achmed had stayed with her and the youngest child that recovered. So Achmed belonged to the household, was one of the ornaments. When the family went anywhere, Achmed came along and carried the coats; he was very decorative.

Paula had loved her uncle's apartment. Some of the rooms were turned into tents, hung with beautiful rugs and brass and copper lamps, Turkish or Persian. She liked the apartments better than the ministerial palace later on.

In the same house lived Uncle O.'s two sisters, Frau von E. and Frau von P. They were of the old order; their collars were high, with a little white edge to them and a big gold brooch in front. They were lively, kindly widows but set completely in their time and class. Frau von E. had been much at the court of the old King of Prussia, brother of Wilhelm the First. She told of the simple court life. The King and Queen would have supper, consisting of sandwiches and beer, at one end of the room, the King smoking his pipe, and the Queen knitting socks. The young people of the court would be having sandwiches at the other end of the room. Aunt E. never approved of the extravagance of Wilhelm II's court.

Her aunts were fond of Paula, but could not make her out. When Paula had a cold and they wanted her to stay in bed, which bored her, she argued: "If I were a poor washer-woman I couldn't stay in bed just for a cold." They were shocked that she, a member of the family, should compare herself to a washer-woman.

One day she saw from the window a cabhorse that could not get at the oats in its sack; the sack was hanging too low. So she went down into the street and adjusted the sack. Again, they were shocked; these things were not done.

Paula had a gay time. The cousins from the different guard regiments came to her uncle's hospital house, and the young attachés. They danced with her, and sang and whistled for her.

One young, handsome cousin whistled like an artist. They took her to the races; she went to balls and gala performances at the opera.

But she was still very young, and what she loved best was to romp with her thirteen-year-old cousin. They would play hide-and-seek on the stairs, and hide in the niches. One day Paula hid, as usual, in one of the niches. When she heard footsteps coming up the stairs, she took it for granted that it was her young cousin. With a loud whoop, she flew out at the approaching figure, which turned out to be a resplendent man in a gorgeous uniform who nearly fell backwards down the stairs. It was the Grand Duke of Saxe-Weimar who had come to visit her uncle; he was a very shy man.

But Paula had her misgivings. It was no fun being a poor baroness, not really. Sometimes she needed new gloves and shoes to go to a dance, and she had no money to buy them with. She knew her father could not give her a larger allowance, and she would not ask her uncle for money, or her aunts. So she pretended she had a headache. She had qualms on her own account.

"I know so little, and I can do so little; it isn't enough just to enjoy myself and be a pretty girl," though she enjoyed it that people thought her pretty. "I am not only a pretty young thing; I am also myself. What is going to become of this unknown 'myself'?" She was scared. At the bottom, this whole elaborate society was meaningless for her. What was it all about? It had nothing to do with genuine living.

One day a friend of the aunts, a countess from Baden-Baden, appeared and they gossiped with her. They must have forgotten that Paula was in the room. The countess told a story of a well-known prince, heir to a throne. The prince gave a party to his friends. For the fish course, carried in on a silver platter, carried by six footmen, lay a nude damsel trimmed with parsley and lemon. Paula wondered whether the lady looked more like salmon or more like halibut. But the aunts, for all their propriety, seemed to get a great kick out of the story. Morals are strange things. People seemed to think it rather charming that this prince so humanly fell for pretty women, and yet his grandson, who genuinely loved a woman and married her, was treated like a traitor. Just as strange had been the morals of Henry the Eighth, who chopped off his wives' heads when he wanted to marry another one, not to live in sin.

Paula instinctively knew this bubble of glamour of a social life was not for her. She had so much respect fundamentally for men and their genuine activity; but for this show she had felt none, it meant nothing to her, as if she had known that before long the bubble would burst.

This German empire that seemed fixed for all eternity, like the polar star—it would have to go before long.

English Marriage

The text of this chapter is a composite of several manuscripts. Chapter X of the typescript, untitled, treated the marriage to Ernest Weekley in brief, synoptic fashion; most of its text was devoted to the affair with "Octavio." In the composite, a whole new chapter precedes the Octavio chapter. The basic text is that of a separate manuscript chapter entitled "English Marriage." The text of the long second paragraph is from a notebook found at the New Mexico ranch after Mrs. Lawrence's death, which was edited by Albert James Diaz, along with other notebook material, and published in Manuscripts *(Winter, 1958), 11–29, 59. This text was checked against the notebook, and some corrections and restorations were made. A different set of fictionalized names was used: "Gisla" instead of "Paula," and "Vernon" instead of "Charles Widmer." For the sake of consistency, these names have been changed to conform with the typescript and by far the largest number of other texts. The account of the pre-marriage visit to England and of the wedding day is from the basic manuscript chapter. The next portion, the train trip to Switzerland and the wedding night, is again from the notebook text. It replaces a different, less dramatic, and less emotional account in the basic manuscript text, which reads:*

> *Like all people who feel strongly, she was fiercely virginal and knew but the given moral code. Women of her class married and were faithful, if not the*

husband and lover would have to fight a duel. She had all the right old-fashioned ideas. She knew nothing about physiology. In the train—they were going to the Lago di Como—her husband said: "You know we are not really married yet." "I know," she answered brightly, but she did not know, she had only vague knowledge that there was some mysterious rite that would make her really married. They arrived at their hotel in Como and went to their rooms, her bedroom had a balcony over the lake, where the lights danced, reflected from the shores. Her husband came with her and said: "I will go down now, you go to bed and I will come to you in a little while." She was alone and looked around, she stepped on the balcony, then looked at the bed. "No, I don't want to go to bed." She saw a cupboard and on an impulse she climbed on top of it and sat and waited. After a while her husband knocked, he came in, looked at the bed, and then saw her, her legs dangling from the cupboard. "He looks scared," she thought, and climbed down. In the morning she looked at the lake sadly. "So that's that. It's a sad affair, now the door has shut on my life and I must make the best of it."

The brief paragraph on the monotony of life in England is from the basic text. The following paragraphs, ending with her reading, are again from the notebook text. The remainder of the chapter is from the basic manuscript text, with one exception. A longer account of the advent of her children is from still another version of the "English Marriage" chapter.

"Charles Widmer" is Ernest Weekley. The English scene is Nottingham, where he was a professor at Nottingham University College. For their life together, see her letters under "Correspondence." Else Jaffe wrote to the editor on December 6, 1957, concerning Frieda's early attachments and the reasons for the English marriage:

Frieda, though she had a "Backfisch" (teen-ager) attachment to a young military Richthofen cousin and later on a more serious liking for a very decent and cultivated officer, soon felt that she did not really belong to the narrow military world. And in the background there was the feeling that, being girls without any fortune, we could not marry officers. And in our home town, Metz, the second biggest garrison of Germany, we did not meet any men but officers. So there was one reason more to marry Prof. Weekley, whom she was genuinely fond of and who opened to her the access to another world. A world that, after all, was not utterly foreign to us, as my mother, who came from a solid bourgeois family—our grandfather was a lawyer . . . —had literary interests and friends out of that sphere.

In a letter of January 11, 1960, Mrs. Jaffe commented:

Of course we fought as children, especially as Nusch and Frieda were nearer together and liked to tease me. But I still remember our last walk together, before she was married, what a pain it was, that separation! Even then I could appraise Frieda's nature, her fundamental innocence, her noble generosity and fascinating originality, her belief in life.

Charles Widmer had gone for a holiday that he had well earned. . . . They had offered him the headmastership of a small public school in the north of England. So the world felt good to him and he went to the Black Forest and fell in love with its running brooks and the mountain walks and the peasants and the good wine. He met the young Paula and he fell in love with her too. He was no longer in his first youth, but of the age when a man falls head over heels or not at all. He asked her to marry him and she said yes.

It did not seem very real to her. She was engaged, going to another country, life seemed to draw its curtains apart for her to step into it. How he seemed to love her! He trembled when he came near and kissed her! Something big had suddenly entered her world, she knew, though she didn't understand it. He had told her of his people. "They are very simple," he said, "but they will love you, because I love you and I have not been a bad son." The quiet man who was greying at the temples became a youth again under her laugh. He told her of the struggle of poverty in his home, of his parents' unselfish devotion to each other and their ten children. She could feel his sense of responsibility, that had been there and grown strong, when at seventeen he earned his living as a schoolmaster and a hard earning it seemed to Paula as she listened. Later on he had gone on schoolmastering and taken the nights to prepare for a Cambridge scholarship. Then he told her with a smile for which she loved him, "I went home one day and surprised them by telling them casually after dinner: 'By the way you had dinner with a scholar of Trinity.'"

Paula felt firm ground under her feet for the first time in her life. Here was something different from her own home life. There in his English home she felt the solidity of family life, an intimate circle, an ideal to strive after. Her own home had been such a scattered thing. There was no grit. Only the moment's satisfaction, good times, counted. Paula wanted more. She had always battled with her parents and their shallow, cynical outlook on life. In spite of their vitality they had failed intrinsically and obstinately, perversely made the best of things. There was this simple, strong man who loved her. Paula thanked God for him. She would be a good wife to him, she would love him; he was poor, but what did she care, she was not afraid of poverty. His life had been solitary, hard grinding; she would bring him the bright side of life. Her own power she did not doubt. Only sometimes he frightened her. When in a fit of reverence he kissed her feet, which seemed to her rather large, ordinary feet in not too elegant boots, then she felt uncomfortable. It flattered her vanity on one hand, on the other she accepted it placidly as the behaviour of men in love. But dimly, this ideal Paula that she knew did not exist made her uneasy. But she would live up to it; she would try and be that sampler of all the virtues he thought [her]. Paula was thinking over these things as she walked towards the fountain in the wood where she would meet him. She climbed up through the pine wood, where young beech leaves were waving loosely like butterflies in the morning wind, shining golden green in the sun. Two red squirrels with black, beady eyes chased each other in front of the [path] brown with last year's leaves, with sunlit golden patches here and there. She came slowly nearer, watching the squirrels, who, seeing her, ran up a pine tree chattering angrily. Paula got more excited as she neared the fountain. She was conscious of her pink and white frock with the pink and white sunbonnet that [he] loved so much. She thought more of her effect on him than of himself. At last she saw him standing in the entrance of a sombre pine wood, the trees forming a deep archway behind him. He was like a man lifted out of ordinary life. He did not know anything, he was nothing by himself, his sole being was in that approaching pink and white girl. His emotion almost paralysed him. Paula felt slightly uncomfortable, she went up to him. He took her in his arms, gently, tenderly, repressing his passion, so as not to frighten her. "My snowflower," he said. . . .

. . . When she went with her mother and future husband to England to pay a visit to her future relations and met them at Dover, her heart sank. She wanted to cry. "Don't be a goose," her mother whispered. The parents, the old stately father and the lively stout mother, talked away to the son, or rather only the mother talked and she could not understand their English. They were all so foreign, such strangers, what had she to do with them, what could she ever have to do with them? She looked out of the train at the soft green countryside, everything seemed so near, a little village humped in the hedged-in fields with a church steeple showing. "What a wonderful cow one would make here," she said to herself, "or a frog"; everything was low-lying and near horizon where the sun was setting behind heavy clumps of trees. How different the country was from the towns! The towns were not soft and peaceful but grim with an iron determination and power.

Charles's parents lived in a suburb of London, and Paula was fond of them. She had never met people of their stamp. When

Grandpa read a chapter from the Bible to the household in the morning, with an arm round a grandchild, he was impressive like Moses with his square white beard and handsome, rather unchanging, face. The lively Granny really ruled the roost; it only seemed as if Grandpa were the head, and Paula admired her female tactics. Granny adored her clever sons, the girls took second place. There was a warm and cosy atmosphere about the house with big joints of meat and juicy pies on the dinner table. The great event of the week was Sunday-morning church. There was such a bustle and running up and downstairs till everybody was ready. Then Grandpa, all brushed up in his top-hat and tail-coat with a little select bunch of flowers in his buttonhole, set forth down the road, and Granny in her silk cape and bonnet trimmed with violets trotted beside him to keep up with his long straight strides. Then there was church, so different from the services Paula had known at home; here men knelt to pray, which they had not done at home, and she missed the strong soldiers' voices that had filled the church with a great sound. The congregation looked so eminently lady and gentlemanlike in their Sunday clothes; "they don't have to pray, the old Adam is dead in them for sure," thought Paula.

She went to visit three old maiden aunts with Charles. They lived in a small town pretty as a coloured postcard. They kept a little select tobacco-shop. The middle aunt wrote poetry for the local paper, but the eldest was lovely, like old ivory, in black satin with a lace-fringed black silk apron. Their old house was curtained and double-curtained not to let any air in at all.

Their most joyful possession was a doll's house, a perfect doll's house with little lamps and cradles and plates and knives and forks. It seemed a symbol of their own lives. And yet they told Paula the grim story of how their father spent many nights with a loaded gun on the new grave of a dead daughter, afraid of body-snatchers. Queen Victoria was a near and dear potentiality in their lives.

Then Paula's wedding day came. For the last time she shared her bedroom with Manya, the bedroom where they had romped so wildly in the evenings, acting Lady Macbeth and the old Moor of Schiller's *Räuber*. Their clothes lying about like on a battlefield. It was a gay wedding down at the big old peasant inn and they drove into Freiburg where they were married in the little English church. But William the manservant, who had been part of the family and knew all their likes and dislikes, and Emma the cook, whose love letters Manya had written for her in the kitchen, wept aloud when Paula went away and everybody was sad at her going. . . .

And now they were married, the train was sliding along through sunny apple orchards, vines, the earth looked bright and fruitful. Paula felt very happy. . . . Also she expected something to happen, she did not know quite what it was, but it would make her very happy, happier than she had ever been. They travelled first class and were alone. He sat in a corner, ill at ease, miserable, tired. He was married, this happy creature was his wife. Yet she felt so far away in her virginity, he was almost in despair. The question of sex relations was terrifying to him, he was almost virgin himself. In spite of his age and strong passions he had never let himself go. Sex was suppressed in him with ferocity. He had suppressed it so much, put it away so entirely, that now, married, it overwhelmed him. His love had been of the ideal, pure adoration kind, sex he had not let enter consciously. How he suffered now! Paula saw it in his face. She got frightened suddenly. Perhaps after all the lovely thing that she expected would not happen. He hardly said a word. From time to time he gripped her hand with his long, beautiful hand tightly, while his body was held stiff and unbending. Paula began to feel sad, she put her head against the red plush and went to sleep till the end of the journey. She woke with a start. They were at Lucerne. The lights were reflected in the lake, a beautiful warm night, E [sic] was strung to an unbearable pitch. Their two rooms looked out on the lake, carts and people and a happy life went still on under their windows. Paula sat down on the window-seat and looked out, uneasy herself.

"Will you have something to eat?" he asked.

"No, thank you," she answered. "What nice big rooms they are."

"Yes," he said. "Paula," he braced himself to it, "I must tell you we aren't really married yet. Come to me."

She came and sat on his knee. She could feel his legs tremble underneath her, she could smell his homespun.

"My little love, you are not yet my wife."

"Oh yes," she said, "I knew."

The cheerfulness, the frankness of the answer confused him. "Go to bed, my child. I'll go and drink something, then I will come and say good night to you."

He got up and went, almost relieved, Paula thought. She was sad, she had imagined it all so differently. "He used to kiss my feet in stupid boots," she thought, "why doesn't he kiss my real toes? He treats me like an old dowager Empress." A big old oak cupboard, beautifully carved with a stiff Eve and an Adam that looked like the "missing link," held her attention. She had taken some of her clothes off. Suddenly she climbed up the old cupboard, the frills of her knickers flapping from her climbing legs. Triumphantly she reached the top, and sat there, wondering what he would do if he couldn't find her; she laughed, but as she thought of his serious, immobile face, she climbed down again sadly and quickly got into the great big bed that was let into a recess, it seemed like sinking into the earth. . . .

Two hours afterwards she stood on the balcony in her light blue dressing-gown for only comfort. She was in an unspeakable torment of soul. It had been so horrible, more than horrible. "Oh God," she thought. How she would love to fling herself from the window! "Only housemaids jump from windows," she said disdainfully. Couldn't she get away? "No, I am married, I am married," rang in her ears. She had expected unspeakable bliss and now she felt a degraded wretch. Her pride was gone, she was nothing. Why did men marry women they loved, she asked herself, why didn't they leave them and never touch them, that would be real love instead of this horror. And he slept. He slept. She stamped her foot in impotent rage. He was sleeping while she was in utter despair. Oh God, how she hated him for it, hated him helplessly, miserably. She was bound to him nevertheless, that was the horror, she was bound to that man whom she could hear breathing. Her whole inner self was on fire. She could not bear it. "My wedding night," she said in cynical misery. "I wonder if many women have felt my joy!" The lights were still slipping like a scale on the waves of the lake, the water lapped under her window, the night got slightly greyer, dawn was coming. With a shiver it went through her body, she was exhausted by her emotions. She went indoors and slept a heavy, miserable sleep. . . .

Paula and her husband arrived in grim November in the north of England. It was awful. Grey and damp, and her little house was always dark. Widmer was busy and Paula was helpless in her housekeeping. She tried to learn the routine of the English middle-class woman's life. You did the shopping in the morning, after lunch you paid some calls or somebody called on you, there was the ceremony of tea and then there was dinner. . . .

This horrid gnawing at her heart, how irritating, how maddening it was! She believed he was good, better than she was herself, he felt so firm and going his way so sure of himself. Yes, he was better, he knew what was right and wrong, she didn't. She could understand how a person could steal, lie, murder, love another man when one was married. To him there was an absoluteness, she knew he simply could not have done any of these lawless things. It impressed her very much and yet somehow she felt so different herself; she knew for certain that never could she have his rigid code of morals, she even did not really want it.

But it was nice to feel him at the back of her days, solid and firm, her rock of ages. He bored her a bit occasionally, she felt again today that curious sensation that she must run, run away. And in the evening she put on an old hat, ran out of the house, tore up the Mapperley hill. The lanterns gave a cheerful light; in rhythmic distances the burring noise of the trams as they boiled up the hill came near and passed again, and she [had] a glorious feeling of escape, of freedom as she ran on and on the dark road where the wind was catching the trees on the top of the plain. Then she would go back to her house quietly, sane again. . . .

She entered the front door. In the hall the gas was turned

down and the curious undescribable smell of the sunless hall damped her spirits. She went into the study where a bright fire burnt; the walls were books, the whole room seemed books, books on the writing-table, books on the floor. And then the smell of his pipe, it was so evidently a man's room, his room, she liked it. She threw herself down on the hearthrug with a novel, one side of her baking comfortably at the fire. These evenings when the children were asleep and he was lecturing were a treat to her.

She had got utterly absorbed in her novel when he came in, tired to death after his two evening lectures. He ran up the stairs, his step so much like his father's. His face was white with exhaustion, his eyes brilliant with his effort. A wave of tenderness rose in her at sight of him, so tired, working so hard, so uncomplainingly for the children and her. The maid brought a plate of soup for him on a tray. He gave her a look and sat down eating it, the spoon so neatly held in his beautiful hand.

"I am a damn good lecturer," he said, wiping his drooping moustache with his napkin, shaking his head proudly.

She admired him then, when he exulted in his work. She could see him rousing his hearers, trying to get some understanding into them, grateful for the slightest sign of progress, slaving for years and years. She could never have that patience, that faithfulness in small things, duties and so on. Then he ate some bread and cheese, he made neat little "breads" as Paula called them, a little piece of bread, butter and cheese. Paula snatched one for herself, they looked so appetizing. He laughed happily. He emptied a glass of beer at one go, she seemed to hear it sizz down his parched, tired throat. Then he drew up to the fire, she slipping out of his chair's way.

"You condescend to speak to me tonight," he said. "Yesterday you were so absorbed in your book that you did not answer my questions except with an occasional grunt."

"Sorry," she said, "is it as bad as that? Lord, but this is exciting. I love Stendhal."

"He is supposed to be something wonderful," he answered.

"I don't care a twopenny damn what he is supposed to be,"

she burst out, "but I have not read anything that's got hold of me like this *Le Rouge et le Noir.*"

"I daresay, it's the kind of modern stuff you like," he said, "with your Nietzsches and Platos."

"Do you remember," she laughed, "when I had my Plato fit on and I began at breakfast, 'Socrates says.' You banged the table as if it were Socrates and said, 'Curse Socrates.' "

"Yes," he said, "you get your measles late, most people have done with Platos at your age, but your fits!" And he sighed wearily, comically. . . .

At last the spring came, the lovely English spring with its primroses, the sea of bluebells under the ancient oaks in Sherwood Forest, and the violets in the hedges and the ferns uncurled. She was waiting for a baby to be born. She knew nothing about babies. She was frightened for the baby. But otherwise she was immensely glad. Her son was born in June. Like most mothers she was convinced it was the first and only child born in the world. When he drank so eagerly, grasping her breasts, she felt she was feeding the universe. She adored him with a secret passion and would have liked to take him away to a hidden place and have him all to herself. She played games with him, popping up behind the curtains and saying: *"Bonjour Monsieur,"* and he laughed with his whole little body, gurgling at her. Two little girls were born, and she was amazed how good the children seemed, how considerate and how they amused her! She loved embroidering small clothes for them, and their neat clothes hung on the fender in the nursery at night ready for the morning. On Sunday morning they all had breakfast together in her big bed and they would listen to her German fairy-stories, that were often sad; then they would hide their faces in the sheets with distress for the fate of the little princess, and Paula felt mean at having made them sad. Their existence seemed a joy in itself, when they ran on such light feet after a ball or jumped dripping wet out of the bath to the nursery fire. They spoke English and German, but when she spoke German to her boy in a tram or train, he would pull her skirt and whisper: "Don't speak German, people are looking at us."

In the outer world a Boer War was going, people were singing: "The soldiers of the Queen, my lads," and Boers were being confined in concentration-camps and there were a few pro-Boers in England. England loomed large and powerful, much more grim than its gentle landscape. Paula admired the English tremendously. Their restraint, their discipline, above all their awareness of the other person, seemed so truly civilized to her. She pondered over their ideal of fair play. Fair play seemed to her that you helped the little fellow against the big fellow, but that was not English fair play. You only stood by and saw that neither side had an advantage or played a mean trick. But she also realized how ironclad was the form of the very minds of the people. Their laws were more set than Moses's Ten Commandments, especially the unwritten ones. One's life was moulded and set and one could not get out. That was terrifying. Paula knew she would never become a good middle-class Englishwoman. It seemed medieval, you were born into a class and a million to one chances you would die in it. Why a class at all? Not like America where the poorest devil dreams that he might be president one day, where every workman felt he had a right to a house, a car, a radio, an icebox, a bathroom and a cottage in the country. No European workman would have the cheek to claim in his wildest dreams so much, and yet why not? There was political freedom in England, but it was not social freedom. Only America had known so far what actual personal liberty meant, a possibility to become anything you wanted to be. When Paula went into the kitchen, Laura the cook resented it, the kitchen was her domain. When Paula asked politely after her family, Laura snubbed her, that was her business. And the routine! On Monday the cold Sunday joint for lunch, and Tuesday washday, and Wednesday ironing, and Thursday and Friday cleaning, and Saturday the kitchen premises. Thursday was Paula's "at home day" and on Friday afternoon she sang at a women's choir, the St. Cecilia. Women's suffrage was in the air. Paula never understood about politics or races or armies. . . .

Octavio

. . . How well she knew later on the form of English life! One
landed at Southampton, and one could know what day of the
week it was. This was a Saturday afternoon because the men in

white flannels were playing cricket, or were mowing the strip of lawn of their semi-detached houses. There was the Dorothy Perkins blooming over a little arbour, and the beds of marguerites and geraniums were flourishing more or less, according to the house. There were the same curtains in the houses, of art linen, the good daddies were wheeling perambulators in the street, there were the fields so unbelievably green in the moist climate that you longed to be a cow or a frog. Young people would be climbing over the stiles. Had it been a Tuesday, washing day, the semi-detacheds would have the washing out. How long, often, the washing took to dry in the damp air! Everything was on so small a scale and so known.

She had seen train after train pour into London in the early morning. There were bank-clerks and small officials and shop assistants. "Hallo, George. Fine day today." And then the whole compartment would be buried behind newspapers. "And in the evening," Paula thought, "George will go home to his little semi-detached in the suburb, to his little wife and a little George, and mow his lawn and, for excitement, collect stamps perhaps. One day George will fall ill and have pneumonia and die, and the other men in the train next morning will say, 'Have you heard about poor old George?' " And that would be the end, and poor old George had not had much of a show.

Paula had tried hard to be a good English *bourgeoise* and do as the other women did. She went shopping in the morning, because to shop in the afternoon would have been unthinkable. She called in the afternoon on other women, and in the evening there would be a dinner somewhere. But she was not happy. The winter came so dark and grey. In her small house, the beautiful wedding presents she had had of Bohemian glass and old silver and beautiful rugs looked out of place. . . .

She had so far lived in the spirit of her people. Never had she been in contact with the issues of life. Neither death nor illness nor poverty, none of the things that hurt mankind deep into living, had come her way. She had spent her days an unbroken, sleeping force. People had loved her, she had loved them. But she had longed, longed madly for things she did not know, could not express. At the bottom of her being lay an uncertainty, everything was so puzzling. She did not know what was right. She argued fiercely with the men, she gripped with keen hands anything that came her way. The strength of her emotions often made people misunderstand her. She threw her whole self at them with the force of a battering ram; she was too much for them as a rule, they did not want such fierce contact, so they did not understand her as she thought and she used to feel humble and a fool. People seemed to her mostly concerned with the accessories of their lives not with the life itself, that they seemed to leave severely alone. This Paula did not understand.

Today she was in one of those cross, longing, nothing-is-right moods. She had seen her sister Manya and it made her sad. Manya had married an officer in one of the crack regiments, and the Manya of whom as a kid she had been so fond, whose blood was her blood, how could she have grown like that? Paula had met Manya at the station of the little village. Never had such an elegant person stepped out of the little, slow trains of this side line. Manya in travelling costume. Shepherd's plaid perfectly fitting, her figure, the ideal of all tailors. A little travelling hat, well shoed and gloved as the French say, she stepped forth from the train. Her swaggering movements calmed down at sight of Paula.

"How are you, dear?" she said. Her hard voice took on a softer tone for the sister she was fonder of than anybody. Manya talked. Paula in her simple, white garments walked round her, watching every detail of her dress; it pleased her, this perfection. Only the face, where was the face of the little sister, the dreamy eyes and the freshness and the something that had made her so dear? She was a beautiful woman, the scale of exquisite colouring that rejoiced painters was there, but the cheeks seemed too broad over the tight, high collar, and the eyes that had animated the face had lost their importance.

"And now," asked Manya, "tell me, are you really satisfied in your life, have you got all you want?"

"All I want; good God, but don't you see I try to, to," Paula stopped.

"Ah," said Manya. "No, your life gives me the creeps, you poor dear. I must have change and the fittings round me and the men. Paula, you have no idea how they spoil me. The flowers I get, and the women, how jealous they are of me. Their faces are a study; oh the frumps, the frumps, I don't wonder men are bored to death with the tame cats!" Before Paula's eyes rose scores of humble, thin, unattractive women. Paula felt sorry for them, yet laughed. "Yes," Manya went on, "the girls, the stacks and stacks of unmarried girls." She pulled down her full mouth in disdain. "Anyway, it's something to be married! How the men hate them, the poor virgins. We married women have a better time! I don't think!" I laughed [sic]. "And you, how are you, tell me about you?"

But Paula heard the pity in Manya's voice. . . . And Paula almost felt a pitiful figure. She wanted to explain to Manya that she did not mind so much about garments and motors and grandeur, but she knew it wasn't true; she did like clothes and nice things, but they were only a part of life, not a small one either. Paula thought of Manya's little girl, Henrietta, who would be another Manya some day. Little Henrietta was already the image of her mother, and suddenly Paula saw a procession of Manya-Henriettas down the ages. She wondered at the futility of it. The why of these temporary beings distressed her fearfully. She would have liked to say something to make Manya understand what she felt and thought. But to her horror she knew, was convinced that never as long as the world stands could she have explained to this dear creature, whom she still loved. Down in her heart Paula held the picture of an adorable little girl; to this picture Paula clung, she could still see it through Manya's elegance, the hard voice. Manya seemed to have drawn a horsehair net of fashion over her very soul. Yes, she had a horsehair quality about her. But instead of saying anything Paula talked *chiffons*. None of her garments deserved that elegant term, but Manya, good-natured as she was, often gave

Paula some of her own garments that she had tired [of]. These made Paula perfectly happy. A real "Paquin," a wonderful creation of shrimp colour and a steely blue mixed with chiffon, was Paula's special joy. It had to be freshened up and to Paula's distress let out in places, but in spite of all it was perfect joy. Manya had only paid a flying visit; she made a grand stage entrance and the exit had been quick. . . .

Paula had one great friend who had one of the first automobiles in England. He would drive into the forests with her, where the great hoary oaks stood apart from each other. There were pools of bluebells between them, and the primroses were big as pennies! Then she felt alive again; there weren't only dull teas and servants and grimy towns. But she always longed to go home.

As often as she could she took her children with her to Germany, to the security of her old home. On one of her visits she went to stay with a friend at Munich, the Munich before the war. Laura, the friend, seemed like a woman of another age. She was like an archaic Roman figure. She had the most astonishing, fine, honey-coloured hair. When it was not piled on her head, it covered her in a great mantle to her feet, like a Lady Godiva. Her face was still, with simple lines; her nose a little long, like an Etruscan's.

The first morning of her stay, Laura said, "Come and let's have breakfast." Paula looked around. There was no sign of breakfast to be seen.

"No. Put your coat on. We have breakfast at the *Kaffeehaus*."

At the *Kaffeehaus* Laura had breakfast and wrote her letters and telephoned to her friends. Paula was introduced to an anarchist friend with the most ferocious ideas; but he looked as though he would not hurt a fly. An emancipated young countess joined them; she wrote for the *Jugend*. More and more people appeared: socialists and painters and poets, and they were all full of talk, and they seemed to come to the *Kaffeehaus* to let off steam. Paula was thrilled. As they were mostly more anxious to talk than to listen, they liked Paula because she was a grateful audience. She did not swallow all they said, but their keenness in itself was exciting.

She met a young psychologist who had been a pupil of Freud's. Octavio talked to her about Freud; she had never heard of him before. "Yes," thought Paula, "these clever Jews." They know where the crux of humanity lay, in love and work. Right from Adam and Eve they had known it.

"You see, my story of Adam and Eve is quite different," she told Octavio. "The Lord can't have been such a bad psychologist as not to have known that Eve would want the apple the minute it was forbidden. He really wanted Adam and Eve to eat it. And when they had eaten it, they weren't ashamed of their nakedness at all. 'Look, Adam. There is a pool down by those willows and we will have a swim, and then we'll dry ourselves in the sun. Hurrah! I shall have a small Adam, and you will make him a cradle out of the willows, and then you'll work to get us something to eat while I sing to the baby.' As for Freud's complexes and Karl Marx's labour, that is all the wrong side of the medal. Call it love and work and it all looks quite different."

Octavio was amused. She told him Mark Twain's saying: "What a pity Adam hadn't swallowed the snake instead of the apple."

Octavio, with the help of his research in psychology, had built up in his imagination a new form of living for human beings. Octavio came from the Austrian Alps and had the light strong frame of a mountaineer; he was the first vegetarian she had ever met. "I won't eat your nasty carcasses," he would say, and he drank no alcohol.

Paula's old world was tumbling about her ears. She had accepted, more or less without thinking it out for herself, the human society she had been born into. It had never occurred to her that it could possibly change. But now she believed it could, and it must. She was all for it. People were choked in their lives; it was all set, the whole show, from beginning to end, from birth to death, and there was no fun and no adventure and no mystery.

Paula fell in love with Octavio and his vision of a new society. She began to question the old order. She read the great writers with a new understanding. The world had suddenly become a large growing place with endless possibilities.

Paula went back to England and her children. With the uncanny second-sight of children, one of her little girls said to her, "You are not our old mother. You have got our old mother's skin on, but you are not our mother that went away." The child was right.

Octavio's letters came.

My dearest:

I am grateful that you exist and that I have been privileged to know you. Thank you for all the strength and courage and hope that has come to me through you. Only now that you have gone I slowly begin to understand what a renewal of all my forces you have given me: you who have shown me living and coloured what has so far been only a bodiless dream to me, a vague longing for fulfilment. I have actually seen and loved what previously seemed only a possibility, a vision I hardly hoped to see in the flesh.

In the past all the paralysing doubts had attacked my vision of a future, of all mankind's future. But now these doubts have no longer any point of attack. Now I know. The woman that I have dreamed of for coming generations I have known and loved. Is it really possible, can it exist? Am I dreaming or is it really true? It is like a miracle, like a greeting from the future that you have come to me. Now I know what men will be like who will no longer be tainted by all the things I hate and combat. I know it through you, the only living human being today that has remained free from all the false shame and sham Christianity and false democracy, free from all the accumulated bunk, remained free through your own strength.

How did you accomplish this, you golden child, with your laughter and your love, banishing from your soul all the curse and dirt of two thousand sombre years? Have you then no idea, dearest, of the great thing you have given me, no idea of the incomparable strength that came to me in these days? It was given me to see actually my dream of a future; and when it proved more beautiful than I had ever thought it possible, do you know how glad and strong it made me? You have taught me to laugh. Now I am sure of myself, sure as I never was before. Thank you, dearest.

O.

Another letter:

Dearest:

First of all a thousand thanks for your last letter, that you always let me see afresh the lavishness of your soul. Have you then no idea of what you yourself are, of your own genius, and how elementally power and warmth well out of everything that you have filled with your life? It is as if out of your letter streamed the warmth of your body, so sweet and powerful, like a wave of happy, liberating bliss, as you live and give, you whom I love with such joy!

I felt the richness of your soul in every moment of bliss; particularly then your soul unfolds itself, don't you know it? You are so free, so open, and yet is your soul shy, dearest; only the most intense, most intimate feeling reveals it. It is so wonderful that in those moments of utter bliss one senses your great capacity for friendship, one feels the light of your spirit fill one's soul. When consciousness is lost in deadening bliss, above all then one feels the nearness of your soul. You are wonderful, my dearest, wonderful.

O.

Paula did not for a moment think that she was as wonderful as Octavio thought her, and it did not interest her; what thrilled her was his vision, his new approach to human problems. She was passionately grateful. He had given her a new faith: the human

world could be happier and better than it was, and more
charitable. People were tight in themselves and could not get
out; they were like closed oysters. She would not accept a phrase
she had read: "The inquisition is dead, but its soul goes
marching on." People could change.

Octavio wrote again:

Dearest:

This is one of the moments when I have need of the talisman
you gave me, when I have need of faith in myself, need of the
surety you have given me. Just now I need the conviction, the
solace that in you, dearest, my dream has found its fulfilment,
my dream of the future.

Do you remember from the Bible how none of those that had
been slaves in Egypt were allowed to enter the Promised Land?
All those died in the desert and a new generation was born.
Only that new generation would enter the Promised Land. This
is a wonderful symbol. Nobody is allowed to enter this new life
who has borne the old chains, not even Moses the liberator himself. Only those were destined who were actually born in freedom,
no matter whether in exile and misery. Only those seekers who
had consecrated heart and soul to freedom. Those who knew freedom as a sacrifice and solemn pledge, those who knew all the
dangers and suffering of their wanderings, those who had passed
through the grinding daily struggle: those alone would enter the
Promised Land. They may know every pain, every anguish except
that of slavery. Only those may enter. Only this new generation
will constitute the future reign of a free nobility.

Another letter:

. . . I implore you for news. I am anxious, very anxious about
you. Not that I am uneasy about your love. Since that night on
the ship fear is no longer permissible, but I fear for your courage
in the future, that your strength may not be equal to the an-

nihilating, strangling smallness of life in that dead, grey, cold milieu. I know that you can never adjust yourself to that world and its destructive strength. I am afraid for you, afraid for your power of resistance, your power to remain whole, just as hardly any of the free, proud animals can survive captivity. Just because of your marvellous nature, just because you are free and born for freedom, because of this I am afraid for you. What will become of you in this eternally foreign and, for you, impossible world? Remain strong and free. You must not go under. Help must come.

O.

Paula had met Octavio again. Together they had crossed at night from Holland to England. They had sat in the still, warm night, and it seemed to Paula they were crossing over into an unknown world. She was frightened, but it could not be helped. Her old world was gone.

"Dearest one," he wrote,

"Now I can see how the highest and the deepest is liberating itself in you, how you are growing conscious in quiet strength, how a proud harmony is completing itself in you. You have the great simplicity of expression that is a sign of the rarest beings. I am not far enough on yet to speak of it. I only know that my love is filled with immense gratitude for your being and your growth. You know that you are the affirmation in my life, the flowering fruitful yes, the future that has come to me.

"You know my belief that only out of decadence a new harmony of life can spring forth and that the wonderful time in which we live is really an epoch of decadence, the womb of a great future. And out of it will come complete health and new strength. And in this new strength I love you. And all love is miraculously beautiful. Also this: I believe in the coming shining day, when so long it was night.

"Yes, I know you as far as you can be known. You are so close to me and yet always so marvellously new, and ever new. I saw

your soul blossom. I didn't only see it vaguely. A man can look
into the light if he has eyes for it; but the gift for looking into
the light is not given to all. So I saw in you the treasures of a
soul that rests on its own integrity, treasures that I saw and
rejoiced in.

"I love you as I love our time and its signs of promise. Soon I
will send you my last work. It is last year's child, and I like it.
Our children, Paula, are not born yet, except one and it is such a
tiny one. But I carry in me projects in which I have found myself
at last and my own course. I call them 'cultural perspectives.' In
them I will declare the programme for my life. Now is a moment
like no other ever before. Through a practical method, a technique of research, we can look into the very essence of all
spiritual life. And who has eyes to see can now see in this newly
opened perspective the future itself at work. In this direction my
road is free; the enormous shadow of Freud lies no longer over
my path.

"Paula, you will come. I send you two pages that I have carried about with me, but there is no longer any need for them;
you have found yourself what I wanted to tell you. You are free
at last from the danger of deceiving yourself, and so the most important part is won. And now I believe the second decision is
ripening and you will come. Paula, the battle is worth while to
free one's self, especially today. The world is wide and deep and
wonderful, especially today, especially for you. It is well worth
loving the future with a trusting heart. What do a thousand
'good' people and all their being and doing amount to compared
to one who lovingly gives himself to the awakening of the unknown future? And you and I love each other in this secret, immeasurable love, in this ecstasy of early comers. Come, Paula,
come. I love you as I love our day and its signs of spring.

                                                            O."

It was not true when Octavio wrote her that she was free and
harmonious—far from it. Chaos raged in her soul. How could
she stand all alone against all the millions of other people, their

weight and power. She loved her children; they fascinated her, their difference of character, the things they said and did, and the fun she had with them. When her boy went to school, she would stand at the window making faces at him, and he would look up a little anxious that nobody else saw her. She seemed so much nearer to them than the grown-up people. "They are so good, these children," she thought, "so considerate with me! They must never be aware that I am going through this hell."

Octavio wrote:

I fear you want to commit self-deception to be able to deceive others, not to have to tell an honest lie. This I fear, that you lack the honesty for an honest lie. You say as you did before that you have no right to destroy the existence of a good man. But don't you see that you destroy your own right of self-determination, this right that can never be lost either through pact or sense of duty? How can you overlook that, if you don't want to overlook it?

And another torturing letter came:

I have come to know what a fateful influence you have become in my life, what dominant powers pour from you into me, and how clearly your image fits into my world and all I strive for. You give me the wonderful strength to make me a genuine human being, and at the same time live for an idea. One must have both to be worthy of loving you.

As we stand with each other today, it is no longer permissible to be cautious. Caution no longer must enter in, as it still did in my last letter. I can no longer try to deny this love. Only with it can I construct the possibility of a future. I can no longer arrive at a picture without its being there. My thoughts do no longer follow that path. So I can talk to you clearly now, without reserve; and you yourself may need clarity.

Paula, I need you because you make me sure and great. You bright fire, you. . . . That is what I had to tell you about myself. As things stand with me now, you have to know it.

Dearest, and how is it with you? I implore you, send me news. It begins to weigh me down that I know nothing of you at this moment. Dearest, surely, especially now I ought to be with you. Surely there is an unbreakable bond between us!

You also can no longer put me out of any phases of your life. We have found each other, Paula. You bright fire, don't let yourself be stifled. Give your flame to me. Don't, for God's sake, reduce yourself to smouldering ashes!

I long for this unspeakable, inexhaustible possibility of triumph, where no strange power, no outside order can interfere with our course that necessity itself is leading onwards.

Think of the night on the boat. There we looked on this vision of a future happiness. You said, "I only go to return." Then you knew where you belonged. Your belief and mine, Paula, of striving together, of recreating together from the innermost driving force of life. Since that night, I must think of those tropical nights when on deck I looked upwards at the stars. There were always the same great constellations at which I stared. Over the prow of the ship always in front in the direction of our course the Southern Cross, always leading the way in the unchanging empty sea. Since that night destiny gave you to me, you, my Southern Cross.

O.

Paula sat by the piano when this letter came. She was trying to make a noise to drown the uproar in her heart; and the tears dropped on the keys. She wanted to go to Octavio. She wanted to live that bright life that he held out to her. How she wanted to go, now, at once. He had wakened up her soul in her, that had lain coiled up and asleep, and now it had become a frightening tiger and she had it on her hands. She could not go to him. How could she leave her children? They were so small! She could not burden him with them. He lived for his vision. The everyday life he ignored. On visions alone you can't live. He hardly knew whether it was night or day. She was no Bohemian. How were they going to live? She would let him down, he who had given her her own soul. She would not help him. He would have to go his way and she her own that looked so grim and miserable. She would be quite alone with that tiger of a soul on her hands. She knew somehow that something was wrong in him; he did not have his feet on the ground of reality.

His last letter came. "I can never lose you because you will never lose yourself."

Then later she heard that he had been a doctor in the World War, and had died. How he must have suffered! He, who had dreamed of a glorious coming day for all men, saw before him the torn bodies and broken spirits of the young that he had dreamed his dreams of happiness for! No wonder he died, as so many had died with their hopes denied and broken.

Andrew

This was the last chapter in the typescript. It was unnumbered, and the last pages were missing, so that there is an abrupt break. The account, which follows, of the trouble over the children has been taken from the notebook fragments. This text contained a wholly new set of fictionalized names—"Theo" for Paula (Frieda) and "Aylmer" for Andrew (Lawrence)—which have been changed to correspond with the rest of the memoirs. The technique and the heightened tone suggest that here she was really attempting fiction. An ending that suggested suicide has been excised. ". . . She sank back in the gently swaying water. Some fishermen found her next day." The final portion of the text, the meeting with her son Monty, whose name is not fictionalized, is also from the notebook fragments.

Paula at the time found herself in the dilemma of Huckleberry Finn when he was in an agony of doubt whether to be a lawful citizen and return the Nigger Jim to his lawful owner or let him be free. She being the nigger, she decided like Finn for the nigger's freedom. She felt cut off and alone in a world of millions, living her inner life unrelated to the outer one. She was a fanatic. She had believed that all people had an inner life or wanted to go on and get more out of their living on this earth, but she found it was not so. Most of them hung on like grim death to their known selves and would prefer death to changing. But in her heart she listened to a little persistent voice: "You have had much, and you will have more."

And one sunny spring morning Andrew walked into her life, naturally and inevitably as if he had always been there, and he was going to stay. In a sovereign way he took her for himself; she was his and he would never let her go again while he lived; he would kill her rather. She liked it. He wanted her, he needed her, and that was bliss. Nothing else mattered; all the misery of loneliness, of unconnectedness was gone. Together they took hold of the earth, the solid earth, never to lose it again entirely, neither of them. He was at home in both worlds, the material and the adventurous spiritual one. He was so much of a piece, so simple, that it took her some time to realize that he was a great man. He was trusting with her, completely generous. "Take me, all of me, I am yours." It almost frightened her. He forced the responsibility of himself on to her; she did not want to take it. She was not as sure of everything as all that, especially of what she thought. She had found that thoughts were shifting and contradictory things. And he would hammer away at her, trying to make her commit herself finally, and she often would not. He lived what he believed, and believed what he lived. There was no discrepancy, no compromise; and she had to be the same. He had written:

A plant has strength to burst its pot. The shoots of London trees have force to burst through the London pavements. Is there not life enough in us to break out of this system? Let every man take his own, and go his own way regardless of system and state when his hour comes. Which is greater, the state or myself? Myself, unquestionably, since the state is only an arrangement made for my convenience. If it is not convenient for me, I must depart from it. There is no need to break laws. The only need is to be a law unto one's self.

And if sufficient people came out of the walled defences and pitched in the open, then very soon the walled city would be a mere dependant on the free tents of the wilderness. Why should we care about bursting the city walls? We can walk through the gates into the open world. These states and nations with their ideals, their armaments of aggression and defence, what are they to me? They must fight out their own fates. As for me, I would say to every decent man whose heart is straining at the enclosure, "Come away and be separate in your own soul and live. Your business is to produce your own real life, no matter what the nations do. The nations are made up of individual men; each man will know at length that he must single himself out, nor remain any longer embedded in the matrix of his nation, or community, or class. Our time has come; let us draw apart. Let the physician heal himself."

Andrew did not only preach these harmless sounding words to others, he lived them. He had walked through the "gates of the walled defences" and found himself in the wilderness and was cutting a path through it for others to follow if they wished. So together they were gloriously alone. It was adventure all the time. His writing was adventure in the wilderness of human experience; so little was really known of what happens inside us, we were only at the very beginning of consciousness. What happens inside of others remains always [a] vague mystery we get at best a glimpse [of] now and then. Andrew's genius gave him a deeper understanding. Instinctively people knew that his words were not so harmless, and neither was he. Society insists on its members being "embedded in its matrix," and it will not let you "walk out of its walled defences."

Paula was so sure she knew little about others. It was as much as she could do to feel right about her own self. She did not really want a connexion, especially not an emotional one, with others. Yet in her own way she passionately wanted people to be happy. She felt responsible for humanity in a vague, helpless way. And there was Andrew who felt more responsible than she did. It would be a fight, and she never thought of possible defeat. Most people think of their own welfare first; not so Andrew. The bigger task always stood first. He needed so little for himself: enough decent food, good water, a simple but clean and healthy place to live in, not in a town but on the land. He had very few personal belongings: a few shirts and underwear, all very tidy, and a few clothes. On the few occasions that his socks had holes.

in them—he was so light on his feet—Paula would mend them with red and green and blue wool. "They are more fun this way," she told him as he looked at them in astonishment.

His movements were so sure and to the point. She never remembered him breaking anything accidentally. He had his own life under complete control. Poor as they were he always had enough money to buy a book he wanted, or a box of paints, or a present for somebody; there was always enough for both of them, but there were no luxuries in their lives.

Especially at the times when Andrew worked, Paula felt alive with the richness of her days. After lunch they would go for long walks and find flowers and berries and mushrooms; daffodils and bluebells and primroses in English woods; almond blossoms and asphodel in Sicily; big ferns and mimosa, so many different kinds, in the Australian bush; red-hot-poker and Mariposa lilies in New Mexico. The house was full of flowers. As a friend had written: "Always when I see foxgloves, I think of the Elmers. Again I pass in front of their cottage and in the window, between the daffodil curtains with the green spots, there are the great sumptuous blooms. 'And how beautiful they are against the whitewash,' cry the Elmers. As is their custom when they love anything, they make a sort of fiesta. With foxgloves everywhere, and then sitting in the middle of them, like blissful prisoners, dining in an encampment of Indian braves."

The very fact that they were poor seemed to give them a more immediate connexion with the things that don't cost a cent. The sun and moon and stars and trees and clouds and contact with people and animals. Most of the very rich people Paula had known were longing to get out of their sumptuous homes, to put on old clothes and get into the wilderness somewhere and rough it in a hut, and broil their own steaks over a self-made oven, and moaned when they had to return to their riches.

Andrew had written:

There is no evil in money. If there were a million dollars under my bed and I did not know of it, it would make no difference to me. If there were a million dollars under my bed and I

did know of it, it would make a difference, perhaps, to the form
of my life; but to the living me, and to my individual purpose, it
could make no difference since I depend neither on riches nor on
poverty for my being. Neither poverty nor riches obsess me. I
would not be like a begging friar to forswear all owning and having. For I would not admit myself so weak that either I must
abstain totally from wealth or succumb to the passion for possessions.

Had he succumbed to the "passion for possessions," he, with
his great intelligence directed that way, would have made
pots. . . .

They had been together for nearly a year. . . . There had
sprung up no grand passion between them a year ago. They had
not wanted to fall in love, but inevitably, against their will, they
had to submit to something blind and strong that drew them
together. They had fought, they had suffered a great deal in this
year; for days they were quite swamped by the misery they had
inflicted on so many people by their union, but always triumphantly rose that love between them and justified what they
had done. They were sitting in the great, white room with the big
windows looking over the lake, ultramarine blue in the sunlight,
the bamboos at the side bowing in the slight breeze. The lake
was dotted with white and pink and yellow sails like butterflies
breathing quietly. Across, Monte Baldo sloped into the lake,
brown and lazy, like the back of a prehistoric monster. Some
windowpanes opposite were brilliant suns reflecting the setting
sun rays. Andrew was absorbed in finishing a sketch. A bold
bridge leaping in one bound easily, gracefully, over a deep
chasm. The white, frothing water rushing underneath, cypresses
pointing up out of a mist of olive trees. Andrew stepped back
from his easel, put his head slightly on one side, then quickly
took a step forward and gave a darker touch to the cypresses. He
stood back again, yes, he was satisfied. "Come and look," he
said, "now aren't those cypresses wonderful?"

Paula rose lazily from the couch where she had been reading,
curled up in comfortable, cat fashion. She looked at the picture

critically. "Not quite soft and misty enough for me," she answered, "but the bridge is a joy. I want the olives different though."

He resented her lofty criticism, but reluctantly effaced some hard parts. "*La posta*," rang from the gate the deep voice of the Italian postman that they liked so much. Paula went to the door. "*Buona sera, signora*," he said to her, handing her a letter.

She looked at it frightened. On the big couch she sat down and opened it. She could not believe what she read. The husband whom she had left promised her the children from time to time. "I could never be quite hard on a woman," he had written at first. However, she had suffered at the thought of her three children who had meant life to her, till Andrew had come. She had looked on their spending these Easter holidays with her as a certainty. But now her husband wrote, "I have done with you, I want to forget you and you must be dead to the children. You know the law is on my side."

"The law," Paula cried with blazing eyes, clutching at the nearest thing to vent her rage. "The law! Can they undo the fact that those children are mine, that I bore them, that they are flesh of my flesh? The law," she said bitterly, contemptuously, "it takes much count of human nature."

Andrew was irritated at the form her deep disappointment took. "It's no good going on like that," he said, tapping the table with his fist. But Paula went on, let loose her anger on the universe at large, at the injustice that was done her as she thought. Andrew felt helpless, her grief was something beyond him, he could not cope with it. His oversensitive, oversympathetic nature could not bear the suffering imposed on her and on him. He shut himself off from her. But she did not notice, she was blinded by the pain of her disappointment.

All night she lay looking across the lake where in the blue night one solitary light shone; she was conscious of nothing but this light and the pain in her limbs, her arms, that had longed to hold her children. Tomorrow would be Sunday. She thought of the Sunday mornings, when the three had come to her bed, when

she had pillow fights with them in spite of the disapproving
nurse, when they rode on her raised knees and she made them
tumble down. She saw Joy's little neck, the head thrown back
laughing like nobody in the world laughed when she tumbled off
her seat.

The next day Paula went about blind and dumb, incapable to
think, to act, just doing household things, the tears running
down her face; she did not notice them except when they touched
her hands or tickled her nose. Andrew suffered to see her like
this. He could not get near her, he might as well have got near an
avalanche. Anaesthetized with suffering Paula went on for two
or three days thinking of the children. She was one great wound
where her children had been bleeding her to death.

Andrew was getting beside himself. He was a delicate man
always. On the third day he developed a bad cold and had to stay
in bed. Absently, mechanically Paula looked after him. At last in
self-preservation, knowing that they could neither of them bear
this, he said to her in a detached voice from his bed, "Paula, we
really cannot go on like this. You see for yourself that it makes
me ill; if things are as they are between us, if you behave like
that, I think you had better leave me, go to the children
altogether and leave me."

Paula was stung into reality for the first time for days. "Oh,"
she wailed, "don't say it, don't. Don't leave me in the lurch now,
don't send me away. You know I love you, you know I can't leave
you. But can't you see what it means to me, the children?"

"No," he said quickly, "no man can understand it."

"Oh, but you won't try," she cried, "you are jealous of them,
you kill me when you don't recognize the mother in me."

"Very well," he said, "I can't then, and so we had better
make an end."

"Oh," Paula cried crouching on the floor like under a blow,
holding her arms. "Oh, but what of our love, that should not fail;
you told me you would die if I left you!"

"That phrase has done a lot of harm in our lives already, you
know it isn't true now," he said.

"Yes," she cried bitterly, "I have made you stronger."

"Yes," he said, "and if a thing is a failure, it is better to acknowledge it than to go on being miserable."

These last words seemed to kill Paula's remaining wits. She became a wounded animal. The mother in her bleeding, and the man whom she loved so deeply giving her this blow was too much for her. She was ashamed, a hunted animal that nobody wanted; she was utterly alone and ashamed; she wanted to creep away somewhere in a dark corner where nobody should see her misery and shame. Him, whom she had loved and trusted, he told her to go. She felt ashamed to be sent away as if she had some disease, nobody wanted her.

She put on a hat mechanically and wandered out of the house, slinking along the walls like a dog afraid of a hiding. A bell started ringing, hitting her raw senses like a blow. She went along the walls through the narrow street of the dark Italian village, slowly, mechanically. At the end of the village she turned to the road leading along the lake. On her right rose the bare layers of rock. The road lay in front of her white in the sun; far away the sky melted into the lake in a haze, the lake lay blue at her left. She left the road and walked on the sand and stones to the water. Little waves were lapping, coming on the land with a wicked little sound. The sun and the clear water were weaving little moving patterns of light over the round stones. Paula's heart beat when she saw those stones. She had become an unconscious mass of life; she did not reason, she did not feel resentment; life went on in her in spite of herself. Only staring at those stones with the pattern of moving light over them did she know that she trembled all over. Something had gone down in her, something was broken that would never be whole again. She accepted it all, the suffering that had left her so raw, she accepted it, but she could stand no more. She envied those stones with their skin of limpid water that protected them from the air and wind; there was shelter down there. The waves were lapping, gently swishing at her feet. She felt so flayed herself, her misery was like a shameful disease to her. She wanted to

hide, to creep away from things. The water was licking her feet
rhythmically. Slowly, mechanically, she took off her things, her
boots, her underclothes. She wanted to be one of those stones
under the clear, protecting water. She would creep into the
water. Slowly she sat down, slipping into the shallow water
gradually, slipping deeper and deeper. Now the waves touched
her breast; she caught her breath, then the waves went over her
gently lapping. Her arms and legs relaxed, she sank back in the
water. . . .

I met him in the dark passage of Colet house. He looked so big
in his grey long flannel trousers and blue blazer. He ran easily
towards me, stopped, came nearer and stopped again. "You," he
said, "you," in a voice wavering with unbelief.

"Monty," I answered, "can you come with me now for half an
hour without anybody knowing?"

"Yes," he said, "but I must ask Mr. Wicroff first."

"Tell him it's your aunt," I said.

He ran away and soon came back, his cap on his head,
joyfully. "We will go and have tea together. Where do you come
from and are you alone?"

"I have come from Germany to see you. You are a big
boy."

He did not dare to look at me; at first only sideways he
glanced. We ordered tea and strawberries and cream from a nice
barmaid who smiled at us. Then I wept when we sat together so
near and I had to ask him for his hanky and he gave it me, a
big grubby school hanky.

"There, I mustn't make an exhibition of myself," I said, and
he looked at me full of manly love and support. Then we talked. I
asked him how I could see the little ones, without anybody
knowing, and he thought and made a plan calmly and self-
possessed. Then he looked at me full of love.

"You look pretty fit," he said admiringly. His eyes filled with
tears. He asked me what I did, what I lived on, and I said, "I
wrote a novel." He looked with his old impish smile at the

ambitious mother. Then he said, "You know it's a bad look-out, you don't make much money by writing. Now I'll show you St. Paul's, the grounds."

"I want a photograph of it."

"No, I'll draw you a picture," he said. I always felt his love strong and whole.

I told him, "You know I couldn't stand Nottingham and the life any more, you can't understand things now, but you will later on. I want to be able to see you," I said.

"Shall I ask Papa?" he said. "I will," his big grey eyes again full of tears and a manly love shining in them as I have never felt before in my life. It was the most wonderful thing I have seen and I humbly thanked God in my heart for it.

"I don't know," I said.

We walked round St. Paul's, I so proudly by the side of him, with a red rose for a brooch. We passed a bitterly weeping kid, I gave it a penny and it stopped like clockwork. It pleased Monty. I gave him half a crown.

"I'll share it with the little ones." He told me, full of pride, that Elsa was so clever at school, always first, that Barby was a little lazy but that she drew so well. Then I took him to the station, where he [slipped] away quickly. Afterwards I saw him sitting on the platform, reading a letter I had given him, his eyes full of tears. . . .

[*After Andrew's Death*]

The remainder of the memoirs has been put together from manuscripts scattered among the papers. The attempt has been made to adhere to the chronological sequence suggested by the narrative framework and technique of the typescript: further memories, the return from Buenos Aires to the New Mexico ranch, and the ensuing months. A chapel was built in the summer of 1934; Ravagli traveled to Vence, arranged to have Lawrence's body exhumed and cremated on March 13, 1935, at the Cimetière Saint-Pierre, Marseilles, and, after great difficulty in obtaining a visa, brought the ashes to the United States. Alfred Stieglitz, he remembers, helped him find and claim the ashes when the ship docked in New York. Taos legend has it that the ashes were also temporarily mislaid at Lamy during the excitement of the arrival in New Mexico in April. The ashes were enshrined at the ranch under the symbol of the phoenix.

In this chapter, the "eagle-eyed" lawyer is C. D. Medley; the judge is Lord Merrivale. The date of the trial was November 3, 1932. One of her witnesses was John Middleton Murry, "friend G." in the text, who with Katherine Mansfield had signed the missing will. Harry T. Moore, in his account of the trial in the Epilogue to The Intelligent Heart, *tells that during the trial, when Frieda's lawyer was sentimentalizing her relationship with Lawrence, she exclaimed: "But that's not true—we fought like hell!" Medley's correspondence with her*

*has been preserved among her papers, and a letter of
1938 acknowledges her giving him the manuscript of
Lawrence's* Goose Fair *and the corrected typescript of*
Wintry Peacock. *In a letter to the editor of September
24, 1959, Aldous Huxley said of Frieda's situation and
state of mind following Lawrence's death:*

> *One of the most curious facts about Frieda was her
> extreme helplessness when left alone to cope with
> a practical situation. She seemed such a powerful
> Valkyrie—but, as I found out when she came to
> London after Lawrence's death and had to deal with
> business and stay to herself in a hotel, she was
> amazingly incapable and, under her emphatic and
> sometimes truculent façade, deeply afraid. She had
> relied totally on Lawrence, and felt completely lost
> until she found another man to support her.*

*The text here is a composite of two manuscripts; the
second begins: "Paula thought of her dead husband."*

After [Andrew's] death, there was the publishing of all his
unpublished work to be done and then she had a shock. She had
of course known all about her husband's affairs with publishers,
all the success and all the disappointments, both in business
relationships and in the way his work had been received by the
world. She had shared in it all in pleasure and in misery and now
she was confronted with the question: "Did Andrew make a
will?" He had made a will in the terrible war days, when he and
a friend were likely to be called up. She remembered when
Andrew one evening in their small cottage by the sea had
proposed to friend G. to make a will. So both had made them,
both wills written by Andrew, his own signed by the friend G.
and his future wife, and Paula and Andrew had signed G.'s.
Paula remembered seeing the will years later in her trunk pocket
with other documents just as they were leaving the ranch in New

Mexico for Europe. Andrew was packing and sending manuscripts away to New York and his agents. Paula ran with the will to Andrew's room and said: "Look what I have found." She returned to her packing and since that time had never seen it again. She had never thought much of the will, because they had been so poor at the time; she had liked her husband's manuscripts because they were mostly so neatly written, but she had never thought of them in terms of money. She had left the responsibility of the money problem entirely to Andrew, he wanted it so, and only after his death did she realize how worried he often was, when funds sank very low.

But in his last years, money was more plentiful. Then she remembered a few days before he died Andrew was reading a Chinese book where a man made a will. "I ought to make a proper will," he had suddenly said. He looked at her. But in his eyes she seemed to read a fear: "Now if she says 'yes,' I know she thinks I am very sick." So quickly Paula answered: "Why should you make a will? Don't you bother about wills." "Anyhow," Andrew had said, "all I have is yours, you know that."

After Andrew's death Paula was too bewildered to realize her situation. According to the law only the income of what by now had become Andrew Oliver's estate was hers and the rest was to go to the Oliver family. And this was not the worst. Andrew's eldest brother Jim was to be administrator with Paula. All the decisions about Andrew's work had to be made with Jim. All her own cheques had to be signed by Jim. Andrew had never liked his brother, they had not met for many years. Paula had seen Jim only once and now she was to be tied to his decisions, he who had known nothing of Andrew and Paula's life, of their friends, their whole scope. Andrew's sister Margaret had told Andrew, when she had first met Paula: "That's the kind of wife I would like you to have." When their mother had died, Margaret had hoped to fill the place of the mother in the family. But she was not the person her mother had been and she soon hated Paula for her influence over Andrew. Margaret had adored Andrew blindly and possessively. She did not understand his writing nor like it and Paula remembered how this hate had affected her when Margaret stayed with them. She did everything wrong and badly. She wasn't able to boil an egg, without boiling it too hard or dropping it. She couldn't be herself. Margaret was generous in her own way, but she hated Paula. When Andrew was dead she had an access of affection for Paula and said to her: "You had the best of him." She sympathised over the fact of the will with Paula and told her, "I am sure Andy meant to leave you everything and it is only fair that a wife should have all her husband's money." But in her secret heart she felt Paula was an outsider in the family and that Andy belonged to the family, as well as Andy's worldly goods. They were complicated affairs. There was the lawyer for the administration of the estate. He was on Jim's side. In her literary difficulties Paula had fortunately found the help of a famous lawyer. He was of the type that had made England what it had been in the past, incorruptible, standing for straight justice. The first time she had met him, she said to herself: "I would not like to tell him any lies, he would see through them right away with his eagle eyes." Paula worked hard for her dead husband's work, to do the best she could to make it known. She had always believed in it and felt as married to his work as she had done to him. With Jim Oliver as co-administrator it made every move doubly difficult. She did not live at all as she wanted to live, her time was spent deciding and quarrelling with publishers and agents and persuading Jim. The time went by, nothing was settled, everything in a muddle; Jim got more and more difficult. Paula had spent all the money in hand, the amount from publications went into the fund of the estate and Jim would not let her have any. And she was not extravagant. She tried to sympathise with Jim's attitude. He had all his life earned a few dollars a week and here was money and he had the control of it and later a third part would be his and now he was a person of some consequence. But now he had gone too far.

She got a letter from her eagle-eyed lawyer: "I am sorry to hear about this hitch about the payment of the royalties. I had understood that the whole of the royalties would be paid as received to the credit of your account but when Mr. S. (the lawyer for the administration) saw me recently I found that this was not being done and I now find that it is because Mr. Jim Oliver raised objection to it. I discussed this matter with Mr. S. and as mentioned to you in my letter of the 3rd inst. he agreed that instructions should be given that £50/0/0 of the amount received should be paid into your account. I now find that he has not given any such instructions and Mr. B. your agent tells me that the only instructions they have got are from Mr. Jim Oliver, that all amounts received are to be paid into the account of the administrators. I have been trying to get over this difficulty, but at the time of writing I have not been able to arrange for the payments to be made. I cannot get hold of Mr. S., and Mr. B. your agent naturally says he cannot act without instructions. I am now communicating in the plainest manner with Mr. S. and I must if necessary tell him that if Jim Oliver raises any further difficulty about the payments being made, we shall have to take proper steps to see that you receive the income to which you are entitled."

Then a letter from the agent, who had handled her husband's work for years: "As you will see from the attached letter to Mr. S. sent yesterday, I am still making desperate efforts to obtain their authorization for us to pay royalties to you rather than in the estate's account."

This was nearly two years after her husband's death.

And then came a letter her eagle-eyed lawyer had written to the lawyer Mr. S.

Dear Sirs,

We are very much disappointed that you have not been able to write to us that arrangements have been made either for payment of the royalties direct to Mrs. Oliver's account or even for payment on account. We think we had better say now that we will write by the mail tomorrow to Mrs. Oliver asking for authority to take proceedings against Mr. Jim Oliver. Matters cannot be allowed to remain in their present state. Mr. Oliver is committing a breach of trust by refusing to carry out his duties and pay over moneys to which Mrs. Oliver is entitled. Mr. Oliver must please understand that people cannot keep money belonging to someone else without disagreeable consequences ensuing. We think Mrs. Oliver has exercised great patience in the matter. Your client has been given every opportunity of complying not only with our repeated requests, but, as we understand, your own repeated advice and if he now finds himself involved in litigation it is entirely his own fault.

Paula began to be exasperated. Was there no way out of this mess? Was she not able to get her freedom of action and take what was hers by all the human rights; did she not know in her bones that Andrew had wanted her to be heir to him? Was she to be punished so cruelly, that she had not asked Andrew to make another will? No, she could not regret, whatever happened, that she had saved him some suffering. But she was so certain that Andrew's genius had been rooted in her, his writing had been the outcome of their life together, she took her part of the glory and the blame. And his family had no part in his genius. She thought where the will could have got to. She remembered friend G. who had told her that anyhow he had his will, that Andrew had written and signed, the twin will made the night of the war. Could she try and bring a case, that there had been a will, though she could not produce it? Would the law be with her or against her? She would try. She left her ranch and went to London and went to see her lawyer. "I cannot promise you success, but we will try," he told her.

She approached all Andrew's friends and hers; many were with her, but few believed she would win, as there was no actual will that she could produce, and many were hostile. So another year passed by and the day arrived when her case was to be decided. She went to the law courts, an old, beautiful, impressive building, into a court where, under the great carved arms, "the Lion and the Unicorn" with a ribbon of carved wood, written on it *"Dieu et mon droit,"* sat the dignified judge in his curly wig. When she came into court with her lawyer a divorce suit was going on. The people seemed to be lying, and occasionally the judge made a short, sharp remark to a witness. "If he speaks to me as rudely as that, out of this court I go, judge or no judge," thought Paula. Then the counsel for the divorce case made a speech that almost convinced Paula that these people were innocent. But the judge pronounced otherwise. Then it was her turn. Her barrister in his straight wig began, "The widow of Mr. Andrew Oliver," etc. The atmosphere in the hall seemed to change. "A very distinguished name," said the judge. Paula's heart rose. "I will convince crocodiles that Andrew gave me all that was his, for it is the truth," she determined in herself, "when the moment comes." She was asked to go into the witness box. She went timidly, but determined.

The barrister asked her a question. She answered it with her whole story. From the time the will was made and the time she had seen it last at the ranch in the pocket of her trunk, had taken it to Andrew who was packing in his room, and then she knew no more of it. She could not find it. But Andrew's papers had been left all over several continents. She had won. The judge granted her her will. She looked at her lawyer. How pleased he was! She did not think he could be so glad. She had won, she had won! The law had pronounced for her. How grateful she was! Now she could begin to live, without the ugly haggling and resentment; she would now be able to do as she liked with Andrew's work and her own life. . . .

Paula thought of her dead husband. Why had be been great? What was it that made a human being great?

A great man is something new walking on this earth. He rejects much and accepts his own inner prompting from the unnamed, unknowable source that all creation springs from. A great man looks at the world and what it has to offer. "This I reject and this I take." There are all the already trodden paths of past great men, but a new great man has to cut out a new path out of the jungle of the present and the future. Paula thought of her husband's inborn power. He might have done anything, reached any of the so-called social or political heights. He rejected them all. That was not the meaning of living for him. He knew, how well he knew it, that eminence and fame are not worth having, ambition is a mistake. In the social order he would for ever be nothing, nothing at all. The world well lost for a profounder satisfaction, and nobody, no human being, had got more satisfaction out of life than he had done. In many parts of the earth he had felt the individual, immediate impact of the place, a contact, a comprehension that was magical. The whole world that he sensed as his real home was but a background for the people he met. The ever present universe with its sun and rain and trees and flowers and creatures, the intensity of his reactions, these had always been his solace when the human element, when his friends, failed to understand what he was after. The fact that life *was* in so many shapes an unending delight of newness inexhaustible, this delight he would not forgo for any ambition or promise of so-called success. Had he wanted power in the ordinary sense, he would have had to pay the price. The price of his joy in the exploration of life, in the freedom of his movements. He didn't think it good enough to be ambitious. He had written because he lived, he did not write to live. This had been his greatness. What he had seen and felt and known he gave in his writing to his fellow men, the splendour of living, the hope of more and more life he had given them, a heroic and immeasurable gift. Her spirit exulted over his achievement. Let the dull of wits belittle him, it didn't matter.

To her, Paula, had it been given to share this intense awareness, this pure apprehension of every living thing. How amazing it had been! She remembered the terrible hole his death had dug in her life. She remembered the strange ecstasy in which his death had plunged her, the bright, short, meteoric light of his life now complete. It was only now that he was dead that she could see his greatness whole as if a supernatural light lit up what he had been. "Be yourself," not "know yourself," he had said to her often; he had been himself and that was enough. His intense, proud self. No theories, no messages, nothing named and nailed and fixed, just a man, and his word.

She had learnt at school that Greek drama had been born out of the death of heroes. Paula understood it, the dead hero and the response of the still living. She had gone to Westminster Abbey.

"You ought to be here among your equals, the great of your race," she had said to him, "but they don't want you here, my dear. They have not seen you yet in their blindness. You wouldn't be happy here either, you, who so loved the open, all these stones would weigh heavily on you. You must come and rest at the wild little ranch of ours in New Mexico, where you were so busy and happy. When I can afford to have you there and make a place for you, you will come. Your splendid effort is ended, so soon, so quickly, and now there you can rest."

Paula sat in the British Museum in London with the timeless beauty of the Egyptians, Ramses and gods and goddesses, here she felt peace. So her desire was born to build a simple shrine at the ranch in New Mexico for her husband's ashes, a simple place on the top of the hill among the pines and cedars looking towards the sunset high above the Rio Grande and Colorado.

On the Boat Back

The narrative of the 1933–1934 trip to Buenos Aires resumes. The text is from a titled manuscript fragment found among the papers. Although Angelo Ravagli's name is fictionalized as "Dario," in keeping with the typescript chapters, Paula's narration is in the first person. This gives the text a more directly autobiographical flavor.

At our table are two young women, one small, neat, tidy and pretty with a cold kind of prettiness; the other is a tall, gawky, very young also rather pretty girl. They are sisters-in-law. The father is a missionary in Brazil. The young wife is joining her husband, in New Orleans. The cabin of the young women is next to mine. We are getting near the Equator, I lie on my bed in my cabin and read or embroider some tropical birds and brilliant flowers on to some blue linen. My door is on the hook to get more air. Dario hovers round on deck to make himself agreeable.

I have little desire to be agreeable. Meal-times are enough for me.

I am reading Fenimore Cooper, *The Last of the Mohicans*, and it takes me back to Cornwall, when Lawrence and I read Fenimore together and were wanting to come to America to escape the killing experience of the war; as we could not escape actually we did so in our imagination. Beautiful wild America! And we found it, the essence, the savage perfume of the America of long ago, in the mountains and high plateaux of New Mexico; I believe they could never be tamed. Nature is too independent here. Sometimes it snows in June and then we have to fight the torrents of water, then again it is dry, dry as dust for weeks. It is always a fight with the elements. Never any rest. Nature lets you know she is there all right.

In the next cabin there is a fierce arguing. I can't hear the words but the voices of the two women are angry. What is it all about? The married woman at night, I see the quick passing of her skirt, goes to a furtive intelligent young man on the boat. It shocks me for her young sister-in-law. She is crying. But the hard little wife doesn't care. And tonight in a kind of despair I see the young one dancing on a bench in the dining-room with her shoes off, kicking her legs high in the air for the benefit of the stewards, who are laughing.

Now the young one is coming along the passage to her cabin. One of the stewards, about forty, who whistles and imitates birds wonderfully, follows her. "Give us a kiss," he says. She is reluctant: "No, I don't want to." Now, why do they go on like this? He doesn't want a kiss really and she doesn't want to be kissed. I feel like jumping into the sea to be with the cool flying fishes to get away from this meaningless performance. . .

Coming Back

The basic text is from a titled fragment. The inter-polated texts are from other manuscripts containing material that is pertinent to the return to the New Mexico ranch and Mrs. Lawrence's feeling for Taos. In all these texts real names are used—a characteristic of early versions. "Beck" is Rebecca James, an artist in Taos. "Spud" is Willard Johnson, a very old friend who had published Lawrence in his student, little-magazine days at the University of California and had been ex-pelled for that, among other iconoclasms. "Mabel" is Mabel Luhan, and "Tony" is her husband. The time is early 1934.

We come to Taos, up the slope to the plaza. There, a shock, the left corner, the most ornamental one where the "Don Fernando" was, is a black, burnt heap of adobe and iron, only a small piece of adobe wall left with "Don Fernando Coffee Shop" on it remains.

But already the undaunted proprietors have turned the next corner of the plaza into the "Don Fernando Tavern."

"Hallo—you back," greets the voice of Tony Mirabar, the Indian. Angelino imitates his immovable voice and face when he says "Yes Ma'am" to me. I want to see Spud, the old Spoodle friend, known so well for so many years. He is editor now of the *Taos Valley News;* I turn the corner of the Taos bank to go to his office, the door opening into the printing shop. Only his official corner with his desk is gay, with flowers, a pink rose

painted delicately on glass by the fair hand of "Beck," a yellow
majolica horse, and there is Spud, thin and alert, "Benjamin"
Angelino calls him, in chestnut velveteen trousers and a yellow
and brown check shirt. I ask Spud, "How is Mabel?" "Ever so
well, she is in the big house again, she is younger than ever,
giving parties and lots of people are coming to stay this summer;
she is in New York now for a little while, but is coming back
soon." I think of Mabel's long adobe house on the low mesa near,
the adobe walls round the entrance, the pigeons on her Venus-
berg: it has something enchanted, the paved long enclosure with
its masses of irises in the spring, and some red fluffy plant
growing out of the stones in the patio; it is a rare place. You go
to a party and she meets you in a creamy, cobwebby lace dress
and turquoises, guests arriving; always new people come you
have never seen before. This night she is Circe casting a spell.
The group of Indians come and dance their turkey and war
dance to the drum in splendid feathers.

Then there is the other Mabel, that at sunset drives me to the
pueblo before Christmas just as the sun goes down. "Look, here
is Nell Gwynne," she says, pointing to a small white dog that
appears from behind the wall, and it *is* a Nell Gwynne. We sit
quite still in the space between the two *pueblos*. Ice edges a
narrow strip of running water of the dividing stream, slowly in
their wide boots the beshawled women come from their houses
with cans to fetch water for the evening meal. Slowly they bend
to the water. The afterglow turns the icy water rosy. The chim-
neys begin to smoke. And now all the little neatly built squares
of ocote wood that I had noticed when we came are being lit as it
grows dark. Unnaturally clear and bright, the fires blaze without
smoke up here near us, and all along the plaza and on the roofs of
the *pueblo* it flares up, and on the *pueblo* of the winter people,
across the stream. We are staying this side, the summer *pueblo*.
Powerful like an ancient fortress the mass of dobe springs into
the firelights; the rhythm of life in the *pueblo* gets us, we sit very
still. All the last green light has gone out of the sky, children and
dark figures stand by the fires, a little boy clapping his hands at
the flames that leap without smoke. Then Mabel sits in a big

room of Tony's nephew. It's a bare whitewashed room, only rolls of bedding along the walls, very neat. Indians sit round the walls, still and centred on themselves as only Indians can sit. Children roll about sleepily, it is right, nobody bullies them and they are good and at ease. Mabel sits and knits. An old man, last year's governor, sits by the fire. The groups of young dancers, dressed up, some as whites, one in evening dress, come and dance and collect from the Indians special cakes as a gift to the new governor. A baby is being handed to its mother to be fed. It has the softest darkest fluff of hair on its shapely small head. . . .

Coming back and feeling happy I know that this country suits my very soul. I love my Taos and Santa Fe friends. I am at home with them. Not that I see so much of them, sitting on my mountainside an hour's motordrive away from Taos and nearly three from Santa [Fe], and often the road is so bad that when the snow is melting in the mountains and comes down in torrents of fierce, rushing streams, we are inaccessible prisoners, but cheerful ones. The faithful Diego rides up with food and mail, through any weather. I love my American friends. They have known the hardships and the trials of this hard country, and their friendship is truly a helpful one. It's different from European friendship, not so dependent on thought and feeling, but a practical one if you need it; it's there and you can ask them to do things for you and they do them, your friends, as a matter of course. We are supposed to be a queer lot out here. We do queer things according to ordinary standards and we get into states and strange relationships. But I like it, everybody stands on his or her own feet and tries to live according to his or her own way and so we quarrel. And there is so much space for us all and much to do and always the fights with the elements and we are all in the same boat. You love this place or you don't, there's no middle way. Some of us are rich and some of us are poor, but it doesn't matter, either you belong or you don't. Nowhere have I seen shams disposed of as they are here, in a hand's turn, it seems to happen unconsciously. Now I shall enjoy living in the new house we built last year.

How glad I am to be back!

I go to the grocery store, where the butcher and the other employees greet me with fervour. I don't give them much trouble, so they like me.

Now across the desert up to the ranch. Nothing has moved yet, but it is warm and soon everything will come up. The alfalfa, the oats and corn and wheat and the cottonwoods and aspens (I don't really know the difference) will turn into their lovely light and yet strong green.

We have crossed Arroyo Hondo, it looks like winter still, all the trees still silver and grey only, like drawings, no colour, and the horses so thin in the fields, when I think of our roly-polies on the ranch so fat.

At last we are back. The two black cats, my aristocratic ones, rub themselves against my legs; his brother has departed to another ranch and the wild mother has also left, but her wild, black daughter is staying and has a romance with the aristocrat.

We are back, we are back. There's the new house that we built last year. The house has no soul, frozen and lonely all winter it needs us badly to put life into it again.

Last year we built it, this year I mean to enjoy it.

How much there will have to be done. Fruit trees planted, the garden sown, a garden started in front of the house. . . .

Last Chapter—Friends

The title is a combination of the titles of the two manuscript texts that make up this chapter. The time is 1935, after the 1933–1934 trip to Buenos Aires which constitutes the narrative framework of most of the memoir. Here, among the numerous, often fragmentary manuscripts in Mrs. Lawrence's posthumous papers, the possibility of a continuous, connected memoir ends. A few short pieces that could not be fitted in appear in the Appendix. It is clear from Mrs. Lawrence's correspondence that she worked on the memoirs until the last few years of her life in the 1950's, but there is very little new material, probably because most of her attention went into revising the account of the crucial episodes in her past. Her concern about World War II is expressed in the prefatory material which appears in the Introduction. For her life after 1935, the letters are the principal record.

Dario was going to Italy and Paula was returning to the ranch alone. She remembered the time soon after Andrew's death when she had met Dario and told him, "I am not fit to be with people." But he had consoled her. For hours she had cried and told her agony between her tears. Her grief was not only for herself; it seemed an eternal impersonal grief. In Andrew the whole world had lost a power for good, something that rarely appears, a new edition of the species man. She did not seem to weep such bitter tears for herself only but for all people, who had lost such a guide and friend. He had been unique. There would never be another like him. [Dario] had let her talk and cry with such sympathy and it had given her new courage. And she had loved him gratefully ever since.

Now he was gone and she missed his cheerful presence, she longed to drive in the car with him while he was singing at the top of his voice, but also she wanted to be alone and think. Never since Andrew's death had she been alone. She knew that she had not accepted the fact that Andrew was really dead. She thought of his dying. He was the first person whom she had seen in the agony of death. It was so different from what she had expected death to be. She remembered when she had for the first time had an inkling of what she thought was death. It had been on Good Friday in the *Garrisons Kirche* at home when she was fourteen. She had worn her new pink and white striped frock, a floppy Florentine straw hat with a black velvet ribbon hanging down the back, a black narrow ribbon round her throat, a little black enamel heart with a wreath of pearls hanging from it, that she had loved among her mother's things. The church was filled with groups of soldiers. She stood between some officers in uniform, she saw their high shiny boots, their hands in their gloves were resting on the hilts of their swords. The church was bare and grey except for the large crucifix on the altar with a tall candle on each side. It was so different from the big cathedral, whose body seemed like the vast skeleton of a mastodon. Through the enormous rose-window came the subdued light and threw patterns on the floor. The scent of incense lingered and groups of candles on the side altars flickered dimly. The atmosphere seemed to turn you inwards and soften you.

It was chilly and more intense in the *Garrisons Kirche*. From the choir above rose the muted but large volume of soldiers' voices singing:

> *"O Haupt voll Blut und Wunden*
> *Voll Schmerz und voller Hohn,*
> *O Haupt zum Spott gebunden*
> *Mit einer Dornen Kron."*

All the suffering, all the agony of all humanity seemed to utter itself in the song.

Then the preacher mounted the chancel and read the story of the crucifixion. "And when the sixth hour was come, there was darkness over the land until the ninth hour."

And the temple curtains were rent and the whole dramatic story was brought home to her. She looked at Christ on the crucifix, the bowed head, the crossed feet nailed down, the blood on the naked body. No, it was too horrible. This could never be for her the last truth of men. She looked at the officer next to her; what was he thinking, standing there so upright and handsome? No, she would never accept this defeat, this agony and shame of a man as the apotheosis of life. She had been right. Andrew's death had been so quiet and proud, so still, and inevitably his life had stopped. And death was there. He had given her so much of life, the glamour of all creation, he had made her feel and now he had given her the last and supreme gift: death in its dignity. She had felt death's silent splendour. Andrew's life was accomplished, his sincere efforts were ended. Nothing would disturb him any more. She remembered singing quietly to him in the night by his bed where he lay dead, he had always listened to her, even when he was angry. But now he listened no more. She had felt a curious exultation. It was fulfilled. Her own self seemed to fall away from her. There was not only the little everyday personal world, there was the great universe, the great whole of creation to whom all belongs, plants and animals and men, alive or dead; the universe was one forever. For the first time she felt the wholeness of the world as if before it had been a flat coin, now she had a sense of its depth, of its roundness. But the live man, he had gone, she could hear him still and feel his presence in her soul. She had lived so absolutely in his world, the bright, noble world that had been his, she was still living in it. But now she was alone. Dario had gone and stood no longer between her and her loneliness, and like a dark figure she saw Andrew standing in front of her bed as if asking her: "Come and join me." She became ill and was taken to a nursing home. A great fear was upon her, she could not fight it. A crisis came, would she live or die? The engines of the trains were screaming their arrival, but there was nobody in the train for her; Andrew was dead, he couldn't come, and Dario was far away. A struggle went on in her between life and death. Then slowly in the centre of her a sweet, patient small impulse rose and asserted itself. No, she was not going to die yet. The number of her dead had grown larger and larger, friends and parents, people she had loved were dead. But she herself would live still and see the clouds and the rain and feel the warmth of summer and doubly would she be grateful for being just that, alive. Let people fight about communism and fascism, in the end the two were the same, a mere fight for control, and what then? You had to live from a deeper self than mere will. They missed the point of living, these would-be controllers. When you had control, what did it amount to? "They have missed the bus," Paula thought. We are not born in little black shirts, nor little red ones, but in our skins. And we live in it and then die in it. Even if everybody had ten cars and twenty radios and forty iceboxes it would not make them rich inside themselves. You had to get your own natural inheritance back, your own joy in the living universe round you. It was this that was lost, nothing else. However much you took away from other people it wouldn't do you any good. There were those who wanted to hang on like grim death to what they had and the others who wanted to take it away from them, and it wasn't the point at all. "Forget about it," Paula wanted to say to them, "it won't make you happy, begin really to live from your own best human inside and see what happens. Resentment and having fixed ideas won't get you anywhere."

Especially resentment Paula wanted to conquer. Let people be mean to her personally, she would not let it alter her nature and sour her life. That's what they wanted: to bore a hole into her wholeness; she would not let them triumph but would cut herself off from this new devil of malevolence. This was her fight, now, not to fight others, but fight to keep her own integrity. . . .

Dim and drowsy the days went by, Paula was feeling very weak. Impatiently she waited for Dario to return, but he could not come at once. He was bringing her husband's ashes from

Europe. How grateful Paula felt that Dario had a respect almost as her own for Andrew's memory. She had after Andrew's death wanted to take his remains to the ranch to which he had meant to return.

In the autumn Dario had built a small chapel, very simple, on the hill under the steep mountains. The hill had wild flowers growing on it, sunflowers and red and pink cactus and michaelmas daisies and little cypress trees. Andrew had loved the spot. The chapel was finished except for the inner decoration. Paula tried to restrain her impatience. "I am too weak to be impatient," she told herself, "I must get better." It helped her convalescence that she was aware of the real concern for her health, that many of her friends felt. "They care that I live," she thought gratefully. Young friends looked after her and took her for a drive in the early spring weather every afternoon. She loved the country, the New Mexico round Santa Fe, Frijoles Canyon with its cliff dwellings, Chimayo where the apple trees began to bloom, Truchas on the hill high up, which her young friend had taken as a setting for his *penitente* novel. Many and infinitely varied were the drives they took.

Now finally Dario was coming. She met him at the station. He was very quiet; she knew he was like that when he was moved. Yes, he was profoundly glad to be back. They drove up to the ranch, up through the Rio Grande canyon where the apricot trees and peaches were already in bloom. But at the ranch spring had not made any signs of coming. For three weeks Paula and Dario were almost prisoners, the car could not be used on the road that had turned into a mudhole with the melting snow. Only the horses could make the trip to the valley. But Dario was painting furiously and was happy. Paula was still feeling weak and lazy after her illness, but she got better and stronger as the cottonwoods and aspens began to sprout their young green and the oak shrub leaves appeared golden brown and the first pale hairy mauve anemones came out near the road in the woods. She was at peace now, Dario was there, he made it possible for her to live the simple life she loved on this spot of the earth that she loved; this spot that they could turn into a living centre, this meant genuine living to her. Dario loved the place as much as she did and he had put so much of thought and elbow grease into the place, with the passion of a pioneer.

Dario had brought Andrew's ashes from Europe. The little chapel they had built the summer before. Up on the hill it was looking far over the land below, where in past summer nights Paula and Andrew had slept out of doors under the pines. Paula thought: "Andrew has come home now." It gave her peace to have his ashes near. She was getting old now and was glad of it. "I am a lucky old woman," she said to herself. "I have what I need and want. Through every window the out-of-doors comes right up to me. There is this ever changing great sky and the desert below and the dark line of the Rio Grande. I never get tired of seeing it. And my past life is spread out before me like this great view. Now I am old I can look over it as I do from this mountainside over the valley below. I have known love and passion and ecstasy and hate and pain, but now there is peace in me, I have pulled through all the difficulties of my own nature and all the other difficulties from outside." She saw herself young again and muddled, living in a fog of uncertainties, now she was sure in herself and clear. Life itself had hammered her out. She clung to her vision of what life could and should be. Nobody would be able to muddle and muddy her again. If people hated her, well and good, let them hate, but she would not respond with hate, because it took one's freedom away. Hate or love, she was not going to be a slave to either. She wanted to be free to live every hour that came along in its fullness and change. . . .

Paula thought with bitterness of Andrew's friends. It had not been given them to understand him, not one. She thought of the many people they had met. She thought of his efforts, so disinterested, to help them in their lives, to extricate them from their entangled situations, to make them breathe in a freer air, but it had always ended in failure. They resented his interference, they jeered at his deeper insight. Some had loved him but had not taken him seriously, like the wayward child of infinite charm he had been to them. Paula had been more

detached, and rested secure in the bond between them, that had
such deep roots, deeper than either he or she knew, they only
knew it was there. That was Paula's reality. A woman like Paula
knows and senses only the reality of her man. The rest was like a
show, a performance that she watched. But he, Andrew, had
given himself, had tried to impart some of himself to others, to
anybody whom he felt had a spark of life. Always and every time
it had been a failure. They resented what they called his
interference, they even thought him evil and purely destructive.
How sorry she felt for Andrew. She knew how "life good" he
was, and she knew how the deathliness in these others called him
wicked. Again and again he tried and always the same result. He
had tried to imbue these phantoms, phantoms they seemed to
Paula, with life, and always they hated him in the end. They had
hated her too, but she had been mostly unaware of it. In the
solemn moments between them he had told her: "Nothing has
mattered but you."

When they were in America two women had determined to
take Andrew under their wing. One of them, a very energetic
and powerful American woman who had learnt all the tricks of
the mind and will, had decided that she was the person to "run"
Lawrence's genius and he was the man to reveal to the world her
great self. But there was no self to reveal, only a terrific will that
possessed her. The very fact that she had no genuine self gave
her this frantic desire for dominion over others. But she had
always failed in her former efforts. She had set herself up as
Paula's rival, though Paula was blithely unaware of this rivalry
that only existed in R—'s imagination. Consciously with her will
R— wanted to "run" Andrew's genius. It amused Paula. How
stupid the woman was! Genius is the freest thing on the earth,
the one thing you cannot "run." Paula knew all the time that
Andrew would rather die than submit to anybody's will. R—
imagined that Andrew submitted to Paula's will. She considered
that Andrew's terrible weakness. She never understood that
between Andrew and Paula it was not a question of will or even
consciousness that bound them together. [As] for the mystery of
Andrew's and Paula's genuine relationship, as any genuine

relationship is a mystery, she could not see it, it was not given to her to see. And in her rage of frustrated understanding she became like a banging door, that rasps the nerves, a mechanical thing, a banging, rattling, nerve-racking, lifeless object instead of a living creature. She tried all her tricks on Andrew, from smart talk and letters to tears and scenes, but none of them worked. Andrew was no sensationalist. The genuine kindly feeling he had for R— as for any human being meant nothing to her. "My will be done," she insisted. So of course it wasn't and she lost his good will.

The other woman who attached herself to Andrew was a different type, the serving self-effacing, adding herself to another's being, but feeling very superior in her self-abnegation. Blindly and humbly she adored Andrew, seemingly asking in return a delicate spiritual recognition of her service. He tried to cure her of her spiritual, false feeling for him, but again it was no use, she stuck to her lollipop of imagined spiritual communion, in that alike to the other woman; both wanted to dominate Andrew, one with a positive will, the other with a negative one. The negative one hated Paula's aggressive nature particularly. Her negative being roused the aggression. S— had got away from her conventional surroundings and had come to stay with Andrew and Paula at the ranch. Paula was impressed with the way S— had thrown over her past, so comfortable and even luxurious, for this simple life. She lived in a tiny cabin with only the absolute necessities, she saddled the horses and helped to build sheds and carry stones, exerting herself like a man. It was admirable and S— was happy. Paula did all she could to make S— happy. Though she knew quite well that S— was not in the least grateful for Paula's efforts. S—'s one-track adolescent mind, that had always, since she was sixteen years old, existed in the adoration, the *Schwarm*, for somebody or other exclusively, the *idée fixe*, the object changing but the emotion remaining the same. She was *parti pris* against Paula from the beginning. She, S—, was the old-fashioned heroine, the "Jane Eyre." "Yah," Andrew had said, "that Jane could only love a man [who] depended on her and [was] mutilated first."

Well, S— was the Jane and Paula was Rochester's mad raving hyena of a wife! It exasperated Paula, chiefly that her own good will towards this incomplete being was so ignored. She put up with her because she helped Andrew in many things, she was a faithful servant but the kind of servant that bosses you in the end with its service. S— did not hear very well, so whatever Paula said was one thing and what S—'s ears heard was another. Every teasing remark of Andrew's turned into a criticism, every argument turned into a tragedy. She encroached more and more on the privacy of Andrew and Paula's daily life, till Paula would stand it no more.

"She goes or I," she had declared one morning. The eternal critical hostile eye on herself had got on Paula's nerves, the hostility took her freedom away. S—'s hatred of her was all the stronger because unconscious. So S— went. But she remained attached to Andrew and Andrew did not know what to do with her, he felt responsible for her as for a servant.

But after he had met her again without Paula and he had felt her heavy leaning on him, his one wish was to remove her from his immediate living. "I can't do a thing, I can't go down the road, without her watching, watching." It had been this police-man watching that had so irritated Paula. But in her humble arrogance S— had explained it all to herself. Poor Andrew was weak, he would go to Paula out of a sense of duty and propriety. He was really lost. There again the two women united in their opinion. Had Andrew submitted to them, he would have been a real, happy genius and now, after all, poor Andrew, he was a failure. Now Andrew was dead. Both women had written to Paula. She thought, "All right, in their way they cared for Andrew, if not for me, but because they cared we can be friends." She had met them, they had talked for hours of Andrew, and Paula believed them her friends, she was sincerely theirs. So the shock she received was all the greater.

When Dario came back with Andrew's ashes, the old situation seemed to come to life again. Quite unaware, Paula gaily lived up on the ranch, finishing Andrew's small chapel up on the hill, when finally she heard gossip about herself and Dario. How she,

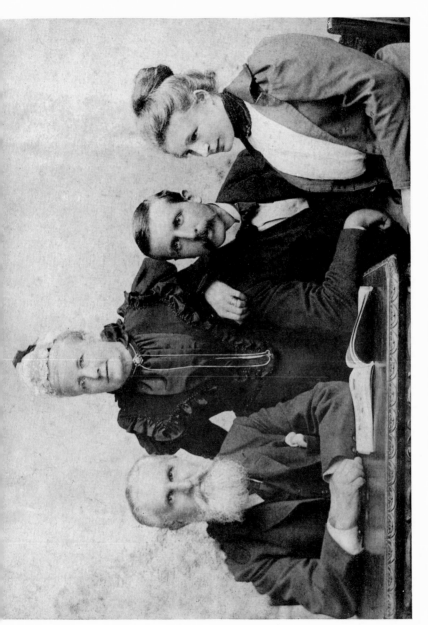

Frieda with Ernest Weekley and his parents.

Frieda with her son, 1901.

Paula, had only brought Andrew's ashes from Europe to enhance the value of her ranch and much more. She did not take much notice till she had a real shock. Just a few days before there was going to be a ceremony held on Andrew's hill, a girl she knew came to her and said: "Can you ever forgive me?" "What in the world for?" asked Paula. "I was willing to help steal Andrew's ashes." Paula felt scared. "And why?" "They told me Andrew's ashes were a speculation up here and I could not bear the thought." Paula shivered all through. Andrew's ashes! The only possession that she ever had considered her own, the one and only in all her life, had been Andrew; had he not given himself to her, and his ashes were the symbol of this, they wanted to take [them] from her, her friends! They had plotted to take the ashes and scatter them! She was profoundly grateful the plot had not been carried out, she could not have borne it. She had trusted them, her two friends, it bewildered her. She pulled herself together. "I will think of Andrew," she said to herself, "and cut off other thoughts. I will be there only for him."

On the day of the ceremony she received some flowers from R— with a note from her, "But when you are dead, I shall have my way and the ashes shall be scattered." But the threat had no more power to touch Paula, she was in her world with Andrew, and there was Dario. She took the innocent flowers to the chapel, but the two friends had gone out of her for ever. . . .

How big the price was that Paula had to pay for Andrew's love. So many people hated her, because he had come her way and not theirs. Well, she paid, but it had been worth it through all eternity. She had been the trusting fool. Of course they must hate her, even if they wanted to be friendly on the surface, and did not even know that they hated her. All right then, it had hurt much, it was sad, but there was consolation in the thought that anyhow they had cared for Andrew; that was true too, she had to put up with the hate. That was life in its mixture of love and hate. She was not going to let it make her miserable, even if she did not deserve this hate; but you never deserved anything, things happen, and it was better like this than if Paula herself had been treacherous and deserved the hate.

Correspondence

The correspondence begins with letters, translated from the German, to her sister Else, who seems to have sensed Frieda's unique qualities from the beginning, and carefully preserved her letters. The first was written at the age of ten, the second when she was eighteen, the year after she had first met Ernest Weekley. The others, to Else and the other members of her family in Germany, along with a few of Weekley's letters to them, trace the course of her married life with him in England. Ernest Weekley became lecturer in Modern English at Freiburg in 1897, and taught from May to November, when he resigned, apparently unexpectedly. Of Weekley's request to be relieved of his duties, Dr. Friedrich Kluge, professor of Germanic studies, said: "I request and recommend attention to lecturer Weekley's application. In the short time of his activity here he devoted himself to performance of his duties with a special enthusiasm and conscientiousness, so that we may disregard and excuse this unusual termination." In a letter to the editor, dated December 1, 1963, the distinguished scholar and educator Herbert Davis recalled a conversation he had in 1924 or 1925, when he was giving lectures at the University of Cologne, with Professor Schroer, who had appointed Weekley at Freiburg and to whom Weekley had come to talk about his romantic passion for Frieda, and the despair he felt as a foreigner and an impecunious lecturer (and perhaps as an older man). ". . . It may even have been that he was so hard hit, that he had decided that it would be better to return to England at the end of that summer semester. . . . Schroer was one of those people inclined to believe in the social prestige of the academic pro-

fession in Germany, and therefore scorned the idea that a colleague of his should not think himself the equal of even a von Richthofen, at once proposed that he should call upon Frieda's parents and make a proposal of marriage." In January, 1898, Weekley was appointed lecturer in French at Nottingham University College; and in September, 1899, when she had turned twenty, they were married. He was, of course, some fourteen years older than she. The courtship, including a visit to his family in England, and the disappointment she experienced on their wedding night are covered in the chapter in the memoirs entitled "English Marriage." The disturbance of their marriage as a result of her widening horizons and the appeal of other men, particularly Lawrence, is treated in the "Octavio" and "Andrew" chapters. Ernest Weekley went on to a distinguished career as linguist and etymologist and is the author of The Romance of Words *(1912), several etymological dictionaries, and various other works.*

TO her sister Else

Metz

4 February 1890

Dear Else:

Don't ever think that we have forgotten you. It must have been terribly funny when Miss Rose stuck her finger in her mouth. I imagine I'll be like that some day. Mrs. Metzger is well. We go very seldom to the Müllers. . . . I was sick on the Kaiser's birthday and Augusta died then. It was very nice on festival night. The Langs were there and brought us bonbons. I would also like to have dancing lessons. I want a lamb for Easter. Recently there was a children's performance at the theatre, and Aunt——gave us a great big bag full of marzipan. Halms and Rohrs are here, it is very nice for they still do what I say. I can now crochet very nicely, and I have made a dress for your poor doll and put it carefully away. Just think, Grandfather wrote me first of all that he would come. 1000000000000000 greetings and kisses from your

Frieda

(*Translated from the German*)

TO her sister Else

Berlin

21 February 1898

My dearest sister!

Finally I write to you, as you see, and want to start at once to tell you everything. Yesterday I was with Trude at a party, not altogether first [?] but in order to talk with Mariele, who with her long-handled lorgnette runs around here in the museums, but Trude is exactly as always. I became very melancholy, she was so nice. I am at the moment as gay as is proper for an eighteen-year-old, life is so beautiful, and I enjoy it completely. I am now awfully glad to be here, a large city is something wonderful. Guess who was here today? Kurt, my first love, just like he used to be; it was very funny. You can't imagine it. I find the society of gentlemen very nice, the way it used to be here. Kurt Elbe has sort of fallen in love, a very nice entertainment. I have so much to tell you. Send me M.'s letters. You must not hold it against him that he is temperamental, he is still young. I am now entirely through with him, perhaps it will come again, who can say anything for sure about themselves? You will be shocked by my awful letter; I am not always like this, I can say for your peace of mind. The notion of being able to become something in Metz is not at all displeasing to me, I do not need to set nearly so high a goal as you! Goodbye, sincerest love.

Your Frieda

How do you feel about Dr. Müller as a faithful, warmhearted admirer, or something like that?

(*Translated from the German*)

TO her family

Nottingham

15 December 1899

My dear family!

My Jane is just going through the room with a wax candle, which smells like Christmas and adds to my holiday mood. Ernest and I are with you in spirit, that you can believe! Everything good, many presents! It was very worthless of me not to have made anything, but one sees such lovely things in England that it would seem very stupid. The tablecloth for mother, the skirt for Nusch, and the lace will do for a blouse; Alti could also trim a dress with it. We would gladly have been much more generous, but I wanted to tell you something so that your grandparently and auntly feelings would be prepared. Weekleys will be three next year. It is to be hoped the little Weekley takes more after his father, and will not be such a nitwit as his mother. I beg Alti, good Alti, not to noise it about. With the Christmas lights, the festival hare, the heavenly "Gangfisch," think of your loving daughter

Frieda

I would fasten the pictures in the frames with the gummed edges from stamps.

A Merry Christmas and a Happy New Year. My wife is stubborn; she wants a boy, but I have ordered a girl. On

Christmas day, at half past one, you must drink to the health of the expected new world citizen!

Ernest

(Translated from the German)

To her sister Else

Hampstead
21 December 1899

My dear Lorella!

Think, in what good odour you are, Ernest and I had just had our Christmas gift-giving and were in a rather sentimental frame of mind when "knocked the door" and the postman hands me your letter. How extremely generous you were, 10 marks; how can you do this, my good old friend, but in any case they made me very happy. You get accordingly the "*Lachtudische*" present! After all you must not consider me crude and unfeeling, I have already thought hard about your getting settled, later on I will be richer, now naturally we have needed a great deal! Many Christmas greetings from Ernest and me, to be sure one becomes melancholy when one thinks of those Christmas Eves in Sablon, weren't they wonderful! Think, my sister, you will be able next Christmas to send along something for a little niece or a nephew, a little Weekley, now what do you say! I am so anxious for it to be nice, Ernest is also afraid, he says, that he will be jealous. But sure, don't tell anyone, it is too sacred to me for people to gossip about. I have been here two days in Hampstead without Ernest; the air here does me so much good and I am often quite alone in Nottingham, three evenings a week Ernest has a lecture for workers. It is to be hoped that Mr. P. will come to Berlin for Christmas. Mama speaks much of "late happiness"; is one at twenty-five truly very old? I would think myself surely very young! We have a rendezvous with Nicholas and Goldsmith.

With sincerest love

Your Frieda

Please, the address of young Gagern!
Greetings to all.

(Translated from the German)

TO her sister Else

9 Goldswong Terrace
Nottingham
[*Undated*]

Dearest Else!

I wanted to write you a leisurely letter today to your old Heidelberg that I love so much, then there came a letter from Nusch,[1] she is engaged! Engaged! Not yet publicly, and I am to act as if I knew nothing, but engaged! They want to be married in October, hardly eighteen years old! I hope she will be happy, she writes so charmingly, very solemn and full of love! I am anxiously awaiting the next news! Poor Mama, I almost wish she would not come, it will be too much excitement for her. The story has even upset me a lot! Otherwise I am always healthy and have spells of absurd happiness! Woman, have a child, and you are happy! I am so sorry for your Mariana Weber! The title which she gave you is really beautiful if one knows you.

You see how long ago the letter was begun. Your "lovely little birds" make me happy today. I have everything ready for the little one; the nurse arrives on the 10th, I am wildly looking forward to Mama! I hope she gains strength in the quiet and good air with me, for since I am feeling as well as a washer-woman, everything runs smoothly! The young one will get married already on August 2! Hold your tongue, but according to all that Mama writes me, I don't like him very well; in any case he is no Ernest, I am happier every day, we have no squabbles, much less quarrels. I would like to go to Metz at the beginning of September, *it* [*sic*], of course, goes with me; in August Ernest will probably have work to do in Cambridge, I don't know yet whether I will go with him, stay here, [go to] Hampstead to his aunts, or where! Perhaps in the autumn we will go to Liverpool where a very good position is open! Do you know a nice German *pension* for an English woman from ——? A friend of Ernest's asked me to recommend something for his niece. I am "scrubbing" in expectation of the Alti. I thought it

[1] Her younger sister.

would be nice to be at Mama's when the Schreibershofers are on their wedding trip. Will you come too?

In love
Your Frieda

A lousy letter but better than none!
I am so happy over the little picture of Gagern.

(*Translated from the German*)

TO her sister Else

9 Goldswong Terrace
Nottingham
4 July 1900

Exalted Aunt!

Yesterday evening the good Alti departed, the time passed much too fast, but—another knot tied that holds fast! I could [write] you volumes about the lady in black who just now sits on the sea and has burst upon Nottingham. I hope very much that the Baden [?] administration at the earliest possible moment realizes how necessary it is that you come here; I have thought so much about you and "yours," and I will certainly like him better than Max, he seems to me much more aristocratic although without "von" and General Staff stripes. But now to the creature who calls himself your nephew, the nurse affirms that he looks like *you*, has your spirit so hovered over him? In any case he is clever, he soon discovered the "false pretences" of his pacifier and holds it with disdain! He has my hair colour, darker eyes and a "nobby" little body. He will be named Montague Karl Richthofen.[2] Mama wrote "Montesanien." Ernest is terribly proud of him. I was allowed to go out today for the first time; farewell, my dear, my mind still doesn't reach very far!

In love
Your sister

(*Translated from the German*)

[2] Charles Montague Weekley had been born on June 15, 1900.

TO her sister Else

Metz

My dear Sistersoul: [*18 June 1901?*]

First of all I thank you, [I am] deeply moved by your extremely generous gift; the little head is sweet and I want to put it on an easel, it will certainly look pretty! Today, as the "height of generosity," came the lovely material. Think, how fine, it will make two blouses, the other I will make for you, you can also use it! If not, then give it to me, for the winter with white lace, altogether a very pretty party dress. You are the "gift-giver" personified, that I must say, have a thousand thanks, I am so pleased; also the little skirt will serve me for a long time. It is a very good idea that you want to spend three weeks with us in Switzerland and not go to England. Of course I would not have had so much time for you, as the boy must first gradually get used to his new nurse, and then the house is so awfully dirty. Also Ernest has much to do at the beginning of the term. I have enjoyed myself tremendously here, nothing to think about and to do. I would have so liked to send you Monty's picture on his birthday; unfortunately they are not yet ready, but be prepared soon for something nice. Think, the excellent Nuschs want to take the boy and Elsie while we are in Switzerland, that will be much better. The boy is exactly like Ernest in temperament. I find the parents grown sadly older, for the first time it bothers me, Mama can be so excited and Papa so very absent-minded; the vacation will do them good! The boy was charming on his birthday, he received so many presents and was beside himself over a dog from Mama. Now he goes every day with a little wooden bucket and shovel along the Esplanade. On a little cake there was a candle, how can one be so ridiculously young. I think Nusch has become so nice, she only acts coarser than she is; still, she is much prettier too. I have gone out quite a bit, witnessed a festival with de Drachoner; it gave me much pleasure at first, but now I have [had] enough. I am overjoyed to be able to be with you in Switzerland.

Love,   Your sister

(*Translated from the German*)   Frieda

TO her sister Else

Nottingham
5 October 1901

My dear sister Else:

For your birthday I wish you everything fine and good, "give her eternal youth, strength, etc." The cravat is a gift for you, together with two silver serving forks, which, however, you must fetch yourself. Your fine "goodies" cheered my heart and incidentally saved Ernest and me from dying of hunger; we had taken a long walk, lunch was not yet ready, then appeared the postman like the raven of Elijah with your "goodies." Sering's speech pleased me so much; he speaks exactly like he looks, but what kind of a dirty fellow is that, to get so personal? Still it is vulgar for a decent person to have to associate with such fellows. I would be very happy if you would send me a newspaper now and then; the parents wanted to send me *Velhagen und Klasing*, but I don't want to remind them about it, they had us all summer long. Too bad that I cannot make arrangements for your birthday so nicely as you did for mine. The beautiful waterlilies. I suppose you will invite the woman with the children. It is to be hoped you like the *Forestlovers*. I have recently read much Eliot and like her very much. Ernest and I are learning Italian in the evenings together, it doesn't seem very difficult. I have been through a thorough house-cleaning, and enjoyed it very much. The house is still not entirely ready, but already we are so far along. I had the seamstress, the light-blue blouse is so pretty with white and [with] gold buttons. Both homespuns have been dyed black and have made a very handsome dress. We were with very nice people for dinner; she is also a little bit Socialist and you must get acquainted with her; he is especially nice, and what surprises me so is that the assertion that educated women are poor housekeepers is very seldom proved true. They have a more over-all view, to manage a household successfully is no small thing, as I note again. The boy develops splendidly under his routine; he is really dear, and it is wonderful for me that to him no one is above his "Momamo." Come early next spring and stay long, for we miss each other very much.

So in the new "life year"

Your loving sister
Frieda

Many happy returns of the day.

Ernest

(Translated from the German)

TO her sister Else

9 Goldswong Terrace
Nottingham
25 November 1901

My dear Ellerich:

I savour with great enjoyment the fame of my sister. I hope you will report your activities to me. It seems to me as if I had not heard for quite a while from the youth group in Baden. How nice it would be if we could sit down together once in a while; in times like this one misses one's sister. We live peacefully in our little house, the boy is our great joy and worth an entire study (he is certainly not at all stupid). I have also [met] some nice people, sometimes there is a concert, and in general I find life worth living. Imagine, I even dabble in writing; it is, to be sure, very modest, but it fills me with great pride to produce something "brainy." A little exercise does my rusty brain good. I receive 100 M. for very little work! I can very easily use a few hundred. You can imagine that I have already bought for the first hundred (which I don't yet have) a villa in the Schwarzwald for all of us, a dowry for Monty, etc. . . . Are you going home for Christmas? Good-bye for today, write when you have time.

In love,

Your true Frieda

Ask Mrs. Seidelset. . . . I can send her a few things as articles without value for 'Li'l' Else.

(Translated from the German)

TO her sister Else   9 Goldswong Terrace
                                                   Nottingham
Dear Ella!   *Monday*

I was deeply touched by the St. Nicholas Day gift from you,
the boy was delighted with the soft bunny, and immediately gave
him a kiss. In any case you still look back on the impressions of
your trip; you can certainly put up with a lot from people, I
always quickly have enough of them. *The Time* has just come;
thank you, I like it; it is not extreme and yet progressive. My
little book about Schiller has given me tremendous pleasure. It is
mean that people try to keep us women away by force from
everything "brainy," as if one didn't need it just as much when
one is married! A household after a time runs all by itself, and
now nearly every day I say, "What shall I do?" (Nearly fourteen
days later.) I had the seamstress and a little dinner; therefore
this letter has been laid aside, which is just like Frieda. For
Christmas one of Ernest's sisters, who is perhaps going to South
Africa, is coming. Such a single person really has it good, can do
what she wants or let it alone, doesn't need to take anything into
consideration. Just you be satisfied. My dear single girl, maybe
you sometimes feel a little lonely but that is only because you sit
in Karlsruhe and your friends are not near you. Is that happy
fiancé still at your luncheon table? The child Monty is turning
into a really wild boy, quick-tempered but good-natured and
easily appeased. He is very much like Ernest only livelier. How
happy he will be at Christmas! Thank God, there is a little one at
our celebration; this is what gives the thing its real blessing.
Here it will be complete. I often think how lonely it must be at
Mama's, I will be glad when you have her in Karlsruhe. To be
sure it is better for her nerves that she is alone. You know, in the
family, one does not appreciate your scholarliness enough, or is
it because one does not expect anything else of you than that you
will become Minister of State for Internal Affairs?

                                          Love
                                          Eichfried
                                          your very own

(*Translated from the German*)

TO her sister Else

> 9 Goldswong Terrace
> Nottingham
> [*Undated*]

My beloved sister,

Your Christmas package pleased me *so*, I have crocheted only a bit on the little skirt and it is now very useful in the cold weather! I don't understand where you found the time to make it! The little angel head is charming; warmest thanks for everything, my sister. I would have already written you but was not certain where you were, now you are surely back at work. How do you like my son? I have just heard from Nusch a sweet remark which pleased me tremendously. You can imagine what! I am looking forward to home! Bertha Niebeleisen will soon visit you, I hope she doesn't bore you too much. She wrote me a Nietzsche calendar,[3] if you own a Nietzsche (I believe you have *Zarathustra*) I would be so glad if you would send it. Everything, everything good in the New Year, in love,

> Your true sister
> Frieda

(*Translated from the German*)

TO her sister Else

> 9 Goldswong Terrace
> Nottingham
> *Friday*

Dear Elle!

So you are again alone and I write to you. Until now I have tried in vain to discover some books for you, our modern novels seem much cleverer to me. And probably you have everything of Eliot and Thackeray. I want to confide to you only a part of my good news, for I know that you can hold your tongue. We hope that next September a little "Else" will come, but it is not yet certain, for I was quite miserable and it must still be proved

[3] Probably quotations from Nietzsche in fancy lettering on a calendar.

whether it is a baby. Therefore I don't want to say anything to the others, and then too I would like Mama to come in the summer and not September, for I would rather be altogether quiet. Could you then still come in the autumn? At the same time for the baptism as godmother? I am looking forward to having two; if you have an old pedagogical book give it to the next one who comes here. In England one is not required to send children to school and perhaps I could teach them at home until nine or ten. Actually I am quite disappointed that you could not come in the spring. I am again feeling pretty well. Monty is sweet, wild and healthy and yet sensitive. It is touching how attached he is to me, and it does one good when they think one is a kind of little god; when he hurts some place, I blow a little and then he is sure it doesn't hurt any more. Ernest is well and working hard, Cambridge delights him. He goes there every Saturday, the distance is very slight. I wrote to T. Elisabeth in January and sent her a picture, she never answered me; perhaps she received nothing, for I wrote to Friedrich Wilhelm St. Could you ask her when you write? I don't very much want to have Rösele in Nottingham, because I would always feel under obligation to have her here (at my house), but still I want to try. I am just now reading a fine book by a Jew, Zangwill, *They That Walk in Darkness*, only Jewish stories; unfortunately it is expensive. At Easter we will probably go for a little to the seaside, what are you planning? How bleak Karlsruhe must sometimes be! Goodbye, it is getting late,

Your sister Frieda

(*Translated from the German*)

TO her sister Else

Nottingham
3 March 1902

My dear Elle!

Deeply moved I unwrapped my little box, you were but too generous. The appealing little skirt won me over, and Monty looks sweet in his little boy's smock. The little underslip will also be welcome to the "Little Else." How suddenly the dear person Schlusser died, "quickly death assails mankind"; you will miss him very much, he was like a nice big boy. I am well; the first months are thought to be the worst, and besides I had to overdo things and get worn out, but the doctor put me in bed, so as to prevent trouble, and now everything is again all right. I am glad you are coming in the autumn; in October too you can even see my ducks and how I live and go with Ernest to Cambridge. Ernest has recently, full of rage, spat out a Victor Hugo article; it [he?] is however also a circus horse [?]. It would be well for you also to be vaccinated before you come, it is certainly safer. We are going for a few days to the sea at Easter since I cannot get away in summer. I would so like to send you my light-blue blouse (material from you) it is so pretty, and if it is laid away through the summer I am afraid the silk will break. Say whether you want it! I hear little from Nusch, also there is not much to say of me; I am as healthy as possible, read much, and again diligently practise the piano. Monty so often says, "Mama sing." Mornings he gets up in his little bed and says, "I see you, Mama." Animals are his delight. He is very loving with me, and if he hasn't seen me for 2–3 hours he runs in every room after Mama. It touches me always, as he thinks me a little god; I wish it could so remain. How unpleasant I find the hate articles against England, it is truly very ugly the lengths to which they go; I see Papa, how he abuses and believes everything. Isn't it often lonely for you? I wish I could come and stay with you once, for a long time, it was so harmonious the last time. We were very good as old maids living together. I have had flower-boxes made for the windows; the little garden gives me much joy, tulips are coming and crocuses are blooming. Adieu and many thanks, always your true

Sister.

(*Translated from the German*)

TO her sister Else

9 Goldswong Terrace
Nottingham
[*Undated*]

Ma chère Mademoiselle Elsen!

My first thought when I heard it from Mama was, what has she suffered all in silence, the II. Hurrah, now she [exists] altogether for herself and her children. How in the world did such marriage ideas enter your head? One does not expect such selfish desires from you, and anyhow it wouldn't be the right thing for you at all. You never would have been happy; first, you are too peculiar to find anyone to suit you; second, one gets one's wings clipped quite a bit because one has to think so often: the dining-room windows are dirty and also the bedroom curtains have to be washed; you see, one has to. Then also you are too much an idealist; it makes me unhappy often enough that one is like all people, not only soul but also body, and you are not so thick-skinned as I am! Now then, the little Weekley girl, if she ever arrives, will be called Else and be your special private property! You will like my little rascal of a boy so much. I can hardly wait until you see him. The seaside is wonderful, it would almost be nicer still if you came then. I shall find a *pension* in London for you and, of course, come and live in Hampstead. But you must tell the good Mr. Goldsmith yourself that it is over. In Hampstead they are looking forward to you. We must also go to Cambridge together. How nice it will be when you sit in Ernest's study where I am writing now, it is always a mess! I am really afraid of Nusch, she seems to me so coarsened. How did the Niebeleisen woman appeal to you? Ernest *hated* her. Ernest half plans to start a doctor's dissertation while you are here. My hyacinths thrive too, but I do court them quite a bit.

In true love
often thinking of you
the Weekleys

(*Translated from the German*)

TO her mother

> 9 Goldswong Terrace
> Nottingham
> [*Undated*]

Dear Mother:

Many thanks for your letter. You seem to have had a gay time together, the Willingers and you. I have good news, they have given Ernest 1,000 M. more per year and by chance there came also today from Cambridge an invitation to give a weekly lecture there; for each lecture he gets 80 M., it makes him very happy. I will then go with him, Cambridge is so pretty and you must also come. Tonight I am going to an amateur performance, next Tuesday there is a big University dance. Monty is outside in his little French coat, he looks like a little dwarf. He is always gay. Paula has him under good control and he is already quite a person in his own right. If only I knew what I should do with Rösele? I believe I could find a place for her, but whether she would meet high English demands? In any case I will make an effort, for she is in any case modest and conscientious. Paula sometimes cooks and straightens out the messy drawers, and is exactly what we need. I am glad that Else is not staying with the Glassner woman, she was an unfriendly person and Else was too good with her. She should look for a brighter apartment. I wanted to send you tea, but now it is probably too late. Old lady Pöhlmann wrote me Mimi's address but the horse didn't write the name; isn't it Schimmelreuter, or something like that? Please answer! (*à la* Nusch). It is touching that you are going to let that Marie go to St. Avold. Did old Schreibershofer leave anything in his will? But Max is silent. . . .

(*Translated from the German*)

TO her mother, from Ernest Weekley

> 9 Goldswong Terrace
> Nottingham
> *13 September 1902*

Dear Mama!

Since I cannot yet telegraph, I am using the time to give my message more fully. All went off famously. The child gave signs towards one in the night and was here before 4 o'clock. I had to get the doctor and nurse in a hurry. All goes very well with the mother; she suffered very little, much less than the last time, and was very gay immediately afterwards. She has courage, my wife. Now she is sleeping very peacefully. The nurse is very nice and undemanding. The child is, as was after all to be expected, a fine specimen. Immediately on its arrival it said, "My name is Frieda Elsa Agnes, and I despise Nottingham." At least I got that impression from the long-lasting and powerful exercise of her voice. [She is] large and strong and well built. How we despise people who do not have children, we are arrogant. We so much wanted a girl and it seems entirely natural to us that it is a girl. It seems to me that Frieda is much less exhausted than last time. She has been very careful of her health in the last weeks. If the little girl grows up like her mother then I consider myself a happy man. Greet everyone for me and spread the good news. It goes without saying, I will send you daily reports. I have just awakened Paula, so as to send her and Monty to Kippings.

Your faithful
(Translated from the German)   Ernest

TO her sister Else, from Ernest Weekley

9 Goldswong Terrace
Nottingham
15 September 1902

Dear Else,

Many thanks for the telegram received this afternoon. Please excuse my not having wired to you at once; a poor man has so many things to think of on these occasions! You will be glad to hear that your godchild and her mother are both progressing excellently. They send their love to you and to Edgar. Monty is with the Kippings and the house is very quiet. The newcomer is better behaved than Monty was: I tell Frieda she has more of English gentleness and less of Prussian arrogance, which would no doubt make Papa sniff indignantly. We have decided that the arrangement Elsa Agnes Frieda sounds more melodious than that first proposed, and we can decide later which to call her; if learned, it will be Elsa, if impudent, it will be Frieda. She is a fine healthy child, and, though she at first seemed to resemble facially that august *vieillard* ex-president Krüger, she now looks quite pretty. My father and mother are of course delighted, and will, I hope, come to the christening. With my kind regards to Edgar,

I am,
Your affectionate brother,
Ernest Weekley

TO her father, from Ernest Weekley

9 Goldswong Terrace
Nottingham
16 September 1902

Dear Papa!

Your letter pleased us very much, and I use the first opportunity to answer it. My time is pretty much in demand even though this afternoon mother and child are sleeping peacefully, as the crush of Nottingham women has already begun and I must always smile pleasantly and receive them with warm handclasps. Stafford was here this morning and in his opinion all goes as well as possible. Frieda is simply overjoyed; the little girl is very pretty and will soon be altogether lovely, has dark eyes and hair, cries very little, has a hearty appetite and is noticeably strong and healthy; she grasps the source of nourishment firmly and moves her little head back and forth for joy. I sit close by and beam like an old donkey. Mama's and Johanna's letters came at noon; have them write as much as possible, for it gives Frieda so much pleasure. We have definitely decided to christen the little daughter Else Agnes Frieda. What she will later be called depends on her behaviour. If she becomes very learned, she will be called Else; very bold, she will be called Frieda; very gentle, she will be called Agnes. That is what the proud mother has determined! Monty is very happy with Mrs. Kipping, who, between parentheses, is worth her weight in gold and is a true friend. He was there again this morning, always goes at once to the cradle, and makes desperate efforts to climb in and take his little sister out. You would be delighted with him, he is strong and well-co-ordinated like a young lion and is afraid of nothing. Only when the "Babi" crumples up her face to howl, does he appear somewhat confused and undecided. We will probably send him later for a few days to Hampstead. We have, fortunately, very nice weather, though a bit windy; the child goes for walks as soon as it is calm. The nurse is quite a nice person, the cook works very well, and everything is completely peaceful. Frieda owes her rapid progress to her own good sense. She was busy and happy up to the last days. We went for a walk every evening, and even on the day before the arrival we did not come home until nine o'clock. If every woman had so much sense and courage, things would go better in the world. I was in the room ten minutes before the new lovely life began, and even then Frieda said to me she was all right and I need have no anxiety. Now she looks so wonderfully beautiful; in short, the undersigned is of the firm conviction that our good Lord, as Mama says, often watches over us, especially if he has caused a meeting to occur in the beautiful Black Forest. I will send you another postcard tomorrow. We have not been able to decipher Brandt's Munich address in Mama's letter; please, write it again and I will send him a newspaper. With heartiest greetings,

Your faithful son,
Ernest

(Translated from the German)

TO her mother

9 Goldswong Terrace
Nottingham
[*Undated*]

Dear Mother!

Many thanks for your beautiful long letter, how happy I am that you enjoyed your well-earned vacation so much. I have also received the delicious chocolate and gobbled it up in a hurry.

The ribbon is also so nice. I would of course have liked to be in on your activities, but one can't have everything. How nice you were with old Mrs. Hollend [?], many thanks; she wrote Mrs. K. that she had been sitting in the hotel and anxiously waiting, and the stupid porter did not announce you to her, "he could not find her." Now you are staying with the good aunts, give them my best wishes; if only I could go with you on the pilgrimage to the Kappele Valley. I am feeling fine, Stafford also said wonderfully fine; he ate with us recently, she and the children are at the seaside. It just occurs to me, whether you might not want something from the treasures which Else has intended for me, or have you enough? That is a good plan for next year, we [will be] in London with them, and then I thought you could come to us from the middle of July to the middle of September, and I will go for two to three weeks to Heidelberg with Ernest to Else and you would have the children.[4] That would be exactly in Papa's vacation and hunting season, then he does not miss you so much. Little Monty is very sweet since you were here; touch wood, he has not had the least bit wrong with him; the other day he was invited out, and you should have seen him, how excited he was when he came home. . . .

[Postscript at head of letter: Monty is banging on the door and says: "Policeman, take this boy!" A reminder of you.]

(*Translated from the German*)

Edgar Jaffe, her sister Else's husband, was a professor at the University of Heidelberg. The reference to the letters from Munich is probably to letters from the "Octavio" of the memoirs, with whom Frieda was having an affair.

[4] A third child, Barbara Joy, was born October 20, 1904.

TO Edgar Jaffe

Nottingham
20 May 1907

You good Edgar!

I must always think of you so thankfully. You were so good to me all the time, so understanding and great as truly almost no one else could have been. I have the feeling that you also belong very much to me, and I will always have a friend in you and you will always understand me. How happy you will be that all went as it did in Munich; I am very, very happy and can only now enjoy all my love. I had promised to burn all my letters from Munich, but I cannot do it; relieve me of my promise, I must still have something. I am nevertheless *very* careful. Come and visit me if you have nothing better to do; I would so like to see you and talk with you, I am very much alone here. When you write to me, write a letter for everyone and a little note for me. The children are unique.

Your faithful friend
Frieda

(*Translated from the German*)

Frieda met D. H. Lawrence in April, 1912, when he sought out his former French instructor at Nottingham University College to ask about obtaining a post at a German university as a teacher of English. She had planned to visit Metz in May for her family's celebration of the fiftieth anniversary of her father's entering the army. She left her son Montague with his father, and her daughters Elsa and Barbara with their grandparents in Hampstead, and she made the journey with Lawrence, loving him openly, as he insisted, though she was not yet fully committed to him and was very disturbed over the separation from her children.

FROM Ernest Weekley

> Cowley
> Private Road
> Mapperley
> Nottingham
> *10 May 1912*

I did not mean to write again, but I must. I had a letter from Lawrence this morning. I bear him no ill-will and hope you will be happy with him. But have some pity on me. Do you want to drive me to suicide to simplify things? I will not do it. I shall write to or see the Hampstead people today. I am quite clear what to do, but you ought to help me. The children will never come back to Nottingham. I shall take a house somewhere outside London—get the old people and Maude to move to it—they will do this for me—and I shall live between there and Nottingham as Oswald does. The children will go to school in London and form new friendships and there will be a family home. It is the best thing. All compromises are unthinkable. We are not rabbits. Do not let all generosity be on my side. Have some remorse for all your deception of a loving man. Let me know at once that you agree to a divorce. The thing can be managed very quietly, but unless you help by an admission, this will be difficult. And then it might cost me my post here and our children could starve. You loved me once—help me now—but quickly.

> E

TO her father, from Ernest Weekley

> Cowley
> Private Road
> Mapperley
> Nottingham
> *11 May 1912*

Dear Papa!

Many thanks for your friendly letter. One can do nothing against fate, and we must all have faith with one another. I only want to beg your pardon for the frantic letter I wrote you. I know you will forgive it in such a distressed man. I was insane for ten days. Yesterday was the climax and I was really not responsible. You see, I had to bear it all alone, and the mind is as though gone. Tonight I finally slept, the pressure is somewhat gone from my head, and I am again a human being. Say that you forgive me. I am trying now to make plans for the future. We must see if we can save something out of such a shipwreck. If only I had kept my self-control to the end!

Your loving son,
Ernest

Do not be hopeless. Frieda is young and I hope she will have only happiness in the future.

(*Translated from the German*)

TO her father, from Ernest Weekley

Cowley
Private Road
Mapperley
Nottingham
12 May 1912

Dear Papa!

Your second letter came this morning. Yesterday I telegraphed to say that my last letter to Frieda is not to be opened. I had written incredibly, but one mustn't judge a man in my state too harshly. I have now recovered a little, and I hope she will have no ugly memory of me. You know, without my saying it, that I have the deepest sympathy with you. It is so sad to think how many innocent people must be wounded to the heart by such an event. My sisters know it, that is, they know that Frieda and I are separated, and I have asked them to tell my parents. They have to know it but I am afraid it will kill them; if they had only died earlier. I could no longer bear it alone. I had to do my work, get used to lying, and then there are terrible reactions when I am quite out of my mind. But I hope that is past. I have only a sadness of which one has no conception. As far as the divorce is concerned, I have only two goals—to make Frieda free so she can marry the man, and to provide for the future of my children. But it will go slowly. I have not yet heard anything from the lawyer, and I will do nothing without your advice and the consent of my family. If it is not possible to accomplish anything without everything coming out in the paper, I will give up the idea. I hope we will see each other during the year. I want only to say that I will always be thankful to you and Mama, and that as long as I live Frieda will have a friend to whom she will never turn in vain. As soon as I know anything I will write you again, and if it is not too embarrassing, please write me. I always believed I was too proud to need sympathy, for I did not know what kinds of sufferings exist.

Your faithful
Ernest

Monty is healthy and good; the girls write so nicely and contentedly from Hampstead. My people are ready to do everything for them.

    (*Translated from the German*)

TO her mother, from Ernest Weekley

Cowley
Private Road
Mapperley
Nottingham
13 May 1912

Dear Mama,

My parents know it since this morning. Maude [5] told them—I was too cowardly. She writes that they show their old courage, but it is unjust that in their old age they must again suffer so, for them it is ten thousand times worse than death. Today two letters came from Frieda; in one she speaks of a compromise, in the second she says she will come to help me with the moving.

[5] Ernest Weekley's sister, the children's spinster aunt, who was characterized in Lawrence's *The Virgin and the Gipsy*. Her own shocked letter to Frieda follows.

Dear Mama, please make her understand what a state I am in: I cannot see her handwriting without trembling like an old cripple—to see her again would be my death. I would kill myself and the children too. It is terrible when one so longs for death and still must live for others. I will not kill myself, but she *must* leave me in peace. She knows that she can depend on my honour. Today I hoped that the clatter in my head had half disappeared, but these letters have again robbed me of my little reason. She *must* leave everything to me, if only on practical grounds. For hers and the children's sake I must keep my local position, although the place to me is more hateful than hell. Today I had to lecture for four hours and take part in a long session of the Senate. I have desperately to stretch every nerve in order not to cry out hysterically, and then I am weak as a child and can only lie there and think—if only for a quarter of an hour I could not think! I will fight with my despair and find the best way out. She must understand that she has no more rights but she knows I am honourable.

Ernest

(Translated from the German)

FROM Maude Weekley

40, Well Walk
Hampstead, N. W.
May 14, [*1912*]

Dear Frieda,

You see I put that for I cannot be fond of a person for thirteen years and then suddenly cease to think them dear.

What does all this mean, what are you doing and why!

We are so in the dark here and shall be I suppose always for Ernest will not blame you in any way for this disaster and knowing him it is impossible to think it is his fault. What did you want more than he gave to you, for you must know that he has always been your slave in every sense of the word.

It has been a very great shock to the old folks but thank God their chiefest anxiety is for Ernest and his for them and the little ones so that I hope they may all pull round.

For him there would otherwise seem nothing but wreck.

Is it possible that you can not see the mischief any more than the Titanic Iceberg did. I know that you have strange views of life, selfish views as you know I think, and I am so sorry that you have collapsed.

Ernest will not want me to write unless it is kindly and as I said I do love you still but oh! that you had chosen any other life than his to smash. He deserves better things of life.

If you care to write to me and if as I fear this parting is inevitable and we do not meet again, remember that any thoughts are sorrowful not angry now, truly "ye know not what ye do" and if things should come quite right no one will rejoice more than I.

The children are well and enjoying the Heath, they are very good too and useful.

I had no time to write yesterday so I am writing now before getting breakfast while the house is quiet and though it is impossible to write all one would say perhaps it is as well for you [to] know what I would say to you if you were here.

You have somehow missed the best in life and the best in love, for love that cannot suffer is unworthy of the name of love.

Poor Frieda make the best of the wreck and make for the light.

Maude

FROM Lily Kipping [6]

40, Magdala Road
Nottingham
[*Undated*]

My dear Frieda,

Surely it is all a bad dream, and we must soon wake up. I want you to write to me. Dear, do come home. I am sure you will regret it all your life if you don't. I have just been up to Private Rd. I think if you could have looked in you would have come back. Not a word of reproach in any way, only a broken hearted

---

[6] The wife of Ernest Weekley's closest Nottingham friend, Frederick Stanley Kipping, F. R. S. (1863–1949), Jesse Boot Professor of Chemistry at Nottingham University College, later the University of Nottingham, and remembered for his work on silicon.

man. Do think of the children—the dear little girls and Monty— if you don't think quickly remember you ought never to see them again. It would not in any sense be right to them. I don't know *anything* about the trouble, only "It is *all* over," but don't let it be all over. Whatever you have done, said or thought, *come back*, back here to me if you like and then tell me everything and let me keep you, but don't spoil your own life and the lives of all the others—the little girls without a mother, no mother's love, and Monty, he *must* have a mother to protect him. Frieda dear, our friendship is a true one, but do, do listen to an older woman, a woman who *really knows* that there is only one true happiness in life. Hold by your responsibilities. His life is not to be ruined like this. You took it into your care and the children you brought into the world can't be cast off like this. Don't you remember the night Monty was born? Don't you remember when E. was so ill and you thought you would never see him again? Come back. No one knows. The children would rush to meet you. I almost feel I must come and *fetch* you. Don't say I am old fashioned or anything like that; only be quite quite sure from me that when you are my age, 44, you will bitterly regret it if you don't come back. My love, dear.

> Your affectionate friend,
> Lily Kipping

Lawrence's friendship with Edward Garnett, the distinguished editor who helped and encouraged so many talented people, had begun in 1911. Lawrence's second novel, The Trepasser, *had been revised under Garnett's supervision, following Lawrence's dissatisfaction with Ford Madox Hueffer's poor opinion of it. In March, 1912, just before the first meeting with Frieda, Lawrence asked Garnett if he would care to see the "colliery novel" which became* Sons and Lovers. *The following letters indicate how much Garnett's friendship meant to Lawrence and Frieda during the first months of their relationship. They are gay, teasing, Rabelaisian, but at the same time reveal the anguish and dissension caused by Ernest Weekley's refusal to let her continue to see the children. The letters also indicate her intimate participation in the revision of* Sons and Lovers, *and her resistance to Garnett's editorial preoccupation with form.*

TO Edward Garnett

% Herr Baron von Richthofen
Mantigny bei Metz
[*May 1912?*]

Dear Mr. Garnett,

I think of you often and your friendly cottage and the apple-blossoms and your own wonderfully hospitable self, you have a *genius* for hospitality. It has helped Lawrence and me through a lot of horrors that we had to go through. I love him with a 1,000 different loves, I want everybody to love him: he deserves it. There is no fight between us, we want the same thing and our fighting will be against other people, *never* with each other. I see you laugh, and I am serious, but I am not taken in; I think you are awfully good. Have you written what you were going to write? May I come to see you again some time? Don't laugh at me!

Yours gratefully,
Frieda Weekley

Of course you must laugh at us. I am terrified of you when you are serious—you're rather like other people then.

D. H. Lawrence

TO Edward Garnett

Icking
bei München
Isarthal
[*July 1912?*]

Dear friend and patron,

I feel how really you take part in our riggle, it is a riggle to keep going at all, sometimes.—Your boy [7] is so nice, quite a

[7] David (Bunny) Garnett, who was to continue the family tradition as editor, memoirist, novelist, and publisher.

The Lawrences with John Middleton Murry,
photographed by Katherine Mansfield at Selsfield Terrace, 1914.

The Lawrences with Witter Bynner
at Bynner's house in Santa Fe, New Mexico, 1922.

treat; I feel him so much akin to me, he seems to have the same sort of whole-hoggerish generosity (if I may swank); where it will land him God only knows, I hope not in quite such tight places as myself. My husband is a perfect agony, the loads of crucifixes here seem joyful round-about-horses [In D. H. L.'s hand: She means merry-go-rounds.] compared to him. I wanted love, now I have more than I can bear. Perhaps I will go to England soon and see Ernest; you would see me then, wouldn't you, it would be a great help, it will be so hard to see him suffer so. Yet I can't be only sorry. Lawrence is great in his way, that seems so little sometimes, but always human, always alive. He has taught me the feel and the understanding of things and people; that is morality, I think. Sometimes our car gets badly stuck and the spokes in the wheels are clogged, but it all comes right in the end. I won't give in—neither will he. Even the money does not seem a worry; we have jolly little, but I think we shall soon have a . . . place somewhere, because L. wants to work. Don't worry about us; even if things went wrong, and they *won't*, we have had an honest try. I wish you would come out, you will soon, please, will you? Good-bye and thank you so much, that you are there, somewhere, with a friendly feeling; I don't believe I have anybody really, who can put up with me. This sounds quite whiny.—You must get out of London, there is too much ink spilt all in one spot.—Don't think me anything out of the way, please; I don't even prance theories or anything else of the sort any longer. L. says he did it for me, I call him a liar, but there is some truth in it, I am afraid.

Yours (I will *not* say gratefully, if you put me in a "sark" nothing but a miserere will do).

Frieda

[In D. H. L.'s hand] Your letter has just come. Don't bother about my stuff—it's a fearful shame to worry you.—And you always sound so miserable. F. says—"Does he hate women?"—I say: "I think so." Then she says, "So will that boy of his, before long. But he wouldn't if *I* had him." She's naturally vain, I'm sorry to say. As a matter of fact, we are fearfully fond of one another, all the more, perhaps, when it doesn't show. We want remarkably the same thing in life—sort of freedom, nakedness of intimacy, free breathing-space between us. You don't know how fine it is between us—whatever either of us says.

We want now—we are going now—to take some little cottage in Italy, by Lake Garda, furnish it with a few things—we really need very little—and live the winter there. We shall manage to have enough money to live on, I think.

You don't think the quality of my work is going down, do you?—It isn't. I want soon to be settling down, to have a go at it (Paul Morel). But we have lived so hard lately. Don't be cross with me about Secker. I know you don't care much for the Paul Morel novel; that's why I thought you'd perhaps be glad to be rid of it.

Bunny is coming here on Sunday. He won't swim, it is too cold. We *do* try to keep him out of danger. I wish you sounded jollier.—I sent you another letter—perhaps you'll get this first.— Still the tragedy simmers. This is a bellyful. But I pay without regretting.

D. H. Lawrence

TO Edward Garnett

[?] Villa Leonardi
Viale Giovanni-Prati No. 8, Riva
Lago di Garda
[*September 1912?*]

Dear Mr. Garnett,

Do come, you will be in Brittany [sic], it will be *so* cheap and we would love and adore to have you! Though I am frightened of yours and L.'s male talks, he *will* give me away so! But I suppose that's being a blooming artist! When I detest him, he *always* makes that his excuse. You have written me such a letter I am quite proud of it, swelled on the strength of it and can't come down. It is a good thing there are men like you (I tell L.) who *do* appreciate women! Yes, he is many things, but his great points are for a woman, the absolute freshness of things; nothing is ever stale or old and in spite of his lots of unrealities he is simple and real underneath. Life *is* good with him, *je ne demande pas mieux*, yes and it is *love*, but thank the Lord *passion* as well. It has *really* been a success, in spite of the misery left behind, in spite of the always missing the children, in spite of the no money, and I could say: "Lord, let thy servant depart in peace," though I don't want him to do it just yet. Your boy is a dear; he walks just like you, he has a lot of you in his composition, it will be so interesting to watch him and he *is* original. *Do* come; your boy said you weren't well off, but there would only be the journey and it *is* such a place.

I hope "auf Wiedersehen",

Yours,
"Frieda"

I have quite forgotten that I am *not* married to L.

I think L. quite missed the point in "Paul Morel". He really loved his mother more than anybody, even with his other women, real love, sort of Oedipus; his mother must have been adorable. He is writing P. M. again, reads bits to me and we fight like blazes over it, he is so often beside the point, "but 'I'll learn him to be a toad' as the boy said as he stamped on the toad." He has written heaps nicer poems than those "baby ones", some about his mother, and lots since we have been together. My sister, who is elegant, has just sent me 4 baldachino hats. L. is trying them on in an undescribable get-up and the most beautiful Asphodel pose!

[In D. H. L.'s hand]—by "get-up" she means "sans anything". She always was a brazen bitch.

TO Edward Garnett [Postscript apparently detached from the letter to which it belonged.]

. . . I also feel as if I ought to say something about L.'s formlessness. I don't think he has no form. I used to. But now I think anybody must see in "Paul Morel" the hang of it. The mother is really the thread, the domineering note. I think the honesty, the vividness of a book suffers if you subject it to form. I have heard so much about "form" with Ernest; why are you English so keen on it? Their own form wants smashing in almost any direction, but they can't come out of their snail house. I know it is so much safer. That's what I love Lawrence for, that he is so plucky and honest in his work, he dares to come out in the open and plants his stuff down bald and naked; really he is the only revolutionary worthy of the name, that I know; any new thing must find a new shape, then afterwards one can call it "art". I hate art, it seems like grammar, wants to make a language all grammar; language was first and then they abstracted a grammar. I quite firmly believe that L. is quite great in spite of his "gaps". Look at the vividness of his stuff, it knocks you down, I think. It is perhaps too "intimate", comes too close, but I believe that is youth, and he has not done, not by long chalks! Don't think I am impudent to say all this, but I feel quite responsible for "Paul". I wrote little female bits and lived it over in my own heart. I am sure he is a real artist; the way things pour out of him, *he* seems only the pen, and isn't that how it ought to be? We *all* go for things, look at them with preconceived notions, things must have a "precedence". We have lost the faculty of seeing things unprejudiced, live off our own fat [?], think off our own free mind. Good gracious, what a tirade! I think you are just *awfully* good to ask me to the "Cearne" but wouldn't my unmarried married condition be awkward for you?

TO David Garnett

> [?] Villa Igéa
> Villa di Gargnano, (Brescia)
> Lago di Garda
> [*November 1912?*]

Dear Bunny!

I did enjoy your letter! About Godwin and London and X; it just was a little bit of life! I thought it was quite a great letter! I am glad you left X, it is the *only* thing if one can't *really* go on; look at the lie and indecency and all; no, if I adored a man till

I was black in the face I would rather he went than stay because he felt he ought. But don't give in, dear Bunny, *le jeu vaut la chandelle* [interlined above this in Lawrence's hand: the game is worth the candle]; if I can say it, I am sure anybody ought; when I think of all, the children, and Ernest, who says: "No man can do more than give his life, but I would have gladly been tortured for you and laughed, and now I'll do more, I'll live." It makes me quite ill every time.—I was cross with L. about the play, he makes himself the strong, silent man, the *wretch;* he *did* hang on to me, but not quite so unflinchingly and I did *not* wobble so; he wrote the play when he was in a rage with me! [Interlined above in Lawrence's hand: No no!!] So there, but I think it *is* a good play! Do come, can't you, at Christmas, it would be a treat! I am *not* going to England before Easter now. Icking and Mayrhofen seem quite a long way back and this place is so beautiful, really a fairyland. [Interlined in Lawrence's hand: I am Bottom.] I lie with joy out of a window [an asterisk calls attention to a footnote in Lawrence's hand: She means on the window-sill] that looks on the road and watch the Italians. They are beautiful creatures. The men so loose and soldiers with such hats, a *foam* [interlined in Lawrence's hand: Good god!] of cockfeathers on them, I long for one, a hat not a soldier. I have found two women friends, most eminently and superbly respectable, but they bore Lawrence, though the one's rows with her horrid mother-in-law rouse me deeply. They *will* think we are well off, the irony of it! I hope L. does not write the same stuff as I am! How we would love to have you here! Yes, I am proud that most of my people had pluck and made Germany what it is; of course I am an anarchist, and a beastly "aristo" [interlined in Lawrence's hand: a fool!] at the same time, but then these women!—I never look at my scarves without thinking of you and our acting and what a God forsaken idiot — — looked as Holofernes! Good-bye, I must stop.

> With much love,
> Frieda

Such macaroni and good things.

*David Garnett and Harold Hobson, the son of the
economist J. A. Hobson, walked with Lawrence and
Frieda across the Tyrolese Alps in 1912, and Hobson
visited them later that year. A mutual physical attraction sprang up between Frieda and Hobson, who was
very handsome, and she admitted this to Lawrence. This
first challenge to her fidelity to him was followed not
many years later by the friendship with John Middleton Murry.*

TO David Garnett

> [?] Villa Igéa
> Villa di Gargnano, (Brescia)
> Lago di Garda
> [*December 1912?*]

Dear Bunny!

I am really quite hurt that you think me so tragic! It's all
because of L.'s play, that is *misleading*, to put it mildly; some of
Harold's language would be more appropriate! Can't you see
what really sad and tragic blokes Harold and Lawrence are?
Both of them! Harold's cheep (as L. calls it) is only bluff; that
type of creature is *all* tragedy, it's got no outlet for its energies,
its strong virility; they are sensitive, miserable consequently,
touchy, to the last degree of decency; don't you be humbugged
by them, just because you are a male yourself, though fortunately
of a different, more restful sort. If you only knew how in
Lawrence I discovered abysses of elusive, destructive spiritual
tragedy [written over this in Lawrence's hand: balls!], that it
took the strength of several St. Georges to fight the dragon
(there's a serpent in the grass; fight it down, fight it, fight it
down!). My tragedy is tangible though [?], floods the bed and
chews the sheet, it's child's play compared to his. [Written over
this in Lawrence's hand: Shit.] They called Harold "six foot of
misery" at the works! I had a hell of a time with them, L.
torturing me, Harold being that humpy, but now we have had
some jolly days, peace and good will all round [written over this
in Lawrence's hand: I don't fink]; I am really proud of us, it

wasn't easy! We saw a red berry that sits on a leaf, is called Butcher's broom, and said you ought to have it; there are primroses, huge bunches of Christmas roses in the hedges; I put them on the table and stick them in my hair and get called names for the effort; they *do* abuse me and have no chivalry. We went to see Ibsen's *Spectri* in a tiny theatre; we sat in a tiny red box, I fancied myself in a huge, soft velvet hat with huge feathers, black garments, Christmas roses, and the pretty red of the box. The boxes are tiny and close together; we watched the butcher boy flirting with a pretty damsel, but she was also flirting with a yokel and Harold. It's jolly to know the sailor who brings the parcels [?] (Lawrence is jealous of him, I *do* love him, the sailor) [Written over this in Lawrence's hand: balls-aching rot] the proud post-office lady, the cheese-monger boy in his Sunday best. They all carry on their conversations, while the conversation on the stage goes on as a secondary pastime. You will hear of Harold's plans! I wonder if they will come off. . . . How you would love this place, Bunny, and what a restful person you would be, no tragedy about you now anyway. Don't think nasty things about me Bunny, I haven't deserved it, I am really quite good and weep no more! [Written over this in Lawrence's hand: Bitch!] A merry Christmas you had and I wish you a happy year and that we shall see something of you.

Good-bye, Bunny, my love to you, I appreciate your letters, though they don't appreciate me. [Written over this in Lawrence's hand: Arse-licking.]

Frieda

TO Edward Garnett

Villa Igéa
Villa di Gargnano, (Brescia)
Lago di Garda
[*January 1913?*]

Dear Mr. Garnett,

Your books were quite a Godsend to me. The tragedy was in its zenith just at Christmas; in spite of heroic efforts and loftiest sentiments one feels more like mincepies and parcels, *almost* Christmas cards, at that time, and of course I was ignored by all my friends, the outcast; even if one says to oneself "*tu l' as voulu, Georges Dandin,*" George doesn't feel no better for it. But things are looking up; I like my people-in-law, the children will be happy there, and I must wait; after all they are my flesh and blood and I must trust in the Lord,[8] it's really wonderful how things come right if you only trust enough. I am really rather dense in so many things, but the sort of blind, stupid trust has always brought me through. We are having a good time with Harold, he is good stuff; we say very nasty things to each other, told H. for instance that he would never have the hospitable spirit of the Garnetts. Every day an hour before the postman comes, Harold goes about crying, "Nobody loves me, nobody loves me"; if there is no letter, you should just hear him, perhaps you would rather not. Between them I did have a time, Lawrence *is* wear and tear. I am cross with him just at present, he chases my poor emotions till they drop like panting hares, [here Lawrence has scrawled "bleeder!"] and if I feel an emotion coming miles away I'm all of a tremble. But still it's worth it and in the end we shall be a quiet, respectable (Ernest offered to help me to live down my past) couple, quite dull; fancy marrying again, it gives me creeps. [Here Lawrence has scrawled across the page "Stinker."] Many good wishes for the new year, do remain the good spirit over us, as you have been so far; we are *really* happy; though we fight like blazes, we shall bring it off. Yes, my theories have sadly altered; there are two sides to human love, one that wants to be faithful, the other wants to run; my running one was uppermost, but it's going to be faithful now. I used to think I should never have enough love, now I think I have got as much as I can swallow. This letter is all about "I". I apologise!

With many thanks for the gift and the spirit and good will of the sender,

Frieda

[8] Lawrence has circled "Lord" and written large across the page: "Who's he? Some new bloke?"

TO David Garnett

[February, 1913]

Dear Bunny,

It will be so nice for us to have Mrs. "Tony," [9] as I only know her. We are always just us two and we live so hard on each other, one day like the lions that ate each other, there will be nothing but two tails left. We will do what we can for her, and if we go away from here, I think she might be *too* lonely; then I suggest *München* to her, where I am sure my brother-in-law would do what he could for her. And she ought to have people. Poor Harold, yes, I hope he and Lola [1] will hit it off! Don't you talk like that about women, one day your turn will come and I bet you will have a decent try; women are *not* like the tooth-ache, though you would have us so, and if women are undecided, what about men? But I shall be interested what you will do. I wonder if you read my last wild letter to your father; I do feel like bursting sometimes about the children, Lawrence is in a state of utter misery then and I can't help it much. Rejoicing on the one hand like *anything*, that he cares so much; on the other, the children and the misery of it. *I* am coming to England anyhow, if I can have the children, *alone;* if Ernest *won't* let me have them, L. and I will both come, so that I can see them on the sly. It will be nice to see you! You have only seemed to be fond of L. lately, not a bit of *me*, and I don't think it's nice!

Auf Wiedersehen,
Frieda

[9] Tony (Antonia or Anjuta) Cyriax, otherwise Mrs. Almgren, in hiding from her mentally unstable husband, a Swedish painter. When he followed her to England, the Garnetts sent her to the Lawrences in Italy. She described Gargnano and San Gaudenzio in a book of prose and paintings, *Among Italian Peasants*, 1919. She is the Mrs. Anthony of David Garnett's memoirs *The Golden Echo*.
[1] The younger daughter of the Russian author Alexander Ivanich Ertel, who became the manager of an estate, and was visited in 1904 by Constance Garnett and her son David. Lola Alexandrovna Ertel came to England early in the summer of 1912. Harold Hobson fell in love with her and visited the Ertels later that summer in Moscow.

TO Edward Garnett

[?] Villa Igéa
Villa di Gargnano, (Brescia)
Lago di Garda
[*March 1913?*]

Dear Mr. Garnett,

I feel that you ought to be cross with me, I am such a lot of bother, but please don't, because you see, it's so hard. For the first time really in my life, I am undecided, I *don't know what to do.* Of course I don't think it's desirable that I should see the children in the street, but what can I do? I am entirely cut off from all, Ernest or the children. Ernest used to write my mother, not now. My last communication from him was, "Well, I'll spare it you." He loved me absolutely, that's why he hates me absolutely; he will keep the children from me, I know he is a whole-hogger! And his people love the children; he has got a vicar brother, they are all pious. I was fond of them, but I should sooner get some feeling out of the inkpot before me than from them. I know they will tell the children, "Your mother has left you"; I want to tell them, "I left your father, not you." If they ask Ernest, "We want to see our mother," I think he cannot say no. Once I had seen them, they are old enough to hold their tongues for a little while, I would write and tell Ernest, "Arrange for me to see the children or I will come and see you!" That would frighten him! There is Lawrence, who hates the idea of England, who dreads my seeing the children; I feel them slipping away into nothing from me and I simply can't stand it and *won't* stand it! It is good of you to give me so much sympathy and listen to my tale of woe!

Yours,
Frieda

TO David Garnett

[?] Villa Igéa
Villa di Gargnano, (Brescia)
Lago di Garda
[*March 1913?*]

Dear Bunny,

Your last letter was *so* nice! But sad, I thought; what's the matter? You want to be my Dutch uncle, so let me be something like it to you! Have *you* drunk of some bitter waters of knowing? I think you are quite right, you have too much to give later on, to throw yourself away on mere sensationalism, and that is what those modern damsels want of you; wait, only wait and *she* [?] will come! Yes, I like it that you are so keen on your work, we think of you at every new flower we come across! Harold and Lola! she has been flirting and he has felt righteous! I hope for both their sakes, they will make a success of it, but Harold is an *enfant gaté*, and like in the *Land of Cokayne* he expects the roast pigeons to fly in his mouth! It isn't as easy as that! I like Tony for many things; she is chasing greatness as if it were a rabbit and she wants to put salt on its tail! But I *do* feel sorry for John, he must have taken her seriously and she is cold to give one shivers; even with the child, she is cold and it's cold too! I had a pang of jealousy because of her, but the bubble's pricked; L. approaches all people (women specially) as if they were Gothic cathedrals, then he finds that they are little houses and hates them for it! But I admire Tony for her independence, she goes her own way! But couldn't anybody tell John that he is a blithering, blighted imbecile, duffer and idiot to want her back? She is a sensationalist, loves all this chasing game, wouldn't, couldn't do without it now! He *must* leave her, with an effort of will get rid of her inside or he will be quite done for soon! Lord, the messes people are in! I have given Lawrence a hell of a time, that's to say he took it over the children; I was so *very* sure to see them at Easter, it was a picture in my head; when Ernest wouldn't, it was like dangling with my feet in the air! Now we are going to Rome! Can't you come? I am anxious to go! Tony is very likely going to Icking, our flat; she ought to have people and a good time! Your mother seems to have been superhuman to her; I am looking forward to see your mother, she sounds so awfully nice; Harold and Tony seem to love her! Lawrence *has* been having a hump; it's quite killing when he goes about an incorporated doom, *nothing* is any good and he asks a dozen times a day in all keys, "Are you miserable, dear?" [Interpolated in D. H. L.'s hand: I never say "Dear"—that's Frieda's marital term for me.] *Most* cheering, when one's got to fight one's own hump off! But still we are going to bring it off in spite of odds and the shortcomings of this world! My love to you, Signor Davide; come and see us in Rome, there are trips, can't you manage one?

                    Auf Wiedersehen,
                    Frieda

Dear David,

I have been seedy as the sickest ass that ever groused, hence the hump. But Frieda sits on top of the hump, and then it's as big as the "doom of St. Paul's", as my father always says.

You are suffering from "genitoritis"—the affliction of one's parents. One goes through it like measles. It's hard all round. The only cure is "love"—*à la* Harold. We have heard of *your* flight to Moscow—and to love—God bless you. Is Harold in the same frame of mind, only rowing another boat, I wonder, as you when you recovered!—We liked your last letters, and I am awfully sorry not to be seeing you just now. You must scramble to Rome later. I'll send you the address when we get to the Eternal City.

                    Love,
                    D. H. L.

TO Edward Garnett

> [?] Villa Jaffe
> Irschenhausen, (Post) Ebenhausen
> bei München
> [*April 1913?*]

Dear Mr. Garnett,

I feel so apologetic that we came and came and came, the *"ewige Wieder Kehr"* of Nietzsche, and then never turned up. I am sorry and it was mostly my fault and Lawrence was seedy! Don't be cross with us! We feel awfully at present as if nobody would have anything to do with us, quite outcasts we feel! I am disappointed about L.'s poetry, but mind you go on believing in him; even if he isn't a success *now*, he will be in the end, I know. He is not so easy to swallow, and to understand, because he is an absolutely original, new plant. I found it hard to understand! Miriam's letter hurt me; [2] that she should only think with bitterness of all the good things they had together, seems hardly credible! L. *had* loved her, and when she sent his last letter back, he *wouldn't* believe; the generosity lies on his side, seems to me! She says: my aim has been to preserve the integrity of the spiritual values! Oh, those spiritual values! People must be mean and pigs to want spiritual values as if they weren't there! He never did her the wrong of spiritualizing her altogether, but she idealized him, the worst of crimes in love! Don't you think one wants to be loved with one's littleness, one's everything of shame and all; but after all he left her; and her world is nothing now, quite empty, after he had made it full for her! He left her behind in her old world of "spiritual values". I am trying to get Ernest's promise to let me have the children in the August holidays, then I will wait; if he *won't*, I shall come to England and try and see them, so please don't tell anybody that I will come, if I do! We

[2] Apparently Jessie Chambers (the Miriam of *Sons and Lovers*) had been in correspondence with Garnett about her own novelistic version of her relationship with Lawrence, since at about this time Lawrence asked Garnett to send him her manuscript. It was first titled *The Rathe Primrose*, later *Eunice Temple*. She ultimately destroyed the manuscript, but used the initials E. T. to stand for the author of her 1935 memoirs *D. H. Lawrence: A Personal Record*.

are just reading some "Wyspianski". Mrs. Garnett knows him, I am sure; he did frighten me! All guilt and bad conscience, conscience mad. I wonder how you will like L.'s new novel! I read it again and quite adored it; before, I wasn't sure. It's so quiet and different, you will be surprised, I think.

Good-bye and please forgive us our behaviour!

I think Mrs. A. is not so very cautious herself, the romanticism of her situation gets the better of her caution, which after all is natural!

Yours,
F.

TO Edward Garnett

Irschenhausen
(Post) Ebenhausen
[*May 1913?*]

Dear Mr. Garnett,

We roared over the "remarkable females"; you just hit them! The worst, it's like his impudence, they are *me*, these beastly, superior, arrogant females! Lawrence *hated* me just over the children; I daresay *I* wasn't all I might have been, so he wrote this! I know now why Goethe wrote *Iphigenie;*[3] so superb she is, but I'll be hanged if any man wants to love her, as well be married to the tablets of the ten commandments, though mind you a man looks for that in a woman too! The book will be all right in the end, you trust me for my own sake, they will have to be women and not superior flounders. I say the book is worthy of his talent, but not of his genius. "Miss Houghton", whom I am reading now, is a 1,000 times "more", but improper! You will love it (I don't mean for that); sometimes it's witty too! You wrote me such a nice letter, it warmed my inside and I am grateful; Lawrence was so seedy, and he goes on working and

[3] Footnote by D. H. L.: Iphigenie, according to Frieda, is a noble statue to the frosty Frau von Stein:—noble, but done in hate; the cruellest thing a man can do to a woman is to portray her as perfection. D. H. L.

it's simply ghastly; he becomes a writing machine, that works itself out; it made me quite frantic. [Interpolation by D. H. L.: a lie—I've written very little.] Not a word about the children for months now, Monty will be 13 [interpolation by D. H. L.: 14 I think.] in June, so I must go on waiting, but we are coming to England; it depends on L's health now. [Interpolation by D. H. L.: Not true. It depends on Frieda's will.] It will be nice to see you and Bunny, we think of him a lot here, where he was with us in the Isartal! Miriam's novel is very lovable, I think, and one does feel so sorry for her, but it's a faded photograph of *Sons and Lovers;* she has never understood anything out of herself, no inner activity, but she does make one ache! I only just realized the amazing brutality of *Sons and Lovers.* How that brutality remains ["remains" a correction by D. H. L. of her "is" and his own "is there"] in spite of Christianity, of the two thousand years; it's better like that, than in the civilized forms it takes! It's only a top plaster [interpolation by D. H. L.: the civilization], and I'm sure brutality ought to develop into something finer, out of *itself*, not be suppressed, denied! Paul says to his mother, when she is dying, "If I'd got to die, I would be quick about it, I would *will* to die." Doesn't it seem awful! Yet, one *does* feel like that, but not only that after all! There I'm "Ellaing" again. . . .

[In D. H. L.'s hand] I was glad of your letter about the Sisters. Don't schimpf, I shall make it all right when I re-write it. I shall put it in the third person. All along I knew what ailed the book. But it did me good to theorize myself out, and to depict Frieda's God Almightiness in all its glory. That was the first crude fermenting of the book. I'll make it into art now. I've done 256 pages, but still can't see the end very clear. But it's coming. Frieda is so cross, since your letter came, with the book. Before that she was rather fond of her portrait in straight pleats and Athena sort of pose.

Send me the first part back, will you.

Auf Wiedersehen.

D. H. Lawrence

TO Edward Garnett

> [?] Villa Jaffe
> Irschenhausen, (Post) Ebenhausen
> bei München
> [*June 1913?*]

Dear Mr. Garnett!

So we are coming! I feel quite glad! It's like me, I ought to come in sackcloth and ashes and I feel only pleased at the thought of seeing the children! I ran away from L. for two days after having broken a plate over his head, while washing up! I was astonished. I thought I was mild and good! My small nephew *was* shocked at my departure, he loves L.; he said: "Tante Frieda, now you will get tired of this man and three uncles from one aunt are too much!" He was distressed! However, we are, L. and I, such friends, I will wear a fragment of that plate in a locket round my neck! At first I wanted to come alone to England, but of course I am glad, in a way, that L. wants to come, and that he can't bear to be away from me, hardly for hours, you will understand rejoices my heart! Even he stays to abuse me! I shall enjoy the Cearne; I hope to see Mrs. Garnett and David, I want to read his novel, and L. has made my mouth water with all the books at the Cearne! No, no, love is no crucifixion, or if it is, then it will rise from the grave on the third day (after a broken plate or two!). I hope our coming is not a nuisance; deep down in me I feel that you *ought* to be cross with us, for always putting our coming off, it's not human to quite forgive us!

> *Auf Wiedersehen*
> and many thanks,
> Yours, The One and Only
> (Phoenix L.'s name for me!)

[At the top of the first page, in D. H. L.'s hand: We arrive Thursday morning, from Harwich, at about 8:30 in Paddington.—It is Monday evening and we haven't heard from you.—I wonder if you didn't get my letter.—Ugh, how I hate shifting. We leave here tomorrow at noon.]

TO David Garnett

> [?] Villa Jaffe
> Irschenhausen, (Post) Ebenhausen
> bei München
> [*August 1913?*]

Dear Bunny,

A big bunch of "Alpenrosen" I had given me reminded me of you and the microscope! Were you glad to get back to it? We will find flowers for you. L. and I are friends at present and the Lord has been good to me in letting me not be so miserable any more about the children. I do enjoy things again. I am sorry you saw me so much steeped in misery and I think you helped me over it a bit, I don't quite understand how, but you did. Yes, you would enjoy being here; so big everything seems, there is breathing space and nothing to make one feel *not* oneself. What's the novel doing? I am quite in love with my niece Anita; she is a beautiful, big creature, something so strong and fresh and simple about her. She is only twelve but seems quite womanish. Edgar is here; we see a great many more people than we used to last year, it's rather jolly. Edgar sends his love; he has just brought me a pair of gorgeous sandals, I have just danced in them, knocked my heel and ooh, it hurts still! And my sister gave me a new Bavarian dress, gorgeous bright colours. I *am* grand. I wanted to write a *nice* letter to you and now it doesn't seem a very exciting one after all. I am glad you had a good time camping. The Isar is *so* green, this place of Edgar's is so nice. Good-bye and good luck to you, write to me if the spirit moves you. Is Harold cross with us? He wanted to come to Margate, then never wrote and never came. (L. asks if I want to send this "lot of stuff" as manuscript.)

> Love,
> F.

[Lengthwise in the left-hand margin of the first page of this letter, and then larger across Frieda's handwriting, as space ran out, Lawrence wrote the following letter]

Dear Bunny,

It seems an awful shame to make use of you like this. I shall send you half a crown for stamps. You won't mind. After a day or two, everybody will write direct here to me. The two MS. that the Northern Syndicate sent back—will you send "The Sick Collier" to the *New Statesman*—10, Great Queen St., Kingsway, W.C.—and "A Christening" to Ezra Pound, 10, Church Walk, Kensington, W. I enclose a note for the *New Statesman*.—Then the *Westminster Gazette* says that last year they sent back a couple of sketches of Frieda and me in the Tyrol, to the Cearne. I have seen nothing of them. I wonder if they are at the Cearne, and if you could send them to me. They are two short sketches— rather good. Frieda is frightfully keen on them, and desolated for fear they are lost.

I am working like a nigger here. Lord, but I mean to get some work done this autumn. It is a pity you can't come here. You could have had a bed—and it is *so* jolly. We think of staying till the end of Sept., then going to Italy, on the coast above Leghorn. I hope it comes off and is a success. What a lovely place for your mother to come and see us. Where we next go, I want to get a more or less permanent abode.

Tell Constanza Davidovna I am sorry she is so pestered by my letters continually arriving. Soon they will stop.

Send the note to your father.

Love,

D. H. Lawrence

Lady Asquith and her husband, the Hon. Herbert Asquith, whose father, H. H. Asquith, became the Liberal Prime Minister, had met the Lawrences in England in the summer of 1913. Along with another aristocratic patron of the arts, Lady Ottoline Morrell, she became deeply involved in Lawrence's wartime difficulties and bitterness, and shared in his hope of leadership by a vitalistic aristoi and in his plans for the establishment of a community apart from the European violence. The friendship with her became especially crucial when the Lawrences were expelled from Cornwall on suspicion of spying, and were placed under police surveillance. In a later letter, Frieda—the German aristocrat—makes a daring plea to Lady Asquith to save Herbert Asquith, her husband, from the danger of war service. She was later similarly moved with regard to her son Monty. Lady Asquith's memoir of Lawrence appeared in Remember and Be Glad (1952).

TO Lady Cynthia Asquith

> Lerici per Fiascherino
> Golfo della Spezia
> Italy
> *23 October 1913*

Dear Mrs. Asquith:

One of my first thoughts in this lovely place were [*sic*] you! How you would like it! The Mediterranean coming into our little bay, where the women wash and the fishing boats are! We have a little pink house standing in vines and olives and lovely smelling pines with red earth under them! How stupid people are to be bothered with lots of money and houses! We live like princes on £8 a month! Elide the maid is so overwhelming in her good manners, every meal is an exertion of politeness! And the people in the shops have such grand names. We buy biscuits from "Dante", "Achille" is the postman, "Ettore" (I wish you could hear me scream it with a string of sentences like his wife, it would please you) is our landlord! It's so fresh and warm! I loaf, for which I have a talent! L. has just put your black *crêpe de Chine* blouse with the big opal in a story! It's jolly, to watch the stories coming! Your son John is a person one doesn't forget. It's curious that you can be a real person at his tender age! Did you go to Venice? Do tell us! There's a fisherman here that looks like Mr. Asquith—he rows standing up, and it looks nice! I hope you are well, L. is getting fat here!

With every kind regard,

> Yours sincerely,
> Frieda Lawrence

Henry Savage had reviewed Lawrence's first novel,
The White Peacock, for the Academy, *and had received*
a letter of thanks that began a friendship. He was the
friend and biographer of Richard Middleton.

TO Henry Savage

Lerici per Fiascherino
Golfo della Spezia
Italy
December 1913

Dear Mr. Savage:

If you knew how *lovely* it was to find your literature when I
have climbed to Tellaro (our post office) there to sit on the rocks
and unwrap the literature (yours and the books) you wouldn't
mind all the bother we are. I am lying in my hammock looking
over Porto Venare, how you would love it. If you could see it,
you would—but you simply *must* come, beg or borrow or steal.
Abercrombie, Gibson, Trevelyan turned up the other day, when
we were at the peasants' wedding here. They were so English
but lovable, especially Trevelyan's eyes seem to shine with
kindness. L. is lazy, I am glad, we are so happy on the water too
in our boat with real Turner sunsets in the flesh. Your boy, *do*
enjoy him, when I think of the joy mine gave me and now I
haven't got them. Is he either you or your wife? Is he an anxiety?
Don't let him be, with a first one never knows what to do; I am
feeling so beautifully stupid today. I never saw Middleton's play,
we have *no* paper of any sort, what you send us is all we have
read since we are here. I just read some Ernest Dowson, he is
another melancholy blighter. I don't believe you are decadent,
it's only a phase.

Good-bye in the sunshine, my love to the wife and the infant.
Yours,

Frieda L.

Bring your wife in the Spring! Awfully many thanks!

TO Lady Cynthia Asquith [4]

> Lerici per Fiascherino
> Golfo della Spezia
> Italy
> [*December 21, 1913*]

[In D. H. L.'s hand: "The shortest day." In Frieda's: "his temper short as well."]

Dear Mrs. Asquith,

You wrote me such a frightfully nice letter, don't be too sympathetic, I warn you, or I shall come and weep to you when we are in England. Don't be too sorry either, after all we are very happy too, (I'm *not*—D. H. L.) and I believe in the miracle too; (I don't—D. H. L.) only it's hard, I miss them so, like one would miss a leg (L.: one wouldn't, after a fortnight). It's still gorgeous here (L.: It isn't—it's cold and dark). I know such a lovely little villa with a torrino here "with a beautiful, beautiful" view for you. We hear of you through Eddie Marsh,[5] a Kipling performance was the last [*sic?*]. Barrie [6] wrote such a nice letter to L. (L.: he didn't). This is to wish you all three a Merry Christmas. L. must write, being an "autore" he does it so much better than yours, (L.: what a hateful way of ending)

> Frieda L.

TO Edward Garnett

> Fiascherino
> [*February 1914?*]

Dear Mr. Garnett,

I have been so cross with you! You attacked me in your letter and I was cross, but I am afraid you were right and made me

[4] This letter accompanied a letter from Lawrence to Lady Asquith dated December 21, 1913, which appeared in the Huxley edition of Lawrence's letters (1932) and was dropped in Harry T. Moore's *The Collected Letters of D. H. Lawrence* (1962).

[5] Edward Marsh, who had met the Lawrences in England during the summer of 1913. He was the editor of the *Georgian Poetry* anthologies in which Lawrence's work had appeared. *A Number of People* (1939) contains his memories of Lawrence.

[6] Lady Asquith was to become secretary to Sir James Barrie, from 1918 to 1937.

realise my wrongs in a way. I hadn't cared twopence about L.'s novel. Over the children I thought he was beastly; he hated me for being miserable, not a moment of misery did he put up with; he denied all the suffering and suffered all the more, like his mother before him; how we fought over this. In revenge I did not care about his writing. If he denies my life and suffering I deny his art, so you see he wrote without me at the back of him. The novel is a failure but you must feel something at the back of it struggling, trying to come out. You see, I don't really believe in *Sons and Lovers;* it feels as if there were nothing *behind* all those happenings as if there were no "*Hinterland der Seele,*" only intensely felt fugitive things. I who am a believer though I don't know in what, to me it seems an irreligious book. It does not seem the deepest and last thing said; if for instance a man loves in a book the pretty curl on the neck of "her", he loves it ever so intensely and beautifully, there is something behind that curl, *more* than that curl; there is *she*, the living, striving *she*. Writers are so beside the point, not *direct* enough. I am going to throw myself into the novel now and you will see what a *gioia* it will be. There is one triumph for us women, you men can't do things alone. Just as little as we can *live* alone. I have got over the worst, terrible part with E. and the children, so I shall enjoy L. writing. So don't pitch into me any more, I have suffered very much for the love of men! You ought all to be frightfully nice to me! It is jolly to have Mrs. Garnett here; I go to her and pour out my Lawrence woes to her and she listens patiently and feelingly, so I never feel I am disloyal to L. It's *pouring* with rain, I wonder if Mrs. Garnett will move on. She said she might. I think it is rather nice of L. and intelligent to accept your criticism as he does, because it is not easy to swallow criticism, but you need never be afraid and mind what you say; he would always much rather you said it! You mustn't *mind* saying it because you are really the only man he has any opinion of. I do think you are good to him, only your second letter was too cross; perhaps it was a good thing too! Thank you for the book! I was so glad to get it. Something "goy" in it pleased me very much. Cannot you come out soon; when I think how you sit in Henrietta Street and how you would enjoy the sunshine and the sea; you *ought* to come!

> Good-bye.
> Yours with love,
> Frieda

Dear Garnett,

I didn't send those other pages, because I thought I'd do the whole thing again. We'll see how it turns out.

Mitchell Kennerley wrote to me he'd offered Duckworth some sheets of the play. You must tell me how it is decided.

Thanks for *The Bookman*. W. L. George had already sent it on. They are exclaiming here on the truth of what he says. But the truth of what is said about oneself, one can never see so completely.

The Consul in Spezia is typing my new novel—for fun. Kennerley asked me for a copy, so I shall be able to send him one direct.

It is sunny again today.

> Yrs. D. H. Lawrence

In 1915 the philosopher-mathematician Bertrand Russell, now Lord Russell, was involved with Lawrence in a plan to give anti-war lectures. Frieda's letter indicates that she took an active role in their quarrel over the soundness of Russell's faith in man's rationality, and his pacifism, which, in Lawrence's evolving "blood consciousness" vitalism, was pernicious at this stage in history. As late as 1953, Russell violently attacked Lawrence as a proto-Fascist; Frieda's reply appears under the title "Bertrand Russell's Article on Lawrence" (see page 447).

TO Bertrand Russell

> Greatham
> Pulborough
> Sussex
> *1915*

Dear Mr. Russell,

Isn't this coalition government thrilling? Surely it's "hate"

that makes the world go round, nothing could ever have done
this except hate for the "Huns". Does it affect you much? To me
it seems so *good;* they are the same old boot really, and now there
is a chance for a new element, true opposition; it is extraordinary,
surely. You wrote me a very nice letter, thank you; I know you
must have suffered bitterly from inquisitive impertinence, but
surely you might have told me something that I would have been
wiser for. Your 2 + 2 is 4 argument meant such a great deal to
L. and me, if one applies it, then it becomes a reverend, big
thing. But I did want to make a drawing that 2 + 2 can be
6—*speriamo!!*—

[Sketch of two tiny figures—male and female—clothed and
hatted—female in front of male, half obliterating him—both
facing forward.]

I *must* illustrate the philosophy! When I wrote that you were too
much *of* the English Constitution (look, I write it instinctively
with capitals), I did *not* mean that you were *not* human enough,
but too much you represent the English *as they are*, and you
want to kick them, but it is too much yourself that you must kick.
I hope you don't mind my saying this. I shall be grateful if you
say something critical to me!

I thought Windmills was jolly, but rather like Smollett.

Yours sincerely,
Frieda Lawrence

TO Bertrand Russell

Greatham
Pulborough
Sussex
1915

Dear Mr. Russell,

Your visit was very stimulating to me. L. told me what you

said of me; I think it's rather true, but you have left out the impersonal me (I don't know what to call it), the impersonal that is in everybody. I think I have shed so many personal things, that I am not very individual in a way. You, you were a little cross with me. It seemed to you that I did not respect enough your work, which I could never understand; that particular manmade thing, you call it intellect, is a mystery, rather a thrilling one to me. But I think you are a Stanley, you confuse people with your intellect; it's rather jolly, it's your form of *Wille zur Macht*. I should always be frightened of your intellect, I feel it against women, at present anyhow. I think what you represent is your national passion; it makes you unhappy because you are too much in the old form of it which has had its day, you are in it and really it needs a wider, more inclusive ring. So perhaps you believe in the war. Don't you think one might? And besides the rotten Prussianism I think that Germany has got something good and a new ideal to give to itself and the world. If nations would only, only allow each other's best characteristics to come out, and take and learn from each other. It's all so tight now, these little nations, so unembracing. All the people are so ugly now, but the other is there, in the nations and in the individuals.

Good luck to you,
Frieda Lawrence

I am afraid you must *guess* what I want to say.

TO Lady Cynthia Asquith

Greatham, Pulborough
Sussex
1915

Dear Lady Cynthia,

It was so nice to get your letter. We have so often spoken of you since we saw you last. I could and cannot yet believe that John has a brother, you must have him *aus dem Ärmel geschüttelt*. But isn't it a vile world to bring children into, just at present? Nowhere anything to make one happy for a single moment. I think it's terrible that sensitive men like Herbert Asquith must go and fight, I am sure it's a violation to them. And I do not think that we any of us feel anything glorious and splendid in this war. I think we are really different nowadays. Last time we were in London I very much wanted to see you and the [great?] John and his brother, but as you were not there I am glad I did not have the disappointment of not finding you. It would be so nice if you could come and see us here. We are almost on the downs, the cottage is like a monastery, the refectoire the sitting-room, and you would have a little cell for your room. Come and we will try and be happy or miserable, we must keep *some* life going, "the flag flying." You know that sort of thing, out of spite against all the misery heaped on us. Lady Ottoline Morrell and Bertrand Russell are coming. . . . Lawrence used to know some of the Portland servants, she is the Duke of Portland's sister, so over this they have struck up a friendship!

We are sending you this ridiculous little box, it's our latest rage, painting them.

Yours,
Frieda Lawrence

Samuel Solomonovich Koteliansky was born in the Ukraine and came to England on a research grant from the University of Kiev. Lawrence and Frieda met him in 1914. Lawrence collaborated with him on some of his translations of Russian writers, polishing and heightening the English. Frieda's need to defend herself against him indicates a cause of difficulty with such literary friends that came to a rather violent climax in the letters of 1923, when Lawrence remained in America while she returned to England.

TO S. S. Koteliansky

> Greatham, Pulborough
> Sussex
> *9 February 1915*

Dear Kot:

Thank you for the cake, it was good, but I hardly like it, when you give me things, because you don't really like me. I was not *cross*, when you did not come with me to Golder's Green, but I could not help thinking if L. had been there, you *would* have come. Also I think, L. would be fonder of you if I were not there; your attitude to me is not really and truly a good one. I can feel it. You think I do not count besides Lawrence, but I take myself, my ideals and life quite as seriously as he does his. This you will not allow, and it is our quarrel, you think I am conceited. I can't help that, but it hurts me very much when you think I do not count as a human being. But you do not think much of women, they are not human beings in your eyes. It's *your* fault, not mine. You will not have me for a friend. Yes, I like Katherine, there is something exquisite about her mind and body, and a great power for affection. You were not nice or patient with her.

Will you come for the week-end? Jack is here.

Don't mind what I say, it is better to be honest.

> Frieda

TO S. S. Koteliansky

> Greatham, Pulborough
> Sussex
> *February 1915*

Dear Kot:

I liked your last (no, the one before last) letter very much! So you wish me to write my "Xanthippe" lectures down instead of delivering them orally to poor Lawrence. But you see I am also his wife on this earth, the wife to the *man* as distinguished from the *artist;* to that latter I would always submit but, you see, some things I just *know* and he doesn't. Don't talk as if I were such a bad wife and he a blooming angel. But I think you like to make me cross. But we will really all be fond of one another and the quarrelling is just for love. It is so beautiful here and I want you and the Murrys to come here together, we would have plenty of room and it would be nice. Our poor, very charming servant Hilda rushed into my bedroom this morning: "My poor brother is killed at the war." It seems so awful. He was only 18. Her mother is very ill.

L. is writing hard, we go for long walks, the estate is very beautiful, much the most beautiful country I have seen in England. Such a nice letter from Katherine. I am glad the Lord made her. Lady Ottoline is nice, she is coming on Saturday with Bertrand Russell; our Rananim [7] will come off in some form or other. We had a correspondence with Forster,[8] very strange, quarrelling with L. and me of course, saying to me, "I will have no dealings with a firm," because I had written in L's letter. Don't you want to have anything to do with a firm either? I believe everybody feels like that, I feel everybody against me, but then I can stand up to it, thank God. And you will be my friend too, soon.

Yours,
Frieda

TO S. S. Koteliansky

Greatham, Pulborough
Sussex
1915

Dear Kot:

No, I won't pity you, how could I, when every time I look at the dried orange with the cloves, I laugh and expect your "uncrowned princess of Judea's" spirit to speak. She stayed till Friday, it was very trying because I couldn't even be cross to her, she is too much a nothing for me. We have had lots of people.

---

[7] "Rananim" was the name for the new community Lawrence hoped to establish as a retreat from the war and an answer to it.

[8] E. M. Forster, whom Lawrence was inviting to join him in a war on the contemporary Mammon.

The Ottoline is really a nice simple person; we are *not* going to have the house done, it would cost too much. We shall have a littler place, I am glad. There are still more Meynells. I try to dodge out of the house, but I get caught, like a mouse in a trap. Francis Birrell and Garnett came. David I loved, but the Birrell is *not* good. I laughed that Katherine came back so soon—"*Je le savais* [?] *bien*". It's lovely weather, I do wish I had a rabbit hole of my own to creep into. There was a *very* nice but ugly Miss Farjeon who sang very funny comic songs with her brother. She had made them up herself. One began: "Thank God I am an Englishman, thank God the earth I tread is English earth." Katherine would have loved it. Lawrence has spent two days trying to make me cross. I feel very happy in my skin, the weather was so lovely but he has been seedy, so he will make me cross. I wish I could become an animal, I am so tired of human beings. I would like to be a nasty animal that frightens people.

Good-bye Kot.

Have you got your crown yet?

Frieda

TO Lady Cynthia Asquith

Vale of Health, Hampstead
21 October 1915

My dear Lady Cynthia,

I cannot write you a consoling letter,[9] I feel much, much too bitter. I cannot bear the thought of it: the hole in the family, the agony for your mother, the shock to that jolly little sister of yours that danced with such absorption in the water at Margate. No, I cannot say anything that would not hurt you more. I wish I could. Only you have my deep sympathy and affection.

Yours ever,
Frieda Lawrence

[9] The occasion was the death of Mrs. Asquith's brother. Lawrence said: "How long will the nations continue to empty the future—it is your own phrase—think what it means—I am sick in my soul, sick to death."

TO Bertrand Russell

Porthcothan
St. Merryn
Padstow
Cornwall
1916

Dear Mr. Russell,

I am so worried about Lawrence. He isn't at all well. I really don't know what to do. If you have a few days to spare it really would be kind of you if you came down. I know he would very much enjoy seeing you, and to me it would be a help. I feel it such a responsibility, it's too much for me. He might just die because everything is too much for him. But he simply mustn't die. It's not as if it concerned me alone. I know you are not extra cheerful yourself, but then at present who could be? I think Florida is the only solution. I resent it bitterly that all life has got the lid on. Lawrence is full of ideas to write and is very seedy and can't. Do come, it might do you good and I would be very glad. There are so few people Lawrence can bear the sight of.

Yours very sincerely,
Frieda Lawrence

TO S. S. Koteliansky

Padstow, Cornwall
13 February 1916

Dear Kot:

I have been thinking of you lately reading Dostojewsky's *Possessed*. I thought Shatov (do you remember him?) was like you. Am I wrong? The book made a great impression on me, the people are all so very cruel and Dostojewsky brings it home. But Lawrence got very cross with it and says Dostojewsky is a liar. He makes people *angels* on one hand and "Supermen", and as if the other were not true at all, instead of just making them human beings. I don't like D.'s women, they really are quite off their chumps and stupid. The feeling Dostojewsky gives me is rather like *Nietzsche*. Lawrence is better, but things have gone very badly with him. I am glad you enjoyed your afternoon with your uncrowned princess of Judea, she never said to us that she was displeased with you! I am glad, Oh so glad that Joy's last conquest is a "rosebud"—though I suppose not as bad as you say. It was good news to me. It will be very jolly if you and Gertler[1] turn up. Gertler would enjoy the sea and colour of things, and it would make you bark your most beautiful bark. The wind is howling now. Lawrence loved your "Kümmel" and if you can afford it *really*, send him one. The Murrys haven't had our letters, they wrote today. I like Heseltine,[2] he is like a boy sometimes and sometimes like the boy's grandfather!

Good-bye and I hope you will come and see us soon.

Frieda

TO S. S. Koteliansky

Porthcothan
St. Merryn
N. Cornwall
1916

Dear Kot:

In great triumph they brought the Kümmel *and* the Sherry home—and my cigarettes. But it was as usual too much. I don't think Shatov was a serf or his soul was not that of a serf. But anyhow you are not like him. I thought your belief in Lawrence was like Shatov's in Stavrogin, but I don't think it is. He wanted something to believe in and so do you. You used to believe in yourself once but you say you are dead, but I don't think it's true. You don't, do you? Shatov is the most living and real person in *The Possessed*. Stavrogin and Piotr are more shadowy and unliving, Piotr is mechanical. Varvara and Stepanovitch are like the Ottoline and Bertie Russell! Exactly! It will be nice if you

[1] Mark Gertler, a painter, educated at the Slade, who had met the Lawrences in 1914.

[2] Philip Heseltine, whom the Lawrences had met in 1915, was a friend and disciple of Frederick Delius, and a composer under the name "Peter Warlock." Lawrence and he were engaged for a time in a plan to publish books by subscription, beginning with Lawrence's previously suppressed *The Rainbow*. Shortly after this, Heseltine turned against Lawrence.

come. The Murrys will stay with us for some time. L. is full of plans and feels happy! Miss Channing (Heseltine's friend) will be in London soon (she is *very* pretty) and it would be nice of you if you saw her. You will like her—I will give her your address. With many thanks for your gifts, we shall have a feast tonight!

With kindest regards,
Frieda

TO Lady Cynthia Asquith

Porthcothan
St. Merryn
Padstow
Cornwall
1916

My dear Cynthia,

I never thanked you for my lovely Christmas present. I loved it but the fuss in the papers about your mother-in-law and German officers struck terror into my heart. I saw you being martyred on account of my Hundom! You really can't tell anything in these days. This is a beautiful place. Tristram and Isolde and King Arthur country. I wish you could come! We have quite a swanky house. We can look on the sea, a great enormous sea, sometimes it's rather horrifying, the black rocks and expanse of sky and sea and the wind pulling and enormous waves. But today was a gentle, sunny spring day. I think that the idea in *The Rainbow* is: *Love the ideal* as a background to these marriages which are really all failures to some extent. Hence the Rainbow between the ideal and these partial failures, because they are not *complete* failures. In the end the man fails Ursula because he has no ideal beyond the old existing state, it does not satisfy her nor him. For perfect love you don't only have two people, it must include a bigger, universal connection. An *idea*, something outside themselves, and it is really against individualism. What makes Lawrence so frantic is that he thinks there is no germ of a new idea in Europe anywhere. I must say I am wild that not a single critic or writer has broken a lance for *The*

Rainbow. That they attacked it well and good, but not a soul, not
a soul stuck up for it, it is maddening. I am full of black
revenge!! Only it is not even worth it. I am so glad you have been
happy! Lawrence has scared me by being very queer, but he is
better. . . .

TO Lady Cynthia Asquith

> Higher Tregerthen, Zennor
> St. Ives, Cornwall
> [*May 24, 1916*]

Dear Lady Cynthia,

What are you doing? We want to hear from you. Think, we
had a shipwreck practically on our doorstep—in the mist a big
Spanish ship—it *was* thrilling. This is very lovely here and I
hope we shall see you soon. The spring is so beautiful here and I
have been very happy in this wide open country of air and sea
and gorse. L. has almost finished another novel, it's a much
jollier one and won't shock the good people so much. The
Murrys are in the next, the tower house; we drive miles into
Penzance and go to sales and come home hanging on to chairs
and cupboards and things, but lovely things, practically for
nothing. I had a great "rumpus" with dear Lady Ottoline,[3]
finally; I told her what I thought of her. All her "spirituality" is
false, her democracy is an autocrat turned sour, inside those
wonderful shawls there is cheapness and vulgarity. She wrote
how unfeeling Mrs. Bonham Carter was about the Irish! Oh,
those stunts humanity and kindness; they are really for the
people whose inside is frozen! How is your young generation? It
would be so jolly if you paid us a visit. Would you like some
flowers? There are millions here!

Frieda Lawrence

[3] Lady Ottoline Morrell, a noted hostess and friend of writers and
painters. Frieda's view of her here is strikingly like Lawrence's charac-
terization of Hermione Roddice in *Women in Love*. Lawrence's letters
to her, before this time, are full of the great hopes he had that she and
his other aristocratic friend, Lady Asquith, would understand his advo-
cacy of a vitalistic religious revolution and the establishment of a new
kind of community.

TO Lady Cynthia Asquith

> Higher Tregerthen, Zennor
> St. Ives, Cornwall
> *1916*

What a treat—a telegram! The whole countryside will rush up and ask what's happened! In my thoughts I have written many letters to you, but L. has got a world phobia and has become a real St. Anthony. But in between we have had a jolly summer, when we have been able to forget everything, it's the only way nowadays. We have been furnishing joyfully and wildly, a lemon-coloured tower-room that we love, and got some jolly nice things at the sales in St. Ives, where the fishermen's wives sell their "old" things for nice new bamboo furniture. Do you remember a nice white blouse with frills you gave me? I have such an "air" in it. Also I seem to have blossomed out into stockings, such stockings. L. ordered me some rose-pink and orange, lemon-coloured and grass-green. Katie Berryman, the little shopwoman at Zennor, has to walk round the counter to stare at them, every time I appear. I hoped there was a chance of your appearing. The only temptations I can hold out to you are blackberrying, and lovely bathing in rock pools. The people here, the Lord bless them for it, are extra nice to me for being a Hun; it would be jolly to see you here. So it is very simple, the heather is just out and we have some beautiful days. L. is writing another novel, *so* different, not at all like his other things; what people will say to it, I don't know. And you are in black, I really dare not think, and cannot understand why all Europe isn't frightened out of its wits; but surely the war has rolled itself into such an avalanche that it must burst and bang somewhere. Your poor sister-in-law, so terrible, where a person has been that one loved there is nothing; it is not for the dead but for the living that it is so ghastly to think of. I feel that we might see you soon, I would enjoy it.

> With love,
> Frieda

Michael must be nearly two now, I remember his birthday last year, when he looked truly archangelic!

TO S. S. Koteliansky

Higher Tregerthen, Zennor
St. Ives, Cornwall
4 September 1916

Dear Kot:

No, you have quite a wrong idea of Barbara; [4] she is not loving, what I like in her is something untamed and quite individual, but I know she is very overstrained and her "womanhood" is stupid in understanding, but she was jolly here except she talked too much for me, but *you* ought to like that, it's *à la Russe.* Yes, that was a scene.[5] I can see Katherine, you three, emerging triumphantly, I am sure it did Katherine's soul good; she will have to fight a little again in Londra [*sic*], I know. Before long I shall come to London to have a look at the children, I want to see you then. Don't be too cross with Murry,[6] he has surprised me sometimes how venomous he is, quite beside the point, and *à propos de bottes*, but there it is, it is better so than sweet lies. And you can also be disagreeable enough if you choose. There, Lawrence is worrying that the letter must go.

With kind remembrance,
Frieda L.

TO S. S. Koteliansky

Dollie Radford, 32 Well Walk
Hampstead
20 September 1916

Dear Kot:

Don't be miserable about things. Nobody could or would believe such small things of you. I think we had no true

[4] Dr. Barbara Low, a Freudian pioneer in England, author of *Psycho-Analysis: A Brief Outline of the Freudian Theory* (1922), and a practising analyst.

[5] The "scene," re-created by Lawrence in *Women in Love*, is that in which Katherine Mansfield discovers a group of Lawrence's enemies ridiculing his book of poems *Amores* at the Café Royal and intervenes in his behalf.

[6] John Middleton Murry—"Jack" in the following letter.

proportion last night. We both felt so bitter. You see, Jack has a terribly jealous nature. He was jealous of Katherine, pretended like the sneak that he is to be your friend, and his hate worked underneath all the time. There is a very great cowardice in Jack, I still feel very bitter about them both. It is so ugly. But I also remember once when Katherine said last year, "Frieda, I am very fond of Kot, he is really good"; and I have said disagreeable things about you, no lies, but I was hurt because you did not like me. I don't want to see Katherine, and yet I feel that Lawrence is their only moral support; he wrote to Jack: "You, Jack, are a little phenomenon of meanness." Can't you tell Katherine, have it out with her? But I know she will not face anything. Yet there is so much that is good in them, must one not *fight* their dishonesty? I have had so many good hours with Katherine, for that I owe her to *make* her more honest with me. Her duplicity is not all, it's a small part in Katherine, but if I love her I will hate her lies all the more—I will tell her. Shall I see her again and tell her?

I shall see you tomorrow, anyhow I think *we* shall be friends now, and I am very glad.

Frieda

Please ask Campbell [7] to come Thursday night. I want to see him very much!

TO S. S. Koteliansky

Higher Tregerthen, Zennor
St. Ives, Cornwall
4 October 1916

Dear Kot:

It was so jolly seeing you in London. I thought we had only been friends for the first time, and I was very glad. Times are sad now and one can't live till the war stops, but you seemed to

---

[7] Gordon Campbell, son of the 1st Lord Glenlavy, a London barrister and, after the war, director of the Bank of Ireland. His wife Beatrice is referred to in other letters.

me not at all "dead" and I hope we shall have some jolly times yet in our lives all together. I know Lawrence thinks so too. Also I hope you and Katherine will be friends again, you see she really loves Murry and then also she plays other people against him. But in the end she sticks to Murry. She must become simple, as we all must learn to be. But I do love her, if she tells lies, she also knows more about truth than other people and don't let us see too much the *ugly* things. I was very happy with you and Gertler at Gustave's. You see everybody is Lawrence's friend and nobody seems to like *me* and I daresay it is my fault to a great extent. I can't express myself, when I speak I am a fool, but I want so much to have a good life with people. Were you cross with me at Dollie's? [8] You see I knew that Murry was jealous of you, that's why he told lies. I must stop, the postman comes in a minute, let us know what happens to you, I do hope it will be all right for you and Gertler. Lawrence has a cold, how I hate all this wet weather, it always makes him seedy. I am so tired of being here alone, but I think it was good for L. to be a hermit for a time.

> With affection,
> Frieda

TO S. S. Koteliansky

> Higher Tregerthen, Zennor
> St. Ives, Cornwall
> *15 October 1916*

Dear Kot:

As Katherine does not write to me, I believe you must have told Jack what I said. I am *glad* if you have. I should have had to have it out with them sometimes. It is time that Jack stopped the lies he tells about people to satisfy his own meanness. They are as mean as they can be to everybody, *then* they turn round and say: "Aren't people *vile?*" And Katherine never opposes Jack's vileness, but rather enjoys it. To me they have been so

---

[8] Mrs. Ernest (Dollie) Radford, a poet, often provided a refuge for the Lawrences, in particular when they were expelled from Cornwall in 1917 on suspicion of spying.

mean, especially Jack; wherever they have been, they have turned people against me, tried to regard me as a *quantité négligeable*. Well, from my point I am not going to put up with it a minute longer. Only I want to know about you and Jack, I suppose now they put all the blame of his meanness on to *me*, but you know how it is. I don't mind if you repeated every word to them I said. You know I love Katherine, but I blame her when she believes Jack, when she knows better herself. But enough. I always *knew* it all, and I am no angel myself, but they have done me infinitely more harm than ever I did to them, so let there be some kind of justice. L. *loved* Mark's picture. We are very happy in spite of *vile* weather.

We both send you kindest greetings.

F.

How are things going with you? Let us be happy or let us look forward to happiness. It will and must come. I feel since London as if I had got real friends in you and Gertler and it makes me very glad.

TO S. S. Koteliansky

Higher Tregerthen, Zennor
St. Ives, Cornwall
14 November 1916

Dear Kot:

How are you? I have a lovely book of Savonarola and he looks like you! I don't think he is as good looking as you, but he *is* like you! We have a little (*poco*) money so I shall not be happy till L. has got to Italy, we want to go to *Rome*. I am very glad, can't you come with us—it would cheer you up. But you are not to tell a soul. We want to slink out of England without a soul knowing. Please be so kind and find us an *old* Baedeker of Rome. I am surprising L. with it and don't tell him I'm writing, and tell me how much it is, *not* being Murry I will pay you. I still feel a deep *rancune* against that young man. She never wrote, well then not, *vogue la galère!* But I always feel them saying nasty things about us, it's horrid! I awfully want to read "Mendel",[9]

[9] A novel by Gilbert Cannan that Lawrence regarded as "journalism: statement, without creation."

be nice and let me read it if you have a copy! I will send it back quickly. I do not *know* Carrington.[1] I believe she is genuine, only the rotten people she sees must make her try to be *not* herself. It's been so foggy, so wet, Oh Lord! L's novel [2] is finished, it would just suit your bitter, cynical mood. It's by far his best!

Good-bye and don't mind that I bother you. Have you been to Gustave's again?

[Frieda]

TO S. S. Koteliansky

Higher Tregerthen, Zennor
St. Ives, Cornwall
Before 12 December 1916

Dear Kot:

It was nice of you to ask Shearman for those Italian books. L. will read them aloud to me. I never thanked you for your *nice* letter, but I was very glad to get it. I always knew we *ought* to be friends, and it grieved me that we were not, but now we are. Anyhow I hold that as a fact and a very pleasant one. I heard a day or two ago from Mrs. Carswell that there was a portrait of me in "Mendel". I suppose I am the murdered woman. We live and learn, I never recognized myself! Except some of L's speeches I recognized. I was sorry that Gilbert made me quite so horrid, so vulgar. But there. We are coming to London after the New Year. L. wants to. I am afraid it will be very depressing, even Cornwall feels the war at last. Poor Asquith, his speech today seemed to me the *oraison funèbre* "of the great old England". But I, being German, cannot help feeling that now at last a better spirit may blossom in Germany, it was time. What do you feel about Russia? Did you ever really believe in it? I thought not, you put your hope into England, and personally I have had a lot from England. But now it is sad. I just read *Peter*

---

[1] Dorothy Carrington, who had studied painting at the Slade with the Hon. Dorothy Brett, was the girl friend of Mark Gertler, who had furnished Cannan with the story used in *Mendel*.

[2] *Women in Love.*

Simple, it is so jolly and proud, then it hurts one that it all should be a thing of the past. God help us all. When we come to London we shall take a room for a week or two. Murry wrote to L. after a long time, but it's no good. I do wish L. and I could go to America, but I know L. can't, somehow he belongs to England till the war is over. He does not feel *free*. And I feel like bursting. But I am getting used to it. I want you to read L's new novel. It is so *good* and to my satisfaction I am a nicer person there than Gilbert made me. Gertler writes you are sad. I wish you would come and make me laugh. I do *so* want to be happy. But with the New Year we shall meet.

Yours ever,
Frieda

Forgive pencil!

TO Lady Cynthia Asquith

[*December 1916*]

Dear Lady Cynthia,

You really must be worn out with anxiety. You have had a special mountain [?] of personal misery in this war, don't you think it is enough? Really, I must say this and you mustn't think me "fresh"! What is the good of being the Prime Minister's son and you can't be any different than other people. Really I think, and it is *true*, it does *not* matter whether hundreds of dull young men die early instead of going into a dull old age, but the few that matter ought to be preserved. If you think Herbert Asquith is worth *not* being risked and if he thinks so himself, well then he ought not to go to those hellish trenches. I know there is all the old stuff of "duty" and so on, duty is a deeper and more individual thing. Please forgive this, but you have some advantages over other men's wives, do take them. I know it *seems* low, but it isn't. I can *feel* you being so worried, and now really peace ought to come soon. When I think how women in the past, Catherine of Siena, put popes and kings in their places, then it grieves me deeply that there is no power on earth to stop this war. I personally want peace and I am quite disinterested, one way or the other, or equally *interested;* sometimes I think I simply *must* do something, go to Germany and see what peace terms they would give. I suppose nothing can be done or is being done? We *all* want peace, why don't we get it then? Catherine of Siena looks, in my picture, like you! But there is no room in these days for *big* people, you must be nicely average and mechanical. "The Thimble"[3] has appeared in America in a paper called "Seven Arts", but they didn't send us a copy! Thank you so much for the hat, but I think it would astonish the natives too much. The woman in her little shop has to walk round her little counter and look at my stockings as it is! I might only wear it out of sheer joy by myself! We are very happy here. I saw the children at the beastly lawyer's office. They were *so* natural and really just the same. It left me with every hope. The boy[4] is quite beautiful, suddenly a youth, nearly six foot already. They *were* nice, I thought. Otherwise I feel the world does *not* love L. and me very much. And I *do* think they treat L. shabbily. Men of guts and originality are not so plentiful that they need treat him as they have done. Will it be the same with Herbert Asquith? It would be so jolly to have a long talk with you!

Yours ever,
Frieda Lawrence

to S. S. Koteliansky

Higher Tregerthen, Zennor
St. Ives, Cornwall
6 February 1917

Dear Kot:

We also thought of you hard about Christmas time and sang (Ranani Tzadikim) Ranani Tza die kim, but it hadn't the proper

[3] The reference to "The Thimble" dates this remarkable letter in December, 1916. That story was later developed into one of Lawrence's most poignant, complex, and symbolically expressive longer stories, "The Ladybird," which, in a sense, imaginatively and emotionally gathers together his experience of Lady Asquith's and her husband's sufferings during the war.

[4] The letter is made more understandable by the reference to her son Monty, now coming into manhood and thereby, to her, also threatened.

flavour without you. What will you think of the novel? There are lots of bits in it—Café Royal, Katherine Amores scene, Heseltine, just a bit of a party where Campbell was in Paris at Ann Estelle Rice! Campbell will tell you about L's quarrel with the Ott. She played Salome to L's John the Baptist!! I *hate* L. in that role, she is a fool. But we are off, dear Kot, *soon* off. Yes, one would like to see things finished in this Europe, but I have a terrible feeling that then the real horror will begin. Poor Russia. I still think Germany *might* become less stupid, they have evidently *learned* from their misery, but England *will not* learn. It is so cold and windy outside but our little cottage doubly cosy, with furze burning, then we read Italian. When you send *Women in Love* to Russia, say it may be first published in Russia, because L. thinks it *won't* find a publisher and L. does not care at present. Also he has *lots* of fine new stories, enough to make a book; but I think Pinker [5] is afraid and also he may think it is better to wait. At present *nothing* will be read. I think Russia would appreciate Lawrence. Our Rananim *is* coming off! What is Gertler doing? I am *so* nice in L's new novel, anyhow I *think* so, Gilbert Cannan etsch!! I am so eager for *jolly* things to happen! The nice young cows are just going by, they are so attractive, and I must say, in watching the animals, they are *not* brutes *but* gentle. The young bull always goes with the cows when they are milked, evidently much distressed that he is out of it. It makes me *quite sick* that nobody in this country will do *anything* for L., they *won't* publish this novel, you will see. One day they will come, the wretches, but then I will kick them downstairs.

Monday

Dear Kot:

I got so far. Is Campbell very cross with Lawrence? I think a genius' greatest gift seems to be to make other people cross. I hope *you* are not cross with him? Will America declare war? If we go to America I shall be in London on the 24th; I may see the children for a *whole* day—perhaps more. L. is not coming. I wanted to ask the Campbells to put me up but if he is cross I had better not. I shall see you, I hope. Will ask Dollie to have

[5] James Brand Pinker was Lawrence's agent in London from 1914 to 1921.

me. It is *so* worrying, we felt *so* hopeful about America. I wish you could see the children for a minute or two, I want you to see them. *Don't* write anything about them or this plan; Lawrence feels much better about it but still he is sore and the less said the better, but it will all come as right as lies in us all concerned. L. will write to you.

Yours ever,
Frieda

TO S. S. Koteliansky

Higher Tregerthen, Zennor
St. Ives, Cornwall
June 1917

Dear Kot:

Indeed you are no longer dead! I can imagine how good it must be for you when you had *almost* given up hope to find what you strove for from your boyhood in your Russian village has come. It is marvellous for everybody, this new Russia that is a *fact* now and not only a dream. *What* may not happen if that has come to pass. I roared at you and the General. I'm sure he was much more frightened of *you* than you of him. I wish we could go to Russia. I was wondering if the "Peace articles" would have any chance of getting the *Nobel* prize? I think they are lovely, the articles, but perhaps you are not much in sympathy with that kind of thing just at present. Campbell is a fool and a *cheap* fool. *Surely* he was not like that 3 years ago. Lawrence has been seedy but is better. It's a heavenly spring, the coocoo "goes" it at this very minute and I am happy all day long. Tell Gertler not to hop about at Lady so and so's too much, they take the guts out of him.

Much love from us both,
Frieda

P.S. I didn't like Gorki's thing much in the *English Review*, he is such "old" literature, not a new opening out anywhere, but perhaps on his paper there will be some young blood.

TO S. S. Koteliansky

Higher Tregerthen, Zennor
St. Ives, Cornwall
[*September 11, 1917*]

Dear Kot:

We always seem to rub each other the wrong way. You are cross at my letters and I am cross with you. Now I am coming to London next Saturday, staying at Dollie's. I can ring you up there. Shall we try and be *nice* with each other for once? I *know* you have quite a wrong idea of me and I daresay it's my fault—and I don't really know you. All right, we will try and see if we can't get on better. I should think we are both terribly obstinate. I shall see the children for half an hour at the dirty lawyer's office; I am very glad. It's been the loveliest day, we went up on the moors, all covered with heather (do you have heather in Russia?), in the autumn mist the world was a real *zauberland* and L. and I were so happy! I should like to see Gertler. Is Campbell in Ireland? But I don't want to see Hutchinsons and God save me from W. L. George. As to our uncrowned princess of Judäa [*sic*], let us bury this bone. And we will *not* have very serious talks; shall we go to the Zoo and look at the animals, instead of the Café Royal? The animals are nice. How difficult it is to live, and one has just a simple idea of life, it might be so easy and everything is so difficult.

With kindest regards,
Frieda

TO S. S. Koteliansky

Chapel Farm Cottage
nr. Newbury, Berks.
Tuesday
12 February 1918

Dear Kot:

Dollie wants this cottage in about a fortnight, I understood we could have it till the end of March. Do you know *anybody* who has a cottage empty? The Wolves [*sic*] have one but do they use it? There's no money, no house, nothing, but I don't really care except when L. is seedy. Does Gertler know of any cottage? We have been very happy here. L. had a letter from your friend *Lewis*, he is patched again, it seems. I will let you know what happens to us. My love to the Farbmans. It is quite a struggle now to exist—getting food and everything. Bertie got what he wished, I think. I just see that there is peace between Germany and Russia more or less. Thank God, may it be a beginning of the end.

Will the Farbmans go back? Will you go to Russia? How lovely it will all be if Europe is free again.

Yours,
Frieda

TO S. S. Koteliansky

Hermitage
nr. Newbury, Berks.
19 February 1918

Dear Kot:

L. says I am not to say anything about your offer of money, but I do think you are a faithful friend. You know L. would ask you if it were *absolutely* necessary, but Amy [6] said she was sending a cheque. I only get a bit frightened sometimes when L. is seedy. He is getting better, but it's been a *horrid* week. About the cottage, L. will write himself, it is paid till *May*, so they mustn't pay anyhow. I would like them to have it, as they are nice. How are the Farbmans and your last hope in life, Fox? I read the paper and *watch*, some lovely things are happening, I think. What does Campbell say? Arabella [7] may be coming to

[6] Amy Lowell, whose acquaintance dated from the Imagist anthology days, was generous to the Lawrences during these difficult times, but she feared the consequences for him, and the difficulty for herself, of his hope to be asked, through her influence, to give lectures in America on American literature. These lectures eventually became the essays of *Studies in Classic American Literature*.

[7] Dorothy (Arabella) Yorke was an American friend of the Lawrences and of Richard Aldington.

stay. Poor Princess of Judäa [*sic*] was nearly frozen to death down here, but she was nice, we made her a lovely hat.

Write sometimes. I do want to feel we have friends.

L. will write.

Yours with love,
Frieda

TO Lady Cynthia Asquith

Chapel Farm Cottage
Hermitage
nr. Newbury, Berks.
[*Early 1919?*]

I shall go to Germany soon now I hope, it feels already holidayish, in spite of everything, but alas they sound very poor, very hungry. I think there will be *no* money, but anyhow the world feels freer, or will be soon. Lawrence is miserable, will go to America, where I shall join him later. I am always grateful to you, when I know how horrid so many people have been to anything Hunnish, that you were so broadminded. Is Michael well? Will he have a brother or a sister? I hope they will have better times when they grow up, than the horrible stagnant pools we are having. Still I feel like setting out for new adventures.

With very best thoughts of you,

Frieda L.

TO S. S. Koteliansky

% Mrs. Clarke
Grosvenor Rd.
Ripley, Derbyshire
Monday
February 1919

My dear Kot:

He is really better. I hear that Mrs. Farbman and Ghita have been ill too, I am sorry. The doctor is still afraid of after effects, but anyhow we are *so* far out of the wood. We have £16 from Cornish furniture, some *English Review* money and a story in the *Strand*, £15—so we are all right, you *know* I would take your money. It's been pitiful to see him try so hard to *live*, if he *hadn't*, it would have been all over. I feel so bitter, so bitter against the world, if they had only given him *some* response, he would be happy!

I feel two hundred years old—haven't slept at all. If you hear of *anything* nice in the world tell him. I am worried about my sister in München too. Will you also send some good chocolates, he is so thin, the doctor says, and must have plenty of sugar. The world is so awful now, won't it almost revive you out of spite?

Yours ever,
Frieda

Your bottles will come tomorrow, I suppose.

> *Cecily Lambert and her cousin, Violet Monk, managed Grimsbury Farm near Hermitage, Berks, the scene of Lawrence's* The Fox.

TO Miss C. Lambert

[Postcard]
Picinisco, Prov. di Caserta, Italy
17 December 1919

We are in the wilds here I tell you, men like brigands, fine women in bright peasant get-ups, and the most heavenly sun and clear mountain air. I hope you are getting well through the winter and have a merry Xmas.

My love to you both,
Frieda Lawrence

I was happy in Germany

TO Miss Violet Monk

[Postcard]
Capri, Napoli
[*January 1, 1920?*]

Dear Miss Monk:

Let us know what kind of a Xmas you had. I have still got a shabby Italian Xmas tree in the room. We had a high time on

New Year's Eve, there's a big famous cafe near us where all the world goes, Italians, Russians, Americans, short-haired women, long-haired men, rich, poor, and then the local people came with a band and danced the Tarantella. We found Mrs. Cannan here, you remember us speaking of her, Mrs. Barry [*sic*] that was.

> Good luck to you in the New Year,
> Frieda Lawrence

TO Miss C. Lambert

> [Postcard]
> Palazzo Ferraro, Capri, Naples
> *1 March 1920*

But I did send you a card from Germany. We were glad to hear your news, it's nice to be here. All kinds of people, Compton Mackenzie, have you read his book "Poor Relations?" We often say how it would interest you to have seen all we have seen. We can *bathe* in the sea actually when it's fine. I was very happy to see my people, especially my mother, but it's sad there I can tell you. I got quite *thin*. My love to you both.

> Frieda L.

FROM her daughter Barbara

> *Tuesday*

My dear Mother,[8]

Thank you for your letters which came one on top of the other. I had a terrible fear that perhaps my letter would reach you too

[8] At the top of this letter Frieda had written: "*Behalt den Brief.*" It was probably written in 1920, when Barbara was fifteen and the Lawrences were in Sicily. In her memoirs of her mother, "I Look Back," published in *Twentieth Century*, March 1959, Barbara Barr wrote: " . . . we saw our mother next as a kind of apparition on the day when, creeping by the back way into our London house, she entered the nursery and found us at supper with Granny and Aunt Maude. She put her foot in it that evening; the law was invoked to restrain her. And while she stood at bay before our relations, we children gazed in horror at the strange woman she had then become. The stuffy old show: yes, indeed."

late. I mean that you would have plucked us from your heart and buried us forever!

Please don't worry about my health. I am very healthy and getting quite fat—not a bit aneamic, I mean anaemic or aenemic. Papa is spending Easter in Switzerland with Elsa. She has her hair up, he says, and is a bit more solid. She and Yvonne Edwards (her great friend at St. Paul's) are out there together. They went last August. They, and several Dutch girls, live with four ladies and attend the classes at the college place. Elsa adores the Dutch girls and is going to stay with one in Holland for a fortnight on her way home, in July. I have written to Monty and her and told them I wrote to you and have sent Elsa your address. Monty has gone back to Oxford. He plays for his college rugger team and gets on very well. Elsa gets into no end of scraps with the Dandirans (the four Mesdemoiselles), who are very proper, but she is very happy.

I am, too, and love Aunty Lucy. She never runs you down. She says she will always remember how sweet you were to her after her father's death.

Do you remember Jackie Bennett? I wonder if his hair is as curly as ever.

Your description of Sicily sounds *bliss*, but the country round here is angelic, too.

Yes, the primroses are out. The woods round here are full of them. I gathered a bunch of them one day and then I remembered that bunch you gave me which I smelt when we were watching "Figaro." The catkins are dears, too.

I try to paint the flowers but they are too pretty and I am never satisfied with my paintings of them.

This afternoon Uncle Ted and I bicycled to Bulmer to see the great point-to-point horseraces. The course was 4 miles, partly ploughed fields and the poor horses looked nearly dead when they came in. There were lots of hedges and ditches to jump and several men were thrown.

Mr. DeVere Stacpoole was there collecting material for his new book. He is very funny but quite amiable. He had been "backing" indiscriminately.

I am going to be confirmed in May.

I am sorry Monty wrote you a nasty letter, but it wasn't from his inside. He is nasty, though. I expect he'll swear at me for writing to you but I don't care.

People round here, some of them, are very nice. So jolly and natural and sporty. Some are awful, though. There is a dear boy just near called Tommy Miller, who takes me for rides on the back of his motorbike, much to the horror of Great Mapleshead. Aunt Lucy lets me, however. She isn't *half* so prim as I used to think her, in fact, sometimes she strikes me as being positively disreputable!

I decorated the screen in church, for Easter, with cherry-blossom. It looked ever so pretty and everyone liked it.

Papa hasn't decided an art school for me yet, but perhaps it will be the Slade. I can draw all right, but as yet I haven't much idea of colour. The other day I saw two dear dirty little girls sitting on a wall, blowing bubbles, with a bowl in between them. When I got home I tried to make a picture of it but couldn't and got very angry.

The trees are coming out everywhere and the fruit blossom is lovely. But the farmers say things are too early. They are, frightfully early. That is because of the hot weather all through February. Yes, 49 Howard Road is still going strong. Aunt Daisy has given up her shop and come home. She is *rather* thinking of marrying! She was engaged about a year ago to one Pat Maccintaggart who, as his name suggests, is a beastly Irishman. Well, they decided to break if off and stay just friends. However, lately he keeps on going to Chiswick and they all say she'll cop him in the end. He has lost a foot in the war and is a rolling stone so I suppose she'll have to keep him, I don't know what on.

Aunty Kit and Uncle Lummy are very happy, and quite well off now. Uncle Lummy has gone back to the merchant service.

The garden here is ever so big and chock full of daffodils. The snowdrops and violets are over now, though. At the bottom of the lawn one looks down the valley (we are on a hill) into cottages nestling among the trees and then the ground rises into another hill. The view isn't appalling, but serene and happy.

All the village people love Uncle Ted. They say he has *such* a nice round face, they could almost kiss it! They don't say it to him, of course!

Good night,
Barby

P.S. Don't go too near Etna, for Heaven's sake.
P.S.S. I am not dirty nowadays.

> *Much happened to affect Frieda's relationship with Lawrence between the postwar year 1919 and the resumption of her correspondence here in 1923. Lawrence had made various attempts to leave England during the war. There had been severe illnesses, bitterness, and revulsion related to the wartime suspicion they had been subject to. At last, in November, 1919, they had left for Italy. In February, 1922, they began the long voyage, East to Ceylon briefly and then to Australia, that was to culminate in the attempt to establish Lawrence's long dreamed of community in the New World. On their arrival in New Mexico in 1922, they first stayed at the home of the distinguished American poet Witter (Hal) Bynner in Santa Fe. Mabel Luhan had interested Lawrence in the religion and way of life of the Indians at Taos, but serious difficulties developed with Mrs. Luhan and her circle; these involved, in part, Lawrence's friendship with the Danish painters Knud Merrild and Arnold Götzsche, whom he undoubtedly had considered, hopefully, as the nucleus of his community. In March, 1923, the Lawrences went to Mexico, where they were joined by Bynner and Willard ("Spud" or "the Spoodle") Johnson. Bynner disagreed with Lawrence's ideas of leadership, as they were now being developed in* The Plumed Serpent, *and began to champion Frieda against Lawrence, particularly in view of Lawrence's periodic outbursts of violent anger. Bynner be-*

came Frieda's lifelong friend and correspondent. The
letter to him that follows signals a serious separation
from Lawrence. Several old friends, John Middleton
Murry in particular, had been urging Lawrence to return to England to collaborate in The Adelphi, but Lawrence went on to California and thence back to Mexico
with Götzsche. Frieda, however, returned to England
from New York. The letters to S. S. Koteliansky which
follow this letter to Bynner reflect more clearly than any
other extant material the nature of her quarrel with
Lawrence.

TO Witter Bynner

> c/o Mary Cannan
> 42 Queen's Gardens
> Hyde Park
> (I have her flat.)
> *Sunday 1923*
> [R.M.S.P. "ORBITA"]

Dear Hal Bynner,

Here I am on the boat, "all by mineself" on such a dull boat.
Chapala seems a dream, an impossible dream. I was not happy in
New York or New Jersey. It may have partly been the Seltzers; [9]
they are very nice, but I don't know what it was, I felt such a
poor little night light, hateful.

I met a few, very few, people. The nice ones all knew you, but
everybody seems so tired. I am sure all those layers of people put
away in their apartments on top of each other like boxes of gloves
or hankies make the air dead. It makes me feel drugged. Lawrence you *knew* wouldn't like it.

I loved some of your poems, but the plays were *too* black. I
hope you don't feel like that any more.

I don't think Europe will be gay. It may not be possible to go
to Germany at all. I do hope my journey won't be useless,

[9] Thomas Seltzer was Lawrence's principal American publisher from 1920
to 1925.

especially as far as my children go. Lawrence wouldn't come, he is going to wander. Where we meet again, I don't know. If Europe is possible, he will come. I will also let you know how it is, that you don't go just to be miserable.

There was one interesting evening with a few people. Macy [?] very nice, but again "from the head". I wish you were with me in Europe. It's lovely weather and a lovely sea, but I can't feel it because of the feel of these boats.

How was your journey, and how did you stand it, and are you really well? I was very sad to part with you and especially you not well. I was very happy with you and the Spoodle; I hope we shall have good times together again, we will have that monastery, when we find the place; but in the few people we met I thought there was genuineness and a kind of readiness to live, if they found it worth while.

Let me know all your news. Did Spud get a letter from me? I was amused at his shots of sentences to Lawrence. How is Santa Fe? It's a thousand million times better than the East.

It's just about the time when you mixed us a cocktail! Can you get me that blue necklace? I should love it. Lord, I am not at all gay on this beastly boat.

A Bernardine knew you, and a Lovatt, and a Benet (is that the name?). You forgot to give us Mrs. Simeon Ford's address.

How is Mabel?

With my best wishes and love,

Frieda

TO S. S. Koteliansky

110 Heath Street
Hampstead
Wednesday, 1923

Dear Adelphis:

Why did Lawrence write that article? Because I told him he was the golden calf round which he danced and wanted me to dance too. And I was sick of it. And so are you all, all golden calves or even "tin ones" round which you dance. If you were *really* religious men, if the Lord were above you and you weren't little gods yourselves, you would also know that man was meant to have a woman; I am supposed to be impressed by your chastities: I am not, it's male conceit. How little you must understand of Lawrence's books, Kot, when you can say that I am the "Porter" in the firm! Why, my faith has been the heart of it! And as far as being a man, I know to my sorrow, that I am six times the "man" that any of you are! Now call me all the names you like, I don't care! And detest me, but if you were "real" men, instead of tin gods, I wouldn't have to say these things! And I think you all treat that generous Brett[1] *vilely!* Especially Jack! And you make me feel a sneak when I come to the "Adelphi", nobody can have an open and free relationship with you. You make me feel as if I wanted to rob the safe or play the temptation of St. Antony. No, there is no fun in temptation, one can't play the game for two! Why can't you simply treat me as a human being?

Now you have made me telegraph to Lawrence and I am not at all sure that he thinks I feel lovey-dovey; I don't; I am cross in my heart with all so-called "men!"

Frieda

TO S. S. Koteliansky

110 Heath Street
Hampstead
Tuesday
4 December 1923

Dear Kot:

You said it, when you told the fact that you didn't like the law and order in yourself *disordered*. And that's just what I like to do: upset people's applecarts! They get such a surprise about themselves. And then they can make a new order! *Sons and*

---

[1] The Hon. Dorothy Brett, daughter of Viscount Esher, who had chosen to become an artist, and who alone of Lawrence's friends came to America with him in 1924. Her fierce loyalty to Lawrence brought her into frequent conflict with Frieda. Her side of the story is told, in part, in *Lawrence and Brett, A Friendship* (1933).

Lovers is *not* so great a book! I had more to do with that, than any of his others; but you don't want to accept the struggle and chaos of *Women in Love*, it's so upsetting!! And when I "boast" about myself, I know that my religion is that I want people to *love*, genuine and whole and paradisically—*not* like Christ but including everything! And I know I can love. When you say Lawrence has loved me I have loved him a thousand times more! And to really love includes everything, intelligence and faith and sacrifice—and passion! People don't think as I do, they have such other gods, but for all that I stick to my own to the bitter end! If the day came, which God forbid, that I should see Lawrence as the "great man", he would be a dead thing to me and it would bore me. Greatness is a thing of the outer world, where I indeed am nothing and don't want to be any more! So I grant you that in the world of men Lawrence *is* and I am *not!* But *that* world is nothing to me, there's a deeper one, where life itself flows, there I am at home! And the *outer* world isn't my affair! All I really want you to admit is the greater importance of the deeper world! Well, Kot, we will have a solemn feast one day! It's no longer: "I have found thee, oh mine enemy!" but, "I have found a friend."

Frieda

Another letter from L. *Why* can't he say he will be glad to see me? Always a misery and pain! It makes me *sick!*

> *Lawrence rejoined Frieda in England in December, 1923, and returned to America with her and Dorothy Brett in March, 1924. His visit might be described as savagely brief. The articles he sent to Middleton Murry for* The Adelphi, *his letters to Murry, and such stories of this time as* "The Last Laugh," *"Jimmy and the Desperate Woman," and "The Border Line," all have as their target what he understood to be Murry's philosophy, and, by implication, the threat of the strong attraction between Murry and Frieda. Frieda's next letter may date from the immediate return to New Mexico and the ranch Mabel Luhan had given Frieda; how-*

ever, the concern for Lawrence's health also suggests the period just after the Mexican sojourn, from October, 1924, to March, 1925, when he had fallen seriously ill after finishing The Plumed Serpent.

TO Witter Bynner

> Kiowa
> Del Monte
> Taos
> [*Undated*]

Dear Hal Bynner,

Quite out of the blue your little parcel was handed me and when I saw the new cigarette box, I thought you had sent me some specially good ones, but no—inside was the lovely jade. I am making myself a green linen dress for it, so many thanks. I like the thin animal on top.

I hope your play will be a success, and do come up some time in the middle of June or after. We have got 9 chickens, an irrigation ditch that looks like a brook; tomorrow comes a black cow. Lawrence is much better. It's *raining!* We have also 4 grown up Indians and 2 little ones. *Embarras de richesse!!*

I am enclosing a letter to Mrs. Hughes.

> Yours gleefully with my jade,
> Frieda

TO S. S. Koteliansky

> Villa Bernarda
> Spotorno, Riviera
> Ponente, Italy
> *Monday, March 1926*

Dear Kot:

This is the village paper! Your book on Dostoevsky came today. Lawrence is in Ravello, I have Elsa and Barby [2] here, they are loving it and the Italian youths hang round like bees! And I feel like the proud old hen! No, if we try to be friends don't let's

[2] Her daughters.

be "Christian" ones! I don't like Christ, hanging there on his beastly cross for 2,000 years to frighten one! Calling *that* love, letting people kill you! Had he said to me: "Woman, what have I got to do with thee," I would have boxed his ears and said: "That's what you have to do with me!" And letting his feet be wiped with hair, disgusting! So that much for Christ from me!! No, I suppose I am a savage!! And that I understand. Lawrence wrote such a good play on David and Samuel and Saul! I am translating it quite well into German! Lawrence was so pleased that you like the Quetzalcoatl hymns! It's his best book [3] but more will come out of him! If only his health were not so worrying! Greet all your housemates! I don't think Lawrence is *fit* to go to Russia, he learnt quite a lot and sat in the evening making Russian noises. The spring is here pink and white!

> Yours sincerely,
> Frieda

TO S. S. Koteliansky

> 25 Rossetti Garden Mansions
> Chelsea, S.W.3.
> *Monday* [postmark *9 August 1926*]

Dear Kot:

Thank you for your note. Lawrence went this morning, much better in health. We only came back yesterday from the country, on the stairs we met Monty, and he stayed till 6 o'clock. It was as if something had broken through in him and there was all friendliness and love—all round. So I can't come tonight as I had promised Monty to go to his bachelor place. Of course this is what I have always longed for, and feel "Lord, let thy servant depart in peace!!" But not too soon! I am sorry I can't come tonight but write me some other time when you are free. I hope Mrs. Farbman is getting well! My mother saw the doctor at Baden and he was reassuring about Lawrence.

> Yours ever,
> Frieda

[3] *The Plumed Serpent*, published that January.

The following letter to her son Montague Weekley and other letters of this time signal Frieda's reconciliation with her family and show Lawrence's sometimes sympathetic, sometimes exasperated, participation in this reconciliation. The sojourn at Villa Mirenda, near Florence, from 1926 to 1929 was immensely productive. It reached a climax in the publication of Lady Chatterley's Lover *in 1928.*

TO her son Monty

> *Sunday*
> Villa Mirenda
> Scandicci

Dear Monty,

It was nice to get your letter, and I'm so glad you are feeling better. From my window I can see a procession of lights going along, some Saint's day or other. Lawrence goes into the woods to write, he is writing a short long story, always breaking new ground, the curious class feeling this time or rather the soul against the body; no, I don't explain it well. [Ooray!!! Eureka. D. H. L.] What are you doing? We are just getting such a jolly room ready, white, and lovely stuffs you get in Florence and the sun shines in all day, [(some days) D. H. L.] warm as toast! Oh dear and you are sitting over horrid gasfires and dark England. [Poverino!! D. H. L.] But next spring we'll take a place in England and you must come for weekends and we'll have a connected life. Lawrence wants it too, wants to see something of the younger generation. I hope Elsa really has done the right thing and won't be bored with her Teddy. Don't be too spartan, but keep a steady core in yourself; but you'll get bored with my preaching. The Huxleys came, very nice he but such a weed. "*Weh Dir, dass Du ein Enkel bist*," Lawrence said; and she was one of Lady Ottoline's protégées and never got over it. Lawrence says he'll say a word; *do* come at Christmas if you can!

> Your mother

Dear Monty

Your Ma is wonderful at giving advice, and even more wonderful at taking it! In which latter, I think you're like her.

I haven't heard any more from those Stage Society people, so don't know if we shall come to London in December, for the play. I emphatically don't want to, but "England expects" etc.—What about your coming here with Mistress Barby at Christmas time? If we're here, it might be fun. Your Ma is pining for somebody to think the house is grand: she gets no satisfaction out of me, that way. Anyhow it's Sunday evening, we sit in the kitchen with the lamp on the table, your Mother eats a persimmon with a spoon and offers me "the other one"—while I write. So much for grandeur.—I have painted windowframes by the mile, doors by the acre, painted a chest of drawers till it turned into a bureau, and am not through, by a long chalk. This is living heroically *à la* Frieda. Mussolini says *Vivi pericolosamente!* and then makes millions of laws against anybody who takes a pot shot at him. *Siamo cosi.* Hope you're well!

D. H. L.

TO Witter Bynner

Villa Mirenda
Sunday, 22 April

Dear Hal,

We read "Cake" [4] and it was amusing! I see you have the same notion. When Mabel wrote: "In a book where I come in, it mentions that I have had 9 lovers," I wrote back: "Don't worry, my dear, alas, alas not one, not one." She has made a myth and a golden calf of herself, and is so strong that dancing round that golden calf she can persuade others to do so as well. But I like *much* about her and you ought to try her from a new angle—try again and don't be taken in and you'll like her.

Lawr. is not well enough yet to risk the journey. Why aren't you a real nice Hal and come and see us here? Bring us some of your hospitable, generous spirit, and a breath of New Mexico, it would do us both good in our souls. We have had a thin time, L. the worst, but it was no joke trying to keep his body and soul together. You might enjoy Europe for a little while. You know that I always think of you as a real friend.

Frieda

[4] *Cake, An Indulgence*, a satirical verse play (Knopf, 1926).

I didn't tell Lawr. I wrote this letter, but I know he would like to see you.

TO Witter Bynner

Ludwig Wilhelmstift
Baden-Baden
[*Undated*]

Dear Hal,

Your letter to L. came just as I was reading the "Bullfight" of *The Plumed Serpent* in French, a sample translation. It took me back so vividly; you are right, the end is muffled, the religious part isn't religious, but desiccated swelled head.

I am glad you think of us (I include myself) with fondness. Some of L's horridness to you was the green-eyed monster and sickness; he is very frail, but much less nervy and cantankerous! Indeed I'm scared of the "heavenly Twins" Brett and Mabel in Taos. If I come, it will be to ignore them, to have done with them. Brett's last letter to L. that I was responsible for his sickness! So *vile*, but I suppose mosquitoes must bite and bitches bark! Mabel is I, I, I, spreading herself on the face of the earth in houses and self. But you exaggerate her importance. The real living place, where a woman can help to make new things live and flourish, does not know her, there she doesn't exist. And one does so *long* for a little delicate warmth and good will and understanding, I am just unspeakably sick of this eternal spite and assertion and intellectual bunk. We have been in Switzerland, L. is better, but *always* it's scaring, his health.

How I would love to stay in your house, and get the breakfast; and you have made it bigger. I always wear a white chain you gave me, and the other day it fell down [the] W.C. in Diablerets. But after being sad over it, I got it back. Wasn't that a good omen!

So all good things to you.

Frieda

TO Witter Bynner

Villa Mirenda
Scandicci
Firenze
Easter Monday

Dear Hal Bynner,

It was nice to get your note in Baden-Baden. You know I had never noticed that woman treating me "atrociously"! But it pleased me that the *Nation* stood up for me! You know it hurt me when you called me the "housekeeper" in that poem, but, alas, you were right; but I am not by nature the "housekeeper", and *nous avons changé tout celà!*

I did *not* like the Brett's photograph, she is a fish anyhow! Christine was in Rome. Lawrence saw her! Why do you never come? You know there is a cousinship between us!!

It's the most adorable Tuscan spring, and something in me just insists in being blissfully happy! My daughter Barbara is here. I wish I could make her as happy as myself, but then she is so young!

Lawrence paints and has written a novel! Is it the *David* you would like? Lend us yours!

Somebody said you drank too much this winter, I hope it isn't true, or only a passing thing! It would be sad! We'll come to Santa Fe some day again! But you pay us a visit! and we would wander a bit once more!

Friendliest remembrance

from Frieda

Mrs. Juliette Huxley was the wife of Julian Huxley, biologist and scientific humanist, the brother of Aldous Huxley. She helped type the final version of Lady Chatterley's Lover, *the novel mentioned here. Lawrence's paintings, which explore the theme of the novel, were shortly to cause him further difficulties when their showing in London was closed by the police.*

TO Mrs. Juliette Huxley

> Villa Mirenda
> Scandicci
> Italy
> *Wednesday, 1928*

Dear Juliette:

Only today Lawr. gave me your letter out of an old pocket. We often talk of you and it made me so terribly sad that you didn't seem happier, but now you will be more so; but England is such a difficult place to be happy in anyhow. Lorenzo is really better, but we will hop off to Switzerland and he will get much, much stronger. Yes, you must look at his pictures, you won't be so shocked after the novel. I feel that novel might really do some good in the world. There should be some glamour again in the relationship between men and women. We have grown so pettifogging. Is your mother with you still? She is real anyhow. I had a few beautiful days with my sister and Barby in Alassio. Do ask the children to come and see you: Miss Elsa Weekley, 49 Harvard Rd., Chiswick—I forget the telephone number. I send you this phoenix, it will rejoice your embroidering heart and I wish I had seen Adam and Eve. What a good time Diablerets gave us! and that Lawr. is better. I am not a letter writer, so don't please think I am horrid not to have written; like that parrot who was supposed to talk and didn't, "I think all the more".

> With much love,
> also to your mother,
> Julian and the children,
> Frieda

TO Rhys Davies [5]

Dear Rhys Davies,

Do you see Lorenzo in his new dressing-gown? looking not only like one prophet but all the prophets of all climes and ages

[5] The Welsh novelist and short-story writer, who had visited the Lawrences shortly before this. This letter was written on the back of one from Lawrence dated Christmas Day 1928, and was illustrated.

rolled into one—those are his pansies with him. On the top is the
sun shining on you and on all your un-born books, this is the
brook underneath where we made the daisies float. The flowers,
they are *not* Welsh, are to enliven your path. I wanted to do some
butterflies but they went wrong—now you know all about it. My
daughter Barbara is coming so I *don't* think we shall come to
Nice, as she will be here Wednesday or Thursday. I hope you
will have a very nice trip into the hills. Lorenzo will tell you all
the other news. I shall love having Barby here and then I suppose
it will be Spain. Having to speak Spanish again—the spirit is
willing but the flesh is weak.

All good wishes,
Frieda Lawrence

*One hundred and three letters to Mabel Luhan from
1926 to 1954, and seventy-three to Dorothy Brett from
1931 to 1954, are in the Yale University Collection of
American Literature. Under the terms of purchase, they
may not be microfilmed, and there were restrictions on
what might be quoted. The excerpts from these and
other letters to Mrs. Luhan, and the remarks about her
and Dorothy Brett in letters to others, further reveal the
bitterness of the quarrel centered on Lawrence and also
the efforts made to maintain the friendships. Mrs. Luhan was instrumental in getting the Lawrences to come
to New Mexico in 1922, and Brett, alone among their
English friends, loyally followed him in 1924.*

TO Mabel Luhan

Paris, Hotel de Versailles
5 April 1929

. . . You seem to think I hang on to Lawrence like grim death;
it's the other way about. He hates to be without me nowadays,
even for hours. Much too much for my taste is he dependent on
me, and the Brett's fixed idea that Lawrence doesn't care for me
is so queer. I don't understand it, except I was sorry for the

Brett, was very decent to her, and then she does detest one for it. Poor thing. Isn't it jolly for me? Ada, L's sister, and I are friends; she detested me too. . . . I am so glad my enemies are friends!

TO Witter Bynner

Hotel Beau Rivage
Bandol, Var, France
10 November 1929

Dear Hal,

Well, it's sad to know you aren't really fit, but we were glad of your letter.

Lawrence is much better here by the sea in a comfortable hotel. We need comfort too, what with the great fuss of Lady C; it would take several days to tell you, and some "pansies" [6] Lawrence has written; pansies indeed, they are very revolutionary, and trouble again!! What with his health and all this, it's a fierce life. Still we live quietly enough, day by day.

This is a sun to shine on you, and flowers on your path, and this is a firebird but it's rather like a wild chicken, and that's a moon in one of your poems! with the Santa Fe house. [Over her drawing of the moon: "I am not quite dotty!"]

Our Taos turtle doves are in New York—Mabel being "psyched" as Spud calls it—Gurdjieffing, Leo Stein, Orage—a boredom, infinite and worse! They must be proud of the result with Andrew and Ida! [7] Spud [8] is pining to get into his own house. A young man came to see us from California; his name, Brewster Ghiselin. [9]

I hear that Mabel thinks she is the heroine in *The Plumed Serpent!!* But, the Owen is not *all* of you, Hal, and also there's something else that isn't you.

[6] *Lady Chatterley's Lover* (1928) and the book of poems *Pansies* (1929).
[7] Andrew Dasburg, the painter, lived in Taos; his wife was the former Ida Rauh Eastman.
[8] Spud (or "the Spoodle") was Willard Johnson, writer, journalist, editor of an amusing and iconoclastic periodical, later a column, *The Laughing Horse*, who had known the Lawrences since 1922.
[9] American poet, now teaching at the University of Utah.

I am flourishing, better looking in my old age, I think, except my hair is no longer an unmixed colour. I shall have to dye it. Lawrence is still the San Francisco; the Huxleys have just been— I like him!

Why do you never come over the ocean to see us? Let's have a cocktail!

Yours ever,
Frieda

TO S. S. Koteliansky

Beau Soleil
Bandol, France
Tuesday, 26 November 1929

Dear Kot:

Tell that doctor how glad I would be if he came to see Lawr. He might suggest something more. Max Mohr [1] worked out a system with me. It's about 7 in the morning an apple, prunes and almonds put through the mincing machine, at 8 breakfast, much *raw* food, no salt, or very little, that is the newest German idea. It's a very bright sunny little "Beau Soleil", we have a very good cook, I am the housemaid. Lawr. was very ill in Germany; Christ rose only once but Lawr. has done the trick many times, it seems to me. Carter [2] is here, there are long talks on the Apocalypse and the Jews and ancient all sorts. Lawr. getting better. I am so bored, with publisher stuff. *Lady C.* in Germany: the tricks they play not to publish her and let nobody else publish her, sickening—if only L. were strong. And what are you doing? Has your youth and enterprise been buried with Fox? Now you have a little money, why don't you *do* something? You have "schimp-fed" me such a lot, it's my turn now, I feel. Barby was so cross with you that you went for me so hard. I don't think much of

[1] Dr. Max Mohr was a German physician and playwright who had first met Lawrence in Bavaria in 1927.

[2] Frederick Carter, an English painter and writer who had met Lawrence in 1924 and shared his interest in the symbols of the *Apocalypse*. He wrote *D. H. Lawrence and the Body Mystical* (1932).

Turner,[3] as to your friend Smerdjakoff, how *patient* God must be! How *bored! How* impudent he is, he does need his ears boxed *hard*. We only saw a review. I think Carter is an interesting man. I liked the Rosanov, a beautiful outside book, but I like things clearer and brighter and less Christian! and less sloppy. It's nearing Christmas time, Kot, greet the Farbmans. I wish I could drop into your drawing-room and smoke 7 of your cigarettes! and hear you tell me *what* bores we are!!

Many greetings,
Frieda

TO S. S. Koteliansky

[Postcard]
Bandol, France
26 January 1930

You will have heard from Pollinger [4] that Dr. Morland [5] thought L. *very* ill. He must have perfect rest. But he won't go into a sanatorium. But no business at all—Poll. will do it all. But I have pulled L. through many times; he'll get better. Love, F.

TO Mabel Luhan

Vence, France
[Undated]

. . . I am very troubled about Lawrence. This is a sanatorium, a nice one. But he is very thin, only weighs 44½ kili, and can't eat and is so weak . . . this winter he wrote something on the

---

[3] Probably Reginald Turner, English writer, friend of Oscar Wilde and later of Norman Douglas, and for many years a resident of Florence.
[4] Laurence Pollinger handled Lawrence's literary affairs while he was with Curtis Brown, Ltd., and later in the firm of Pearn, Pollinger and Higham. After 1958, he represented the Lawrence estate, with his own agency. During his last illness, Lawrence asked him to look after Frieda's financial welfare.
[5] Dr. Andrew Morland, a specialist in tuberculosis, recommended that Lawrence enter Ad Astra sanatorium in Vence; he refused to accept payment for his treatment of Lawrence.

Apocalypse, or rather before that time, so good, but now he can't write and is so unhappy. . . . Can't you make her [Brett] realise that she is *not* important to either L. or *me*, that she wants to force me into an intimacy I don't feel or want? She imagines I am jealous of all sorts of things I don't feel. In my own world she doesn't exist. . . .

Lawrence died on March 2, 1930, at Villa Robermond, Vence, the day after leaving the Ad Astra sanatorium.

TO Witter Bynner

> Villa Robermond
> Quartier Chabert
> Vence, A.M.
> *12 March 1930*

Dear Hal,

You will know that Lorenzo is dead. Right up to the last he was *alive*, and we both made the best of our days; then he faced the end so splendidly, so like a *man*, and I could help him through, thank God. Dead, he looked proud and at peace and fulfilled. We had a simple, cheap funeral; he would have liked it cheap, wouldn't he? Now I have one desire—to take him to the ranch and make a lovely place for him there. He wanted so much to go. Do you think American admirers would pay for the transport? There is very little money for me; he didn't make a will, according to English law I only get the *interest* on the £4,000 that there are, but I hope the pictures and manuscripts are mine. I have enough, I hope, for my few wants. Would you help me, is it too much to ask? You know he had practically no money from America. Would you ask Miss Green of Morgan Library what a Lawrence Mss. is worth.

Do you remember our glamorous time in Mexico? Yes, you do, we read the poems together, and he loved the one you wrote about him. How it took us back to Chapala, they *are* good.

The world is changed for me. You will be sorry to hear that

my adorable daughter Barbara is also threatened with tuberculosis. It's almost too much.

Write to me, there was something vital between him and you. Aldous Huxley is editing his letters with little impressions by different people, would you do one?

With love and sorrow,
Frieda

TO Mabel Luhan

Vence, France
[*Undated*]

. . . Thank you for your friendship, we will come later. Yes, our Lorenzo is dead, but up to the end life never lost its glamour and its meaning. The courage, the courage with which he fought. I am so full of admiration that I can hardly feel much else. Dead, he looked so proud and so unconquered. I didn't know death could be *splendid;* it *was.* I didn't know anything about death, now I do. He opened a door into that place of the dead, and it's a great world too. He had given me a world here on this side, now he has given me the world of the dead. He was a great giver. Mabel, I want to bring him to the ranch, and we must have the Indians there with drums and singing, a real funeral. Tell Tony he must tell the Indians how Lorenzo made them live in his things. You will help, won't you, Mabel, and I want to make the ranch lovely for him with all that will grow. . . .

TO Witter Bynner

Monday
Villa Robermond
Vence
[*Undated*]

My dear, dear Hal,

There's no end to my sorrows. My lovely daughter Barby is very ill and the horror of it, it's her brain. I cannot tell you what

I've been through. I can't think of anything, not even Lorenzo. Only the affection of friends helps; think of me, I'll write later.

Sadly I send you my love,

Frieda

TO Edward Garnett

Vence
Monday

Dear Edward,

I was so glad to get your letter, we neither of us forgot ever, what you meant to us in our first being together and what you meant to Lawrence as the midwife of his genius! I can't say anything yet about your doing the letters. The will isn't proved yet, so I have no right. Then I must ask Aldous, as he is doing it. But do send me copies of the letters, I should love to see them. About my own, I have my doubts, but as you think. I loved seeing Bunny and I wish I had seen you; I see no reason why you shouldn't bring out those early letters, I'd like it; there are a great *many* letters—*more* than one book. I'll let you know as soon as I can. It's good of you to offer me so much money, but you know, there may be quite a lot; it seems strange after our poverty—but how rich we really were!

Sincerely yours,
Frieda

TO Mabel Luhan

London
1 April

. . . Lawrence is dead for a month, but he doesn't seem dead, not a bit. They are arguing and quarrelling about him just as ever. He seems serenely riding above it all. The dead will love and understand him better. He gave me so much life. . . . I don't know whether he would have liked me to write about him. Can't you hear him jeer at me as the "famous author's wife"?

TO Mabel Luhan

Vence
Villa Robermond
28 April 1930

. . . No, Mabel, we were all *more* than that. I know we were! It isn't fair to all of us to put only our sicknesses down, and meannesses, and not much else. It all had more meaning and affection and tenderness. It's the failure in tenderness especially that makes me so very sad, especially for Lawrence. You see, his last years and his death, and why did you not see him again, were enough to melt the hardest stones. He was so given over; the courage and the facing it, yet never denying the splendour of life and wanting to live and yet seeing death coming nearer and looking it straight in the eye, is such a miracle of human greatness to me, I stand amazed. I did give all I could, we were always generous with each other in love and hate. But I had to restrain it all, all my affection; he needed all his strength and mine just to live, and he worried very much this last winter that we had quarrelled so, and I had to console him and tell him, as we were with our characters it couldn't be helped. I weep over *Lorenzo in Taos*. Why was I such a fool and couldn't manage the situation, why did I doubt that he loved me? How wrong of me. And why were you so bossy, and didn't show him your real understanding and tenderness for him! Lord, what fools we were, and now it's too late, as it always is. His death has left me so full of love; it is very strange, no bitterness, no regret; I feel his love and protection, his "ambiente", more complete and whole than in his lifetime. I have got him like one has the sun and the moon and the earth and is of it. And then all you wrote seems as if we had been playing rather terrible charades. Write it again, Mabel, with all the meaning it had for us; knowing the Indians changed us all; into deeper realisation and connection with the earth it drove us, it wasn't only a *mental* experience. Write it from a deeper self, I am sure that's what Lorenzo would say to you. And you so generous too! and how he tried to help you in your living. Think how nice we also were. If I did think you horrid sometimes and wicked, I didn't judge you with narrow guts but thought, well, she is like that, she has the right to be what she is. And I never denied Lawrence the ultimate freedom to choose any other woman he liked better than me. There I was a fool, because when a real man has given his final allegiance to a woman, he has given it, and *basta*. And when I think that he, with his great achievement of living, said to me: "Nothing has mattered but you," then I feel I must love and serve humbly till I die, to rouse in other people the tenderness that is so often buried in them, and they don't know they have got it. How strong his spirit is! And yet I love his bones in that grave also; those bones that were his straight, quick legs once, how I loved them in the past. Then they got so thin, so thin, and how it grieved him so, also because he knew how it hurt me to see them so thin. How we suffered, and then I had to let him go finally into death. But death isn't at all terrible, as I had imagined. It's so simple really. One moment I held his ankle so alive, and then one hour after it was different, it was death, and I daren't touch him any more. He belonged to death now. It has changed me completely. I know something now that he always knew since his mother died. He had this advantage over me. Now I know about death, and it's good to know it. I can't say any more today, somehow reading your book got me. . . .

TO Witter Bynner

> Kingsley Hotel
> Hart Street
> *23 July 1930*

Dear Hal,

Yes, I knew you would write as you have written, and that you haven't forgotten him or me. But your letter was even *better* than I thought, and *lovelier*. When you didn't write, I read your "Red Earth" again and I could almost *smell* Chapala. How good those poems are. I still feel as if for years I had looked into a terribly strong light and now I'm dazed. He grows bigger and clearer for me and his death was so marvellous in its simplicity and control and belief in life. And now his bones are in the earth and he has become of the elements again and I feel everything more alive because he is part of it. I do admire him so, you know, the way he managed his frail body and life, little and big, and he saw so far and so deep, through and round the world. And my pride is that I saw him right through, and you know it was diabolically hard at times. In every way you know!

I want to bring him to the ranch, yes; I want to come early in October and there is a mess in New York about Seltzer and Boni. I shan't be *poor*, but for all that I would *love* it if his friends and admirers paid for his transport to the ranch; the Americans, the English, have treated him so *badly*. I told you I asked George Seldes and he said he would help. (I wrote on the spur of the moment, I don't know him.)

Send your letters to Mrs. Enid Hilton [6]

44 Mecklenburg Square

London, W.C.1.

(I'll write to George Seldes—to write to you.)

She collects them for Huxley and is *quite* reliable. I am so looking forward to coming. You won't be in New York by any chance in October? My daughter Barbara will come with me; she is an exquisite creature and you'll love her. I want to make a life at the ranch, am a bit scared of Mabel and Brett. Mabel wrote a book, *Lorenzo in Taos*, Oh dear! Oh dear! Anyhow I have the satisfaction of knowing that we were *all* nicer, even she, than she makes out. How jolly it would be to arrive in Santa Fe! Greet Christine Hughes.

> Yours ever and gratefully
> Frieda

If you call me a "grand girl", neither are you "small beer", and *he* knew it too.

Sir Richard Rees, author and painter, was the editor of The Adelphi *from 1930 to 1936, the period when*

---

[6] Mrs. Laurence Hilton was the daughter of Lawrence's old friend in Eastwood, William Hopkin. She had also helped with the distribution of *Lady Chatterley's Lover.*

Frieda was making a new life for herself after Lawrence's death. John Middleton Murry had long been associated with that periodical, and Rees would, of course, be linked in her mind with the struggle between Lawrence and Murry and its challenge to her loyalties. The occasion of her second letter to Rees was a meeting of the Chelsea branch of the Independent Labour Party, to which, at his persuasion, she had given a lecture. In 1959 Sir Richard published Brave Men, A Study of D. H. Lawrence and Simone Weil.

TO Sir Richard Rees

> Villa Bernarda
> Spotorno
> [*Undated*]

Dear Sir Richard Rees,

Thank you very much for your letter, when I come back to London I want to see you again. I really love Lawrence's *cross* letters to Murry, they make me laugh. I think Lawrence was only so terribly but *alive* cross with Murry and me, nobody else. It is *always* a fight. I have been in Florence where the lawyers came to take Douglas' and Orioli's evidence.[7] I *must* win this case. Lawrence would hate me, if I let all he left me be taken from me. How *dare* they, really. I *bet* you are fighting and I am sorry for you and Murry. Still, not *really* sorry. It's only the dead fish one wants to annihilate, they are to be pitied. Yes, can you imagine how I miss Lawrence, and his guts. Now I am alone, but I won't give in; no, I won't.

[7] Giuseppe ("Pino") Orioli, Italian bookseller and publisher, had arranged for the printing of *Lady Chatterley's Lover* in Florence in 1928. Frieda was trying to establish that Lawrence had made a will, which had been lost, that made her his heir. She was also attempting to recover certain of Lawrence's manuscripts which were in Orioli's possession. The story of the friendship between Norman Douglas and Orioli, and of Douglas's hostility toward Lawrence and his probable influence on Orioli's attitude, is told in Richard Aldington's *Pinorman* (Heinemann, 1954).

This is a stupid letter, but a small child insists that I play with it. Murry will have to help me such a lot. I would be lost without him.

Hoping to see you again soon and good luck to you,

Frieda Lawrence

TO Sir Richard Rees

[*Undated*]

Dear Richard Rees,

The meeting was certainly educational, but for me.

I felt like a squirrel chattering to fishes out of a tree.

I felt so sorry for them, they tried to get a bit *mentally* and that was all.

And yet they feel so without any direction, any raison d'être, and life is nothing to them but an economic question. I had thought my life and Lawrence's would give them hope and vision of another sort of life. All I felt was a bit of envy and hopelessness that their lives can never be different; Lord, I felt like a fool! Really! I didn't know they were like that, I thought everybody had a spark; but they haven't. And I am cross, cross with Jack. He knows better than anybody the dynamic and tenderness of Lawrence. He ought to use it and then he goes chasing those old hats of Marx and Morris. I believe I know better than anybody the tenderness in Jack's heart. His destiny was and is to stand with Lawrence, but no, he denies it and has *pity* instead for those dried haddocks and pity for the poor. *Pity isn't* love or tenderness. It's an insult to living stuff.

He evades his own pure destiny and sidetracks and chews the cud of old stuff, that he does not believe in. I am cross with him, because he is part of my life.

He doesn't love those people. Love is different. And he *is* capable of love. And you can do *nothing* with intellectual talk. It's the dynamic that does it. If he could only come free, that it isn't safety and self preservation and higher wages and economics that's needed. I hope I shan't develop a social passion; it must be terrible. Bad enough to love individuals, but to try to move that mass of inertia must be hell. But I feel sorry for you. It's a hell of a job. And the richness of life wasted for economics and politics and all the other ics.

But it was interesting!

Please don't mind this explosion! and good luck!

Yours ever,
Frieda L.

TO Witter Bynner

Vence, A.M.
15 May 1932

Dear Hal of Hals,

Yes, you were quite right. I implored Mabel, "Write that book again, it's not doing Lawrence justice, it's small beer!" But she wouldn't; then I thought, all right, give yourself away in all your cheapness.

We would have been so happy in Chapala, *don't* make me think about it. I am kind of fighting for Lawrence all the time. I am having a case to prove that there was a *will* leaving all to me.[8] Pray for me to all the decent gods you know. I told you, I wanted you to write about him. But I fear the letters are nearly out; I read them and also thought them marvellous, his book of letters will be great, but couldn't you use them *again?* Any permission of mine you have. I shall have enough money if all goes well. But I'd like to have enough, to get Angelino out. I want to come back; oh, this Europe! I think they'd like to treat me like the Lindbergh baby!

[8] The story of this "case" is told in the memoirs, in the chapter entitled "After Andrew's Death." Represented by the barrister C. D. Medley, Frieda was trying to establish her sole right to Lawrence's estate by showing that Lawrence had made a will, now lost, in her favor. John Middleton Murry testified to having witnessed this will. She won her case, and Lawrence's brother and sisters were permanently alienated. In 1938, as a token of her gratitude to Medley, she gave him the manuscript of "Goose Fair" and the corrected typescript of "Wintry Peacock." His letter of thanks, and much of his correspondence involving the estate, were among her papers.

Your letter made me happy! We know each other in all friendliness, don't we?

I am going to London for the will business.

Kingsley Hotel
Hart Street
London, W.C.1

Ever yours,
Frieda

The following letter, probably written in 1933, marks the beginning of the final phase of her life—permanent residence in New Mexico with Angelo ("Angelino" or "Angie") Ravagli. Lawrence and she had met Ravagli at Villa Bernarda in Spotorno in 1925, when he was a captain in the Italian army. It was chiefly he to whom she turned after Lawrence's death (see the chapter entitled "Leaving for South America," in the memoirs), and in the spring of 1931 they reached a decision to go together to the New Mexico ranch, he on six months' leave from the army. This stay was interrupted the following winter when he was recalled. The difficulties concerning Lawrence's will and estate occupied her in 1932. In the spring of 1933 she and Ravagli returned to the ranch. Their house, just below the Lawrence cabin, was begun May 30.

TO Witter Bynner

[*Undated*]

Dear Hal,

Thank you always that I just may come to you and feel welcome. We were in deep snow but how wonderful! Come up soon and see L's pictures.

Does motoring hurt your neck? You know we ought to see each other; life runs away so quickly. Love to Bob and you, and *come*.

I have worked so hard blissfully and leave my "friends" ya! alone.

> Ever yours,
> F.

Excuse this lousy paper, all I have. Love from Angelino. He is ploughing and building. We will be quite grand.

TO Sir Richard Rees

> Kiowa Ranch
> San Cristobal
> New Mexico
> *June 6*

Dear Richard Rees,

I did like the article, also for *your* sake, that you have the courage to come out with your opinions, but I am sure you have lots of uncompromising courage—and patience, my word. . . .

I am happy, building a log house; it is such a wild, fresh place; I get up at five and *live* anyhow according to Lawrence's idea, and it's good. Your article was the first thing I read for some time. I had to abuse John once more, reading *Son of Woman;* it's not a generous book, not his best self, nagging and fault finding, and I have always found him generous with me. I am glad those children are going to a school. It didn't work at Larling. I can quite imagine *how* fed up you must be at times. If ever you feel you want to refresh your soul and forget about the rotten part of humanity, come here. You can have a log-cabin and you would like Angelino, he is so natural. One lives with the sun and the desert and the cowboys and Mexicans, my bread is so good, and the vegetables, and the horses have just eaten a lot of corn, and the coyotes one gorgeous moonlit night tore a young sheep to pieces, and a weasel has bitten my two kittens to death. That is also nature sweet and pure and don't let's forget it!!

> Yours sincerely,
> Frieda L.

Mrs. Henry Dax, the wife of an Eastwood pharmacist, was one of the women close to Lawrence at the time he met Frieda. Clara Dawes in Sons and Lovers *is based in part on her. This remarkable letter on the occasion of the publication of Frieda's memoirs* Not I but the Wind . . . *(1934) attests to the painful complexities of Lawrence's relationships.*

FROM Alice Dax

> Station Road
> Shirebrook
> *23 January 1935*

Dear Frieda,

Last week I spent with Enid at Cookham Dean and there I saw your book. I am so glad that you allowed yourself to be borne upon a wind so fresh, fragrant of simplicity and sincerity. A story moving and so terrible, yet so rich and beautiful, written by the one person most competent to know, must surely displace the calumnies—the stenches which have blown from all quarters to sully the reputation of a man whom men have feared and envied.

On the wireless recently a clergyman said that the lamp of truth was in all ages carried by the prophets, and that it was to the prophets men must look up. "And how," he continued, "you may ask, are we to know the prophets?" I ejaculated, "Oh you can pick 'em out all down the ages to today—the men who have been hounded out and stoned and spit upon and starved and discredited with every sort of lie," but he continued, suavely, "Each one of us has something of the prophet in him and 'deep calls unto deep' when the true prophet speaks!" Sic! My God! Had he forgotten the vast shallows? Or, as I suspect, were shallows the only depth he knew? I suspect it.

The "Wind" nearly broke my heart with sadness and with gladness and other conflicting emotions. And I was grateful to you—really grateful.

I had always been glad that he met you, even from the day

after the event, when he told me about you, and I knew that he would leave me. I was never *meet* for him and what he liked was not the me I *was*, but the me I might-have-been—the potential me which would never have struggled to life but for his help and influence. I thank him always for my life though I know it cost him pains and disappointments. I fear that he never even enjoyed morphia with me—always it carried an irritant—we were never, except for one short memorable hour, whole: it was from that one hour that I began to see the light of life.

Unlike you, I could never quarrel with D. H., the probable truth being that I felt unsure of him and feared to lose him, whilst he in turn, I suppose equally unsure of me, rarely quarrelled with me, but when he became extremely angry would turn and walk out. It was not honest—I know it, and I know too how much sooner I should have achieved myself had I given vent to the feelings I had, *when* I had them. And then I expected of him an honesty which I myself did not render, which was impertinence, so that always between us there were under-currents which we could not cross. He needed *you*. I remember so well his words: —"You would like Frieda—she is direct and free, but I don't know how you would get on together" and his voice trailed off into "I wonder", whilst his mind compared us and his eyes left me in no doubt. You had, without doubt, all the things that he needed, and his sensitive soul knew it without an inventory.

My own childhood had been much nearer to D. H.'s than to yours, but even in his poverty he was richer than I, for the poverty of my life was shut in behind clean faces and gloved hands; a father's silk hat and frock coat, and a table which carried fair linen and crocheted doyleys even though every cake on it had to be halved or quartered to make them go round—a damnable crippling poverty, base and dishonest, which had no room for thought or books or recreation, but which demanded that every moment must be devoted to mending and making and scraping to keep up an appearance.

I happened to be the most unlucky bird of the brood—damned from before my birth and doubly damned after it. I was conceived during a long period of unemployment, and the sordid story of those pregnant months, as well as those which followed, I heard time after time after time repeated by my mother throughout my childhood with tears of thankfulness to the good God who had always provided her with *bread*—she seemed to have had little beside! When at last *knowledge* came to me, I loathed and detested my father (I had never been very fond of him); I swore vengeance on his sex when I should myself be married, and since *everyone* said that no man would ever marry me, I took the first who offered lest I should be cheated. Luckily for him I had developed a rather strong sense of justice before the marriage day so that he didn't suffer so much as he might have done. But this! All this! *Was* it the vessel from which D. H. might drink to his joy and wellbeing? I ask you! And I do believe that my revenge, unconsciously and unintentionally, hurt *him* far more than it has ever hurt my husband. Alas! I loved him. But now I think you will understand why I was glad that you loved him too—you who could give him so much, but my cup was bitter when he wrote from Garda in the richness of fulfilment. How bitterly I envied you that day! How I resented his snobbery and his happiness whilst I was suffering in body and sick in soul, carrying an unwanted child which would never have been conceived but for an unendurable passion which only *he* had roused and my husband had slaked. So—life! And with its irony that same unwanted child is the most enduring and precious joy of all my years.

I think you won't mind my having written to you. After the "Wind" I wanted you to know and I wanted to thank you for it. I am going to give a copy of it, when it comes out here, with a copy of *Lady Chatterley* to my son and future daughter-in-law before their marriage—to me they seem a fitting gift.

You would love C. A.—a straight lithe little body, a quick intelligence and swift unconsidered actions—he is delightful. Like Enid to look at—fair with blue eyes, but he has a broad rather large head. The cottage is a lovely place for them to live these first years, fairly isolated with plenty of open space around and a nice big garden. Enid is not awfully well—seems never to have recovered herself properly since the boy came and she makes terrible toil of everything. I think it better to have a family whilst one is young and vigorous, rather than later. Laurence is very good with him, but a bit scared I think, and the environment is not so casual for a child, as it is good for it to be. Maybe it will be better as time goes on, but Enid treats him a good deal as her mother treated her—over carefully. The weather was beautiful all the time I was there, but when I returned to the Midlands on Sunday a dark grey pall hung low over the land—a most depressing sight after the clear hills and dales of Berkshire with a sliver of silver away in the distance which is the Thames—it's a charming countryside. C. A. and I were very good friends. We had a day alone whilst Enid went to town and never a murmur until I put him to bed. Then I made the mistake of lighting his gas (which he loved, but was seeing it alight for the first time). When I put it out he howled and howled for nearly 20 minutes, and the next morning pointed up immediately asking for it to be relighted. They have a delightful little maid of just 15, who when told that I was Phyl's mother, looked me up and down and said, "No! It isn't credible." She has the most complete *savoir-faire* that I have ever seen in a child of her years. She is one of the *very* few children who make marriage at 15 seem possible!

All my best wishes for your health and well being

Yours sincerely
Alice Dax

TO Witter Bynner

28 February 1935

I have been remade into the new "35 Ford".

I was thinking with pleasure of you all winter and down there 25,000 words!! And this is my most favourite photograph of you and the lake, and tomorrow Lawrence died. I do know and feel that you help and support me, *such* a lot, and I won't say any more, because I won't cry.

My book is called *What's the Big Idea*, and *cheeky!* [9]

If your mother is a virgin, after all the only thing you can say to her is "Woman, what have I got to do with thee?" And if you have no father you invent yourself one in heaven. And that old serpent in our "ancestral home". It's amusing.

No more or I will cry some more. Well, we'll have such a reunion. Much love to Christine,[1] to Bob,[2] and the Stevensons [?]. Think of me with all your benevolence.

F.

TO Mabel Luhan [3]

[1935?]

Mabel,

I puzzle over the mystery, that you must do such awful things to people, as you did to me. I had such a genuine good will towards you and wanted you to "come off" in your own way. You are playing at Mme. Tussaud's waxworks and you put us all in your chamber of horrors, but some of us aren't wax, nor horrors. If you didn't care about me, you might have left me alone. You have done me no harm but you tried to. You never cared for anybody and you never will, that is your tragedy. Do you know what a shock it was to find that you wanted to steal Lorenzo's ashes? When I had stood at his small, ugly grave and telling myself: here lies all that I could really call my own in this life, because he gave himself to me, body and soul? You didn't

[9] The title of her memoirs became *And the Fullness Thereof*. . . .
[1] Christine Hughes, a close Santa Fe friend of Witter Bynner.
[2] Robert Hunt, a writer and Bynner's companion for many years.
[3] Of this letter Witter Bynner said, in a letter to the editor dated February 1, 1962: " . . . Incidentally, now that I have read Frieda's memoirs in which she talks freely and fully about her situation with Mabel Luhan and Dorothy Brett, I feel that I may release one last letter of hers to Mabel which Frieda tore up in my presence when I had agreed with her that it would be better not to send it but to try rather for continuance of as friendly relationship as possible with those particular Taos neighbors. She had brought the letter here [to Bynner's home in Santa Fe] from Taos to ask my advice as to whether or not to send it. However, after tearing it in two, she handed it to me saying: 'Perhaps you had better keep it for me in case the situation changes for the worse'."

care for him or you could never have written *Lorenzo in Taos*, where you make him look a fool, and all of us. How deeply I sympathised with you when I felt, she doesn't get all she wants from Tony; then I thought, she is so big, and has her own white life too. I have come to the conclusion that you really hate me, God knows why. Yet you seem to ask for one's affection; when you get it you destroy it, inevitably. I don't understand the meaning of your nature.

Lawrence never told me he wanted his ashes scattered. Wouldn't I have done it if he had?

As for Barby,[4] she does care for me and I think her old rancour, that I left her as a child, has almost gone. This was justified—the rancour. Have you known so little about life not to know that here [sic] are knots in the string?

I was so genuine in my trust and my affection for you. I still grieve for something that was Mabel to me.

Life means, that others care about you, that's all.

Frieda

I was so shocked and angry, now I feel the loss of my destroyed affection.

TO Dorothy Brett

[*Undated*]

. . . Also, I am glad to say, I feel no longer bitter about you. You have the merit in my eyes to have cared for Lawrence, but that affection was balanced by hatred in your case and Mabel's. You both hoped for Lawrence to leave me; that again is human nature. But then it is better for me, certainly, not to have anything to do with you any more, you *couldn't* do me justice ever! . . .

> *Angelo Ravagli had maintained relations with his family in Italy—his wife, Professor Yna-Serafina Astingo, who taught in a high school at Savona, and the three chil-*

---

[4] Her daughter.

dren, Stefano, Magda-Micaela, and Federico, who was Frieda's godson and was named after her. The situation in part was ironically parallel to hers with Ernest Weekley, her first husband, whom she had left for Lawrence. At the time of the following letters, Ravagli was making one of his periodic visits to his family. Since the winters at the ranch were severe, and Frieda had fallen seriously ill in Taos during a separation in 1935, he had settled her in Albuquerque, to the south. They were not married until 1950, when both, for a time, desired citizenship. Ravagli is the "Dario" of the memoirs And the Fullness Thereof . . .

TO Angelo Ravagli

> Central Park Court
> W. Central, 11th Street
> Albuquerque
> [*Undated*]

My dear,

Today you leave and your long letter came. I hope you can rest on the boat. You must have been very tired; I hope the sea won't be rough.

Very funny about Maria.[5] I have not heard from her again, I hope she is not ill.

I am quite happy, so don't worry about me.

I get up at seven and make coffee and go to bed again to have it. Then I have a bath, and tidy, and write. I write with pleasure, this book will be better than *Not I but the Wind*.[6] It is good to write about our life together and all my past, I believe I can write simply and beautifully (I hope so!). I have written in a new book, all very tidy, nearly 100 pages.

Then I go out and shop and sometimes to the cinema and sometimes one of the nice men takes me in "Henry" to shop.

I am making some Christmas presents. I took some whisky

---

[5] Maria Huxley, Aldous's wife.
[6] Her earlier memoirs, published in 1934.

bottles and dressed them as ladies. I made their faces with a piece of white cotton and painted the hair with black shoe polish and rouged their faces. They look very pretty, you wouldn't believe it.

I have not seen Christine, but the Maltzahns [7] are coming for Christmas; he writes if we sell those tapestries I must have a commission; very decent, so you see he isn't so mean.

I live very cheaply here, this is much cheaper than Taos, about 5 dollars a week for food.

Yes, it will be a very good thing if you can make your own money, because as you know I have not so much. And the Maltzahn place may be good for your enterprise later on.

So now you are on the sea. I will write to Antonio Luna. Maybe you get this letter for Christmas. I will send a cheque for a 100 dollars and not forget the cheque for January.

I am very glad the Hutchins will come to the Bernarda, a bit of America for you.

I think of these 3 years and the good time we have had. And when you come back full of a new energy for the pottery, it will be fun.

I saw Eric Rhodes on the film, very good. Zeitlin [8] wrote that a very good publisher wants to see my book. How do they know I am writing? But I am pleased.

I was very glad you wrote me such a nice long letter. I hope all goes well with you, you will enjoy seeing your children.

A letter from Marshall Best,[9] very sweet, but it tastes bitter to me.

[7] "Baron" Maltzahn, from whom she was to purchase a house and land in the valley near Taos. He is said to have been at the center of a plan involving Mabel Luhan and other old Taos friends to steal Lawrence's ashes in 1935, on the assumption either that Ravagli was going to capitalize on the memorial chapel at the ranch by charging admission, or that Lawrence would have wished them scattered.

[8] Jake Zeitlin, Los Angeles book dealer, who in 1937 exhibited her collection of Lawrence manuscripts, and offered them for sale. Dr. Lawrence Clark Powell compiled *The Manuscripts of D. H. Lawrence: A Descriptive Catalogue*, with a foreword by Aldous Huxley.

[9] Marshall Best was an officer of Viking Press, who held the American rights to most of Lawrence's works.

I sent cheques to Rachel and Gregory.[1]

Give my greetings to your wife and children. I can read your English!

Ever yours and keep well!

F.

TO Angelo Ravagli

3 December 1937

My dear,

Today I had your letter from Gibraltar, now I want to know how you are in Italy.

The Laskoffs were here for three days. They want me to go with them to Hollywood on the 15th of February but I don't want to. I *like* them, but I can't live with people. They are lazy and don't get up till 12 o'clock. If I can I will stay at the Maltzahn place, if it is too uncomfortable I come down here again. I am very comfortable here. The food in Albuquerque is very cheap and good and I walk to do my shopping and Betty Cottam[2] and he come often. Paul Horgan[3] is coming tonight and we go to dinner to the Fergussons.[4] Tinka[5] came; just the same. Today for the first time is bad weather, rain and snow; it will be snowing at the ranch very much. I have an idea you are at Tredozzio now. Tinka and Mrs. Weiler are going to do something with Tinka's house, Tinka will have the Heptagon there at her house and give people tea and lunch. Ruth Swayne[6] also wanted to drive me to California and I must give something to

[1] Rachel Hawk, wife of William, son of the owners of Del Monte Ranch, where the Lawrences had spent the winter of 1922–23, and her nephew.

[2] Mrs. Louis Cottam, daughter of Mr. and Mrs. A. D. Hawk, owners of Del Monte Ranch.

[3] Novelist, dramatist, and regional historian living in New Mexico, who won the Pulitzer Prize in 1954.

[4] The friendship with Erna Fergusson and her mother, whose German origins were a source of mutual interest, became quite close and intimate. Erna is the author of books on Mexico and the Southwest.

[5] Divorced wife of Nicolai Fechin, the painter.

[6] Owner of a small dude ranch at Talpa, near Taos.

the "Sentinel". Had a letter from Bynner in New York, not a word from Esta.[7] I am glad you have already bought a return ticket. I enclose a cheque. Dear Angie, our life together is so good and I miss you very much, it is not really any fun without you, but this month has gone very quickly and I hope the others, till you come back, go as quickly, or quicker.

It makes me sad when your letters come, then I wish you were here.

Had a very nice letter from Mrs. Hutchins [8] asking me to go to Europe with them.

Americans do that like the Hutchins did to you, it is very "chic"! I am writing my book and I think how you will enjoy making your pottery. I am *sure* you will make a success of it. I don't know what to tell the Laskoffs, why I don't want to go to Hollywood; it won't be any fun without you. You will be very grand when you have your own pottery and your own money.

Lee wants the pasture at the Maltzahn place, but the Mackies [9] say don't let him have it. I won't do anything about it till you come back and we know what can be done with the place. Had a wonderful letter from a young German, saying "A friend of mine told me: I have only one prayer: 'God give me a Lady Chatterley'."

You think I ought to give you more money. If I were rich, yes, but I am not and I don't think it is reasonable. I know there is only the 120 every month, but think of the money we spend. Going to South America and Boston and Hollywood. We spend quite a lot of money, but you don't think of that. Now I pay you for five months when you are away *and* the journey *and* some money for this time. Many times you work hard, but also many times you just paint and *I* do all the work. You never think of money, except when you think of Italy. But I hope that now that you are in Italy you realise what a good life you have in America.

[7] The wife of Dudley Nichols, screen writer.

[8] The Hutchins are recalled by Dorothy Brett as friends of the Blooms-bury group in England. He was a barrister.

[9] Ted and Elmyra Mackie, proprietors of the store and post office at San Cristobal, near the Lawrence ranch, were known as shrewd business people.

I *don't* want you to be grateful, but just to know that you have a better and freer life than most men. So there!

I hope it is not too hard for you at home, not too difficult, but you are coming back. What news from Buenos Aires [1] and Tredozzio?

Much love to you, how is Federico and Puppa and Stefanino? Did the watch come?

I expect Ruth Swayne.

Yours,
Frieda

Will send another 50 dollars soon. I spend very little money here. It is cheap. Have sent your cheque to Boston. There ought to be some money from Zeitlin soon. Can you read all my writing? A letter from Maria saying *why* she did not hear from you.

TO Angelo Ravagli

Central Park Court
21 December 1937

My dear,

It was *lovely* to get your letter today, I had resigned myself to have to wait for a long time. Poor E—! But I *won't* go, I am sick of consoling people after the T—.

I want to do my book, that's what I am here for now; perhaps she might come to me later on. I *won't* go where it's cold, I am all right here.

Merrild [2] wrote to you and me. Frere [3] found him another publisher; it is better, Frere has too much Lawrence stuff. I get many letters: Zeitlin, Diego wanting already 20 dollars for his

---

[1] The home of Ravagli's brother Giovacchino (now dead) and his sister Luisa, Ferruccio Castori's wife.

[2] Knud Merrild, Danish painter whose memoirs of Lawrence, *A Poet and Two Painters*, were published in 1938 by George Routledge and in 1939 in the United States by Viking Press.

[3] A. S. Frere, officer of William Heinemann Ltd., the English publishing firm.

truck. He did not get the lumber job. Maltzahn has had the interview with Mabel and Tony and Brett and Miriam Bright [4] and Kiker [5] and Mrs. Kiker and Beutler.[6] He said they asked beastly questions, but it was hateful for Mabel too.

The Otises [7] came, so friendly, and I lunched with Mrs. Simms,[8] very chic. She told me to call her Ruth, I like her though she is so rich. I listened to the opera at the Fergussons', they are so charming with me.

Dan Wells [9] sent me some paper, printed; I can't understand why he was so cool with you.

I get very excited about my book, Erna brought me a charming woman who will type it. Ted Stevenson . . . asked for an Ms. for Spain.

The Otises have gone to New York for two months.

This night the wind blew hard and I couldn't sleep and I thought of you on your *Conte di Savoia* and I had an idea you were not very well. I wrote Merrild to go and see you at the Bernarda. I sent his letter to Haniel Long,[1] he wanted to know some things. There was a long article on the front page of the *Times* and a large picture of Aldous. But not a word from Maria. People are very strange. And Christine has not been to see me.

Please don't be too economical with yourself. You know I feel what is mine is yours. I don't feel like that about your family. For that you must forgive me, it is only human.

Manara wrote me a very nice letter, please greet him kindly from me; he seemed satisfied in the letter with the cheque.

[4] Mrs. Edward Bright, of Taos.
[5] Judge Henry Kiker, her lawyer at this time.
[6] Floyd Beutler, Taos lawyer.
[7] Raymond Otis of Santa Fe had been very kind to her during her illness in 1935, and is remembered in her "In Praise of Raymond Otis" in this volume.
[8] The former Ruth Hanna McCormick, wife of Albert Simms, wealthy Albuquerque rancher and businessman.
[9] Husband of Jenny Wells, the folk singer, long-time residents of the Taos area.
[1] Poet, long-time resident of Santa Fe, and organizer of "Writers' Editions," the non-profit, cooperative publishing venture.

The people here, those two men, are very nice with me, and the owner of the place was very pleased that Mrs. Lawrence was staying here and he wants to pay me a visit.

I am so glad you put me in this easy, warm place.

Now you will soon be getting home. I have not heard from the man of Puppa's watch. On the 23rd the Maltzahns are coming and I will take them to Mrs. Simms about those tapestries. You have been gone more than a fortnight, the time will pass quickly. Else [2] writes how happy she was to see you and how *nice* you are, and she admired you. I hope you hear how your brother is. I miss you very much, but am happy. The writing does me good. The chapters are:

I. The ranch
II. Leaving the ranch
III. Contretemps
IV. To San Antonio
V. On to New Orleans
VI. Christmas at home
VII. Buenos Aires
VIII. Adolescence
IX. Rio de Janeiro (I have got to here)

Then there are those letters of Otto's and England and more Lawrence.

It will be an interesting book of a woman's life.

So good-bye and be happy. I will write again soon.

One and only, greetings to your wife and children.

F.

Grillo [3] wrote he could not find me here, he will come on his way back from California.

[2] Her sister, Else Jaffe.
[3] R. Grillo, the Italian consul in Denver.

TO Angelo Ravagli

Albuquerque
17 January 1938

My dear,

I have eaten half a lobster (*arragasta?*) and half a large pink grapefruit and I wish you had the other halves!

I am very proud that you are so energetic and are already working, now you are happy! It must be very interesting!

I see already quite a few people; Erna Fergusson had your card, I like her *very* much, she is a true person. I often see her! How *dare* you say my new book will *not* be so good! It will be much better, much more interesting, or I wouldn't write it! Marcella,[4] my pretty typist, says so! As you work hard, I want to work hard too!

The Laskoffs were here again for two days, they are nice but lazy and I am the *serva* and I don't like it! They insist that I go to Hollywood with them but I won't, I would just be the cook! The English actor whom I sent to Grillo told me that King Edward abdicated because they told him they would *stop* her divorce, so he had to choose! Grillo wants me to write something about the exhibition in Rome. *If you go there* you write something and I will translate it! Don't forget that I go to the Maltzahn Place on the 1st of February. My address Taos. Mabel has taken a house here! Enid may go to England to get a divorce, I think her husband wants a divorce; poor Enid does not know what to do.

You will have been at Tredozzio and I am sure it was very sad for you, but they will have been very glad to see you. You don't say anything about your wife and how it is!

Somebody wants to buy the Mss. of Sons-Lovers, I have not heard about the French film of Lady C. Don't forget to have the two Mss. of Lady C. typed. Leave them at Savona and bring the originals. Also the book. I get so many letters and people come and my book does not get on as fast as I hope. I must write to the Hutchins, they asked me to come to Europe with them. I am very well and happy, but I miss you. Then I think what good

[4] Marcella Matson, who had been recommended by Erna Fergusson.

friends we are and I am glad! People are very good to me and bring me sweets and jam and take me for drives! I am a very lucky woman!

Tinka is here, more cheerful this time.

It is so warm, like spring, and if it is like this at the Maltzahn place I shall like it.

Erna lent me a very interesting book about American finance and politics. How 60 families in America have all the money; it seems to me *silly* to have one hundred million dollars, what good does it do you? These millionaires think their work so important and it is just a stupid game. Only the sad part is that the other many people are so poor.

It's already spring and the birds are singing, but I daresay we shall have some cold weather yet. So work hard and we will have a pottery! It will be exciting.

My best love to you and greetings to your family.

Yours ever,

F.

If you need some money for the pottery things let me know.

TO Angelo Ravagli

29 January 1938

Dear No. 1!

Your letter from Tredozzio today made me very sad! Your poor, poor sister! It is too, too terrible! And your father too. I wish we could have her at the ranch and look after her. But I know it is impossible now. She is dying, so young! You have had a sad time, I am very sorry!

I hadn't heard from you for a long time and I was getting worried, I hope you are well. It is enough to make you ill, all that tragedy. Write to me every week or I get frightened that something is wrong, and I am not happy when I don't know how you are.

I have just been listening to Wagner's "Tristan and Isolde" from New York opera at Erna Fergusson's. It was very lovely.

And I thought of Tredozzio and your home and your father and your poor sister, and I wanted to cry.

I have a very good time, but already lots of people come. John Howland stayed with me for nearly a week; he was very nice but I didn't get much writing done. Erna Fergusson is a real friend, *not* like Mabel; she is more loyal, like a man.

I get lots of letters from Harold [5] and Elmyra[6] and Maltzahn comes to fetch me on the *fourth*. If it is too cold, I will come down again. But I would like to make the house nice, so that we can let it. A postcard from Maria, she will be here in a week; I don't know what she will do then. Judge Hamlin came, and the Laskoffs again; they let me do too much for them. *Everybody* is very good to me here, I am glad I stayed here, I have been very well; but now I want to go to Taos, I feel a little like in a cigarbox here. Betty is also very sweet to me, she said she had written you. Grillo sent me an article on the Rome exhibition and Irene Fisher took it for the Albuquerque *Journal*. I was glad. Mabel was here, but the people weren't nice to her, so she went to New York. Maltzahn said he will stay a few days and help me with the house. Zeitlin sent me 500 dollars and more is coming next month and he may sell the Mss. of "Sons and Lovers."

I enclose your month's cheque and another 50 dollars. If you want more for coming back, *say so*. Come back soon, everybody misses you and I most of all.

Yours,

F.

I send a cheque *50* for your sister. My book is very lively and colourful. I *like* it.

TO Angelo Ravagli

Los Pinos

Taos, N.M.

16 February 1938

Dear one,

Here I am. It is surprisingly beautiful. The big room really splendid and the simplicity of this landscape I love; the sky is the

[5] Harold Hawk of Del Monte Ranch.
[6] Elmyra Mackie of San Cristobal.

sky, and the earth the earth, and everything is itself. Maltzahn came to Albuquerque and then he stayed in the hotel here. He was very unhappy to go, he cried and he said how he loved me! He is a little hysterical, I also think she does not care for him and your good nose has smelt something, I think it is true. He told me there was a count that Hanni was interested in, and he, Maltzahn, has been very good to her. We went to see Gerson Gusdorf [7] and Emmetaz [8] and Haskell,[9] and I have been to the cinema, the new one; it is very fine.

You don't know how nice Taos is in winter! Not cold at all, not enough snow on the mountains; it will be a dry summer. I went up to the ranch at 6 o'clock in the morning, so the snow was hard and Joe made it with me. Diego was there and the horses were so glad to see me, they trumpeted at me like *fanfare di benvenuto*. Saw Rachel and Harolds and Mackies. Ted came and he really liked the place, I could tell. He says business is very bad.

Maltzahn took his owl with him and his beastly dogs; I hated them, they stole the butter and made everything dirty. I am sure Maltzahn will be back before long, but he is a good fellow at heart and I *know* this place is a good investment; I don't care what anybody says. It is snowing this very minute, I am glad because the land needs water. I can also have water for irrigation from the Indians; John Concha told me so. I am very happy to be here; the oil stove is wonderful, it keeps the whole place warm all the time. But I wish you were back. Come soon. The ranch was all right and a lot of hay left. Water and everything all right. Joe is really glad Maltzahn is gone; he got tired, Maltzahn wanted him every minute . . . Joe said: "I want the captain to be my boss now." Poor Maltzahn! So I am already fixed here, but I don't think I can manage a bathroom, building it I mean, though Ilfeld might help me, and Edward and Emmetaz.

Please thank your wife and the Puppa and Federico for their

[7] Owner of hardware store in Taos, builder, farmer.
[8] Rich old Italian who took people on camping trips and had a house on the desert.
[9] Muriel Haskell, friend in Taos.

nice letters. I will answer soon. Tell me how your pottery, the stuff from here, came out. Miriam Bright looked very pretty, but not nice, when I went to them.

I enjoyed Bobby and Betty [1] very much. I told you that the Huxleys came and we had a lovely evening at Betty's. Aldous *sang* and I danced. It is snowing softly and I can't see the mountains, nor the ranch, from here.

I am *very* well and have not had a single cold this winter. ("I touch wood.") Your wife writes you get colds; *be careful!* We have had wonderful early spring weather all the time, very seldom a grey day. It is very still and peaceful, Mabel and Brett away, the place seems cleaner. John Howland wrote how he likes our Hollywood friends and how they like me; he saw Dudley, but didn't say how he was. The Hutchins want this house, a 100 dollars for a month. But Maria says they will go away for a month this summer, then the Hutchins can come. A nice letter from my son, his wife is never well. I *don't* go to Europe, it costs too much. Your wife says she doesn't feel well, I am sorry.

Ever your old friend,

F.

TO Angelo Ravagli

Los Pinos
Sunday, 19 February 1938

Dear! One!

This is to say, I am *very glad* you did not send anything from Italy, because you can get *everything in Denver.* A man in Albuquerque makes pottery and he told me you could buy *stoves* for baking and everything. I wanted to telegraph to you but then thought you might have bought the things already. I suppose it will take some time before you can make pottery to sell.

About Lady C., it would certainly be safer if she could be typed. Perhaps the Hutchins could find somebody. But Lawrence's handwriting is very clear.

[1] Mrs. Ted Gillett and Mrs. Louis Cottam, the daughters of Mr. and Mrs. A. D. Hawk of Del Monte Ranch.

I am expecting the Mackies [2] for lunch. I do hope you will love this place too. Joe is very nice, more willing to do things than Diego; I like his wife.

Luna says he sent the *watch*. Have *you got it?*

I shall be very glad, when you are back. Sometimes I am afraid. Europe seems so dark and terrible to me. Perhaps I am stupid, but sometimes I feel you will not come back. I hope it is not true. And your wife writes you have *colds* and *you* don't say anything. Do take care of yourself and *don't* have colds. I am very comfortable and Joe brings water and wood and coal and Edward Bright takes me shopping. The Mackies were very nice. He wandered about the place and made plans as usual, but we decided we won't do anything till you come.

I wish you were here safe and sound.

Maria Huxley gave me back the Mss. of "St. Mawr" that Zeitlin had given to Aldous for me. I didn't like it, I had given it to Aldous and she should not have given it back; but there.

I liked the photographs of your sister and Federico. I looked at them a long time. Your sister's face looks very interesting, the suffering does not show much, perhaps a little wild. Federico has a very attractive face, he will be a real person. One day he must come to the ranch, I like him very much. You will be very glad to have your Signorina daughter with you, but don't love her too much or she will never love another man and her life will not be happy. It is Sunday night and I am alone; it is very still and snowing, but I am warm and cosy. The big room has the loveliest views; the green Alamosa curtains are up and lots of plants in the windows, and I live in the big room. I have the large desk in it. Your last letter was in Italian, do you forget your English? There are always things I forget to tell you; it is funny to live so near Taos and see more people, and I can see the ranch from here, all white now, the triangle.

Tomorrow I send this letter air mail that you get it a little quicker. What about money? Say in your next letter if you want any more, that I can send it in time. I hope this place won't cost too much, but I am sure we can let it in the summer. Mackie

[2] Ted and Elmyra Mackie, of San Cristobal.

Frieda in Mexico, 1923.

D. H. and Frieda Lawrence in Mexico, 1923.

says, "You don't make Diego work hard enough." I think Diego is jealous of Joe, but then I need Joe here. . . .

Ask *Grillo* to look around for things for your pottery in Denver. I have not written a word since I came up, so many things to do.

Good night, sleep well, and come back well and soon.

Yours,

F.

TO Angelo Ravagli

5 March 1938

Dear One,

I was very pleased to get a nice letter from Gigina. Also I had a letter from Tessie Payne, you remember the girl we knew in New York with poor Phil when we first came. She wants me to write about a book her husband wrote; he is a Consul, but his book is about Japan, so what can I say; I don't know Japan.

I am also reading a book called *The Red Knight* about the flying cousin. But it frightens me killing people like birds, it is much better to make pottery.

Trinidad and Ruffina [3] came, and I can have as much water as I like, Trinidad said; so you see I am glad I was friendly.

You will be pleased with the place, I know; only more work for you and more responsibility. A letter from Maltzahn, he is sad to have left. Spud Johnson wrote a subtle nasty article about him in the Sentinel. These people are slaves! Poor Edward is tired of Miriam [4] and will leave her; he said, "She does not care for me, but I can't leave her now with two children but later I will." I think I have even persuaded the Tinka not to love Spud any more.

I am worried about the Lady C's. If they were confiscated, it might be a very great loss and yet you might get through easily.

[3] Indian friends from the days when the Lawrences returned to the ranch from Oaxaca in April, 1925. They worked there during Lawrence's convalescence.

[4] Edward and Miriam Bright.

If you could have them typed, it would be better and yet it would have to be a *person of confidence*, somebody might tell. Surely Lawrence's handwriting is so clear, somebody Italian might do it. I am very glad you want to come back. I *knew* it would be so in the end. I am making you a very nice room for you here, you won't believe it is the same place.

Joe is very good and does everything to please me, I could not live without somebody here. I only pay him 1½d. because he has the house.

I have the Fonso and he is very special about his food, he must have what I have. Eulalia gave me a nice lamp for your room, a reading lamp.

Joe made me a very nice dining-room table and is making a bed for you. I don't like those ugly beds you buy.

I would have liked to have gone to the little chapel on the first of March. Lawrence is dead 8 years! But I could not go, it was very muddy. Betty and Bobby came and Louis; they loved the place, I went with them to the Lockwoods; [5] many people are away, so it is very quiet and peaceful.

Before you come back I think you ought to go back to Tredozzio again; when you are here, you might be sorry not to have seen them again.

I am always very happy and now I am happier to think that soon you will be back. If you were not coming back, it would be different. I would be miserable. I hope you no longer worry about money and you have enough. I hope poor Puppa's watch has arrived. Today was one of the few ugly days, snow and rain and wind.

Today in a months [sic] you start in the Rex. I hope the time will go quickly. I am very well. I have not had a single cold this winter and am awfully well. I hope you are.

Love to you

F.

Greet your family.
I begin to say *Auf Wiedersehen.*

[5] Mr. and Mrs. Ward Lockwood, he a painter.

TO Witter Bynner

> Los Pinos
> Taos, New Mexico
> *23 March 1938*

Dear Hal,

Now I don't know whether you are back, but I don't want to wait anyhow to write to you. I have just spent some hours reading your selected poems,[6] and was in *your* world. You poets have an unfair advantage getting at one's soul. So I am being soulful. They are quite new to me again, your poems, as if I read them for the first time.

I love so many of them, "gods" not made of wood or out of a book; it is such a *rich* book. The one on Lawrence is very good, because you saw something nobody else had seen and one hated it and yet it gave one space to wander about in.

"Charioteer" I just adore.

How are you in New York? Have you seen the glamour girl? If she focuses on New York, Taos may become a mild and friendly place.

I am in my new place and like it very much. Come and see me soon when you come back. You will like this place, and I am happy "fixing" it. Really, this country means so much to me; all the more when I think of poor Europe! It's all so terribly indecent.

Come back soon; I don't like it when you are so far away. So many people are dead and so few of us left.

I have been writing and I think it is better than my first book.

On the 23rd of May I go to Hollywood, the University of Southern California is doing *David*. Angelino will be back soon. I want sheep on this place and [to] grow alfalfa. In May we go up to the ranch again and the Huxleys will come too.

There is nothing but sagebrush between me and the Rio Grande and I can hear the Indians sing in the pueblo and poor Maltzahn will hate it in Austria; he had better not go.

[6] *Selected Poems of Witter Bynner*, edited by Robert Hunt, with a critical essay by Paul Horgan (Knopf, 1936).

I have got a nice Joe who looks after things, grandson of Padre Martinez, and he tells me many tales about the Mexicans; they are strange and interesting too! It is fascinating, this country.

I send you and the Bob my best greetings and am

Your ancient friend,
Frieda

TO Witter Bynner

Kiowa Ranch
San Cristobal, New Mexico
Monday, 28 March 1938

Dear Hal,

I wrote you an affectionate letter the other day, I want you and Bob to come up as soon as it is convenient for you and see this place. Christine was up and told me you were coming back in a day or two. She also told me that you were bringing much of your mother's furniture. If you have anything to spare, give me some; with the new place, I would be very grateful; it is very bare yet. But beautiful.

Did Clifton Fadiman ring you up? He wants to come to Santa Fe for the summer and wants a house and I told him to ask you. 3 bedrooms. Do you know of any? round about, houses I mean.

I hope you enjoyed yourself, but are glad to be back.

When you come I want you to tell me lots and lots about Mark Twain. I think he is so very great. What language, Oh Lord, fresh as a daisy, that has just opened its eye.

Baron Maltzahn has left for Austria; he hated to go. I fear that instead of having done him a good turn by buying his place, I may have done him a bad one. I wouldn't put my head in the Nazi noose.

I hope they fairly adore Mabel in New York and that she stays there.

The winter has been so lovely, but now it's nasty, wet snow, but it is good for the land.

Now, dear Hal, please don't think my last affectionate letter was "cupboard love", because I want some of your things. When I wrote that letter, I didn't know you were having more things; Christine hadn't told me yet.

So come soon and I hope you are well.

Yours as ever,
Frieda

From about 1933 until the war, when gas rationing made travel impossible, Frieda and Angelo Ravagli frequently wintered in California, in the Hollywood area. There was one exception—a memorable stay in Carmel, where they lived with two other unmarried couples and felt shunned except for the friendliness of Robinson Jeffers. Winter high up on the mountain at Kiowa Ranch was very cold, and even after Frieda bought "Los Pinos" lower down near Taos, she spent the winter elsewhere when she could. After the war she went to Port Isabel, Texas, for the winter. Her closest friends in Hollywood were Dudley Nichols and his wife "Esta," and after 1936, Aldous and Maria Huxley, who moved there after a stay at the ranch. Dudley Nichols was a gifted man with unusually high standards of artistic integrity for the films on which he worked. Among these were For Whom the Bell Tolls, Sister Kenny, It Happened Tomorrow *and* The Long Voyage Home.*

Thirty-six of Frieda's letters, dating from June 5, 1936, to May 4, 1956, were purchased by the Yale University Library after Nichols's death (January, 1960). Because of space limitations, only the most representative fragments, and those of unusual interest, are given here.

TO Dudley Nichols

Kiowa Ranch
8 October 1938

. . . It was a real shock, dear Dudley, that you have been so busy and going, rushing it. I hoped you were having a peaceful time, was sure of it. I think you will have to retire into a monastery, a silent one, or you will never get any peace. You are killing yourself and it isn't worth it. It makes me cross. There aren't so many people with such a good will in them as you have got and the wretches know it and want to swallow you up. You *must* have some rest and some peace or you won't be able to stand it much longer, nobody could. Flying to Hollywood again, O Lord!

The Huxleys are there, taking it gently; I hope Aldous won't get involved like you. But he is a wary bird and so is she. She also liked Esta very much. . . .

TO Witter Bynner

2 December 1938

Dear Hal,

What *fun* that you write your memoirs! Do go ahead; that's a book I want to read!! Use all you like, I hope my letters aren't too silly, that's all.

Haniel writes that [the] page in the *Sentinel* will not continue. I am very sorry, aren't you? Can't you persuade Cyrus to go on? It was interesting. I wish *you* had a magazine. But I suppose they are very expensive.

I have made *two* cushions for you and enjoyed it.

We are going to Hollywood on the first of January. Maria and Aldous persuaded us; I wanted to go to Corpus Christi. Angelino has also his bookends (yourself) ready. Kieve has written such a good novel.

Soon we will appear. We will stay a night with Erna.[7] We are too busy getting ready to stay with you. I telephoned you from San Cristobal (the *first* telephone call) on Thanksgiving, but you were out. It's beautiful and I feel like telephoning to say "come up," but then it may snow and be awful.

[7] Erna Fergusson.

We will let you know when we come. Angelino wants to sell some of his pottery in Albuquerque.

Always your friend,
F.

TO Witter Bynner

1230 N. Poinsetta Place
Hollywood
[*Undated*]

Dear Hal,

Thank you and Henri for the glasses.

I will write to Bob. Glad you are working.

Yes, this is a queer place. I lie low so far, have only seen M—, charming but, oh so drunk.

Now when you say nice things about me, don't forget our Christine, who doesn't think me such great shakes!!

I am writing, it's really fun, but occasionally so difficult to say what you want to!

Angie goes to "Highschool" in the evenings to learn English.

Finish your beautiful novel!

I am here with a nice young man who made us stay; he is in the Fox film, "make up" he does. He is keen to get me on the films, knowing what they want. But they make you have a contract for a year, and my beloved liberty? Though it might be fun.

It's an odd place, nobody has any roots. But I'd like the money and you can make lots, then I could build my Santa Fe house. I love Santa Fe.

We'll stay here over Christmas, then take a house in Laguna Beach where you could stay with me, and the sea is a joy, the Pacific, so different from the Atlantic.

Dear Hal, I never told you that when Lawrence was dead, I felt, what is there left now? And besides Angie, there seemed nothing but the pleasure of seeing you again.

Had such a nice letter from Paul Horgan.

Love from me and Angie,

F.

TO Montague Weekley

Taos, New Mexico
6 May 1939

My dear Monty,

Can't you persuade your people that it would be very important for you to see the New York Fair and come and pay your
mother a visit? She is going to be 60 this year.

You have had your nose to the grindstone for so long it seems
to me, isn't it time you had a holiday? I would pay your trip, as
my birthday present.

I hope all goes well with you, all of you. I had a great time in
Hollywood with the Huxleys and Charlie Chaplin. They may do
The Plumed Serpent on the film, but "do not put your trust in
films".

Now there is all the hard work of the two ranches, I do so
want you to see this place. Eddie Marsh sent me his book. I am
fed up with this European powderbarrel that does not go off. It
must wear people just to threads.

With much love to you and Vera and the children. Their
photographs sit in a row in my bedroom, and a faint hope that
you will come.

Your mother

Friedel Jaffe [8] with wife and two children is coming.

TO Montague Weekley

Kiowa Ranch
13 July 1939

Dear Monty,

The day after tomorrow you leave these shores again.

I fear it was terribly hot. I hope you have not lost your tan,
you looked so well.

It is still terribly dry, no rain.

Bynner came and said C— was enchanted with you; when I

[8] Her nephew, Else Jaffe's son, now Frederick Jeffrey, living in the
United States.

told him you were not so with her sons and used the word "oaf" he said, "Exactly my word for them."

It was just wonderful to have you here.

Also Mabel said you radiated happiness, and Ruth Swayne said you had my vitality and warmth. So you see you were appreciated in New Mexico.

I may have some luck. The Library of Congress (MacLeish) may buy Lawrence's Mss. Then you can come next year, *Kind und Kegel* and all.

Have had thousands of people. They must want to come pretty badly to come up this rotten road.

I hope your passage is good and you are refreshed.

Much love to you and yours. Angelino sends greetings.

Your mother

TO Witter Bynner

Kiowa Ranch
25 July 1939

My dear Hal,

We are in a nasty mess. An immigration officer came, asked questions, and about Angelino and my relationship: we admitted it was intimate. But those El Paso people were trying to make out a case of "moral turpitude" against him. Mrs. Perkins[9] came, Mabel of all people took up the cudgels for Angelino. She, P—, was very sympathetic here in Taos. We thought the battle won, but no, she is in Santa Fe later, sees Christine and says: "I don't want to hear any more about this, it isn't Mrs. Lawrence at all, but something *he* did, something immoral. They picked him up!" Now you know it is not true. He doesn't ever get drunk, he is just bewildered about it all and it is so horrible not to know who accuses him and what for.

It looks like a frame-up, who is the framer?

I have never felt so helpless and down in the mouth.

Now, Hal, I know you do not stand for lousiness. Perkins

[9] Frances Perkins, Secretary of Labor, 1933–1945, author of *The Roosevelt I Knew* (1946).

asked after you, Christine said. Write to her, use your goldenest tongue for us.

You have seen Angelino so often and it is so obvious that he just likes to be gay sometimes.

If the charge of immorality is because of our relationship, that is all right, but another one is just nonsense!

I have not seen Bob, but send this to him.

I miss you in New Mexico, but hope your brother is better and you enjoy your Florida stay.

> Ever your old friend,
> Frieda,
> who is in a mess.

It was an awful experience having that officer ask you the most intimate questions. They may want to deport Angelino.

TO Dudley Nichols

> Kiowa Ranch
> [*Undated*]

. . . Now I will tell you the story of our upset. An immigration officer came, very suave, and asked us questions of our intimate life. We answered truthfully (beastly, of course) and first me, then Angie. . . . The official took both our passports and they have not come back. But fortunately Frances Perkins came, and Mabel and other friends talked to her, and she is doing all she can, she said. . . .

Then the officer also said, "Mr. Lawrence got our people into trouble years ago." Lawrence was very ill in Mexico, and the officials would not let him through into this country in spite of letters from the American embassy in Mexico. So Lawrence wrote them how viciously he had been treated. . . .

TO Montague Weekly

> *22 August 1939*

Dear Monty,

I am thrilled at your new adventure! You have a bigger field for your activity and may become a power in the land, necessary too these days.

If you have any influence work for the simplification of things. These governments have become too ponderous and choked. I believe a great deal of the unholy success of Hitler and Mussolini lay in their simplifying things. You can also learn from the devil.

A young Viennese came to see me who had been in a concentration camp for nine months, horrible, just horrible. Young boys, 17 and 18, stormtroopers trained to beat men of 60 with whips. What a crime. I felt like turning into one of those awful propaganda women to help save what can be saved of decency in the world.

I had a grand birthday party, an outdoor fireplace with half an ox practically, lots of lights, beautiful; wish you had been there!

People ask after you; you made an impression here, I tell you!

Next year you must come, all of you! I think America did something to you, a kind of liberation. It was just wonderful to have you here.

I am sending Ian and Geoffrey some Indian chief headresses.

Angelino was so impressed how you adjusted yourself straight from London to finding the right tone for Bill and Rachel Hawk when you found them making hay. It is a gift.

You are working already on your new job. Good luck.

We will have a bathroom and lots of water in Los Pinos. Much love to you all

> Your mother

Your job will give me a new interest. Send me the measure for those overalls.

TO Montague Weekley

Sunday
3 September 1939

Dear Monty,

So the horror has come! On the radio I hear everything! Out there the Azul and the cows are having their noses to the ground, and I told them there was war, but they did not listen! Peaceful and sunny and warm, you can't believe it!

Truly I am grateful you came this summer, who knows if you can come next year? You will be very busy and the responsibility of it! I still hope Germans and Austrians might turn against Hitler and the whole show be over quickly!

If Italy joins war, Angelino will be recalled. *Please*, ask Vera [1] to let me know all you are doing. I guess Teddy [2] has gone; *where* is Vera, and Elsa, and has Stuart [3] joined?

Just a greeting and good luck. Keep well and strong all of you.

With much love

Your mother

It is paralysing! Angelino greets you!

> *William York Tindall's* D. H. Lawrence and Susan His Cow (*1939*) *aroused Frieda's defensive anger as perhaps no other of the many books about Lawrence has. The modification of his views later on, as in his introduction to* The Later D. H. Lawrence (*Alfred A. Knopf, 1952*), *apparently had no effect on her lingering resentment. In making the following letter available, Dr. Tindall, professor of literature at Columbia University, had this to say: "* . . . *I don't care what Frieda thought of me and have no objection to your publishing her slams. I guess I deserved them. I was young and bushy-tailed when I wrote about Lawrence. Frieda wrote me at least three letters.* . . . *The others seem misplaced or lost.* . . . *In a letter before publication she supplied many details of Lawrence's reading in Mexican archaeology. (All these details are recorded in my cow book.)" Frieda's "review" of Tindall's book is included among the essays.*

[1] Montague's wife.
[2] Edward Seaman, a naval officer, husband of her daughter Elsa.
[3] Stuart Barr, journalist, husband of her daughter Barbara.

Taos, New Mexico
16 September, 1939

Dear Mr. Tindall,

I read your book with great interest.

It made me laugh when you cannot explain by "fashion or reason" that Ursula wears red or green stockings. Can't you imagine that she did it for fun and that red stockings might look attractive in the snow?

Was not the purpose of your book to show that Lawrence was a fool and you much too smart to swallow him?

But was he such a fool to hate the machine and try and give a new meaning or an ancient one to his fellow men, of the world around them, in the light of this war, that they have gone into out of sheer boredom! Had the English accepted Lawrence, Lady Chatterley and all, they would not have gone to war.

How you detest him! How unfair you are!

That his vision was not his own and that he sneaked bits from others and cooked them up!

He never stayed with Mrs. Nutall for instance, never had books out of her library, only the one of her own she gave him. We lunched there three times. Also he knew nothing of a general and a Harvard widow. Your Dr. Vaillant is quite mistaken. Also in his novels the events are always based on some actual facts, they are not theories; Women-in-love as "Bunyan" is bunk to me—and too far fetched, your theory!

He was not a fascist. When an Englishwoman shot Mussolini through the nose, he said: "Why don't they put a ring through it?"

He had nothing to do with politics; he just wanted to be free and have his own individual relationship with anything in creation.

How can you say Virginia Woolf is a better artist? Aldous said of her: a highly decorated vacuum.

I think Lawrence's day is yet to come; even your book proves it.

I am old and alone now but the glow of his world makes one

feel rich, richer than ever your wife will be with all your
cleverness.

> Faithfully,
> Frieda Lawrence

TO Montague Weekley

> Kiowa Ranch
> *29 October 1939*

Dear Monty,

I was getting anxious not to hear from you. You don't sound
cheerful and God knows you have no reason to be. It must be
awful, this uprootedness and disorientation. Mabel was quite
distressed for you and said: "He is so sensitive." And Angelino:
"Monty ought to come and make pottery with me!" They have
not forgotten you here. We had a wonderful, sunny, golden
autumn. It seems incredible here to realize that people are scared
of air raids, with the peaceful cows and horses and trees and sky;
I wish I could send you some of the sunshine and peace.

Perhaps if this horror is over, it will be better. It is hard to
hang on to one's own reality and decency, but one must.

I remember Lawrence saying last time he went to Baden-
Baden: "A change has come over these people; I don't know
what will come of it, but something will. It seems I can hear the
wolves howling in these forests, and the towns are gone." It may
come to that. What an outlook.

I will write to Vera. Couldn't you make a bomb shelter for
yourself at Barrowgate Road? You must have such lonely
evenings!

You don't say anything about Barby and Elsa and Teddy and
Stewart.

I send you much love and wish you were here.

What a mess it all is!

> Your mother

TO Dudley Nichols

Kiowa Ranch
4 November 1939

. . . Yes, that awful war, my daughter Elsa's husband is a commander of a cruiser; poor Elsa, she is very fond of her Teddy.

Monty writes, not at all happy: he thinks of the lights of Broadway in the London blackout. I don't think we know how irritating it all must be.

I hope Hitler realises that he has called up spirits that he cannot call down again in Russia's alliance. I hate messes and despise the whole show. They think about everything except human living. . . .

TO Witter Bynner

Laurel Canyon Blvd., 2136
Hollywood
19 January 1940

Dear Hal,

How I wish I were with you! I would so love to see Mexico again. But we are without passports and can't make up our minds to ask for them or let sleeping dogs lie!

We are here in a comfortable house. Heard that Bob had just left to join you.

Have seen only the Huxleys and Dudley Nichols so far. It is nice to be in the green and not the white.

Yes, I will gladly send my book to Faustino, but he will have to wait, tell him, till we are back at the ranch. What a good time we had, in spite of the arguments, didn't we?

Just a line, the ink won't open, so forgive pencil.

Much love, perhaps you will appear here on your way back. Your rooms were taken, so we couldn't have them.

The Huxleys asked after you. Aldous has finished his *Pride and Prejudice* at M. G. M. His last book, *After Many a Day* [*sic*] *Dies the Swan*, is queer stuff.

Much love from Angie too.

Frieda

Thomas Matthews Pearce was professor of English and head of the English department at the University of New Mexico in Albuquerque. He was deeply interested in writers of the region and at this time was trying to create a Lawrence memorial at the ranch and at the Harwood Foundation, a branch of the university in Taos. Mrs. Lawrence agreed to give the university the ranch and her collection of Lawrence's manuscripts if it would undertake to provide perpetual care of the ranch and the chapel containing Lawrence's ashes, and if the Harwood, through its Taos board, would provide a memorial room and a vault for the manuscripts. Mrs. Lawrence's adviser and representative in the negotiations that followed was Willard Hougland. Professor Pearce obtained assistance from the Rockefeller Foundation in the form of a fellowship, held in 1944–45 by E. W. Tedlock, Jr., a member of his staff, to make a descriptive bibliography of the manuscripts (The Frieda Lawrence Collection of D. H. Lawrence Manuscripts, 1948). At this time the university and the Taos board were slow to respond to her enthusiasm, and her impatience is reflected in the letters. It was not until 1955 that the university, under a new administration, reopened negotiations, and accepted her gift of the ranch.

TO T. M. Pearce

Kiowa Ranch
San Cristobal, N.M.
9 June 1940

Dear Matt,
　The title of the lecture might be: "Some More Lawrence." [4]

---

[4] The lecture was given on July 16 at the University of New Mexico in Albuquerque, and dwelled at length on the tendency in some quarters to associate Lawrence with Fascism.

I come with Frank Waters,[5] we drive back the same night. What time is the lecture?

I think you can have the little house, but will tell you for sure when I come.

You dine with me and Frank, and we will talk.

Brett says she wants to pull Hitler's whiskers out. I feel I don't know whether I stand on my head or my heels, I don't know anything any more.

Let me know when the lecture is.

A rivederci,
Frieda Lawrence

I have not stirred from my mountain, but shall enjoy coming to Albuquerque! The Huxleys are coming soon!

TO Witter Bynner

Monday, 9 December 1940

Dear Hal,

Thank you so much for the 50 [?]. I am so glad you like it, Lawrence did some work on it too, I remember, when I got fed up with the pattern that goes all round.

Merrild also loved it. The McCormicks asked us to come down, when they return. We may do so and hope to see you all.

But I don't feel at all Christmasy with this terrible war, which I fear will be worse before it gets better.

Please thank Henrietta [6] for her nice note, we will come and see her.

Mabel trod on some glass and poisoned her foot, but is better.

Otherwise, it is wonderful weather and we are down at the lower ranch. "El Prado" post office.

Many, many greetings to you from Angie too.

Ever yours,
the old Frieda

[5] The writer, long a resident of New Mexico.
[6] Henrietta Harris, then Bynner's private secretary.

TO T. M. Pearce

> 8591 Crescent Drive
> Hollywood
> [*Erroneously dated March 21, 1940;*
> *postmarked March 18, 1941*]

Dear Matt,

First of all, *much* good luck for your coming marriage. I *am* glad for you; bring her soon, we shall be back early April.

Funny that you write about Aldington. He is going to stay with me all summer, comes 1st of May.

We are having a great time, almost feel guilty when we think of friends in Taos having such a hard winter.

George Biddle painted a big, really wonderful picture of me, and a young McKinley also. Mabel has come too, and Tony. We are very gay, Angelino and I. He has had the luck, that a man wants to make an exhibition of his paintings in New York.

Your book on American literature sounds exciting. Would it not be one thread that it frees itself from English literature and becomes entirely itself and American, something new? I remember how Lawrence felt that. You must talk to Aldington, he knows a great deal. American literature is a vast subject.

You always have a lot going on in Albuquerque.

Hollywood is really cosmopolitan. It bucks one up.

Now I would say much more, but will do so when I see you, hope soon.

> Many greetings,
> Frieda

TO Witter Bynner

> El Prado, New Mexico
> *12 December 1941*

Dear Hal,

I have just read some of your poetry again and thank the Lord it made the world "right" again. The one on Lawrence is so good and *not* nasty—in the bigger sense.

So war is here too now, the very air seems different.

I am so glad you like "Singing of Swans", I am sure Lawrence would have liked you to have it, as it were "one poet to another", and some of that wildness in him that you know about is there.

Thank you for sending me that article, it made me write one too, but I won't send it you, I will write it again.

There was a kind of upset here with the Vanderbilts.[7] I will tell you when we meet.

Will you be able to go to Mexico? We don't know yet if it is better to stay here where people know us. It is just on the cards that all aliens are interned.

I feel very American, I think, so does Angelino, his poor Italy has been a victim. Perhaps we are all victims, but of what? One tries to think it all out fairly, but there is no explanation. Perhaps there isn't one. Is Bob free of the army?

I hope to see you before you leave. Write us, like a nice Hal, when you can come up for dinner. We are down, as you know, so it is not far.

Ollie wrote that you had been so nice to them. Ollie said to Brett: "I have known men like Bynner in New York." Brett said to me: "That's where Ollie is dumb, there aren't any Bynners in New York." So there's a compliment from the uncomplimentary Brett!

So much love to you from Angie also. I admired the Americans going into war and Roosevelt, so decent and real.

Yours ever,
the old Frieda

TO Witter Bynner

13 December 1941

Dearest Hal,

I had written this letter when Angie brought your telegram. I was so touched by your thoughtful friendship! We laughed, too, at the ingenuousness of it.

I love the poem "Charioteer"! Do you wonder? I also *love*

---

[7] Joe and Ollie Vanderbilt.

"Voltaire Be With You". Write some more of those, there is a special Bynner note there, light and airy!

One is so thankful for friends these gloomy days. Angie seemed to have completely disappeared and gone under.

Let us meet. We have a new car, we need it with these distances.

Let us meet and drink to a future that with luck we may know.

> With love,
> gratefully ever,
> F.

TO Witter Bynner

> El Prado, New Mexico
> *19 January 1942*

Dear Hal,

You must miss your gay Bob. It makes the war more real. I wondered when I *had* to paint the sailorboy for Bob. I wonder where he has gone.

We have been lucky to have a nice letter from Francis Biddle,[8] it makes one feel protected.

I don't quite understand about the Vanderbilts. I will tell you what I know, then perhaps you can make it out for yourself.

When one looks out on this quiet landscape, it seems incredible that so much war is going on.

Why don't you come up with Christine or someone else? The weather is splendid. Just phone El Prado. I have three bottles of good whisky, but this is bribing.

I have a nice story for Christine about Victor Higgins[9] and Christine's visit to San Antonio, Victor told it yesterday.

This war makes one feel somewhat insignificant and small. But for all that, war is not all of life.

Come up soon.

Love from Angie and me,

> Frieda

[8] Attorney General of the United States during the war years. His letter would have been welcome indeed to someone of German or Italian antecedents who did not have citizenship.

[9] Painter, long a resident of Taos.

TO Witter Bynner

Kiowa
6 June 1942

Dear Hal,

It is too bad I did not write sooner. But we have moved up, just after having finished the building down at Los Pinos. It is always a job, cows, horses, chickens, pigs, canaries, goldfish, and ourselves and goods and chattels.

Thank you so much for your nice letter. Yes, let the man print those two pages. How he got them, I don't know.

I will give them back to you when, I hope, you come soon.

I wanted you to see the other house; it looks so much nicer, with electric light and running water, etc.

I very much feel the urge to write and want to work hard this summer. I was so pleased that you resented my passing through Santa Fe without my prancing in on you. But both times it was 10 in the morning, so I regretfully did not prance.

Come up soon, these awful days it is good to see the ones, and they are few, one loves.

I am so loving being up here, the late spring, so green. Your little plants you gave me have multiplied a lot. I want to hear all the news.

My love to Buena Vista. Won't you stay the night when you come?

Yours as always. Do you know we have known each other 20 years? Let's hope we know each other another 20.

Frieda

TO Witter Bynner

Kiowa
10 September 1942

My dear Hal,

What a feast you sent me! It was such fun and so many things, only too many!

These days I don't buy anything, so it is a pleasure. I wear the brooch and love the bottle, and use the combs and the mat is so Mexican!

Thank you so much, Hal, you gave me a lot of pleasure.

It is real autumn already and I hope you come up when the mountains have put on their bobcatcoats!

Tomorrow is Lorenzo's birthday, twelve years he is dead!

You looked so well and young, Hal, when you came last!

Ever yours,
Frieda

TO Witter Bynner

Kiowa
27 September 1942

Dear Hal,

You are so efficient, like all artists, in spite of what is said to the contrary of them.

Yes, the world is a chaos, but I feel curiously happy and hopeful, as if out of the chaos something new will be born. Surely humanity has lots of possibilities yet. The Nazis will die of their own horror and then if we are wise and follow the best in us, a wonderful people might come.

It is so beautiful, this life, one seems to know the value of it more, with all the horrors going on.

No, I didn't like the corkscrew, *that* was never a corkscrew to me!

I wish you would come up. If not, we will come down one day.

I hated the spirit of that article, the last one, that man doesn't know the simplest thing about living, with his "historic [*sic*] vitalism"; [1] what a phrase, it wouldn't fetch a cat from the fire.

Ever yours, Frieda

Love to the Bob!

[1] Probably a reference to Eric Bentley's "D. H. Lawrence, John Thomas, and Dionysos," *New Mexico Quarterly Review*, XII (May, 1942), which appeared in 1944 as a chapter of his *A Century of Hero-Worship*. Among Frieda's papers were notes for a reply, which, apparently, she did

TO Witter Bynner

El Prado
3 January 1943

Hal, you lamb of a friend,

There Christmas was over and the small Christmas tree put away and there comes another Christmas or a beginning of a New Year, so joyful!

I love those beautiful laces—it is so good to have them. Women are making munitions now and not lace, alas. I have a very handsome white satin dress (that Bridget gave me) and the big lace collar looks splendid on it. And you know I can plan things for the rest. *All* my finery comes from you. I either wear a brooch or a necklace or a feather in my hat or a scarf, or a shawl, always something of yours.

And the nice apron and the fine looking glass and the cigarettes that remind me of Mexico, and Angie loves finding out about the lighter. It was such an affectionate parcel, a Christmas in itself.

So I thank you very much. Can I never do anything for you? You have everything.

I get some money from England, the income of L's books, of that they take half income tax, the investments they keep, but it is enough what I get, we need so little, with the chickens and cows and no rent to pay. I am a lucky old woman!

Maria sent me such a lovely letter, saying that coming to the ranch had changed her life; so she built herself the place she

---

not complete and send to the editor of the *Quarterly Review*. She wrote, in part: "Mr. Bentley has produced such a funny object in his article, not Lawrence, not a man, but a scarecrow to hang his own intellectual rags on. . . . Even great men belong to their day and its problems. They themselves are elementally the battleground of the dying old and the new that clamors to be born. For this heroic struggle Mr. Bentley despises them. He has no use for greatness, lock, stock, and barrel he hates it. What does he wish to put in its place? . . . *Blueprints*, blueprints for the future. He thinks these great men should have had their ideas readymade, jumping from their heads like Pallas Athene from Zeus's head already booted and spurred and helmeted. . . . The 'Mediocre' hope that greatness can be achieved through a formula or blueprints; it can't or it would not be great."

wanted near Llano and she found her "peace and silence" and Aldous does things and is happy too. He is writing about another saint, asked Angie for some help and I had a fascinating book of Italian proverbs, just what Aldous wanted.

Mabel was operated in New York, is getting better. Everybody is pleasant and more or less peaceful here.

When shall we see you? I hope soon. One's life seems to turn inwards these days, one dare not turn outwards.

All my good wishes for you and Bob.

Always yours,
Frieda

TO Witter Bynner

6 January 1943

Dear Hal,

Your letter came and I saw the Benrimos at the Buffalo dance this afternoon. Everybody hopes you will come and see those decorations; you know Benrimo [2] made stage decorations in the past and I told Benrimo that you and he must meet.

I wrote a bit and will try and get it for you. I wanted to bring you in and what you had told me about China, but was not sure enough of my facts, that monastery and all that.

So you feel very superior now and virtuous about your sobriety. I wish Bob would catch your virtue; it would be better for him.

But I know from myself that it's no use going for people.

Have you as wonderful weather as we do?

I daren't ask you to stay the night in case Marina thinks it's her privilege, but we are comfortable and have room for you.

I still rejoice in your gifts; as you said, they aren't stylish, but if I try to be stylish, it is pitiful only.

It was strange at the pueblo to see an Indian as a U.S. sailor with his wife in those Indian boots and a shawl—strange altogether, this buffalo dance and a world at war.

---

[2] Thomas Duncan Benrimo, illustrator, art director, and set designer, particularly active in the 1910's. In New Mexico he had devoted himself to experimental painting, refusing offers to exhibit.

If it would only stop and when it stops, what then? You feel the hatred that Germany aroused will last to the end of time. But I won't end on a note of hate.

So here is my love.

Frieda

Angie liked the article and so did I, and thanks you.

TO T. M. Pearce

Wednesday
[March–April, 1944?]

Dear Matt,

Do let me know when you all come up. I will give you lunch.

I was glad to hear from you your work. I won't say all the things I want to say, we will talk when you come. What about the Lawrence memorial? You don't mention it.

I fear you and Helen may not be able to stay at the ranch, too difficult these days, but anyhow in Taos.

I am glad you like Robert Bright's book.[3] It is good.

Aldous just wrote me: "I only read two chapters of Lady C., but it looks as if it were going to be very good, with a kind of ease and freshness such as only Lawrence at his best possesses. And I loved your preface; it is so touching and even beautiful. And you find the most wonderful phrases sometimes. That one about the asparagus is a classic and ought to go into an anthology."

I was so pleased, was mad with the "smarties" who know so much better than Lawrence.

But the book [4] sold 10,000 already.

So come soon.

Ever yours,
Frieda

[3] Probably *The Life and Death of Little Joe*. Robert Bright was living in Taos.
[4] *The First Lady Chatterley* (Dial Press, 1944), the text of Lawrence's first draft. The third was published in Florence in 1928 as *Lady Chatterley's Lover*.

TO Witter Bynner

El Prado, New Mexico
23 May 1944

Hal, dear Hal,

What a wonderful letter you write and what a specially wonderful one to me! My vanity part would like to broadcast it, but the other me hugs it to myself jealously!

I saw Lawrence as an orchid suddenly and had to laugh.

Lady C. sells very well, but Sumner attacked her, found 92 "spots"; he must be very "pure". But it's the publisher's responsibility and it shows that there is a kick in the book still.

I am so glad you are extra well. You have to be there on this earth, you just have to, I couldn't do without you. I am glad you are there in Mexico, war is dreadful for poets and your idea of the *rapprochement* of races is so good. You made me love the Chinese.

Mind you send me that book. I understood when you wrote me: "It's best for me to be here."

You had to be alone and gather your strength, and men like you who feel responsible for the state of the world are rare and important. Aldous wrote how in England honesty has gone and morals and civic liberties—result of war. He also liked that preface very much, so the two men whose judgment I respect, liked it.

I am sure your Chinese book is good. The winter was long and cold and white, but now it's green and it makes me happy.

I really like my Taos. But Santa Fe is just lost without you, sheep without a shepherd.

I liked your poem very much, you will never lose your spark and your sanity.

But come back; in this grim world of today, the people one loves mean so much.

We have only been to the ranch once. There was still snow.

I am very much afraid of this coming invasion, uneasy.

I could go on, but I hope it won't be so long till I see you. Bring me some poems and read them to me.

Angie works away at his pottery but is distressed about poor Italy, it is such a mess.

Why not leave your fortune to a foundation "for the better understanding of all races"?

Nobody told me about Bobby Hunt, but I am very glad he is a success.

Everybody misses you in Santa Fe.

Dear Hal, my love to you!

Ever the old Frieda

TO Dudley Nichols

25 August 1944

. . . I have your beautiful letter about *Lady C*. There is a change in you, a new high note. I wish to goodness more people "got" *Lady C* as you do.

Your film on Elizabeth Kenny is something quite new, *there* is natural genius for you. I hope it is very good. That you have the production too in your own hands is good, so it will be a unified thing and no tinkering. I wish I were there and could sit and watch you produce it. Yes, it is strange that we love truth; lies can really be cleverer but they are not satisfactory.

Your letter was hopeful. Maybe this horror was necessary to shock us into human beings again. . . .

I was up at the ranch and gratefully thought of you, reading Montaigne and Plutarch's *Lives*, etc., *you* gave them to me and they are good to read these days, the great ones.

To me you are almost a symbol of the best in America—your freedom, your generosity, your sensitiveness.

Do you think that Lawrence had perhaps too much loyalty for his miners, almost an obstinacy? Surely the underprivileged must hate sympathy, and privileges also mean responsibility. But I don't know enough about it. . . .

TO Dudley Nichols

[*Undated*]

. . . There is the actual Christ we love and the man-made Christ whom they made into dogma and church. Read Lewis

Mumford's *Condition of Man*. It is *very* good. So clear and serene.

My Lorenzo (but the fact is he is not my Lorenzo but all the world's Lorenzo) is really a religious reformer. He wanted to put religion, that bond with all and everything, back into living and especially sex, that we don't live like a disturbed ant hill.

Don't you think that real love only begins when the "my" has been surpassed? Now you see Esta as the big being she really is. It takes time. . . .

The war, the actual war, will soon be over. There will be more mess, then there may be a new sprouting after all this horror and suffering.

But America is a great country. There is Angie, who was in the Italian army, and I of the German aristocracy, we couldn't be *worse*, and yet nobody cares and nobody bothers us. . . .

I know what you feel about Aldous. He is, as I have found him, the gentlest, most human human being, and not a bit of that gets into his books. Why? A man has asked me to tell him all I know about Aldous, but I *wouldn't*. It seemed to me a betrayal. The man wanted to write about him. . . .

That [*sic*] that's enough today. . . .

TO T. M. Pearce

El Prado, New Mexico
Monday
4 September 1944

Dear Matt,

It was a pleasure to be with your wife and you yesterday. But Mabel on Mary Austin is too bad. Mabel says Mary was ridiculous, but was she? I say *no*, because what she did came out of a primitive, instinctive individual and that is never ridiculous, only pretence is ridiculous. And all Mary's zest for life and genuine longing for culture and going after it; no, you cannot dismiss a remarkable woman like that.

So let's leave Mabel alone. It is so boring. I like Tedlock very much. Brett will help, I could see. This great scheme will go ahead almost on its own momentum.

I wish now I had written about Mary too, only I thought I did not know enough about her, but anyhow she has my sympathy.

Hope you come again.

Good luck to all your enterprises.

Next time you must stay here. It won't be luxurious, but we can be quite all right.

> Best greetings,
> Frieda

Please don't forget to send the Mary Austin booklet, I want to read what you said.

> *Edward Gilbert read English at Pembroke College, Cambridge, and history at London University, where he received a Ph.D. in 1954. His publications have been in the field of church history*—Saint Peter's Monkwearmouth (*1947*), Deerhurst Priory Church (*1954*), *and others. He was a friend of Middleton Murry for many years. In a December 10, 1963, letter to the editor he said of his correspondence with Frieda in the Forties: "I wrote to Frieda primarily to try and convince her that an order existed wherein Lawrence was predominantly validated as a man, which Frieda did not believe. . . . I wanted to shew her how his philosophy is conditioned by the circumstances of this order, although predominantly antithetic to this order. . . . I forget exactly how the question of failure came up. But obviously the theoretical failure implied above would prevent him from fulfilling himself, from believing in himself, and others from believing in him, all of which happened. . . . Both humanly and theoretically Lawrence's life was a failure measured against his aspirations. But such a failure is not discreditable, nor does it imply lower powers than others. Everything depends on the magnitude of the task you*

are attempting. Lawrence's was supremely great. He understood this, and did not hesitate to admit his failure. I understood it. And I assumed Frieda understood it. But I never made a mistake, that was bigger. She seemed to think I was insulting Lawrence, in spite of the fact that it was quite obvious that I had a high regard for him. She accused me of saying that she had failed him. As I said nothing of this, nor implied it, I was and am puzzled. I can only conclude that she lost her temper. Certainly this correspondence rapidly descended into a quarrel, which I regret, but for which I disclaim all responsibility. Moreover I must warn the reader that all her quotations must be held suspect. . . . I suspect that Murry must have told her that the woman I most respected and admired was Lawrence's mother, Lydia Lawrence. If so, it would explain everything. . . . The reader should not overlook that her reaction to me was very similar to her reaction to Lawrence when she was annoyed with him. I got a good idea of what the famous quarrels were like, from Lawrence's point of view."

TO Edward Gilbert

El Prado, New Mexico
17 September 1944

Dear Mr. Gilbert,

You ask many questions. How am I to answer them?

Since Lawrence died, all these donkey's years already, he has grown and grown for me, and I can see him as a whole, though you are right in saying that many things still puzzle me.

No, I don't think Lawrence was a pagan; he was too English for that.

To me his relationship, his bond with everything in creation was so amazing, no preconceived ideas, just a meeting between him and a creature, a tree, a cloud, anything. I called it love, but it was something else—*Bejaung* in German, "saying yes". All those people you mention seem so unimportant now. I have forgotten so much, and now that I am old (65), I know what a fool I often was.

Lawrence was that, and so rare a thing, genius, and Murry, as he says himself, did not have the least idea what Lawrence "was after." Murry was of the social world and Lawrence had another one. Lawrence was often unsure of himself, but not in the final issue. Everything, especially his own living, was of the utmost importance. He was compelling, he demanded a hell of a lot. I resented that, but I believe my chief merit, as I see it, was that to me not much mattered, except that he should come off, do what he wanted and had to do.

I think a real relationship only begins where the all too personal leaves off, and we fought like nothing on earth ever fought, being both possessive and jealous.

Wives are not respectful, but he was so real to me. I don't think "respect" matters to women. I didn't apply "principles" to him; he was something new on the face of the earth, as you say, and the old formulas didn't work. I have felt agonies of bitterness on his account, that he was not understood and was only reviled, but finally I feel only his triumph, never having given in, his uncompromising pride without conceit. He was a lovely man. The greatest thing he gave was, I think, what they condemn him most for—a new joy in sex—sex as the height of all human experience, just as people in love seem to see the moon and sea and all for the first time. That we had shared. *Nobody* has ever yet mentioned his wonderful letters to me at the beginning of my book. It is significant. One publisher said on reading "Song of a man who is loved", sex and religion should not be mixed. Of course, churches must hate him.

Murry and he had no "love affair". But Lawrence did not disbelieve in homosexuality.

If you could make posterity see him as he was, that would be great. Your wife sounds a lovely person.

Of course I will see you if you come.

Sincerely,
Frieda Lawrence

*Karl von Marbahr is recalled by Frieda's sister, Else
Jaffe, as a young lieutenant Frieda was attached to
when she was about sixteen—a somewhat more serious
attachment than a schoolgirl "crush." When Else was
in Berlin as a student, Lieutenant von Marbahr sometimes met her just to talk about Frieda. The portion
of this remarkable communication which has been omitted concerns the painfully personal problem of his
daughter's behavior.*

FROM Karl von Marbahr

[*Undated*]

My dear Frieda,

That was nice of you to write me at once and we will write to
each other often and when I have time I will come and see you
with pleasure. You wrote of yourself as an old goat, well I am
an old buck too and the emphasis is on "old" and why should not
two elderly domestic animals bleat together cosily.

You must tell me what you are doing, what plans you have,
where your children are. You had as far as I remember three or
more children. Then I would very much like to know if your
Lawrence is the writer D. H. Lawrence. If he is he must have
been a most extraordinary man of the highest individuality. I am
just reading a book by D. H. L., *Lady Chatterley:* it is written
with immense daring quite deliberately and in spite of the clarity
of expression produces a naïve almost chaste effect. I almost
think it is your Lawrence because I had to think of you, when he
says (p. 112), "She is nice, she is genuine, she does not know
how nice she is." That's how you were long ago, when I was
very fond of you; a little bit naïve, ingenuous, and yet strong, but
very feminine, no bluestocking.

After all you would have suited me very well. I would have
absorbed vigour from you and all would have been well.
Altogether I must think of you with Connie and I suspect the
author of having done the same. What else has he written? I
want to read his other things now.

*Frieda, a few years after Lawrence's death,
at her resort in the mountains, seventeen miles from Taos, New Mexico.*

Frieda and Angelo Ravagli, at their home at Taos,
a few weeks before her death in 1956.

At first I did not want to approach him because the monopoly of the English in general is a certain boredom and hypocritical untruthfulness. So you must tell me all this. Perhaps I am all wrong and D. H. Lawrence is not your Lawrence and Connie is not Frieda. As to my life it is all work, because a wife and three children want to live and quite rightly too. I am with the Ufa, that means nothing to you, but it is the biggest German movie concern and we try and with success to amuse the public. I am only an employee, work on censorship and the scripts of foreign films for Germany. . . .

Yes, that's how we have our troubles. You won't be without them either, Frieda. I had a sample in your letter. Have you still got relations in England?

A little while ago I visited my mother in Clareus. She is now over eighty but fresh and gay. Her husband died last year and she wants to stay on in Clareus. My sister Lene, the writer, whom you know, don't you, is with her.

Now I will close, my dear Frieda, and send you many sincere greetings. Twice I should have given you a kiss, once when you had stepped in the mud near the tennis court and you stood close in front of me, and then at the station in Metz when you were going away. I still see you at the open window of the car.

But then at that time we would have got engaged and would have had to wait ten years for a captaincy. Now I know if I had resigned my commission and started something else, together with you, I would have amounted to something as a writer or a journalist. You remain well and cheerful and write again soon to your old

K. v. M.

(*Translated from the German*)

TO Witter Bynner

El Prado, New Mexico
15 November 1944

Dearest Hal,

I love the Laotzu and your introduction and all your words! It was a great deal of pleasure to get this whiff of you, but it is only a whiff!

We are going to Brownsville, Texas, for 5 months. That is not so far from you, but not being citizens yet, we can't come to you, but maybe you could come. I want to get away from the cold and the snow and see mangoes and feel warm. How I'd love to come to Chapala!

A Texas oil friend found me the house and I am her guest. Did you see that Lady C. was acquitted? A good sign.

I hear Bob is with you and that Georgine will visit you. Willard is here and we have some good times, also necessary in these unbelievable times.

I enclose this wonderful letter. Found it in a book on the Jesuits; it made me think of you.

Come back again, we all need you. I hope you are well and Bob.

You will have become a real saint and philosopher by now! With much love to you.

Frieda

Greetings from Angie!

TO E. W. Tedlock, Jr.[5]

Route 1, Box 558
10 January 1945
Brownsville, Texas

Dear Ted! (not Ernest!)

I was so glad to get your long letter! I thought of you all at Christmas! It is so lovely to have young children around then!

Now for God's sake do, do realise that you are doing a very important job that will have its influence on the future and Lawrence is very lucky having you to do it. It may not look spectacular compared to battles or movie-stars, but it's solid. I just read Santayana—"Persons and Places"—somehow it re-

---

[5] An instructor in the English Department of the University of New Mexico, he had been in Taos since August, 1944, making a descriptive bibliography of Frieda's collection of Lawrence manuscripts.

minded me of you. It is very quiet, very solid and—lonely. I think you will always be a lonely bird too. You think too much of other people and not enough of yourself. So there! I shall enjoy going over what you have done!

Now, look, you be thankful, that you have not "carved a place" in the world for yourself yet. That's the "Ernest" in you speaking! You are making a place in the consciousness of men right now which is more than a professorship!

Aren't I scolding you and enjoying it! But that's because I am fond of you, you are a real person to me.

Of course I read the bit I was not to read to Angie, to him and he laughed.

We enjoy it, the sea and the warmth and the oranges and the nice place we have, but Angie has had boils on his neck and gets mad.

I miss my Taos friends, you can't make friends so quickly.

I felt it very badly that the children had nothing from me at Christmas, but it was a rush moving and getting used to this. I am so glad you see in Mabel Degen what I see in her.

Remember me to Agnes, and the birds.[6] Keep well, all of you. Now I will stop or I'll go on.

> Yours affectionately,
> Frieda

TO Dorothy Brett

> Brownsville
> *25 January 1945*

Your letters are really more interesting than you realize; instead of reading a novel you are living one! and I live it too! . . .

TO Dorothy Brett

> Brownsville
> *21 March 1945*

. . . Well, our correspondence goes on flowing. I have never written to anybody so regularly except when I was in love, or to my mother! . . . My good news is that Guthrie McClintic has

---

[6] She had left two parakeets in the Tedlocks' care.

taken the play *You Touched Me;* you remember Tennessee Williams, who made a good job of it. . . . There will never be peace, I fear, till the world changes altogether. You hate the Nazis, so do I, but I also hate any other bullying and stupidity. I sometimes feel as if the whole of humanity were a jungle, all the ideals and morals only a camouflage. . . .

TO Witter Bynner

El Prado, New Mexico
5 December 1945

Dear Hal,

Most stimulating was our "night", for me anyhow. Also, I had never enjoyed Bob so much. I got a real "glimpse" of him that night. Spud wrote how he enjoyed seeing you! Quite a lot for the Spud!

You must repeat the feast! I translated this from Nietzsche for you.

Also just had a letter from Kiker,[7] he wants to try again with those men. It might be very helpful if you talked to Kiker.

Also, if Big Sur is a success, you will come, won't you? You and Bob? We will get the Huxleys and Nichols and soak in the sulphur baths. Tell Bob—it will bewilder him—that Mabel and Brett are friends again. I was "cheap at 3 cents" the next day after you left, but happy. We could just never stop talking and listening!

My love,
Frieda

John Middleton Murry's friendship had been, perhaps, both the most promising and the most bitterly disappointing for Lawrence, from his eagerness to have Murry and Katherine Mansfield live near them in Cornwall in 1916, to his savage criticism of Murry's philosophy and editorship of The Adelphi *in 1925. Now, long after Lawrence's death, the correspondence between Frieda*

---

[7] Judge Henry Kiker was her attorney. The matter under discussion may have been her application for citizenship.

and Murry that begins here, in 1946, makes clear that
their mutual attraction during Lawrence's lifetime seri-
ously challenged their loyalty to him, a challenge of
which he must have been aware. The letters have
been edited by Mrs. Mary Middleton Murry; the elisions
in both Frieda's and Murry's letters were made by her.

FROM John Middleton Murry

> Lodge Farm, Thelnetham
> nr Diss, Norfolk
> *27 May 1946*

My dear Frieda,

I have mislaid your letter. It had an address that was new to me. But I shall send this to Taos, and hope that it will reach you.

I am very sorry to hear about Monty. I have written to him, but so far there has not been time for a reply. When I receive one I will write to you again.

You ask me for a long letter. Well, my dear, if I were to try to give you an account of all that has happened to me since I last wrote, it would have to be a *very* long letter indeed. I will put the main facts quite baldly, beginning just before the war.

In March 1939 I had to go into hospital for an operation on my sympathetic nervous system. What had happened was that seven years of being married to——were killing me by inches. The struggle between us was more than I could stand. . . . After years of this, I found that I was beginning to lose the use of my legs. The condition was diagnosed eventually as a rare dis-ease—sometimes called Buerger's disease—whereby the nerves which control the flow of blood to the arteries of the legs gradu-ally decay. There's no cure. But by a drastic operation the prog-ress of the disease can be checked.

When I came out of hospital I had a longish period of great pain: which ended in a nervous breakdown while I was away from home, in Wales, trying to convalesce. When I emerged from this breakdown, I knew I was free of ——. The emotional and physical bond was finally broken. That left me free to fall in love, which I promptly did—with Mary (née Gamble). . . .

In 1942 I took this farm of 200 acres, and I have been farming it ever since: it is run as a sort of community farm. There have been plenty of ups and downs; but on the whole I have never regretted it. And now, at last, it is a decent going concern. But there has been and still is plenty of hard work. Last spring (1945) I had to go into hospital again for another operation to save my other leg. But I didn't have a nervous breakdown after that one. I can't walk very far; but I can do most other things.

I took the pacifist stand during the war, and edited the pacifist newspaper *Peace News*. That got me into some trouble. But they didn't actually imprison or intern me: and they didn't interfere with my farming. So I have nothing to complain of.

My life with Mary has been one of unbroken happiness ever since it began. She is 9 years younger than me. She was 41, I 50, when we fell in love. And it has been a kind of heaven on earth ever since. I have to confess, in the simplest and most naïve way, that I just didn't know what man-woman love could be until I met Mary. You know I am not trying to flatter you, my dear, when I say that she reminds me of you more than of any other woman I have known. Anyway, with her I have come into full possession of a knowledge which you alone came near to teaching me: what I call the knowledge of the innocent Eve. I trust her absolutely, and have trusted her absolutely from the moment we met. Through her and in her I have finally untwisted myself, and I am now (I think) as simple a person as you are likely to find. Her love enabled me to get over the bitter pang of parting with my two younger children—the little girl whom you saw and for whom you knitted a shawl as a baby, and a little boy who was born some years afterwards. My two elder children came away from home with me. Katherine, the elder, is now 21 and at the University; John, now 20, is in the Navy still, but is hoping to get out by the end of the year. The other two, whom I have not seen for nearly 6 years, are Mary (now 14) and David (now 7). But, as I say, I have got over the agony of being without them.

I continually think about the old times: the pain of them has gone, and only the joy remains. I wish I had understood life then as well as I understand it now; but that's an impossible and childish wish. *Si jeunesse savait, si vieillesse pouvait!* How terribly we hurt one another: how utterly was I bewildered! But I think back, with nothing but love and gratitude, to lovely moments with you. How odd a creature I must have seemed to you, and yet you were fond of me! It wasn't wasted, that fondness—believe me. Those moments of blessedness when I lay beside you fed something in me that had been utterly starved and only now, in the last years, has been full fed.

I don't believe—quite finally don't believe—in the *necessity* of the struggle between man and woman. That is not to say that I know how it can be avoided. I had to go through the same bitter hell, with——: and finally lost all faith in woman, even though I knew that to lose faith in woman was to lose faith in life itself. But, lo and behold, I came through—battered, but alive and capable of love, and able to feel younger in my love than I did at 21.

I have learned that the *only* thing that matters is complete trust between a man and a woman: complete physical trust, complete spiritual trust—there's no distinction between them. Where that trust exists, there is heaven on earth. Life is utterly fulfilled. And everything is so simple, that it's hard to believe that one ever lived in any other condition.

Now you must write *me* a long letter. Tell me whether you agree, or disagree. I feel that I am only telling you something that you knew years ago.

Yours ever affectionately
Jack (now 56, 57 in August)

TO John Middleton Murry

El Prado
Taos, New Mexico
4 June 1946

My dear Jack,

It gave me quite a pang to see your handwriting I know so well. . . . I am very glad you are happy! I agree with you:

why, oh why did we have to go through all those agonies and fights? We were fond of each other, the Lord knows. No blame that I can see—that's how it was. *Guilt* is stupid anyhow! Your farming sounds good.

Brett is quite near. I gave her a piece of my land and she built a house and she comes over all the time.

I am 66! but I am quite well off and don't feel old, except peacefully. Angelino has been a good friend and helper to me. . . . Those adorable children are 21 and 20? Lord, it makes one feel a thousand years old.

Brett just appeared and was excited that I had heard from you and is writing too. It is only 7 o'clock in the morning.

Monty is well again, but he is not coming here. His doctor wrote the Thames valley climate would not do after this.

So you were a pacifist, the only thing to be. People listen to what you say. I saw Aldous this spring. He is all right in his own way. I am very happy only too many people come to see me and I love to be alone and let myself be lost in my wandering thoughts. I am sure Lawrence would have been like we are now. We all of us have a lot to be thankful for. It is fun to be writing to you. If I can send you anything you can't get, let me know. I will try and get it.

My greetings to Mary.

Your affectionate, very old friend

Frieda

FROM John Middleton Murry

Lodge Farm, Thelnetham
nr Diss, Norfolk, England
4 September 1946

My dear Frieda,

I meant to write you a fortnight ago: but one thing after another interposed.

We have had a beastly summer, and it's being a horribly difficult harvest. Rain and wind, rain and wind. All the country folk hereabout put it down to the atom-bomb: and I shouldn't be surprised. Man's everlasting monkey tricks with the universe have to be paid for somehow.

It's nice to be in touch with you again. Everything begins to seem strange in this modern world, and it's a comfort to talk to one's old, real friends. What a queer young man I was, to be sure! Thinking back, I wonder at myself—how naïve I was, and how ill at ease in the world,—thoroughly scared of it, in fact, but trying to keep my end up. The one redeeming feature in that remote J. M. M. that I can see is that he really did have a genuine capacity for love. That was genuine—though may be it was largely a desire for protection: for the safety and security of love.

I wish you would write me a letter telling me what you really feel about love—a love autobiography, so to speak. It seems to me so terribly important. And yet we go to our graves without really telling the *truth* about it. That is one thing I am determined not to do. I will leave a faithful record behind me if I can manage to write it. Above all, it's the *happiness* of love I want to record. I've got booksful of the agonies. . . .

But do you give me some of the woman's truth. You have time now, my dear: every now and then instead of letting yourself be pleasantly lost in your "wandering thoughts", take up your pen and write me a page or two about your experience of love.

As I told you, it's only since I found Mary that I have entered into my inheritance of love,—to the full. The only glimpses I had had of what it meant were those I had with and from you. One is so terribly shy—worse than shy: afraid. *Why* is it so? I remember so well what I used to feel about you sometimes—that you had something wonderful to give me, if only I had the courage to take it. But the kind of courage required was pretty tremendous really, for a shy and affectionate young man with very lofty notions of the obligations of friendship. But looking back, I think that my shrinking from letting Lorenzo down, though it was a genuine feeling, was merely an excuse. I didn't take what you had to give because I was afraid of love itself. It's like taking a tremendous plunge—into a strange, new world. One has to surrender oneself entirely and absolutely to love—at any rate with a woman like you. And I dimly felt this, and was scared: not of you, but of the new world, the new life. That's how it seems to me now. Tell me how it seems to you. I truly want to know.

I don't think casual love-affairs really come into the picture at all: simply because they are casual, they cannot be the real thing. Love, for a man like me, anyway, is essentially a headlong self-surrender; and I don't believe it essentially different for a woman in this respect. But again, I say, tell me how you feel about it all.

Well, that's enough to go on with. I hear from —— occasionally now. We have buried the hatchet, I hope, for good and all. Cath Carswell died a few months ago—I suppose you heard. Then H. G. Wells the other day: and what I chiefly thought of was the night we all went to his party in Hampstead, and the immense preparations we made. Lorenzo's cuff-links were my masterpiece. Do you remember?

Yours affectionately,
Jack

TO E. W. Tedlock, Jr.

El Prado, New Mexico
9 October 1946

Dear Ted,

I am sorry not to have written before, had a cold, but am better. You sent that lovely record,[8] but no bill. I play it when I do the chores, very helpful.

Yes, send me your questions. You ask, why America? You see most other possibilities were again English, and *Delius* [9] had offered a farm in Florida.

Yes, Ceylon was because of the Brewsters. Then his health was bad in Ceylon. So Australia. Then America. Mabel had written, "The Indians say the heart of the world beats here in

---

[8] A recording of English ballads.
[9] Frederick Delius, the composer.

Taos," and she sent photos of *Acoma*. But I expect you will turn up soon and we will talk. Also more about Harwood Foundation. Why don't you stay a night? That you don't get so tired. You will be my guest. I will get you a room, if you let me know in time.

Ever your
Frieda

TO E. W. Tedlock, Jr.

El Prado, New Mexico
18 October 1946

Dear Ted,

I enjoyed your visit very much.

They had a meeting [1] here, discussed the Lawrence memorial, but did not ask me—it was said I was "vague" about it. Now I had talked with Willard, there was a definite letter left on Zimmerman's [2] desk. But nothing happened at all. They can't expect me to run around with my offer.

Lawrence's birthday was on the 11th of September. Yes, we must ask Willard. As for a tea, I can't spread myself around as Mrs. D. H. L. I can't do it. I would come and look at the exhibition as a private person, but no, no tea.

Bring the librarian when you come. I am glad about the cases—25 Mss. does not seem too much to me. We might have special editions too—translations and so on.

Thank you for "widdershins".

Becky James [3] is coming this morning and I want to say a thing or two to her. I am cross. I felt I had done my part and they

---

[1] The meeting involved further, but futile, efforts to reach an agreement between the University of New Mexico and Frieda, through her representative Willard Hougland, on a Lawrence memorial room to house his manuscripts at the Harwood Foundation, and on care of the ranch and the chapel containing Lawrence's ashes. The tea was part of the plan to exhibit the manuscripts at the University Library in Albuquerque.

[2] The president of the university, James Zimmerman.

[3] Rebecca James, an artist.

had not done theirs. And then I am blamed. That's how it goes.

Yours ever,
Frieda

I think they should have asked you too to that meeting, you know more than anybody about the Mss.

TO E. W. Tedlock, Jr.

El Prado, New Mexico
15 December 1946

Dear Ted,

Yes, do come sometime between Dec. 20–Jan. 5. We aren't going yet, because I have a hearing on 14th of Jan. for my citizenship. Hope all goes well.

The books Eddie Marsh sent were *Thomas Hardy*. They produced that essay on Thomas Hardy; you remember, it hasn't so much to do with Thomas Hardy, but I love it. I think when L. was prowling in Charing Cross Road, London, where the cheap secondhand books are, he found some Fenimore Cooper and that and the idea of going to Florida set him off.

Come before the second of January as I may go to Ojo Caliente for a week with Tinka to soak.

Best till I see you.

F.

TO Witter Bynner

Laguna Vista
Port Isabel, Texas
17 February 1947

My poor Hal,

I did not expect this tale of horrid woe. I do wish I were a "citizen", then I would come and see you. *Do* let me know, please, that it is not that radio business.

One always has to worry about one's friends! There I thought you and Bob were having your usual good Chapala fun!

For God's sake, don't burn up yet, it's too soon; let's wait till we do it together when our time comes in hell!

We bought a house here right on the gulf. I love it, it's still wild, and fishermen with sailing ships who bring us fish, and the lighthouse of Padre Island blinks at night, always twice and then a pause. There are pineapple boats and banana boats on the wide channel and I want to go on one. So much to watch—when the boats turn so cleverly in the channel and steam away round the bend and then they look like moving on land and look mysterious and the sun sets behind them.

The world is so lovely in so many places. And you don't enjoy anything just now, it isn't right.

The house is a friendly little house and Angie is happy too, fishing and painting. He painted some fish, really good.

I almost feel guilty of liking it so much here, but in the American constitution it says "the pursuit of happiness", no other nation ever had that.

Saw Christine in Santa Fe, she has really great charm. . . . Lynn Riggs [4] is in Taos in Mabel Degen's house. Mabel Degen [5] went to Paris. Maybe Spud comes to visit us here.

We go back about the 20th of April. I got so fed up with that snow in Taos and so many clothes on one and wet feet and cold nights. Mabel L., you can't talk to her when she is in her bad moods, she just makes statements and that's that.

Such heavenly peace here, not a house in sight, only the lights of the fishermen's boats at night.

Please, get better and let me know. If you get well, you might visit us on your way home.

Those boys,[6] who were in the Navy and then waiters, who

---

[4] Born the son of an Oklahoma cowpuncher, he wrote poetry and plays, in the idiom of his region, on the vanishing cowboy and open range. The most famous are "Green Grow the Lilacs" (1931), which was the basis of Rodgers and Hammerstein's "Oklahoma!"

[5] A painter. Her house and studio near the Harwood Foundation were left to the University of New Mexico.

[6] William Goyen and Joe Glasco. Goyen in particular has since achieved a considerable reputation as a writer.

write now, are building themselves a house on my land next to Brett's.

Willard Hougland has been sick again too.

My terribly good wishes for you, I will even pray.

Angie sends his greetings.

> Ever your old friend,
> Frieda

Greetings to Bob, glad he is well.

TO E. W. Tedlock, Jr.

> Port Isabel, Texas
> *29 January 1948*

Dear Ted,

Thank you for your nice note. I liked the order form.

Now here's a mess. You will understand from this letter what it's about. I wrote to Pollinger that I am sure I had sent *all* the typescript of the second Lady C. to Mondadori.[7] He writes again. Now I thought the original Mss. of the second Lady C. might have the missing page—I mean the writing.

Now, Ted, would you be a perfect angel and go to Taos to the *bank* and look it up? It's an awful chore, I know. Another complication is that Angie isn't here and I don't know where the key of that trunk is. So you would have to break it open.

Angie went to New York for a fortnight; not so "hot", this weather.

I enclose a note to Mr. Secrest.[8]

Would you copy it, the page, and send it to Pollinger?

Here it's cold after heavenly weather. Angie will be back in a few days.

A contract in England with "Pictor" for "Rocking-Horse Winner"—another one for play and eventual movie rights for "Lady C."

Hope you are all well. Spud couldn't take his job any more,

---

[7] For the Italian translation.
[8] An officer of the Taos bank.

has "quit", may come here. Brett in San Francisco, exhibition of her pictures.

I am translating my father's diary in the Franco-Prussian War. I love words. He wrote it in a sort of machine gun style.

The best to you and yours.

Frieda

Nobody but you could do this!

TO E. W. Tedlock, Jr.

23 March 1948

Dear Ted,

The book [9] has come. I think it's splendid! The look of it and the printing and mostly your work. It seems to me so solid and scholarly without the dullness of scholarship, that it so often has. It ought to give you a reputation for all time. I have a hunch it will even sell. I am only sorry Lawrence himself can't see this book and your hard, patient work; he would have appreciated the stuff of yourself you put into it.

Well, there it is, you must be *proud*. Spud is here and is also impressed with the book. But he looked at "Altitude" and said you printed what he had left out!!

The "boys" are looking for work in Dallas, they hated their teaching job with awfully tough kids.

We had a good winter, now it's beautiful, 80 degrees! We go back on the 20th of April, hope to see you soon after that. I have decided to have my sister Johanna over from Austria. Things look grim and I could not bear it if she disappeared behind the iron curtain. We always got on well together. It's a responsibility though.

Have a good Easter. This was a really satisfactory book for me, it did my soul good! I want to send some of them to people like Aldous and so on. It also seems very clear and well arranged,

[9] *The Frieda Lawrence Collection of D. H. Lawrence Manuscripts: A Descriptive Bibliography*, just published by the University of New Mexico Press.

the book; I don't understand so much about that part really, but it seems so.

Greetings to the family and a nice Easter.

Yours ever,
Frieda

I have not thanked you for the Mondadori job! It was good of you!

TO E. W. Tedlock, Jr.

Port Isabel
4 April 1948

Dear Ted,

Isn't fame the damndest thing! But then you can still be proud of your own good job.

A letter from Matt Pearce, I enclose it. God knows he means well, but here is my reaction. Those hours we spent together on this job *meant* something to me and I would feel we were both cheapening this experience. I have an idea you feel the same. Now, to make a show of it—*No*. Do you agree? I might say to —— that I think we would both feel self-conscious; *don't* tell him what I say to you here, I don't want to hurt his feelings; as I said, he means well, but wouldn't we both feel fools! It was such a grand experience seeing you slowly realize Lawrence and then your doing all the hard, plodding work. And this splendid book emerged! I would come with Brett, I hope, but no show—you know how I detest those things and I would come for your sake.

Didn't I tell you this book would make you a name?

Soon our time is over here, we will be back about the 23rd. Come up soon, and talk about the Ph.D.

Spud is here and very gay, having a holiday. He grumbled at your printing that episode, but I think really was amused.

Hope you are feeling rested. Peace here.

My best,
Frieda

TO E. W. Tedlock, Jr.

El Prado, New Mexico
Monday

Dear Ted,

It was a pleasure to see you in your own home [1] and everything flourishing: you and Agnes and the kids and Freckles and the trees and shrubs. I was really so pleased about the whole thing, such a friendly success. The book is beautiful.

We left at 5 o'clock this morning, a lovely drive. While poor Brett had been nagged by Mabel at Embudo.

Just a thought that you might use later on: It is strange that people think Lady C. so shocking. After all the love-act that L. describes is really *scientific*, only wrapped in poetical language. It seems another case like Galileo (it was Galileo wasn't it?) when he said the earth moves, and was condemned for it. Do you agree?

Thank Agnes too for her hospitality. I am a bit tired now. Angie has worked all day. Angie says it all was real and friendly and "unofficial". I shall not forget it!

See you soon.

Affectionately,
Frieda

Do you think I could have a few copies of the book? A letter from a man for Mss. You will see I'll get more requests.

TO T. M. Pearce

El Prado, N.M.
5 May 1948

Dear Matt,

I am still feasting on the lovely occasion. I never expected anything so full of meaning, so I was more than just "pleased."

Thank you so very much, Matt, you took so much trouble; I will never forget it.

[1] She had gone to Albuquerque to be guest of honor at a tea in the University Library. Tedlock participated in the event; his descriptive bibliography of Lawrence's manuscripts had just been published.

It was wonderful to see your new abode and I hope it comes along fast and that Helen is still not at the last gasp.

I have a few books, translations of D. H., I want to give you for the library.[2] I love *my* book. Hoping to see you before very long.

I will write again soon, and thank all those nice people that helped you from me. Angie thanks you too, he had a good time. I am writing to Popejoy [3] and you will come up this summer, with them. Think of an Mss. for *your* self.

You will let me know if anything goes on about them.

Again, dear Matt, thank you and Helen.

Ever yours,
Frieda

TO E. W. Tedlock, Jr.

El Prado, New Mexico
11 September 1948

Dear Ted,

Glad you are back, and that Los Angeles was a success. I knew you would like Merrild.[4] Your book is a success.

Now I have an idea for you. Lately it came to me that to understand Lawrence one should see him in the tradition of the fathers of the church, St. Augustine and even Francis of Assisi with his fervent feeling for plants and animals!

Are there any unpublished Lawrence things for Ortega? I think you know better than I do.

We have had a splendid summer. Stephen Spender is in the boys' house; they have gone to Reed College. You must come and

---

[2] Shortly thereafter these books were received by the University of New Mexico library.

[3] Tom Popejoy, under whose administration as president of the University of New Mexico her hope that the ranch would receive permanent care as a Lawrence memorial was realized in 1955.

[4] Tedlock had spent the summer in graduate study at the University of Southern California, and had gone to see Knud Merrild, the Danish painter, a friend of the Lawrences since the Twenties, and author of *A Poet and Two Painters*. At this time he was forced to make a living painting houses.

see the finished house; it's nice. Also a Leonard Bernstein came, a musician.

Willard is rather sick. He has more misfortunes than anyone I ever knew. He has a swollen neck and has to be operated.

I am still not sure when and if my sister will come. It costs 790 dollars to fly from Vienna and back.

Hope you can turn up soon. Please, Ted, send one of your books to Pollinger and another to Editions des Deux Rives, 9 Quai St. Michel, Paris 5, France. Pollinger: 39–40 Bedford Street, Strand, London W.C.2.

I liked *The Nation* article, also in the New York *Times* there was something.

My love to the family!

> Yours ever,
> Frieda

TO Witter Bynner and Robert Hunt

> Port Isabel, Texas
> *7 January 1949*

Dear Hal and Bob,

The pleasure of seeing you left a glow in me and in the night I thought, "This is the first night they are sleeping here and I hope there will be more!" I am sorry I was not my top self, but you did me good and I have done a big wash already!

Now have a nice spring and summer in Chapala.

You both looked so well and happy!

When my stuff is typed, I will send it to you. There is very little finally done, but lots of notes. I must write now or never. I shall be too old soon.

You have a lovely day for your drive.

Give my love to Christine. And lots and lots to you both. Thank you so much for your lovely visit!

> Ever your Frieda

Angie sends his greetings!

TO Witter Bynner

> Port Isabel, Texas
> *14 February 1949*

Dear Hal,

I am glad to have your address in Chapala.

My great news is that Nusch [5] is here! It is wonderful to have her. She is still so young and gay and good-looking; she has the "grand" manner and all she tells me seems somehow admirable, makes sense and is sane. So we get along "fine" and Angie too! I am looking forward to you meeting her, you and Bob! Your visit was sweet, but, oh so short.

I am not writing much! What a chore it is! But sometimes I love it!

Mabel comes like a stroke of lightning, she likes it here, but not Tony. Long letters from Millicent.[6] I like her so much! That Bob Davidson [7] is a sensitive creature!

Yes, ask about those letters, do! It's 80 today, but a beastly wind! Yes, next summer we go to the ranch and Nusch will tell you some of "her" Lawrence and you will laugh!

Have a nice few months and come back and we will meet, that is something to look forward to!

Love from Angie, and always love from me and to you both,

> Frieda

TO Witter Bynner

> Port Isabel, Texas
> *6 December 1949*

Dear Hal,

I wanted to say good-bye to you before we left. It will be some time till we meet again.

You will be leaving for Egypt soon and you will have a good

---

[5] Her younger sister, Mrs. Johanna Krug, who then lived in Austria.
[6] Millicent Rogers was a close friend of Frieda and Dorothy Brett, and lived nearby in a big house at Ranchitos. Her collection of Indian artifacts and crafts is now housed in a museum in Taos endowed by her.
[7] A sailor during the war, now a lawyer in Brooklyn.

few weeks, I hope, and you and Bob be careful and don't get sick, for goodness sake; it's so boring to be sick.

Laurence Pollinger, the agent in London, and he is a very good agent, would like to handle your book and sell it to Heinemann. I told him about it! . . . Pollinger writes Dieterle would like to make a film of Lady C., but the British censor won't allow a film of that title, after twenty years and so many people have read the book.

We had a nice drive here, stayed at a beautiful ranch near Sonora, a Dr. de Berry, his dead wife was Longfellow's daughter.

Now here it is warm and bright and I really like the peace and no strain of any sort. Penguin are printing a million cheap Lawrence books. L. would have liked the cheapness.

So your book will just be out at the right time. If you are kind to me in your book, I will be happy. Think how many nasty things they have said about me too.

My love to you, Hal and Bob. I can imagine what fun you will both have on your flight. Fly like the ducks here; they twinkle!

Frieda

TO Witter Bynner

Port Isabel, Texas
8 January 1950

My dear Hal,

Here is my wish for a wonderful holiday.

Norman [8] used to like me and he was brilliant fun, but he was down on Lawrence and beware of him—he is wicked. I am really quite excited for you over your trip. Murry will interest you. No, Murry was a witness at our wedding, and Campbell, in Ireland, he is a Lord now. Murry would know his name. A must for you is my son Monty; and Frere you will enjoy (Heinemann). Lady Cynthia Asquith. My sister Else in Heidelberg. I feel you will have such a good time. You will have lots of people to make a fuss of you! You might see Spender. He knows loads of people.

[8] Norman Douglas, best known for *South Wind* (1917).

The Sitwells, etc. There used to be a Lord Berners in Rome—nice.

Yes, your book will be something for me, I know.

Whenever I think of you I get a most pleasant feeling of warmth. Our relationship is safe, thank the Lord. So, my blessings go with you on your trip! Above all, keep well. Don't eat fresh oysters anywhere; they aren't safe. Take warm clothes. You might also look up my very good agent Laurence Pollinger. He would like to handle your work.

I am sure I shall think of lots of people when this letter has gone. Thank you for the photograph. It makes me laugh! How fat I was! What a good time we had.

Write me when you have time. Bob will be thrilled too. I shall be travelling with you!

So have a first-rate time till we meet again!

Nusch had a 6 months' extension. I wonder how long you will be gone!

Ever the old girl
Frieda

TO Dudley Nichols

Port Isabel, Texas
11 January 1950

. . . You write me an interesting letter and say: "Don't answer it," but you make me want to! So much goes on inside you and you know I always expected great things of you: I will read "Job" again, will borrow a Bible from the neighbours. I never quite got the hang of it, who is talking, Job or the friends.

I have been talking to Paris over the phone, to Baron Philippe de Rothschild, who made a good French play with Gaston Bonheur of *Lady Chatterley*. You must meet him, he is nice. It was about filming his play, and it bores me because I don't know enough.

Been reading a book about the Brownings. It seems so *tame* these days, incredibly so, we have come through so much savagery since those days, but also more truth. Rothschild told me how he had been in the "underground", had been at the liberation of "Belsen" and had fainted at the horror of it. He said (I think he forgot I was German): "I felt I could never shake hands with a German again while I lived." It made me miserable for days. But then I thought of Palestine, that is a hope and I am sure the horrors of Belsen helped to make that hope bloom. Francis Biddle said to me, like you: "Why not give the devil a chance?" But he is a cynic and you are not, though I am sure he loves America passionately. He asked me: "What do you think we talked about for the first two hours at the Nürnberg trials? . . ." I did *not* say what I wanted to say: that the virtue of the victor is generosity!

I am trying to write, but it's so hard to find out what you really want to say and then say it in a convincing way!

I was telling you about the unparalleled generosity of Americans (you among them), but here is another story. Angie said there was a fair in Port Isabel. Hoping for a circus (we went to one with you) we went. A sordid little affair. A man got hold of Angie, made him play a game with balls beginning at 25 cents, in a few moments Angie had lost a hundred dollars; hoping to get the money back, I signed a cheque for 200 and we lost it all! We were hypnotised or something! We felt so ashamed and dumb. Now we are being frugal to make up for the 300, serves us right. I think the devil is part of the show too. He keeps us on our toes. I loved Senator Taft's saying: "If we arm to the teeth, it may be like being all dressed up and having nowhere to go." I just write anything that goes through my head, as you notice.

I still think you will do something specially fine one day, in spite of your saying your last film is nothing much. . . .

TO Witter Bynner

[*Undated*]
5 o'clock, *early*

Dear Hal,

How beastly about your finger. I hope it is healing well. What an insensitive, hateful creature to bang the door on living stuff—*damn*.

Now I will amuse you. I think our friend C. came up to "keep me in my place", that I don't swell up. She is so very honest and kind really, and loves you. She told me about a scene you had, soon after Lawrence died, with her and Ida. You said Lawrence was a happy and a fortunate man. This makes me so *profoundly* glad, you *knew*, you *knew* about him and the something else, that we *believe* in, some *glamour* in life. Do, I *implore* you, write about him, it's up to you because you are a *man.* . . .

I don't really think much of what I wrote [9] except as a document, not as *creation*. You must do that. Also it *did* please me that you said I was beautiful. I am *not* beautiful in the society sense, but sometimes I can be, thank the Lord, and will take the responsibility; and C's aim in making me feel *small*, had the other effect of making me laugh inside with *gladness*. I am so *thrilled* that *you* know about that *shiny* part in us few, we won't deny it even if so few see it and have it. Thank you for the lovely beads of heavenly blue. Did I tell you I left you one of Lorenzo's Mss. in my will?

> Yours ever,
> F.

Harry T. Moore had been gathering material about Lawrence for years, and was soon to become the foremost authority on his life and correspondence. At the time of these letters he was teaching at Babson Institute. He later moved to Southern Illinois University as research professor and has been very active in the university press there.

TO Harry T. Moore

> El Prado
> *27 May 1950*

Dear Harry,

Thank you for your letter and reviews.

In England a positive frenzy seems to have broken out—I send

[9] Apparently a reference to her *Not I But the Wind* . . . (1934).

you some reviews. They have not changed an atom in these twenty years! But the books sell!! Tindall is so dry and uninspiring. . . . About his book on English poets! L. talked to me by the hour about Jessie Chambers.[1] He owed her a lot, considering L's home, but the human relation between them did not work, she was a blue stocking and he had more warmth for her than she for him. She sort of wanted to run him too much in that humble bullying way. She would have wanted him to be a nice, tame English little poet!

I shall look forward to your book! I could tell you a lot more, but want to get this off!

Ever yours,
Frieda

TO Witter Bynner

El Prado
13 August 1950

Dear Hal,

It was good to be with you and weren't the people nice with us!

But we didn't talk enough about your book. Mrs. Ruell told me that in it you "come round" to Lawrence, surely that would be very interesting and anyhow you wouldn't be "snooty" like A.

Your meeting with Monty made me think. He must be torn between his father's world and "ours". When I couldn't get on with their father (he didn't know how I felt), I gave myself to the children, it was fun too. When Monty went to school, I stood at the window and made faces at him, and he was terrified that . . . other boys would see me! Then when I left and they were not allowed to see me, Monty couldn't eat for 6 months and was sick. I am glad I didn't know that then. What hells L. and I went through anyhow! Their father was awful to them. If he was cruel to me, all right, but to them, *no*. I couldn't go to England, I

[1] Lawrence's principal confidante during his youth, and the "Miriam" of *Sons and Lovers*.

couldn't. Even for *their* sakes, I would only be a queer creature to them. But I felt pleased that they want me—a coffin would be the same thing!

Thank you for the scarf—it's very nice. I am being the "mannequin", trying it on.

Glad you were so well! Hoping to see you soon. Still have questions to ask.

Much love to you. I hope Bob is not too down.

Frieda

TO Witter Bynner

Kiowa Ranch
Taos, N.M.
[*Undated*]

Hal,

You see I have read your book and I got your two letters, and thank you so much! You'll be on your way to Mexico and I wish we were coming too! I loved your book, Christine didn't, so I was doubly glad I did. It's life, and honest, bold, you didn't spare yourself but risked the show! Can one do more? Or less? Yes, I danced like an ancient waterfall at the cowboy dance and I wish you had been there. It's a comfort to think of you, in a world of so many dull millions, and Lorenzo is a bond between us and our times together. I still get it, that it seems impossible to live without him, the world that he made for me. But it is also a relief to have somebody "on the other side", who keeps the door open for one when it's one's turn to pass through it. You know that; meanwhile I want to live as gaily, and profitably, as I possibly can!

And thank you for your nice letter and Eden tree, and the photos haven't come yet.

Ever and a day,
Yours,
F.

Greetings to Bob.

TO Lady Cynthia Asquith

El Prado
Taos
New Mexico
15 October 1950

Dear Cynthia,

Thank you for your letter. It was wonderful to get it and I went on and on remembering and remembering.

One of my treasures is a photograph of a painting by [Augustus] John of you, but I don't think I like it enough. You sound cheerful and I have ordered your book.

What a handsome family you all were and I hope the grandchildren follow the tradition.

I am 71, but well; I have the life I want.

Lorenzo seems to "get" in his completeness more and more. You and he seemed to understand each other in a strange and wonderful way.

What a lot of things we would have to talk about!

Do you never think of coming to America?

A house in Bath sounds good. Bath is so real in Jane Austen.

All good wishes to you.

Love, Frieda

I knew your handwriting at once!

TO Harry T. Moore

3 November 1950

Dear Harry,

You are really soaked in Lawrence. You mean Victoria Crescent, the house I met Lawrence in? It wasn't called Victoria Crescent but I can't remember what it *was* called.

My mother's name was Marquier, of French origin, her ancestor was supposed to have escaped from the French Revolution in a hay wagon to the Black Forest. My Richthofen grandmother was a Polish countess Lashowska. My uncle in Berlin was foreign minister—Uncle Oswald—we loved him.

No, I don't know of any more L. letters, I did not know there were any more. I also wait eagerly for your book. I am glad Mackenzie isn't bitter. In those [days] he was somebody and L. nobody! I cannot remember meeting Helen Corke—Louise Burrows . . . didn't like me. I never met her. Some of the outer setting in *The Rainbow* is a bit like Louise, but the inside is me. Gudrun has a bit of Katherine Mansfield and my sister Johanna in her. I think the musician was a true event in Helen Corke's life. Don't remember about Mrs. Davidson.

Angelino and I got *married*,[2] to simplify things.

I was very pleased to get the photographs, I like them very much. Yes, you must come, there is much that would interest you in the papers I have—in fact, it is almost a "must".

Else wrote me very enthusiastically about you. She was disappointed not to come.

I am writing in a hurry. Best to you all.

Frieda

Greetings from Angie

TO Montague Weekley

El Prado, New Mexico

10 November 1950

Dear Monty,

I wonder if you heard that Angelino and I got married. Of course nothing is really changed except that we can now both become American citizens [3] and he can go to Italy without danger of not being able to return, and I could come to England. Now the only person about whose reactions I care is you. The people here are to my astonishment very pleased.

It has been a heavenly autumn, but today we had the first snow. I had the Huxleys here; it was a treat, he is so ripe and his horizons so vast, and he knows such a hell of a lot.

Now we are getting ready to go to Port Isabel, Texas.

I heard from Cynthia Asquith a little while ago. You can't

[2] The marriage to Angelo Ravagli took place October 31, 1950.
[3] She later gave up the idea—Ravagli says because she felt she was too old.

imagine how rich and full my life is. For an old woman, amazing. Now if I become an American citizen I shall try and have the courage to visit you. I want to see all those children. I keep my own name, I mean Lawrence, because it would be too complicated otherwise. Of course Angelino had got a divorce; it is valid here, but not in Italy.

So keep well through the winter, and the same to Vera and the children.

Much, much love,

Your mother

Barby has not told me of her troubles. Oh dear! Keep me posted on the children, I do hope they don't have to go to a war. Yes, this amazing sunshine is a compensation. Could you not get a temporary job in America? Wouldn't that be something! I feel Vera would love it in America!

TO Witter Bynner

Port Isabel
25 November 1950

My dear Hal,

We arrived yesterday from Wichita Falls, a cool sparkling day, and I am happy to be here.

Your book has stayed with me all these days. I grin happily when I think of it, and yet I believe that it is one of those books that will live on. Don't you like it better than Boswell's Johnson? It is also so very much *you*, it's got your innermost spark. I feel awfully grateful for that book, not to you so much as to the Lord who made you write it. I agree with you when you say you should leave out what others have said. I read your poetry again in Wichita Falls and enjoyed it, but suddenly I felt you should have been a dramatist, the impact of person on person, you can do it and the outcome of the impact. The Lawrence book would make a play.

Thank you once again for an unforgettable evening. What a place yours is, so much life goes on, a Mecca, I should say, these dreary days. And the turkey was so delicious!

Much, much love

from Frieda
and Angie too

TO Witter Bynner

1270 North Havenhurst Drive, App. 6
Los Angeles 46, California
20 January 1951

Dear Hal,

Those reviews make quite a show, don't they? I have sent the clippings on with my greetings. We are looking forward to your advent.

It has rained terribly, but we have a very "Hollywoodean" place, not far from the Huxleys. Maria has been in a hospital, operation, but yesterday Angie brought her home again. Aldous came for meals and he is a real, wonderful person if you know him; he is really very shy. It's fun here, but God forbid that one should live here, somehow there is no *meaning* to it.

Much love, dear Hal, so we see you before too long! Please give our love to Mirendi, she *will* miss Bob!

Frieda

Tel: Hillside 2802

TO Harry T. Moore

Port Isabel, Texas
24 January 1951

Dear Harry,

Your book [4] came this morning and I have been reading it. I can't say any more than that Lawrence would have liked it. It is a solid piece of work, not just skimming over the top. I was

[4] *The Life and Works of D. H. Lawrence* (Twayne Publishers, 1950).

especially impressed with your comments on *Rainbow* and *Women in Love*. You have facts I had forgotten. But *Gerald* is also like a friend of his youth I never knew. Ursula is mostly me, Gudrun: Katherine, a little my sister, and the setting the Burrows.

I was glad to see an older photograph of Jessie. Louise Burrows, somebody wrote, has sort of visions of Lawrence, who visits her since he is dead. I just read the N.Y. *Times* review. I don't think it does the book justice. But you must expect that.

I think you have so well interpreted *Women in Love* and *Rainbow*.

Lawrence was *not* engaged to Agnes Holt. I could tell you such a lot. A young English doctor wrote to L. after reading *Fantasia*, etc., he praised it—seemingly. Lawrence was very pleased, wrote to the man, and then came another letter saying: "I am very embarrassed. You did not realize evidently that I was making fun of your book."

But now I want to say this—I think you underrate Lawrence's significance and courage to write what he wrote and your *own* courage in writing your book. He changed the outlook on sex for all time and you can "live" by Lawrence—he is a "way of life". *Your* book has some of Lawrence's vivifying quality in it too.

Will you send a copy to Laurence Pollinger, 39–40 Bedford Street, Strand, London W.C.2.

Of course about the guy in San Francisco is one of those charming lies. I was there in San Francisco every minute. Murry suggests that L. had homosexual feelings for him, I know he never did! Murry is so muddled. Tindall is a most uninspired fellow, the way he writes about poets, he might as well write about saucepans. T. S. Eliot to me is like a beautifully carved skeleton—no blood, no guts, no marrow, no flesh.

Also you might have said, how well he managed on the little money he had, how sensible he was in practical things, writers are supposed to be muddlers, which I have not found to be true.

The book looks *very* nice, you must be pleased. . . .

Now, I will stop or I'll go on forever.
I am so glad you wrote this book.

Good luck!
Frieda

TO Harry T. Moore

Port Isabel
Texas
30 January 1951

Dear Harry,

Sorry to tell you that I did not read Pollinger's letter right. . . . But after what you write, it does not look as if Knopf will part with the material he has. . . .

Do you think it would be any use my writing to Knopf? After all I should be allowed to have a say in the matter. Has Knopf read your book? . . .

I was trying hard to remember about "Miriam". There's a pretty young photograph of her somewhere. L. wrote *Sons and Lovers* mostly in Gargnano, the final one. L. felt unhappy about hurting her feelings. She *was* deeply hurt. She was the "sacred love", you know the old split of sacred and profane. She tries to defend her position by insisting on the "purity", which gives the show away. Humanly as a whole she wasn't the person his mother was, so the best horse won. She bored me in the end. There was some correspondence between L. and her about the book, but when she had read it, she never wrote again. In writing about her, he had to find out impersonally what was wrong in their relationship, when so much had been good. But what was insufficient in her, how could she admit or even see it. You see it all. I just had a most charming letter from the *maestra* in Tellaro, after all these years. You are right! L. had to have a woman as a sort of confirmation or test in his writing.

I can't remember who the other "Gerald" friend was. I believe I met him once. O, and *None of That* is more or less *Mabel*—Brett is wrong. I think she said it to *protect* Mabel—

maybe not. A friend said she liked your book so much. It gave such a vivid idea of L's activity. It's true.

I am reading the book again!

> Best greetings to you all
>
> F.

Of course I would share with you if you find a publisher.

TO Harry T. Moore

> Port Isabel, Texas
>
> *18 February 1951*

Dear Harry,

I fear you are finding out like the "United Nations" with the "Russians", that these publishers try to hold the initiative at any cost. That's what's happened to me. When I think how much I was part of L's living and writing and how these people ignore me completely, I am mad. Your book is much too good to be a best seller, but it won't have the fate of best sellers, "here today and gone tomorrow", I think it will live.

I agree with your wife, write your own stuff now and then return to L., if you feel like it. Let your book on L. sink in and then they *will* come to you. "Tindalyana," it's called, our friend's inspiration; they have no sense of humor.

Angie thought your book wonderful! I also think you kept yourself so out of it, not like Richard.[5] I don't know how you did that!

Maybe Frere is committed to Richard. 1 am glad you get good reviews. We will have to do what we can for each other, you and I—or anyhow tell each other the truth as far as we know it. I agree with you absolutely as far as understanding of L. goes. Maybe there is another side or other sides. The religious, mother influence. I got only *one* of your books. Would like *Aldous* to have one. *I may be wrong*, but I think you might wait for more of *your* Lawrence. There is Bynner's book coming now, it's

[5] Richard Aldington's life of Lawrence, *Portrait of a Genius, But . . . ,* also appeared in 1950 (Duell, Sloan and Pearce).

amusing, what he read to me! Of course a man has a right not to like Lawrence. They called Lincoln a baboon (Max Herzberg). Viking have got, by my contract, all the rights to the letters, but of course anybody publishing the letters must have my permission too, they are my property. So any letters published must have mine and Viking's permission. . . . Pollinger has been wonderful. He left Curtis Brown a long time ago and as he looked after L's work always I went along with Pollinger. . . . Poll. is not officially my American agent but is beginning to take over.

I don't think the Viking man is Tedlock. . . . There is an unpublished *Mr. Noon*, first part of a novel—the second part disappeared. I have the first part in Taos.

Now you are in the fight and I am so glad they take your book *seriously;* it was just possible, that they might have said: "Another book on Lawrence." But after all, honesty and truth can't be wiped from the face of the earth—not completely.

You see I am not told that Harper's are bringing out a *Sons and Lovers*. But I don't want these people to drive me nuts! Then I believe things often come out right in the long, the very long, run. I hope you don't work too hard, you sound a bit like it. We are so peaceful here, it's a nice small house.

I hope you find Pollinger helpful.

Best greetings to you all.

My letter seems more like a string of telegrams!

Yours,
Frieda

My sister Else hopes to come in April. She said in a letter you were the most genuine L. admirer she had met.

TO T. M. Pearce

El Prado, N.M.
11 June 1951

Dear Matt,

You were so very nice to us, Helen and you, and I want to

thank you. My sister [6] could not have enjoyed anybody more than you. I am reading every word of the book [7] you gave me, and I am amazed what a wonderful almost revelation it was to me, so much *real* poetry, the feel of this part of the world in it. I hope it has been a great success.

You go your way, it is a good way and you know it, so stick to your own guns. If they have ideas, let them and just do what you want to do. But let them know that you have more insight into this part of the world and have helped to make it known, helped to put it on the map. It wasn't there before!

Looking forward to seeing you and Helen.

> Affectionately,
> and love from Angie too,
> Frieda

TO Witter Bynner

> El Prado
> *27 July 1951*

Dear Hal,

I read your book [8] at one gulp, oh my, oh my, that was just something. What it did to me!

I fear it is your own generosity that sees me and puts me in such a rosy light. Makes me feel humble! How it brings back all those hours and days!

How good you all were to me, I took it all so for granted! packing me off and all that!

I am so glad you wrote that book, so much effort of many kinds. I will read the book carefully and write again, I am so under its redhot impact now!

The only thing [that] makes me sad is the imprisonment of the

---

[6] Else Jaffe and she had just had another reunion in Albuquerque, which had included a trip to Isleta pueblo. They were driven there by E. W. Tedlock, Jr.

[7] *Signature of the Sun* by Ross Calvin (University of New Mexico Press, 1950).

[8] *Journey with Genius: Recollections and Reflections Concerning the D. H. Lawrences* (John Day, 1951).

little bootblacks. I am almost certain I would have known. Lawrence would never go to any police. I think the man didn't like to have those boys around the place himself and put it on to Lawrence. His stories are a bit phony to me.

I want to come and see for myself how you are. It was a shock to hear of your operation.

Much love, the genuine article, to you.

Hope Bob is all right.

Greetings from Angie.

Frieda

TO Witter Bynner

El Prado, N.M.
[Late August, 1951]

Dear Hal,

It is only six in the morning and I hope you are sound asleep. This is a belated "bread and butter" letter and I wish all "bread and butter" letters could as sincerely say how good a time they had and how grateful they were. I loved being in that cosy house.

How is the eye? you cyclop. Is the sight coming back? Bob will have told you about poor Aldous, in a dark room, and he was really ill. When people don't complain, like you and Aldous, one has so much more sympathy than when they do.

The morning has already a touch of autumn in it.

Spud wrote nicely about the book. Now that you are launched on prose, you will do some more exciting work.

But for the love we all have for you, be thoroughly selfish and don't waste yourself on people.

The atmosphere at your place is so charming and warm, that good Rita and those little girls around, one feels so welcome. I hear from Mirendi how you are. Millicent's [9] party was very beautiful with the Indians dancing under that enormous sky round a fire, and lightning, and a few drops of rain, and an enormous moon.

[9] Millicent Rogers.

Angie hangs onto the wine you gave him and my Mexican figure looks at me while I write.

Much, much love as always, past, present and future.

Frieda

TO Edward Gilbert

El Prado
Taos
New Mexico
13 October 1951

Dear Edward Gilbert,

Your fervent interest in Lawrence makes me glad.

I am here at the upper ranch in a golden autumn world where L. and I lived so very simply and strenuously. You should know this place where L. still pervades the air. I try to understand your point of view about the passionate and spiritual. That is a centuries old split. But in Lawrence it was united by a religious and elemental approach. He himself was whole. When he wants to marry me, his marriage is approached religiously. You belittle *him* if you think I was just a passionate female to him and rather dumb. He was a gay bird mostly and not the tragic fish he is made out to be. Life was a thrill always. Life itself, lived from hour to hour to the best of one's ability, was his philosophy. That I never wrote about; *he* did it. I don't think you have gone deeply enough into him, not the elemental part.

You say Miriam was spiritual. She was intellectual. Her passion was the written word. She never realized L's potentiality. But he owed her much as a writer. For me the man came first. It still takes my breath away when I think of the uncompromising fearless man he was: This is what I am, that's what I found out and I am going to say so and to hell with the consequences—and the consequences followed all right! It was lived experience, not theory!

Good luck to your book! . . .

Sincerely yours,
[Frieda Lawrence]

I see I haven't really answered what you say and went off on my own.

I do not agree with you that L. thought life should be based on passion; the aim was to be a complete, all-round functioning human being. L. was no idealist; he did not expect people to be angels. Surely with the horrors in the world one must hate them! I don't think hatred is death to the spiritual.

Of course, I believe the most sublime words ever spoken were Christ's: "Father, forgive them, etc." So logical. "I love you, my fellowmen; crucify me, but I go on loving you." But what about the fellowman? If you truly love him, you don't let him kill you.

There must be anger and hatred, if suppressed they come out in an unwholesome way. Never did Lawrence think he had found *the* solution. There will always be new solutions. If you have found one, I am glad of it.

What you call hatred of compulsion is love of freedom, isn't it? I do not see that he ever sacrificed it, and to what? I agree with you that they try to belittle L. as a thinker, because they can only theorise and don't really think and you are so right, saying they belittle [him] as a *man*. They must feel superior to him; they do that to every great man.

Please don't be down on me and try to fit me into your philosophy of life and Lawrence. I might jump out of them!

Now I stop.

TO Witter Bynner

El Prado
16 October 1951

Dear Hal,

I saw the *Times* letters.

Yes, this is the story. When Mabel took us to the ranch, it was in a bad state and John Evans used it for hunting. I fell in love with the place and Mabel said: "I give it to you." When I told this to L., he said: "No, you can't take such a gift." Then he went to the Apache land with Tony, and while he was away a letter came from my sister Else, that L. had left the Mss. of *Sons and Lovers* at her place in the Isartal and she was sending it. So I thought, I will give the Mss. to Mabel for the ranch. I gave it to her when it came, and then had qualms because after all it was *his* Mss. and not mine. But when he came and I told him, it was all right, and the ranch was always in *my* name; you remember he did not want property.

Pollinger writes and you know how good he is, would you let him arrange the English publication of your book?

Poor Mrs. Crotch! [1] Of course I *did not* give her the headstone as it was on L's grave. Madame Lily's husband (she was the cook), he was a stonemason and I made him put a phoenix in bright pebbles on the cement block. It isn't anything much and she can have it.

Also Pollinger wrote that Graham Greene found Norman Douglas very poor and feeble in Capri and wanted the permission to use a design that L. had done for a cooking book for him. Douglas's title of his cookery book is *Venus in the Kitchen* by "Pilaff Bey". Graham will write an introduction. So it goes. I believe you have put me on the map with your book!!

---

[1] Mrs. Gordon Crotch was a shopkeeper and friend in Vence at the time of Lawrence's death in 1930. Lawrence's body was removed from the grave there and cremated in Marseilles on March 13, 1935, and the ashes were brought to the New Mexico ranch by Angelo Ravagli. By 1957 the headstone, apparently a gift from Mrs. Crotch, was in the care of the town clerk of Eastwood, Nottingham, Lawrence's birthplace, where it was to become part of a memorial. On September 24, 1959, Aldous Huxley wrote to the editor about the possibility of helping Mrs. Crotch. She was then over eighty, infirm, and almost penniless in England. Huxley had in the past aided her financially and now sought to find a publisher for her reminiscences about Frieda in the period immediately after Lawrence's death. These were purchased by the *New Mexico Quarterly*, but have not been published yet. The remainder of Mrs. Crotch's memoirs concerned, in large part, Norman Douglas who knew her well and confided in her extensively.

Yale University wants L. material. Tell him so, I mean Cady.

Mirendi says you are writing on your novel. Much luck to it, you read me a bit once.

Love to you,
F.

People are always wanting things or wanting information. I do get fed up!

TO E. W. Tedlock, Jr.

El Prado
Taos
New Mexico
2 November 1951

Dear Ted,

Thank you so much for the photo. Many people want one. It does not seem much damaged.

Ted, I come with a request. I don't know whether you see *El Crepusculo* and how the younger writers and artists weren't in that *Quarterly* [2] with us old birds in it. They protested in the *Crepusculo*. So I suggested why not have a *Quarterly* with the younger birds of Taos in it. It was Ortega's idea—I mean the old-timer one. Now I don't know whom to approach; will you do that and approach the proper people if they would like another *Quarterly* with the young ones. Dorothy Benrimo, who is a very efficient person, would do the work of editing. She wanted me to help, but I don't trust myself so much in this kind of a job. But I would do what I can. The heavenly autumn is gone and no golden leaves left, but it's cold and sunny still.

I hope the family is flourishing and all goes well.

Ever yours,
Frieda

[2] *The University of New Mexico Quarterly* had published a special Taos issue. Joaquin Ortega was the editor.

No more fishing! We go to California about [the] first of December.

TO Harry T. Moore

> El Prado
> New Mexico
> *15 November 1951*

Dear Harry,

Yes, I was disgruntled when I wrote you last. People think I make undue propaganda for Lawrence, which as you know isn't true. That I am responsible for all that's written about him, they say. For myself I feel that Lawrence is sort of dissected and too much is written about him and *he* is swamped *out*. But then I also feel he belongs to the world and the world will do as it likes with him, it's really taken far out of my reach. I tried to fight the Viking, I protest, but it's no use, so I leave it to the *Lord*. I have my Lawrence fresh and vivid and I want to keep him that way while I live.

You have my permission to do as you like.

You sound very busy. Good luck to your enterprises.

We go to Los Angeles to be near the Huxleys chiefly, he hasn't been well, but is better.

What a pity you can't go to Nottingham to lecture. That would have been something!

We are having a lovely autumn—cold at night, but all day the dear sun.

Several letters by young men who want to write about L.

There has been a rumpus about Lady C. in *Japan*. L. is selling there, but I cannot get the "yens".

Dear Harry: stick to Pollinger about details. He knows all about it and I don't.

Ooh, it was a cold night tonight, but now the sun is here!

Greetings from us both.

> Frieda

TO Edward Gilbert

El Prado
Taos
New Mexico
25 November 1951

Dear Edward Gilbert,

You must be a gloomy man, looking at the negative side of things. You have identified yourself with Lawrence, but you read yourself into him. I agree with you that Lawrence is like St. Augustine. As far as I know you are the first who saw this.

I don't agree that the cause is greater than the individual. Where and what is cause without individuals? L. was much too wise to have a cause.

Lawrence was a "way of life" in himself, his living and thinking were one and the same activity. There were no "thought processes". What he wrote came out of his living and thinking like daisies out of the soil. When you say Christ was no thinker, look at the great truths he stated, as: "To them that have shall be given."

You see Lawrence as a great man and yet in the same breath you affirm that he did not find what he wanted, he could not think, he could not formulate his ideas; so what the hell *do* you see in Lawrence? I was the first who knew of his significance, I saw him unfold, he was my responsibility. You tell me I failed him. Your "thought processes" don't do you much good; they take away your sensitivity or you could not make such a heartless or cruel statement to me. It is my riches, my glory, my deepest conviction that I was part of his work as I was of his life and a vital part. . . . You can read it in his work everywhere. You haven't got L., not by a long chalk. Like Murry, another smart Alec.

Why does L. interest you so much if he was such a failure? The world failed him, yes, indeed, and I saw it and it grieved me. A great deal of his life was fulfilment, the wonder of living never left him, and dying as part of life. No, he did not want for a moment "cold clearsighted thinking". You want that! It is only part of a man, not the whole. If he did not get all he wanted from living, that is also part of the show.

What a place the world would be if there were many such failures around! You cannot make a statement like this one: "L. hid his deep, sad feelings from you." He was no hider. Do you think I did not suffer when people jeered at him and always: rejection, rejection!? The world let him down all right, as they do every big man.

You see how you have roused my opposition! Did you really expect me to say: "Yes, I failed L., and he was a failure?"

Of course you have a right to your Lawrence, and I to mine. But it is yourself you are writing about.

Of course it might mean a lot to you to come here—Indians, Spanish, and Anglos. But it is a small place, and I fear no jobs. Albuquerque has a university.

Today it snowed, but now the clean sun and an enormous sky.

We go to Los Angeles in a few days to be near the Huxleys.

Good luck to you,

F. L.

FROM John Middleton Murry

Lower Lodge, Thelnetham
nr Diss, Norfolk
9 December 1951

My dear Frieda:

I *was* glad to have your letter; so unexpectedly. I haven't the least doubt either that we could all have lived together now happily and at peace. But life isn't like that—or very seldom. Why, even you and I are so far apart that the chances are that we shall never see each other again, though I find it difficult to *believe* that.

How true it is what you say: that our disagreements meant so much more and went so much deeper than most people's so-called friendships. I feel that very strongly. In fact I sometimes feel that I have never had *any* friends except Lorenzo and you. Old Blake talks of "the severe contentions of friendship". Well, we have known them, and now they are a rich and joyful memory. The only thing I dislike about the past is that horrible grinding fear I used to have of not having any money.

Do you sometimes think happily of the times when I was your lover? I often do. You gave me something then that I needed terribly: as it were opened a new world to me. And I sometimes wonder, when I think of that journey of ours to Germany together, and we wanted each other so badly, whether I was not a fool in feeling (or rather thinking) that it would have been disloyal to Lorenzo. Looking back, it seems only an "idea"—something in my *head*—and that the right and true thing would have been to stay with you, if only for a day or two. Anyway, I felt horribly sad when I left you: and the sadness lasted a long, long while.

I am well—really very much better than I used to be 10 years ago. . . .

Mary is just lovely. I have had 10 years of absolutely unbroken happiness with her now. It makes up for everything.

I heard you had married Angelino. (I think it was Paul Dinkins who told me.) And I love to think of you serene and happy: tho' in a way you were always happy, weren't you?

I haven't any rabbits: but I've lots of pigs and cows—browny-red ones, called Red Polls, without horns. And I grow my own tobacco! A 200 acre farm is good fun: but it's the only reason I wish I were a bit younger. Otherwise I agree with you, that it's very very nice to be old.

My love to Brett when you see her.

Affectionately,
Jack

I will send you a few photographs round about Christmas time. Did I tell you we went over to Ireland to see Gordon [Campbell] and Beatrice?

TO John Middleton Murry

El Prado
Taos
New Mexico
19 December 1951

Dear Jack,

Your letter was a feast. I had taken it for granted that Mary and you were married. . . . Your life with her and that farm sounds like a very good life.

Yes indeed, I often think of our friendship first and later of our intimacy with great satisfaction. In the early days you were a friend and I am quite sure both L. and I never had friends like you and K. Then when there grew a greater intimacy when I stayed at that beastly place of —— it was wonderful. On that journey to Germany I also felt sad but without bitterness because I had a hunch you were fond of me too. There was a lot of good will and understanding between us. It was very free, no *arrière pensée*, no suspicion, no vanity. Maybe it was right that way, after all it was my job to see L. through to the bitter end.

I believe my deepest feeling for L. was a profound compassion. He wanted so much that he could never have with his intensity. I felt so terribly sorry for him or I could never have stood it all. Sometimes he went over the edge of sanity. I was many times frightened but never the last bit of me. Once, I remember he had worked himself up and his hands were on my throat and he was pressing me against the wall and ground out: "I am the master, I am the master." I said: "Is that all? You can be master as much as you like, I don't care." His hands dropped away, he looked at me in astonishment and was all right.

You must have had a tough time with Katherine too; so absorbed in you, asking more than any human being could or should give. That may have been the root of your money fear, you felt inadequate to her demands. You weren't a pure intellectual as your farm shows, but she was.

I don't know why it makes me so glad when you write: "In a way you were always happy, weren't you?" Yes, I was and I am.

When I was just forced to be miserable, something soon bounced me out of the misery. I wake up in the morning and the sun rises on my bed and I run around the house happy and grateful to be alive (this is a morning country). I love doing what I do, I like people if I don't see too much of them, I am a lucky old woman!

But that was a shock when you wrote: "The chances are we shall not meet again." Hoo! Now I say, why don't you come here? You and Mary! You *ought* to come! Try hard, do! I *know* the change and the new experience would do you good. You also might see your publishers! You drive a car, don't you? Come next May.

Now we are off to Hollywood. I will send you the address.

Phillippe de Rothschild is making a play of Lady C in Paris.

I am looking forward to the photographs. I have sent you some records.

Did you enjoy seeing Campbell and Beatrice?

Merry Christmas!

Affectionately,
Frieda

TO Edward Gilbert

1270 Havenhurst Drive, Apt. 6
Los Angeles 46, California
[*Undated*]

[Dear Edward Gilbert]

Anyhow your letters make one think. I have to ask myself, "Do I agree with you, if I don't, or don't I?"

When I think of him, there was a splendour, a magnificence about him that I cannot possibly connect with failure. It is just absurd to call L. a sexual weakling, anything but: with his intensity. You don't know how a man like he was, could give himself, body and soul. I experienced this miracle.

I even don't want to think about it too much. But Murry and Katherine Mansfield were the most intimate friends we ever had.

I am very fond of Murry. We misunderstood all around, and only a part of Murry was the smart Alec. Of course there are things I don't want to tell.

In *Women in Love*, Ursula is the most me, I think. When I read it now, I can hardly bear it. How much he cared. Those episodes are practically true. I didn't mind what you call his wickedness. I am no angel of light myself. No, I also know he wanted a real man friend. He never found him. I doubt whether I could have stood it. I would have fought, not now as I am old, but in the past.

I think it is clever of you to say wickedness is synonymous with compulsion. I don't think I meant just everything to him. He had his vision beyond me. This I knew always, and also that there were things in him that were not in my make-up. Yes, I knew that he was more "all round" than Christ.

If you say I don't know the magnitude of the drama I was caught up in, maybe I don't want to know too consciously. It is frightening.

Both Brett and Mabel are my friends. Brett lives near me and comes every day or so and so does Mabel. We used to quarrel, but don't any more. They would interest you!

I have an Italian friend whom I married—easier this way. We are here, chiefly to be near Aldous and Maria Huxley, for two months.

[Frieda Lawrence]

TO Edward Gilbert

[Undated]

Dear [Edward Gilbert]:

You want to be a St. Paul to L's Christ. But I believe Paul made a mess of it. He put so much into Christianity that wasn't Christ.

You haven't understood, being an intellectual, that Lawrence wrote like a tree puts out leaves and grows tall and spreads. It was not a cerebral conscious activity. That was his genius. In my book,[3] I tried to show what he *was* day by day, not so well, I admit, not what he believed. I think his belief is in every word nearly that he wrote.

I am glad Murry has changed; maybe he sees more clearly now.

You are wrong saying L. is disregarded. He is there in the human consciousness all right. You seem to me like the rest of the critics when you say he reached for something that escaped him, and evidently does not escape you, you think. He did not nail things down, but left the door open for others to come along. He was great enough to know that life goes on and there is no ultimate word.

Lo, now I have had my say, and you have yours.

Brett and Mabel are well, and I will give them your greetings. We are getting old, but still going strong.

I believe you do not need any permission for short quotations, but you better. . . .

TO Edward Gilbert

[Undated]

Dear Edward Gilbert,

First you suspect me of playing a dirty trick on you, then I want to use my power to keep you from the British Empire; if you think the British Empire sits and waits for you to explain Lawrence to it, I believe you are mistaken. Then you think I consider the money angle, when I would get some if you had to pay for the excerpts from L. books, otherwise no money from your book. You must have a charming conception of human beings!

I would not have answered your letters if I had not felt you identify yourself with Lawrence, or rather you use him as a dummy to hang your own ideas on. If you wanted to recreate him, you should have done so in his own image, and not yours. You never say a word about his intense relationship with all around him, a hen, a moon, a child, and everything. What

[3] *Not I But the Wind.* . . .

Lawrence would have said to you, would have been: "Go out, man, and live as full and rich a life as you can. Forget about me and what I meant and did not mean. I had my say and I meant what I said. . . ."

TO Dudley Nichols

El Prado, New Mexico
4 April 1952

. . . No, Dudley, you wouldn't have liked Douglas.[4] He was, I think, the only wicked man I have known, in a medieval sense, but, oh, so witty. Once when he said something I did not like I told him: "Douglas, you never said anything like that, you have always treated me like a Madonna before," and he answered quickly: "And now I have let the Madonna out of the bag.". . .

TO Montague Weekley

El Prado
New Mexico
9 May 1952

My dear Monty,

Sit down, when you open this: I have news for you. I mean to come to England, be in London the middle of June. Ida persuaded me, and you saying: "If *she* comes we shall all see her." So I come. I go by train to New York and fly from New York and you meet me. I want to stay at the old Kingsley Hotel if it still exists, also to be near Pollinger. *Don't* let anybody else know that I come except Elsa and Barby, and I want to see all the grandchildren of course. Nobody else. I won't stay long. Now *if* my passport makes me no difficulties I will be there. Perhaps Vera would have us all meet at her house.

I am a bit scared, "all by mineself," but I travel with a friend to New York and [will] be in the same hotel with the Stravinskys, who will see me off.

[4] Norman Douglas.

Will you phone to Pollinger that I am coming and that I *don't* want to meet anybody but him and Frere?

Monty, isn't it wonderful to see you and all the grandchildren, Vera, etc?

Much love till we meet.

Your old mother

Ida [5] could stay with me for a day or two at the Kingsley. When I write again you can reserve a room for me at the Kingsley.

TO John Middleton Murry

Hotel Lexington
New York 17, New York
1 July 1952

Dear Jack,

Your lovely book [6] is very important I think. If you had seen in Texas those enormous fields without a tree or a hedge, so inhuman, you would know. Just production, but you are making a *life* and making things live. The community was an ideal (and ideals never work) and thank God you dropped it. By the way, if only America could learn to be human! They should read your book. It isn't sentimental, thank God; in my old age I am sick of emotions.

It was wonderful to see you and Mary, I could see what she has been to you. A miracle really! I loved England, it was beautiful! Also seeing the children and grandchildren was a great success. At long, long last! I wish you would let Monty come and see you, it would do him good!

Dear Jack, I hope we will live a few years more and that you and Mary could come to New Mexico. Isn't it strange, when people have been real friends they don't become strangers, it was as if I had seen you the day before!

[5] Her children's former nurse.
[6] *Community Farm.*

Now I go back to New Mexico very contented. Brett will be interested. Is your book published in America?

With my old love and greetings to Mary. . . .

Frieda

TO John Middleton Murry

El Prado
Taos
New Mexico
9 September 1952

Dear Jack,

Thank you for your letter, it was just "a treat" to meet you and Mary; she was the gayest person I met in England and I can imagine how her courage has helped you. . . .

I think your book is quite a record and I am cross with us all that *this* was your work and we should have had the sense to know it, you never wanted to be a highbrow. But now you can be happy. It's a fine and happy thought that you will visit me, it freshens one up to go away for a bit; don't put it off, we don't get younger.

Your legs worry me. Would it help you to have alternate hot and cold baths, and massage? I believe so much that nature wants to heal if you help it. Brett read your book and would also love it if you came. Did you enjoy your trip to Ireland? You know that Ida you met, the nurse, is quite a remarkable person, that attachment through all these long years for the children and me is something and now the grandchildren too. She is a violent Catholic and should put me in the deepest hell, but she doesn't. It was wonderful to have the old bond with the children again, I had given up hope, thought it was the price I had to pay for being L's wife.

This is now the best time here, cool nights and quite warm days, yesterday I saw a flying saucer above the house. And there is a big bear up at the upper ranch, he tears down the fences and smashes the apple trees.

Angelino is making his pottery, that is what he likes; he is no farmer by nature, I am sorry to say, but a man can't be everything. Aldous and Maria have gone hypnotist for the time being.

In November we go to Port Isabel, Texas, on the Gulf of Mexico. We have a little house there; it is quiet and warm.

It is good to think that your life is so full and rich. And I am a very happy old woman, there is nothing more I want from this life, only that I can enjoy it a little longer.

My love to you both,

Frieda

TO Harry T. Moore

1 October 1952

Dear Harry,

You write me a lot of interesting things I did not know about. It is very interesting that *men* are chiefly interested in L. now, that is good I think.

It is only just that your book gets so much praise, after all you worked like a demon all those years. But a strange thing, L. himself never got praise from the critics! That's how it goes.

Yes, the outer setting of *Women in Love* is Louise Burrows,[7] but the inner relationship is L's and mine, like the ring scene, where I throw the ring at him; that happened. Skrebensky is a bit like a Richthofen cousin.

Yes, I was in London, loved seeing the children and grandchildren and Pollinger and Frere and Murry. He wrote me about Bertie's [8] unfriendly BBC broadcast.

I think Louie was an escape from Miriam, it was a short affair.

Sir Allen Lane, "Penguin", is opening a place in Baltimore and hopes to print Lawrence there. It might interest you.

What a lot of work a book like you are doing means. Do you know L's criticisms on painting? Very good.

Glad all goes well with the family. I enclose bits of a letter from a "beau" I had when I was seventeen. I never saw him again, but he always wrote to me till the end of his life. He was an artillery colonel and then at the "Ufa".

[7] One of the intimates of Lawrence's youth in Eastwood.
[8] Bertrand Russell.

I feel I can't read any more books on L. He gets further away from me if I do. Of course it is most gratifying that so many people make him their own, but I don't want to lose my Lawrence. My youngest grandson, 11, he is at St. Paul's, said, "Oh, they know all about Lawrence and you at the school!"

Angie is well, making pottery; he was in Italy, enjoyed it but was glad to be back. I think that is really something that they made you a fellow of the royal society of literature. I am very grateful for all the information you send me of what goes on.

Angie and I send our best wishes.

> Yours ever,
> Frieda

TO Montague Weekley

> Port Isabel
> Texas
> *8 December 1952*

My dear Monty,

There is Christmas around the corner again! It doesn't feel like Christmas here, no fires, and the grass is getting green again after a good rain.

Taos is terribly cold, Brett writes, and deep in snow. So I feel we are terribly lucky. Did you solve the Aunt Lucy problem?

We have cleaned and painted like mad. The house was rented, and people don't keep things up when they aren't their own. Angie wants to build on a porch towards the bay; we haven't got one, and this climate asks for it. I heard on the radio England was foggy and cold; I can't believe it after my June visit. I believe in Eisenhower, and I believe he can put the salt on comrade Stalin's tail.

I hope I can write here. Houghton Mifflin [9] wants a book from me. But so much happens all the time. And then the chores. I suppose Vera is getting ready for Christmas. I hope you all keep well.

[9] The editor's letter of inquiry to the publisher brought no reply.

It is such a remote place, this, very peaceful. A. loves it. That is a nice picture: Ursula [1] having lessons from her grandfather.

Now it is Christmas soon, and I am sending you a cheque for everybody. For you 10, that means for each person 2.10. Elsa and Barby, 10 each. (I get mixed.)

Have four young enthusiastic students coming. The poor General Pierce has had a stroke and is mad with himself: "I can't write, I can't talk." He used to talk a lot. And she is awfully nice. You know that bit of money at the Westminster; I don't know about income tax. I pay income tax over here; I'll just let it sit there. It is a shame I can't make you a nice parcel with some marzipan.

Would you like any more "Care" parcels?

Much love to you all

from your mother

If Vera would like to make Marzipan: —1 lb. icing sugar; 1 lb. almonds; rose water.

TO Montague Weekley

Port Isabel

29 January 1953

Dear Monty,

Ida [2] in the hospital! She wrote me rather solemnly: "*Es will abend werden.*" I think that is a hymn. She must have worked very hard and is worn out. I will write to her. I hope she is better.

You are very thoughtful for the children. Yes, I am glad you think Julia [3] should have a good time. I think we all should; I am sure the good Lord put us on this earth that we enjoy it to the

---

[1] Her granddaughter, daughter of Barbara Barr, and now the wife of the English critic and poet Alfred Alvarez.
[2] Her children's former nurse.
[3] Montague's daughter.

full. I had such a nice letter from Ian; [4] he does *see* things, especially architecture. I will write to him soon. It seems terrible that these boys have years taken out of their young lives, for what?

But don't worry about saving, because I am sure you will have something from me when I am under the daisies. It may be a lot and it may be not so much.

I wish sometimes I felt kindlier towards your father. I wish him well, but I cannot forget that he had made an image of me and did not know anything about the real me. But that's how it is. I am grateful to you all for looking after him so faithfully.

I am very interested in this new administration and Eisenhower. I do hope there won't be another war, but sometimes I am scared. Everybody except America and Russia has had more than they can take. The world needs peace so badly. And when I think how pleasant my old age is, and so many will never know it. But the days get longer and soon your cherry tree will be in bloom again! Love to you all.

Your mother.

Glad you are writing. I am just reading Montaigne, he is a sane old bird! Greetings from A.

Dear Monty,

An afterthought. A man appeared a little while ago and told me the "big money" now was in television and that Lawrence's short stories would lend themselves very much for it. I wondered if you could talk to Polly about it, or if you would like to do something yourself.

As so often happens I have not heard from the young man again. I may sell Lady C to the movies, but again I don't get thrilled any more. So many bites and no fish. I don't like television, but I suppose it will get better.

4 Montague's son.

FROM John Middleton Murry

Lower Lodge, Thelnetham
nr Diss, Norfolk
20 July 1953

My dear Frieda,

I almost wrote my darling Frieda—wanted to—but it didn't seem quite *comme il faut*. Three letters from me in a fortnight! You'll be getting thoroughly bored. But how it happened was this. Somebody—some paper—asked me for an article on Bynner's book,[5] and I felt I ought to do it. (It's very seldom anybody asks me for an article nowadays.) So I read Bynner's book again—and oh, how *real* you both became! Then I started reading *The Plumed Serpent*—then *all* your letters to me: those when you were very angry with me, and those when you weren't. So that I have been saturated in you all day, and I just can't refrain from talking to you. I'm terribly sorry I ever gave you cause to think that I wanted to, or did, belittle Lorenzo: believe me, I never *dreamed* I was doing that. I thought I was making him out almost infinitely great. However, it doesn't matter now; but I hate to think I *ever* seemed to you deliberately to have hurt you.

But you see, my dear, I was always utterly bewildered by Lorenzo's bursts of hatred. Even to read of those in Bynner's book towards Leighton, towards the shoe-shine boys—and above all towards you, made me horribly sad. It isn't that I am incapable of hatred. . . . But why should Lorenzo ever have hated *you?* Truly, I know your tenderness. As I've told you, it was from you I learned what a woman's tenderness could be. And you can't say that's a tenderness of the body only—that's impossible—it's a tenderness *of the soul* as well. How can there be hatred? How can it come in? I ask you, my dear, because I am just as bewildered as ever. I am quite sure I could have loved you tenderly, without ever a glimmer of hatred arising between us.

Not least because of you, I was able to love Mary. I have loved her now for thirteen years, loved her steadily more and more, was—thank God—still young enough, tho' battered, to know

[5] *Journey with Genius.*

years of complete physical fulfilment. We have never for one single second ever quarrelled. I don't think I'm an extraordinary man—certainly not a bloody miracle. But if this is natural to me and to Mary, you will understand how bewildered I was—and still am—by Lorenzo's doctrine of love-and-hate.

And, in my inmost soul, I believe it would have been the same between me and you, you and me, if I had had the courage in 1923. And if I had known then, truly, how things had been between Lorenzo and you, I believe I should have had the courage: and I should have been spared much suffering.

It's silly to think like that, I suppose: but I am just talking to you as if you were in the room. You will remember the crazy things I did. I felt you were in love with me; I *knew* I was in love with you. Heavens above, how I needed and craved for you then! And, like a little gentleman, I had to suppress it all. Why didn't I go back with you to New Mexico? You knew the reason, or I supposed you did. Because Brett was going, too.

But I only say this, my dear, because I am still bewildered. I do not, and *cannot*, believe in love-and-hate between man and woman. I have had some, and it is HELL. I know, and believe, that you and Lorenzo had something between you—far above and far beyond this. But why, why did he so often preach, and act, hate?

There's always something that eludes and baffles me in this. I wish you would explain it, if you can: because I feel it was this in Lorenzo that I always,—often blindly and stupidly—resisted. I don't profess to be a genius as he was: and very likely I'm not even a talent. But I suppose I do want to feel that in my way I was trying to stand for something true.

Well, that's enough. I've been all agitated all day because I was selling 23 young heifers. I hate buying and selling. Before the two farmer-brothers who were buying actually came, my heart was thumping, and I was in the dickens of a state. One of them I knew before; but he brought his elder brother—a man of my own age. He was a perfect dear. Quite suddenly, with enormous relief, I felt I could *trust* him. So I said to him, "Look here, Mr. Cobbold, I feel I can trust you. Offer me your price, and I'll take it!" He looked at me—I looked at him. Then he had another good look at my cows—and offered me £7.10.0 a head more than I expected! So there are some good men—even in England. You would have liked him. "All this science," he said to me, "and what do they *really* know? Just how to kill one another by 20,000 at a time!"

Ever yours,
Jack

TO John Middleton Murry

[*Undated*]

Dear Jack,

The *comme il faut*-ness between us made me laugh! Rather late in the day, isn't it?

I loved your letter and I thought how L. would have loved your story about the young heifers and how he never knew that side of yours and he *should* have done. I had a hunch, a dim one, you never were a real intellectual *à la* T. S. Eliot, with his carved skeleton people, who have no marrow and flesh and don't exist except in nowhere! You had a genius for life, and God knows you never tried to spare yourself and took any risk. It's a wonder you weren't broken many times. When you say you came to Mary rather battered that makes me laugh again, I don't know why; anyhow you don't feel sorry for yourself! I felt what a truly wonderful relation there was between you and Mary! We shall never understand L's hatred. It came like an impersonal, elemental thing out of nowhere and it frightened me, but a last scrap of me wasn't frightened and I think now I ought to have handled him better; but how can a poor woman handle a thunderstorm?

You and he were straight with each other and that is so wonderful if you can be yourself with a person, no defences, nothing. One human being with another. I have just realized that people treat me in a special way, as being a bit famous, and I don't know how to behave and it makes me shy and it is not pleasant. One of the great things with L. was that I was not a social being at all. I don't think I ever understood what society meant.

This letter was left alone for a few days. I had a birthday (74) and so they gave me parties! Now I am recovering!

Maybe after all L's hatred was love. It exasperated him so much that people were so unfree and miserable. Do you remember those awful damp cottages we had soon after the First World War and we walked over to you for dinner over those wet fields with smelly decaying cabbage stalks in them in the gloomy twilight and it was the only fun we had! But you were always richer than we were! And Gordon with a thick stick and a cap on would come, and Kot! Spender (did I tell you this already?) has a new paper *Encounter* and Kot wanted him to print L's letters to Kot. Spender says only 6, but Frere and Pollinger resented that he did not send his letters to Aldous's book and when I was in London he had tea with me every Tuesday at 4 o'clock and I thought he was a friend, but he had written a nasty letter to Aldous about me a little while later. Kot has 500 pages of L's letters! Kot wants 75 per cent for himself—he has no right to anything, he might at least *ask!* He must be unbelievably sour!

Now I must stop this babbling or I never will, because I like it.

Now I will cook my good bone-steak and I wish you and Mary were here to share it!

The old one,
Frieda

I think your book on Swift ought to be very interesting. I think people are fed up with that too emotional stuff of our era!

TO Harry T. Moore

El Prado
21 July 1953

Dear Harry,

Your book [6] came today. I had no clear idea in my mind what

[6] *The Achievement of D. H. Lawrence*, edited by Moore and Frederick J. Hoffman (University of Oklahoma Press, 1953).

it would be like, so it was a wonderful surprise to find it so—truly rich.

What a job, all the criticism through the early years, that awful London *Times* was always so snooty and "stuffed shirt" and always will be. Now we can thumb our noses at *those* critics after the brilliant ones that follow in this book.

I am much impressed with the quality of the criticism. Sigrid Undset, but I wish she would not dwell so much on his sickness because he was so sane, and I danced with joy at Leavis putting that poor old carved skeleton T. S. Eliot in his place, *not* the place Eliot has assumed. How clearly Hoffman puts the two views of Freud and Lawrence. Mark Schorer is very good and of course I love Aldous and your chapter too. That Eliot never was alive for five minutes and in ten years he will be forgotten, a phony! I also like Edward Nehls. I cannot forgive Tindall that his stuff is called "Tyndallyana," has he no sense of humor? *Very* very interesting to read the reactions to Lawrence of all these people. Wouldn't he have been pleased? I feel very grateful to you.

But for all that I feel there is an even bigger Lawrence of all time. When I read Laotse and Chuangtse and the real great ones I know he is one of them. We are still to close to him. Of course Lawrence had a cultural background and that English tradition, but he needed a wider, world-wide space to fly around in.

The book has really made me very happy and I thank you very much indeed for my beautiful birthday present (74). I am sure Claude would like one, we go there in an hour or so. Angie is busy making pottery and he has built a glassed-in veranda on the house, very nice. We live in it. And he would like those books very much! Is Leavis English?

Yours ever, with best greetings and wishes to you and yours,

Frieda

Tindall is mistaken, we never stayed with Mrs. Nutall, lunched there 3 times, one awful lunch with Somerset Maugham. Tindall does not know that artists get their knowledge not so much through books, but by immediate contact with the place itself, enough to see the Aztec carvings and *feel* the people and landscape. He is a professor and does not know how a creative artist works. Lawrence had no access to Mrs. Nutall's library. Anthony West speaks like the Lord, so absolute!!

I would think more of Eliot if he said: I don't like that fellow D. H. Lawrence, to which he has a right, but these feeble words! Yes, I can see Lawrence at Cambridge trying joyfully to upset their applecart! I think there ought to be a new approach to criticism, you can't separate a man from his work! Nothing is said about L's integrity.

I want to say more about the book. Sigrid Undset puts too much stress on L's sickness and explains things by it and he was very well much of the time. She also does not like him.

Betsky has not noticed that Miriam nowhere shows any desire for Lawrence the man, only this abstract love for poetry and culture, there lies the crux. I like what you say of *The Rainbow*.

A. West says that L. had an "extremely superficial" knowledge of Lady Cynthia Asquith, that is not a fact. We knew her quite well in Margate. The "Ladybird" is not "poppicock" but phantasy at work. I don't think the political country house world to which Edward Marsh introduced him dazzled him at all, and "all he seemed to notice was the small splash he made in it". What foundation is there for this spiteful assumption? Lawrence saw *people* when he met them, people not their setting or trimmings.

The "Prussian Officer" goes also deeper than race as A. W. affirms. It is a profound, universally human conflict. A. W. still judges on the old social level. The argument that Lawrence wrote badly when he moved "outside the area of his personal experience", well, he never did; there was always a personal connexion, maybe not always grasped by Mr. West! To *The Border Line* Mr. West does not have the key either, because there is a key, so he has to invent one. Frank Amon is very right, I think, in writing: "Rather I have dealt with the subject, the discovery under the social surface of more opulent realms of being."

I read Miriam's D. H. L. again, it is very good and charming, very well written, poor thing. That she could not face the incompleteness of her own nature, that one cannot expect. Did Helen Corke send you the small book: D. H. L.'s Princess? [7] Isn't it terrible when she writes: "David is my Sodom and Gomorrah"? That seems to me enough for a man to leave a woman. She is sure he is lost and miserable . . . when she no longer could keep him in her pocket, that was too small for him anyway! But I say "poor thing." If you have not got the book, I will send it you, it is interesting. Look at the L. letters to me, not so much because they are to me, but as to showing his attitude, almost religious, to marriage.

I have had so many interruptions since I began this letter, that I'd better stop or you will never get this.

F.

TO John Middleton Murry

Hotel Jerome
Aspen, Colorado
2 August 1953

Dear Jack,

Thank you for your letter. I think of you with great satisfaction, you have come into your own. I don't worry about you. Mary and the farm and the writing and children and grandchildren and the past, the puzzling past.

Yes, that was a lovely time, when you stayed with us and Katherine went to Carco; because he had told her: "*Ah, Madame, vous devrez être au soleil,*" that's how it began. And then the wonderful story only she could tell about the woman in the train who had a bird in her hat!

That time with you was good. I believe there *is* marriage, you have it with Mary and I with Lawrence, that elemental, unconscious thing. But then—I think L. had become strange to me, when he came back and I was scared and your warmth was good to me and I was happy about it and deeply grateful. I mean in

---

[7] *D. H. Lawrence's Princess, A Memory of Jessie Chambers* (The Merle Press, Thames Ditton, 1951).

Hampstead. Our relationship was wonderful too and is, all through the years there is that "Puck" in my life. Haven't we been rich?

There is another H. Moore book out—more criticism about L. I like the Aldous one only. I got so cross about the others. And I must say L. has grown for me; when I compare him to Laotse and Chuangtse and St. Augustine, he is one of them. When I read Plutarch I get the picture of a man, but in these critics you get little wigglers, who don't see the wood for the trees and then they aren't genuine trees. You might write a wonderful book about the books on L., a big job!

Gordon's Paddy sounds delightful. He had red hair, didn't he?

I am here at Aspen, a beginning "art" centre high up; it's like the Alps, with high mountains and mist hanging around and wet, with lots of music!

I just read Miriam's book and *your introduction* [8] with great satisfaction. It is well written, but I think it is not quite true . . . and how could she face it, poor thing. . . . You can't. But . . . Lawrence could be tender too. I don't *believe* in darkness and don't want it, but you know: "The sun shines on the just and unjust" and one has to accept all life, because it's there. Do you know that terrible story of L's *The Border Line*? The jealousy beyond the grave?

I am a very lucky old woman, and am grateful!

Greet Mary from me, please, very affectionately. You don't say how you are, so I take it you are well, both of you. Mind you send me your book on Swift, I don't know much about him.

Poor old Kot, sourpuss! I disapprove of him too.

With love,
Frieda

Angelino has just built a veranda on the house in Taos and I wish you could see it.

[8] An American edition of Jessie Chambers's *D. H. Lawrence: A Personal Record* with an introduction by Murry had been published by Knight Publications in 1936. Apparently her correspondence with Murry now had brought it to her attention. He had emphasized the happiness of Lawrence's and Frieda's life together.

TO John Middleton Murry

El Prado
Taos
New Mexico
6 August 1953

Dear Jack,

Your second letter came and welcome too.

I was just looking for *David*, L's play, and came across all the Medley material about the Will [9] and suddenly got very excited and felt *very* grateful! How decent English law is and how good everybody was to me and *especially you.* . . . I think the whole thing is really interesting and wasn't I lucky? I feel the material should be used, *what do you think?*

Pollinger just wrote that Spender got the Kot letters for a new magazine Spender is starting called *Encounter*. So I agree with Pollinger, but I fear Kot is very poor! Kot wrote a mean letter to Aldous about me and you too. So I don't feel generous. He never lifted a finger about the Will and he saw me every Tuesday that time I stayed in London and then is mean.

Yes, you would have liked Bynner. Hatred prevents one to be oneself and going on in one's own way. There was a real bond between you and L. If he had lived longer and had been older, you would have been real friends, he wanted so desperately for you to understand him. I think the homosexuality in him was a short phase out of misery—I fought him and won—and that he wanted a deeper thing from you. I am aware so much as I am old, of the elements in us, that we consist of. Do you know what I mean?

Well, I must stop now and get the lunch! Pollinger is a wonderful agent. When I said to him: "I am grateful to you for handling L's work as you do, I feel safe." He answered: "That's how it shall be as long as I live."

Adios for now,

Frieda

Love to Mary.

[9] C. D. Medley was her attorney in 1932 when she won sole right to Lawrence's estate, helped by Murry's testimony that he had witnessed the lost will.

TO John Middleton Murry

29 August 1953

Dear Jack,

That is a good article and you try so hard to explain L. to yourself and others. Of course from a rational, accepted social conventional point of view he is impossible. But then at the bottom I always felt that there was an inevitable thing there and he had to live by his own laws and I did not bear him any grudge, so [sic] indeed I was unhappy at times. And if it was love or hate or both between you the impact you had on each other was very real and very powerful. I do not believe the shoe-shine story is true, I would have known it and I cannot see L. going to the police, can you? I think they were a nuisance round the hotel or the proprietor told the police. That part of your article: "partly an impassioned endeavour to find a way of life for humanity. This effort of Lawrence's has never been taken seriously enough, because it is too disturbing." There you have it in a nutshell. That was his significance for me. His way of loving. And nobody saw it, and surely it is something! But now they begin to. From that angle you can forget the things that hurt. I believe if he could have come to your Thelnetham, wouldn't he have thrown himself into all you are doing and naturally would have begun "Bossing"! You see Bynner is not aware of L's way of life endeavour. . . . I also think he is too nice to me at L's expense. It makes me very happy that you see it.

If you have a photograph of your house to spare, send it to me. I would like to know what it looks like.

Love to you and Mary,
Frieda

I am sending you these photographs, my favourite one is one with a cat, but it is not clear and Frere said it would not reproduce.

L. said: "Jack ought to get what I am after, he ought to know."

FROM John Middleton Murry

Thelnetham
nr Diss, Norfolk
24 September 1953

My dear Frieda,

Thank you very much for the photographs. I should like to use the one of him stroking the dog, with you in the background, at Oaxaca. (Who is the padre?) I only hope Cape will be able to reproduce it.[1]

I am sure you are right: that there was an "inevitable thing" in Lorenzo. He was a real man of destiny—a genuine "daemonic" man. I am sorry I reheated the shoeshine story, if you do not believe it was true. I thought it had your *imprimatur*. Of course, I forget the things that hurt: or rather I understand somehow that it had to be. Not forget, really. Actually, I still wince when I think of them. I have never been *so* hurt. And for the same reason, I never feel so sad as when I read his books—above all his later ones. *Last Poems* are still almost unbearable for me. If I had known what I know now, I could have understood him (very nearly—not quite)—that's what makes me sad. *Si jeunesse savait, si vieillesse pouvait.* He asked too much of me, four years younger, and with nothing comparable to his experience, when he asked me "to go along with him". I was too "innocent". Why, half the *Rainbow* was completely beyond my ken when it was published. I had a childish faith in Love. (In a way, I have it still.) But there was no *depth* in it. I didn't know what physical love really was, or could be. And Lorenzo seemed bent on shattering my ideal, and giving me nothing to put in its place.

Sometimes it all seems both very complicated, and blindingly simple. Why, I ask myself, was it *you* who should have revealed to me the richness of physical love? You gave me the clue. And then there was no hate in it. It was lovely and tender and so rich. Just a fulfilment. And then, having the clue, I had to go through hell—almost literally to have my legs broken—with a woman, in order to find my mate. Now I am *there*, I can look back, and

[1] Murry's *Love, Freedom and Society* was published by Jonathan Cape in 1957, a year after her death.

wonder and half-understand. For it is *very* strange. What held me back from claiming you as my own in 1923? Nothing else but loyalty to Lorenzo. Precisely the kind of loyalty he despised in me. If I had acted by his philosophy, I should not have let you go. And you will not wonder that I still ask myself: Was I a great *fool?* Or was I simply doing what I *had* to do? Perhaps I did not have to go through my *hell.* . . .

I should never have gone through Hell with you. I know it; in my bones I know it. You and I could never have hated one another. But I suppose for some mysterious reason, I had to go through the agony of —— all over again with ——, only worse, because I had been through it before—and then such hell with —— that I looked back to the pain of —— and —— as *happiness*—in order to find love and the ultimate tenderness and peace. Just in time. In another few years I should have been too battered and too old to love. It took me months and months of healing by Mary before I was able to love her.

I like talking like this with you: somehow it helps to take the pain out of the past.

L. was right when he said "Jack ought to get what I am after": but wrong if he thought I *could* have done it then (I mean in 1915–16). And, as I say, in 1923, the price of my getting it was his giving you up to me. And when I couldn't have you, of course I began to go haywire: and he jeered at me.

It's a *wonderful* story, really—of the four of us. It's so strange that I seem to have finished up where, I suppose, he wanted me to finish up. How I can see him around here at Lodge Farm bossing us all!

And what an extraordinary effect he had upon my life! I married —— because of him. When with —— the same thing had happened as with ——, only worse, I said to myself "Lorenzo is right. I always love from the spiritual centres. And I have come to this appalling, repeated disaster. I will love with my body only—follow physical attraction only." And I married ——. It was the worst disaster of all. . . .

And so I have paid, with blood and tears, for my conclusion. Lorenzo was right *and* wrong. The physical tenderness of love is just as much a spiritual thing as it is a physical. It is both at once—in a new, blessed reconciliation. Was it merely a physical attraction I felt for you? Nonsense. I wanted, needed, *all* you. And the loveliness there was between us came out of the generosity of your soul as much as the generosity of your body. There *can* be no generosity of body without generosity of soul.

Well, my dear, I have talked a lot.

Harvest is nearly over. My brother and his wife have been here a fortnight while he painted Mary's portrait and mine: now they have gone. My son is coming in a week's time. We have 20 acres of barley left to get in. I am busy gathering my tobacco crop: I hope it will be enough to last me for a year.

Here is a picture of our little house. It is the small farmhouse—*Lower* Lodge Farm. The big farmhouse—Lodge Farm itself—is a quarter of a mile up the road: where Donald and Saul and their families and the two pupils live.

Jack

You say in your letter, quite truly, as far as I am concerned, "And if it was love or hate or both between you [me and L.] the impact you had on one another was very real and very powerful." The impact on me, at any rate, was sometimes quite shattering. But what, if any, impact I had upon him, I don't know. I can't believe I hurt him as much as he hurt me. I sometimes went on quivering inside for months after one of his letters. I can remember now, how when he was so furious with me for not coming out to Spotorno at the beginning of 1926—when Violet took ill, and the second baby was on the way—I just seemed to go sick inside for weeks, and I said to myself "Never, never, *never*, will I expose myself to L. again!" And gradually I grew hard, so that he could not hurt me any more.

Mary sends her love: I've just been down for coffee, and she specially impressed it on me.

TO John Middleton Murry

Port Isabel
Texas
[*Undated*]

My dear Jack,

It was a treat to see your "fist" today the 26th or rather your beautiful handwriting. Yes, it had been my turn to write. In the night of the 24th I woke up and thought, I wanted to write to Jack for Christmas. I meant to write actually before, wrote "unactually" several times. I remember I wanted to say after your last letter how wonderful it is that you are so happy with Mary comparably [sic] late in life, mostly it's the other way around. At the end of November we left Taos after the first snowstorm to come here. It is always a chore this exodus, closing the Taos house for the winter and finding homes for the house plants and draining the pipes and so on. Then the house here was in a mess and had to be repainted. Now it is nice and everything works; we are right on the gulf and away from houses, so that I can run in my nightie early in the morning to the water and look at all the seagulls and ducks and pelicans and geese. It is warm and green and we have big white oleanders and pink ones and big cactus with a huge white flower in the middle. And the fishermen (Mexican) bring us fish and oysters and there is a big fleet of shrimpers and all that activity, shipbuilding and so on is fascinating. This is a frame farmhouse, we have had it now for several years and it is good to get to this low altitude and the semitropical climate. There are banana boats that go to England from here, take passengers, not expensive and they give you good food. Wouldn't it be fun if you and Mary could come some autumn. It is very quiet, not many people, thank God!

Your life sounds most satisfactory, a real life *á la* Montaigne, whom I love. I fear I am not much interested in the *Golden Echo*,[2] people get so mixed up. He, Garnett, wrote how he was with us when we found the chapel and slept in a hayloft, but he

[2] The first volume of David Garnett's autobiography, now three volumes, *The Flowers of the Forest* and *The Familiar Faces* bringing the story to World War II.

had left us before. I am much more reasonable now, I would not have burnt your book. You see all those years L. was abused it had inflamed me (not that I abused him too) [sic] and [I] did not see straight—how stupid one can be. That awful pity I felt for him, that I shall always feel, that he had to die and did not want to die. He still holds me, as if he said grimly, "You are mine." Part of me likes it, part doesn't. So your Swift[3] will come out soon. Have you an American publisher?

Love to Mary and may the next year be a lovely one for you both.

Always affectionately,
Frieda

FROM John Middleton Murry

Lower Lodge, Thelnetham
nr Diss, Norfolk, England
3 January 1954

My dear Frieda,

Your "Christmas" letter came yesterday. I was glad indeed to have it. I was afraid you were cross with me for some reason, though I couldn't think what it was. I am accordingly relieved. For I think of you so often with love, and a queer kind of happiness: the kind of happiness which can only mean that all that was, and is, between us, was *good*. And such a memory is a treasure. You are a very real person in our little household. I don't suppose many days pass without Mary and I talking about you—just casually: saying: How Frieda would enjoy this! or something of that sort. So it was with a shock of surprise and pleasure that a fortnight ago we saw your letter and picture in the *Sunday Times*—so unexpectedly! I chuckled over the letter as I read it aloud. "That's Frieda, all over," I said. A good sound sudden *smack*. Wallop!

Tell me more, if you can find out without trouble, about those banana boats: how much it costs for two of us to make the trip. I should like, at any rate, to please myself with the thought that

[3] *Jonathan Swift; A Critical Biography.*

Mary and I *might* make it before we get too old. It would be
thrilling to look forward to. We would have to save up a bit
—which is quite a good thing in itself—for we have just had to
buy a new car. The old one, which has lasted 15 years, was just
falling to pieces. Now we have one with a heater inside, so that
we don't get frozen, don't have to wear big overcoats, and it
seems the height of luxury. I am told there was a broadcast on
"Lorenzo in Cornwall" lately—on what is called the Western
Region—in which a farmer friend of L's (presumably William
Henry [4]) told how he had seen you once "take an armful of L's
MSS and put them on the fire" during a quarrel. I didn't hear it;
but a friend of mine told me about it. I wrote to the BBC asking
for a copy of the script, but they told me I couldn't have one,
because there was no copy. I wanted to kick up a row. Have you
heard anything about it? Without actual evidence I can't be sure
it was true. . . .

   With my best love for the New Year

Jack

TO John Middleton Murry

Port Isabel, Texas
Box 201
8 January 1954

Dear Jack,

   I did not know they had published that letter I had sent to
Pollinger for *The Times!* I am glad it amused you. All through
the years they had been so condescending about L! "He was a
genius but he couldn't think and he couldn't write and he did not
make sense!" I will write to Pollinger about that "Western
Region Broadcast." I wonder if it was William Henry. I was
never aware that he was hostile to me, but he may have become
so. . . . A[—] wrote a nasty review, how he had visited L. at

---

[4] William Henry Hocking, a young Cornwall farmer with whom
Lawrence had an intense friendship in 1917, but who seems eventually
to have been affected by the general suspicion that the Lawrences were
spies which culminated in their expulsion by the military.

the Villa Mirenda and how it was full of flies and spilled bottles of milk, sordid. I found that at the time of [——]'s supposed visit we were in Bandol. You see there never was an "armful of MSS," they were in hard-bound books mostly. I know I did no such thing, but several times I tried to save the MSS when L. wanted to throw them away. Will write to Pollinger.

We also have a new car, and ours has even a radio!! But the lovely news is that you and Mary may come!! Look on a map. We are the lowest point of the U.S.A. near Brownsville, where we shop. It's about 20 miles away and you cross the Rio Grande bridge into Mexico. On New Year's Eve we went with a few people to Matamoros, it was very gay but not rowdy, wonderful acrobats. Came home at 3! We would have such fun, I feel, all of us! I will send you the literature about it! I suppose next autumn would be good. Our house is too small for us all, but there are nice small bungalows; I think getting away for a little while may do you both good. I heard that the food was good, only a few people on the boat, it sounds attractive. You might inquire from your end too! I *like* Texas! So soon I collect the literature for you and send it. The days are already getting a little longer.

Love to you both, I will write a more sensible letter soon!

Frieda

Don't tell anybody you may come, I do so hate it that they talk about one!

TO Harry T. Moore

Port Isabel
19 January, '54

Dear Harry,

Yes, that was a "heartwarming" review. So you have still two months of work on the L. book.

I had no idea you had collected so many L. letters. Do you mean they are not the published Aldous' letters? Angelino says the Viking has the letter rights. Have you written to the Viking that you have all those unpublished letters and have dated and put them in their places. You have my support. I agree with you, you are the person to edit them. It is better you write to Viking, because they detest me. But maybe it would be better (I don't *know*) if you waited a while. So much is published now. They, the Viking, might do a second volume of letters. I do think Frere would do them. I must say I am very grateful to you, for being L's more than Boswell, and so ought the publishers. . . .

But you see how it was with L. in that wonderful chapter of yours on how he was hounded. But I am sure in the long run it will have been worth your while. By the way there was a big family history, done by my uncle Ludwig; you have not seen it, have you, and I have not got it.

For us there is not much to say, except that I am writing a bit very slowly. I would rather have it published when I am dead. I like it down here and so does Angie—another world of shrimp-boats and harbors and fishermen and so on. The Viking know I don't think much of the Trilling; they don't care. . . .

The best of luck to you both.

What a relief when you have finished.

Greetings from Angie and me.

I wrote to Schorer.

Frieda

TO Montague Weekley

Box 201
Port Isabel, Texas
27 January 1954

My dear Monty,

It shocked me to hear that Elsa is pessimistic about your father's health. I know Aldous has shingles; I suppose at his age (your father's) they are weakening. It is such a great comfort to me that you have all been such faithful children, especially Elsa. It shows how "decent" you are. Should anything happen, will you please telegraph me; after all I would like to know.

It worries me about Ursula. Is Barby doing all she can for her? Is it the knee and is it stiff? It would be too bad if poor

Ursula only got a stiff knee out of all that effort at dancing. I wrote Barby, but maybe you can see that she, I mean Ursula, does learn something. I feel a good nurse might be helpful with advice; surely that knee can't be so bad.

Meanwhile I am very well and enjoy this place, the nice clean house by the water and all it means.

They asked me to talk on the British broadcast. I can say a few things. Just got a book from Aldous. Are you writing any more? Yes, I enjoyed my stay at the Kingsley and you all.

I know you will do all you can for your father.

I had a letter from Ida.

Just a line to say "how do you do?" to you all; your own young ones seem flourishing. Vera and you will enjoy their visits!

Much love,
Your mother

I can't help thinking about the old days! Greetings from A.

TO E. W. Tedlock, Jr.

Box 201
Port Isabel, Texas
30 January 1954

Dear Ted,

I am glad all that work you did in the past is not wasted and you get something out of it. Your questions. The only difficulty I had with the immigration health laws was in El Paso. The American embassy in Mexico helped that time, but it was tough, the El Paso people hating to give in.

No, we never suffered from the moral turpitude clause, we had been married a long time.

No, if I remember rightly I did not oppose his colony plan; my reason: I never believed in it.

We are happy here. It is quiet and warm and green, and the water is a source of interest with the fishermen and the boats, and the good fish and oysters to eat.

I am sure the family is growing like mushrooms.

My best wishes to you all.

Isn't it strange about your young man [a student] and the wedding.

Yours ever,
Frieda

TO John Middleton Murry

Box 201
Port Isabel, Texas
13 March 1954

Dear Jack,

I thought of you and Mary getting married on the 10th all along, and I wanted a feast that day and [to] send you a telegram, then I had to talk over the radio that day in Brownsville and forgot. So I am having a feast tonight at the Carlos Café and it will be oysters and Mexican food, very good. Anyhow I am so glad you are married.

Not much to say, except that we start for Taos on the first of April. It has been very hot but pleasant.

You seem to be amused when I get on my hindlegs, so I copy that letter to——for you, how cocksure and arrogant he is!

Now I go to my feast.

Love to both of you
Frieda

TO Else Jaffe

Box 201
Port Isabel, Texas
15 March 1954

Sister Else,

You have delighted me with the Goethe letters. What a charming and kind man he was! And then they call him *"Herr Geheimrat"*—is that stupidity or malice?

We have had such a fine winter. Just right! but the weather is so changeable, one day real heat, then comes a norther and in a

few hours almost cold! Just think, we have glowworms! Has
Arturo Montoya visited you? the neighbours' son? I have known
him since he was a child. They are good neighbours. Lasky
sends me the *Monat*, which I read with great interest.

I must write letters constantly. Lawrence has a vogue again.
What is our Nusch doing? She doesn't write much. She is
probably lonely at times, but she gets along so well with most
people. I hope you are all well. Many greetings to Alfred, but he
should not do too much. Angelino and I get along so well
together, I have learned much from him, he stands so firmly on
his own feet, naturally intelligent, dependable, and [he] cares.

I have just read a book by B. H. Tawney, *Religion and the
Rise of Capitalism*. A great deal in it about Max Weber.

Best wishes, dear Else, and very many thanks for the delightful, stimulating book.

Your sister

(*Translated from the German*)

TO Else Jaffe

Port Isabel, Texas
24 March 1954

My dear Else,

Angelino had just taken my letter to you to the post office
when I thought: so, now I did not ask how Marianna Weber is
and I would like to know. Then I began to dream about the old
days there in Freiburg with you and the Webers. Your letter
moved me deeply. Yes, I knew that, without thinking much
about how you were so deeply attached. Now a silly thought
comes to me, that this relationship which had such heights and
such depths is lost to mankind. But according to my experience,
I am glad for you; for as far as I am concerned they talk bosh
about Lawrence. After all, one has no real knowledge of
relationships which one has not himself experienced, only an
idea. Naturally I wept over your letter, and still weep.

Yes, that was your constellation, with the Webers, it is that
way forever. But you still have Alfred, who needs you like the air

he breathes. And it is indeed wonderful that he has never lost himself, never his own way. In this age, where there was a Hitler and so many base things, it does one good to think of him.

But no, Else, don't think that your hour will come soon, that is because you are now grieved. Now spring is coming, which always makes you so happy, and then you have the children. And maybe we'll see each other again as real old hags! Yes, send Nehls the "Burns novel":[5] I remember that L. had the idea.

Order some flowers in my name for Marianna's grave.

All love,
Your sister

Angelino also said, she thinks that because she is now sad, "*e triste*".

So, Else, live a little while yet!

(*Translated from the German*)

TO Richard Aldington

Box 201
Port Isabel, Texas
29 March, 1954

Dear Richard,

Of course I swallowed your *Pinorman*[6] like a raw oyster. You

---

[5] In 1912 Lawrence began a story based on the life of Robert Burns. Else had now discovered, among papers left with her, fragments of this unfinished work. These appeared in the first volume of Edward Nehls's monumental *D. H. Lawrence: A Composite Biography* (The University of Wisconsin Press, 1957, 3 vols.).

[6] Published by William Heinemann, Ltd., in 1954, and subtitled "Personal recollections of Norman Douglas, Pino Orioli and Charles Prentice," this is a remarkable exploration of the problems of biographical accuracy, with particular reference to Douglas. It dealt of course with the controversy between Lawrence and Douglas concerning the nature and merit of Maurice Magnus, and defended Lawrence as the superior man and artist, if not gentleman, in terms of Douglas's class stereotype and amoral hedonism. In her sympathy for Orioli, Frieda does not mention the difficulty she had after Lawrence's death in obtaining the manuscripts that had been left with Orioli; yet she had kept the cor-

made it all live again. You give this wonderful bit of living, unique, never to be repeated. I laugh when I think what ordinary people will make of it.

You treat Pino with special tenderness. I am glad. How good he was, when Lawrence was ill and I sent for him and at once he came, bringing Dr. Gigliogli mostly. Then came the bitter blow of his meanness. I am sure it was Norman. I don't think Lawrence ever knew how much Norman hated him.

I knew Norman earlier than you when he still had his diabolical splendor, that could not have friends, only slaves. But you are fair to him, you could have presented an ogre feeding on small boys. He saw himself as that finished article the "perfect gentleman," but with wild, unsophisticated urchins, that freshened his weary soul.

I do hope Pino did not die in misery and loneliness. But somehow Pino would always find someone to be good to him. Pino did not write anything nasty about me. I wonder why?

What a lie when Norman says the peasants did not like L. at the Mirenda. They did very much. In their own way they knew

---

respondence, which was in Italian. Also among her papers was a draft of a letter marked "Sent to Editor of *Time and Tide* by Frere"—A. S. Frere of William Heinemann, Ltd., was a friend of all concerned. The letter was a reply to an attack on Aldington's book by Miss Nancy Cunard, which Frieda took as an attempt to glorify Douglas at Lawrence's expense. After remarking that Miss Cunard did not seem "very bright, not profoundly so," Frieda went on: "I did not want to tell this story; it is an ugly one, but I think now I will. When I was in Florence after Lawrence was dead to talk with Orioli about his publishing some of Lawrence's books, I was in Orioli's flat and Norman was there too. Casually Norman said to me: 'I have got a charming boy of fourteen, but I prefer them younger; wouldn't you like to take him on?' He would never have said this to me while Lawrence was alive. I said, after gathering my wits: 'I have children of my own.' I don't know whether Miss Cunard thinks I should have felt honored by kind Douglas's offer or not. I was horrified and never saw him again. . . . Naturally Miss Nancy Cunard wants to defend her friend Norman Douglas. I also, like many others, had experienced his charm and wit. But anybody who knows about Douglas knew that he was no little Lord Fauntleroy. There was a sinister side to him. In the future people will be interested to read Mr. Aldington's account of this period. . . ."

he was somebody. Not in a "frère et cochon" way (as my father would say) but very real. I *love* it when you say: "If Pino said that, I won't speak to him again, either in heaven or hell."

That you defend Lawrence like the cat its kittens is wonderful but surely fair. I don't think L. was envious, you cannot be, when you are so much "yourself" as L. was.

Richard, now I say: mea culpa. I had forgotten that you got Frere to take L.'s books. Ingratitude, but now I will remember— and be grateful.

Good luck to *Pinorman*. I am glad it was written and how it was written!

Ever yours,
Frieda

Had Douglas read Gregorovius?

to Montague Weekley

El Prado, New Mexico
12 May 1954

My dear Monty,

I got your letter. You are going through some sad days.[7] Maybe today you bury him. Write to me all the rest, where you buried him and so on. I hope he did not suffer much. I feel very solemn. He was a good man in every way according to his lights. You were lucky to have such a good father for such a long time and you were good children to him; that must be a great satisfaction to you. To his grandchildren he will be an unforgettable figure. I am thinking of you and the past. I am thinking of how when he tried to explain something to you and you did not get it at once he held his head and said: "Why should I be cursed with an idiot for a son!" And I remember when we first were married and I slithered down those narrow stairs, he rushed out of his study and said: "My God, I am married to an earthquake."

[7] Ernest Weekley had died on May 7. Born in 1865, he was, indeed, one of the last of an older generation.

Did he look handsome when he was dead? His generation is nearly gone. Like the wheat the crops follow each other. You will have much to do. I hope Elsa is not too tired.

All my thoughts are with you, and write again.

All my love to you,

Your mother

Angelino sends his sympathy.

TO Else Jaffe

El Prado
18 May 1954

My dear Else,

You had a visit from Arturo. He wrote happily about his visit with you and about the fireworks. The photograph is nice and cheered my heart, for you look so well and fresh.

Now it is spring and pleasant. Monty wrote a few days ago: "When you get this our father will be no more."

He is dead. I think I am glad. I caused him such terrible suffering! But it is all so long ago, as though it happened to other people. I am glad for Elsa, it was touching how she took care of him, [she] has a charming house and large garden, her eldest already has a good position.

You will no doubt see Ian,[8] he is in Germany. All is well in my neighbourhood. Only Ursula, Barby's daughter, hurt her knee and can't go on with her dancing, and she worked so hard! It upsets me for her. I hope it will get better. You won't believe *how* much we do with the Lawrence thing! All enjoyable. But work. . . .

Angelino helps faithfully with everything. Three days at the ranch with Arturo's mother, who cleans for us, very beautiful up there, then Angelino built a "patio" in the rear of the house with a little pond in which, if you please, a water lily is growing! With help from two Spanish boys, whom we knew as children. They are called Brett's "worm brigade", because they used to

[8] Montague Weekley's son.

bring worms to Brett when she goes fishing. She is really incredibly energetic!

Mabel is in San Francisco, where a very good eye doctor performed an operation on her eyes, she was almost blind, but will again see better. You won't believe how many people come—a diplomat with his wife from Australia, then a poor student, then an Italian, etc.

Now Friedel will soon be with you! Has Alfred rested up? I am doing well financially, better than I ever expected. Have you an idea whether Nusch has her money from that factory? I am indeed very glad that I can help her, but I think when she has an income she won't need my help any more. She doesn't write a word about it, and our Nusch always needed lots of money.

I often think of the Albuquerque airfield, how you stood beside me, that was surely very nice.

In true love,
Your sister

Greetings to Alfred!

(*Translated from the German*)

TO John Middleton Murry

Kiowa Ranch, El Prado
Taos, New Mexico
May (*I don't know the date*) 1954

Dear Jack,

We came up here with my neighbour Mrs. Montoya to clean and I dusted the books and I found your *Between Two Worlds* [9] and instead of cleaning I got absorbed in it and read and read.

It is beautiful with the plum blossoms out and the cherries, and my hands are icy. I dipped them in the swimming pool and it is full of the water from the mountains and everything is new and fresh from the lonely winter.

[9] The subtitle of *The Autobiography of John Middleton Murry* (1936).

I loved *Between Two Worlds*. How wonderful the story when K. says: "Why don't you make me your mistress?" And you wiggling your legs in the air! Lovely! And then the end with the war chapter and your terrible grief! It is a book that should live.

I know you and K. blamed me a lot, but I had to throw myself against that elemental Lawrence and fight him. That somehow was my job and, as you know, when the elements had settled it was wonderful. I think women loved you because you never had that awful "medicinal" attitude toward sex, no whole human being could have.

L. and K. wanted *too* much, and you are very sane. You also knew even then how L. depended on me in every way for his living and work.

Monty wrote two days ago: "When you get this our father will be no more." So he is dead. I don't feel any remorse, but hope he got something out of me as his young wife, before I grieved him so much. It also makes me feel humble. I always thought, he doesn't know me, but maybe I did not know him either, but he was so cemented into his set ideas and he couldn't change. My clever mother always thought too that I tortured L. too much about the children. But now it is all right between them and me, I am so lucky (I touch wood). I haven't heard from you for a long time.

I do hope you come to Port Isabel next winter. You and Mary must be so peaceful about being married!

Write and say how you are.

Love
Frieda

I think K. wanted you all to yourself, I can understand that! I think that fight in Cornwall was chiefly over his disappointment that it didn't work, I think K. didn't want it to work! I can understand that too!

TO John Middleton Murry

El Prado, New Mexico
16 July 1954

Dear Jack,

You are a bad man to write me such enchanting letters that I want to answer at once, instead of answering the dull ones.

Yes, your spring comes late in life, that's all, and why not? When I think of Mary I think of her great serenity as of a woman fulfilled—you would not find such a one in the whole of America. All the women here are always rushing as if they never sat down peacefully, or went to sleep cosily. Is it the men's fault?

Does your kettle take so long to boil? I have a "whistler" too. I should say it is very wonderful and unusual, your love for Mary, and you have deserved it. Because you went on loving and would not be disillusioned, as most men do sort of prefer it, it is easier. It takes guts to go on. Indeed, indeed, I think we were real people!

I went to see my friend Dr. Hausner [1] who said I was in very good condition and also said: "You are a great woman with your simplicity and humility." I nearly fell off my chair. I thought great women are different and I did not think my humility was so "hot" either. Isn't it funny! That's why I am glad you say we are nice people, "great" would be a bore! Marble busts! You might be a good one! I am not "rich", but you know money comes in from MSS also and they are making a film of Lady C., a Major Angel in England. I am not so much interested—not much faith in it. I doubt their ability. I wish you could have put your oar in this! It will be a tame show!

18 *July*

Now I have escaped for a day or two from Taos and am up here at Kiowa. I wish you knew it, it really is something special! It doesn't seem to change, as if nothing could tame it.

Not much worth having seems to come out of English writers. But maybe I don't know enough, nor of Americans either.

[1] Dr. Eric Peter Hausner, Santa Fe physician.

Have a nice summer!

> Love to you both
> Frieda

FROM John Middleton Murry

> Lower Lodge, Thelnetham
> nr Diss, Norfolk
> *13 August 1954*

My dear Frieda,

It's nearly a month since I had your last letter. Anyway, it's dated July 16; but it seems to have come only yesterday. So quickly time flies nowadays. We have a houseful—my eldest daughter, Katherine, who is married to a Belgian actor and playwright, and is here with her little Jon and a lumpish Belgian maid; and my youngest son, David, who is on holiday from H.M.S. Conway where he is training to be an officer. And that is about as much as our little house can hold. But it's very delightful to have them. My small grandson is a real charmer.

I have, you see, become very much of a family man. The death of — — has brought my two youngest children back to me; and, thank goodness, they are very happy in their new home. In spite of all the fantastic abuse of my Mary they have heard for the last 12 years, they have taken to her, like ducks to water.

About ten days ago a nice young man came down from the BBC for me to broadcast some of my reminiscences of Lorenzo, you and Katherine. He told me that you had done something at a local studio near Taos for the same programme. I don't know when it is to be given: but I shall listen eagerly to what you say.

I like what Dr. Hausner said to you: "You are a great woman, with your simplicity and humility." What he meant, I am sure, was that you are a rare woman, and a real one, and a lovely one. Real women seem to me the rarest creatures on this earth. I'm not a bit surprised that you say you don't believe there is one in all America. I certainly don't know one, except my Mary, in

England. And, as I've told you before, it was because I had loved you—and do still, for that matter—that when the time came, I could recognise Mary.

We are having a perfect nightmare of a summer—certainly the very worst since I came to this farm: rain, rain, rain—hardly a glimpse of the sun. We daren't begin harvest, although it's already two weeks later than usual. Send us a bit of your Taos weather. Just as I write, there's the very *hell* of a downpour begun.

I won a bottle of whisky bowling at our village Fête a fortnight ago. Since I don't drink a bottle of whisky in a year, we are well provided for. Moreover, since I grow my own tobacco, I am prepared for the worst.

With my very best love

Jack

Write to me when you have time!

TO Harry T. Moore

El Prado, New Mexico
20 September 1954

Dear Harry,

I never dreamt you would be affected by the hurricane too!

No, I have very few photographs left and you know I must write my book. I have a diary of my father, the war of 70–71; [2] I want to publish it, chiefly to show what a decent war it was, to counteract the Hitler régime impression of Germany! There won't be so much about Lawrence in it.

So now give yourself a rest, you can't go on working at that pressure. I am looking forward to your book. Our great excitement now is the University of Texas. They want to make it the biggest L. centre in the world! And I am told they have lots of

[2] A considerable portion of her translation of the diary was found among her papers, now at the Humanities Research Center of the University of Texas.

money to do it with! We are going there beginning of November on our way to Port Isabel.

Yes, you have my permission to use the record photograph.

Yes, I think there is enough material for another book with the plays!

We are having the most lovely weather!

Angie is looking forward to the Dante!

Yours as ever
Frieda

TO Else Jaffe

El Prado, New Mexico
3 October 1954

My Sister Else,

A sunny autumn Sunday. About this time [3] the apples and pears, one kind was called "passe Kolmar", were being stored in beautiful order in the cellar, and the overripe yellow plums lay on the ground by the small garden gate, and the bees and wasps had a feast. And then it was your birthday, and now it is your 80th! You can be proud of your long, full life.

I hope you have a lovely birthday. Nusch said she wanted to come. You go ahead of me on life's pathway, go on doing it.

We will drink to your health. I think about your visit to Albuquerque. It must not be the last. The University of Texas wants to found a "Lawrence Centre" in great style; they also want to buy the ranch and build there so that students can work there. That will solve the problem for us when A. and I are dead. The richest University in the world. On the way to Port Isabel they want to give us a reception in Austin. O woe! But they are full of enthusiasm. So there is much to do, but Angelino is on the ball. I couldn't do it without him.

I read an article in the *Monat* by Alfred. Regards to him, I too am proud of him.

This winter Angelino will visit his sister in Buenos Aires. I have invited Ida for two months. She has deserved well of me.

[3] Elsa's note: "In Sablon, our home near Metz."

There are freighters that go from Texas to Bremen and back; it costs only $430 there and back. We are both very well. It was a magnificent summer. Ian will probably visit you. On your birthday you will think of many who are no longer here. Continue to enjoy everything enjoyable. I am with you in spirit.

A little gift for flowers.

Always, up to a blessed end, not yet for a long time, I hope.

Your sister
With love,
Frieda

(*Translated from the German*)

TO John Middleton Murry

Box 201
Port Isabel, Texas
[*Undated*]

My dear Jack,

Haven't heard from you for a long time. Is it myself that has not written? Anyhow I hope you and Mary are well. I had an idea I had told you the University of Texas wanted to make a Lawrence centre at Austin, they wanted to buy the MSS I still have and make the ranch into a sort of study place. It is the richest University in the world. So we thought our problem of L's chapel (which I would give them) with the ranch was solved and the MSS. I told them you must have some L. material and the young Prof. Roberts [4] wrote he had heard from you. They gave us a great reception in Austin, we arrived with the MSS and rare books, but nothing was settled. . . . Otherwise we are flourishing, sold *Sons and Lovers* to the movies.

You remember Ida? I invited her here, she is coming on a nice freight boat from Bremen, only costs 430 dollars here and back.

[4] Dr. Warren Roberts, director of the Humanities Research Center at the University of Texas, author of *A Bibliography of D. H. Lawrence* (Rupert Hart-Davis, 1963).

Angelino visits his sister in Buenos Aires while she is here. She comes end of January.

I had hoped you might come and Mary. But it would be so much more interesting for you to come to Taos. In every way; people would interest you, and could you not lecture on the way? How I would love to show you around and you could stay at the upper ranch. There is Brett, and Mabel, and all sorts of people. Here the human element is negligible. I love the sea and what goes with it, the real sea at Padre Island, a lovely endless stretch of sand, seagulls, pelicans, clouds of ducks, cranes, shells. I even swim, while Angie catches a little shark now and then. It's so peaceful and I feel like Barnaby Rudge. I just read it again. That strange Dennis, the hangman, who is so officious in his calling. Dickens is such a good psychologist, knowing about the strange inhuman twists in people. Lawrence said Katherine had a lot in common with Dickens, you know when the kettle is so alive on the fire and things seem to take on such significance. It would be interesting to compare Dickens with Mark Twain, who is so completely American, the first really. Could you get away from your farm for some time?

Are you well enough to take this trip? Would Mary like it? I want to hear from you—and have all your news.

A very good Christmas to you and always all good wishes to you.

Frieda

Don't tell anybody my story of Austin. I don't understand it yet.

Did you hear about poor Frere's trouble?

TO Montague Weekley

Box 201
Port Isabel, Texas
24 December 1954

My dear Monty,

It is Christmas Eve and I am thinking of *our* Christmasses! You were always so thrilled and grateful! You were an awfully nice child! Full of beans and schemes! And I remember one night, you were ill and slept near me, and I woke up and you were looking at me with feverish eyes and I asked you: "Do you want anything?" "Water," you said. "Why didn't you wake me?" "You were sleeping," you said. Nobody had taught you to be considerate. Funny that you say you liked "Nikolaus" almost better than Christmas. So did I as a child. Nikolaus came and we put some hay out for his donkey and a little glass of "Schnapps" for him. He asked if we had been good children and we doubtfully said "yes". Then he threw his sack of nuts and figs and dates and men made of gingerbread with currants for eyes down and departed. But then the thrill, he came again, when we were asleep. Nusch and I shared a gay bedroom. When we woke up in the middle of the night, there was a tray for each of us. We lit our candles and there was such a good smell and just a few presents, little pots and pans and some gloves and slippers, just a prelude for Christmas and the mysterious dark night outside.

I am having a wonderful time here. We go to Padre Island. A long, lovely stretch of sand and beautiful sea. I can even swim, but not far, because of ugly small sharks. Angelino fishes. There are pelicans and seagulls and cranes and shells to pick up and landcrabs to watch and hardly any people. The nonhuman world is so restful. We have early spring weather and soak in the sunshine. It is mean to tell you this, you there in London.

But there is also hard work. We sold *Sons and Lovers* to the movies. I hope you will have a good Christmas with Vera and Ian home.

Julia is all right, Monty. Be thankful that she has so much go. But I am a little doubtful that the place she goes to gets all that work from those young girls for nothing. Isn't that it?

I never hear from Elsa and Barby. I think your father's death was a great shock to Elsa.

I think Ida will be here the end of January. I shall feel at home with her, I am sure. She is deeply attached to all of you, but especially to you.

I do hope Vera is home and getting really well. Her letter

worried me very much. I suppose she did not look after her varicose veins soon enough. She has had a bad time.

Is there no chance of you coming over? this year?

All my love to you and I hope you will write this year. You can write, you know.

A really good new year!

Your mother

Angelino sends greetings!

TO Harry T. Moore

Box 201
Port Isabel, Texas
27 December '54

Dear Harry,

The Intelligent Heart [5] came right on Xmas Day and I have been absorbed in it. You may well be proud of it. It runs along so smoothly and alive and also amusingly. How did you ever get to know so much? At first I had to get rid of my personal self and see it impersonally, it's my life too after all. I thought L. had really a wonderful life, in spite of illness and poverty and quarrels! Of course his genius made it so—and the quarrels loom too large, in between there was so much good feeling too, genuine affection!

We have such a peaceful time here; on Padre Island there is a wild endless stretch of sand and clean water coming in and we get full of sun, Angie fishes. I swim and get shells and watch the birds and the sandcrabs. I hope your book is a great success and you make money too!

A wonderful new year to you and yours!

Best from Angie too!

Yours ever,
Frieda

[5] Published by Farrar, Straus and Young in 1954. It is subtitled *The Story of D. H. Lawrence*, and contains many hitherto unpublished letters and much new information. It is the definitive biography.

TO John Middleton Murry

Box 201
Port Isabel, Texas
January 1955

Dear Jack,

I am so glad the *Journal* [6] arrived two days ago; I spent them and most of the nights reading it. They are the purest joy: her creation of images so entirely her own of human and nonhuman life! How she noticed! No, one could never say: "Poor Katherine," to so rich a person! But you get mad too. She wants to be alone; when she *is* alone, she complains about loneliness. She was so disciplined in so many things, but I think she let herself go in her being ill. And that feeling "sinful" when she doesn't write! Her will, her will! But I am so thankful that I have my own living Katherine, she was not the Katherine *"couvre-toi de gloire"*, so much as the Katherine *"couvre-toi de flanelle, Tartarin"*. I don't think she thought much of my intelligence, but I don't mind in the least. She is so right when she says she was like Lawrence. Our early days were really rather stupid, I mean the age itself was squilchily sentimental, you had to take your miserable little emotions so awfully seriously! I can see Ida so profoundly fulfilled in her martyrdom and Katherine too in letting her temper fly at her! I love herself better than her *Journal*. I am just making marmalade with bitter oranges, that would have interested K.

Yes, Ida is coming. I am very pleased. I also want to pay a debt of gratitude to her, she made my life so easy when the children were small, I had only the fun of them. I took it so for granted at the time. How I wish K. could have had the heavenly time I am having nowadays, peace, very little nonpeace. Your life with Mary sounds wonderful too. Do you think Katherine could have imagined it? I like to think of it—a kind of squire life! You got what you wanted, finally!

No, no sympathy for Kot. Yes, Frere was in trouble with a book, there was a chance he might go to prison.

[6] *The Journal of Katherine Mansfield*, edited by Murry (Knopf, 1931).

So we were on the radio! So Emily [7] is still alive; yes, she was nice! But when I won that lawsuit, chiefly *grâce à vous, Monsieur*, they had no more to do with me. But William Henry was not a faithful friend to L. When we were turned out of Cornwall he was scared and wrote no more to L. And now he spreads himself.

I will close now; no, I must tell you about Harry Moore's book; how he got all that stuff God only knows. Some not true! But it will amuse you.

> Love to you both,
> Frieda

TO Harry T. Moore

> Box 201
> Port Isabel, Texas
> *14 January 1955*

Dear Harry,

The first time I read the book I rushed through it, now I read it again calmly and it *is* an achievement! It also runs along so beautifully like music, your voice as an accompaniment, never insistent. Surely that book will sell. I read the *Times*, loving the gossipy bits of course, but the serious people will see the whole. So much, so many people I had forgotten, and then it shocked me how much spite and gossip and pure lies there were about us! How I hopped over it all comparatively blithely is a miracle to me now! I could write to you by the hour—Violet Hunt about Jessie's gloves I don't believe; just as the visit with me is just made up. I never told you about my friend, a young Austrian doctor who had worked with Freud and who revolutionised my life with Freud. Through him and then through me Lawrence knew about Freud. That horrid Kot, I never liked him. Beatrice Campbell told Murry she had seen him and he was very old and miserable.

The New Republic wrote. They are anxious to honour L. in this anniversary year of his death with several articles. "Would I be at all interested in providing a personal reminiscence, *using*

[7] Lawrence's older sister, Mrs. Emily King.

Harry T. Moore's book as a point of departure?" I said yes.[8]

The terrible thing about Lady C. is that L. identified himself with both Clifford and Mellors; that took courage, that made me shiver, when I read it as he wrote it. I never said: "hein" in my life, that gives Mabel away. And I doubt that I asked anybody for money in my life, that I left to Lawrence.

How badly John Barkham writes!

The Andersons are coming to pay us a visit. Ada [9] loved Lawrence, but she hated what he wrote. First she "approved" of me, then she was very nasty, trying to make me feel small when I couldn't cook. Then she tried to break up our marriage but she did not succeed. Then when he was dead she told me: "You had the best of him." I thought: "I should hope so." Poor Ada, I don't bear her any grudge. She was just not big enough and that was not her fault. . . .

Comments

I think you are fair and just mostly . . . but Mabel Luhan you did not like. We owed a lot to Mabel too. The Hueffers coming: this is *my* story. When they came, he and Violet Hunt, I said to him: *"Wir sind auch Deutsch?"* That made him squirm and he hummed and hawed. It was wartime. So I did not think much of him. I never said: those "dirty Belgians", I never felt like that! Lawrence was not there, there was no outhouse Ford could have retired to, I made no tirade, he wore no uniform, just dislike of me, which I returned, or rather despised them.[1] That was a rotten time. All false, sentimental, the Bloomsburies, so conceited, and not a toe on the ground. What a lot of my-eye L. was up against! It was a load indeed!

[8] See "Apropos of Harry T. Moore's Book, *The Intelligent Heart*," in this volume.

[9] Lawrence's younger sister, Mrs. Ada Clarke, who wrote *Young Lorenzo: Early Life of D. H. Lawrence* (1931), in collaboration with G. Stuart Gelder.

[1] This incident, at Greatham in 1915, may have come to official attention and contributed to the suspicion of pro-Germanism that culminated in the expulsion of the Lawrences from Cornwall in 1917.

But for Ottoline [2] I must say this. When Lawrence was dead and I was in London I went to see her and had forgotten it was her "Thursday". Her maid that I remembered announced me to the people having tea in the dining-room. "Mrs. D. H. Lawrence". For a few seconds there was absolute silence. Then they got up and talked to me. And after a little while Ottoline took me aside and said in her strange voice: "Frieda, I must tell you that I never was fair to you." She had sent Bertie R. to tell Lawrence that he must get rid of me. I think England never liked me, not for a minute. But Ottoline was no small beer. The English are too English, like ingrown toenails. So much I had forgotten that I found in your book. I am sorry there is no photograph in your book of Cynthia, she was so lovely! I always liked her.

As for Caresse Crosby, [3] they must have been relieved when we left: Lawrence breaking all the records and I the plates!! So much crockery I must have smashed through the years!! I did it only once! When L. told me women had no souls and couldn't love! "Christs in the Tyrol" is also one of my favourites and what you say of *Women in Love* I liked very much. I don't think he caricatured the people though, he saw them that way. I wish you would tell me (when you have time) of Ada's end. She hated me, didn't she? She had something very attractive and unusual about her, especially young. But Jessie! American female bossiness is nothing compared to their "superiority", you can only bash it in with a hatchet; but I think you put salt on her tail. I detest her in her arrogance and "virginity", they try to come it over men that way, but this time it did not work! She was "stronger" than he, was she? Oh, how she "humbugged" herself—an ungenerous nasty bit of goods, I find after reading your interpretation. But I do jump about. We never knew that the Duke of Argyle brought those handsome 20 dollar pieces and the gold cigarette case to Florence! Several other things I did not know. I believe that Violet Hunt made it up about the gloves at

[2] Lady Ottoline Morrell, whose friendship had been so crucial and turbulent in the 1910's.

[3] Wife of Harry Crosby, the American poet and proprietor of the Black Sun Press in Paris, who published "Sun" and *The Escaped Cock* in unexpurgated editions.

lunch! I gave the cigarette case to Pollinger! Of course you put your own intelligence into the book as well—that it hangs together—and with no arrogance, which is rare. Most of the people who write about him feel superior, because of L's human weaknesses; they amused me. He "showed off" before others often, and they jeered at him and he didn't see it, which infuriated me, that's why we quarrelled mostly when others were around! Then he was stupidly jealous!

I think *The Intelligent Heart* is your own in this book!

Angie says the only book I have read on Lawrence with interest is this one!

So now I had better stop or I will go on and on!

F

TO Harry T. Moore

[*Undated*]

Dear Harry,

I liked your *Saturday Review* article,[4] as: "yesterday's defects become today's virtues." I was always so sure of L's powers, that I never doubted that he would "live". You did a lot towards that end. I also had letters, how much they liked your book, but nothing from Taos!! That is strange, except from Ruth Swayne, she wrote from Boston. I also had some enthusiastic letters about my article. I never saw what they printed and I did not call it the "bigger heart," they did that. All the gossip will pass away, I do hope, and he will emerge purely himself. What interested me was the new truth he was seeking, that's why so much that went on around us escaped me. I think you have a right not to like Mabel. I don't mind if people don't like L., but I only don't like them either. Lawrence changes all the time for me. He will change still for you too. You see, critics don't affect me very much one way or another. What the English critics said of him long ago was enough, not one with any vision, small beer they were. Now it's easy for them to say L. was somebody; they were

4 "The Return of D. H. Lawrence," March 12, 1955.

forced to it. If they had said it sooner, as you did, I would listen to them! I can see that maybe you will write another L. book later on. Now you have with great labour put down all the facts of his life, now you will put down the meaning, the truth he so honestly extracted from the experience of his own living; that has not been said. A friend came from Brownsville and said the bookseller had many requests for *The Intelligent Heart*, even here! Angie is in Buenos Aires to visit his sister. I have my children's old German nurse with me, and we have a nice man to drive the car! Richard Aldington sent me his book on *Colonel Lawrence*.[5] Very interesting. . . .

TO Dudley Nichols

Port Isabel, Texas
15 February 1955

. . . I am so sad about Maria's death.[6] She was such a friend! She never said anything nasty to me, she never hurt me. She was a rare, vivid person. But she was always frail. Poor Aldous, he will miss her, miss her, and he cannot really express what he feels. He can express what he thinks superbly but not what he feels. O dear, I wish one could help people when they suffer, but one can't. I hope he can go on and grow in stature. We were worried about you, Dudley, so I waited for your letter and was so glad to get it. Now you are really on the way to health. . . .

TO Dudley Nichols

Port Isabel, Texas
26 February 1955

. . . I must write you again, about Aldous and Maria. I had a lovely letter from him and I was wrong, her death did

[5] *Lawrence of Arabia, A Biographical Enquiry* (Regnery, 1955).
[6] Aldous and Maria Huxley were very close to the Lawrences from 1926 to 1928, when, at Villa Mirenda, near Florence, Lawrence was writing *Lady Chatterley's Lover*. Maria typed some of it. Aldous Huxley died on November 22, 1963, also of cancer.

something to him, something burst out of him. He sent me some pages he wrote after she was dead. I can't get over it, so moving. How he helped her to die in utter love and compassion. No slop; he writes in the letter: "It is so difficult to know what one can do for someone who is dying, incidentally for oneself. What I did seemed to be of some help for her, as well as for me. The men of the Middle Ages used to talk of the *Ars Moriendi*—the art of dying.—I also thought very often of that spring night in Vence twenty-five years ago while I was sitting by Maria's bed." When Lawrence died. It is true we have belittled death, have taken the splendour from it. Esta knew what Maria was! A creature of light and yet so human! In these pages he is truly a great man! I have to share this with you both. He will miss her so, in his daily living. He wants to work hard, I hope not too hard. He knew her all right. I do wish you could get in touch with him, but I suppose he has to be alone. He will come to Taos in the spring. Dear Dudley, you write about Lawrence and Huxley with such profound understanding. . . .

TO Else Jaffe

> Box 201
> Port Isabel, Texas
> *26 February 1955*

My dear Else,

I must write you that Maria Huxley is dead. A true, true friend, we never said a rude word to each other. A letter from him, he writes: "I thought very often of the spring night in Vence 25 years ago, while I was sitting by Maria's bed. It is so difficult to know what one can do for someone who is dying, incidentally for oneself. What I did seemed to be of some help to her, as well as for me. The men of the middle ages used to talk of *ars moriendi*, the art of dying." Then he sent me a few pages which he wrote when she was dead, how he helped her to her death, so overpowering and gripping. He is a good, great man. Poor Aldous, how he will miss her day by day. He wants to come in the spring.

Ida is here. She tells me much about Germany which is not so easy for me to understand, and about her circle, but a great competence and often great helpfulness speaks to me through it all. And hardly real poverty any more. I mean not so much worse than before the wars. Now I know too why Ida clings to me so faithfully. I asked: "Ida, how did it actually happen that you first came to me?" "Really through the Flersheims. And do you know what you said then? 'You must stay with me until you are better,' and [you] called Dr. Stafford and soon I was better." This simple human reaction before this pale young thing made the poor pushed-around creature realize one can also be treated well, and developed into her great gratitude. "All that I am I owe to you," she said; she owes it to herself, I think; and how she made life easy for me with the children. So we are peacefully together, we have found a very nice man who drives us around by auto. Angie had a fine day in Mexico City; he will enjoy himself with his sister and her husband and three children. He will return soon. It is beautiful, the big cacti are in bloom. But I long for only one blue hyacinth. Do you already have flowers?

Greetings to Alfred and the children. With love,

Your sister

(Translated from the German)

TO John Middleton Murry

Box 201
Port Isabel, Texas
15 April 1955

My dear Jack,

Not for a long time have I heard from you. I hope you are both well and busy in the spring with your farm. It is a lovely spring day here today. In an old French paper I read a translation of what you wrote about K. and those early days of our friendship! It always makes me feel gay! You know, when I think of how L. insisted that you should get his ideas and you wouldn't have them forced on you, I don't believe it matters; fundamentally you did have a knowledge of each other, but we were not wise enough yet to accept it! We were never bored with each other.

Maria Huxley died of cancer. She was a loyal and true friend to me all through the years. He wrote me a very moving and strange few pages how he helped her to die. He will miss her so much. I dread to see him without her.

In Eastwood they are making a memorial to L. Eastwood! R. Aldington wrote me, they did not tell me. Much they have helped!

Angelino went to Buenos Aires to visit his sister and her family. I had my German Ida with me, she came from Germany by that freight boat, she liked it. It is nice having her! And she is so quickly at home here! Our joy here is Padre Island, a lovely wild spot, clear sand and water and shells and birds and warm, we swim. You would love it—and the birds! The sea is good.

Wasn't that horrid of William Henry Hocking? Well, I never thought much of him! He was no "friend." Forget about them is best. One has to forget an awful lot! I am so glad you and Mary have got such a good life! I believe people misunderstand you as much as L.

My love to you and Mary and all the luck!

Ever the old
Frieda

Ida remembers you well! She goes back 15 May and so do we.

FROM John Middleton Murry

Lower Lodge, Thelnetham
nr Diss, Norfolk
21 April 1955

My dear Frieda,

I was very pleased to have your letter of April 15. As a matter of fact, I wrote you last, so I was waiting, more or less, to hear from you.

We have had a very severe winter,—March was very grim— but now spring has really begun. Yesterday was my eldest daughter's birthday: she is here with us for a week or so—she is married to a Belgian husband, and lives in Brussels. We had tea on the lawn; it was marvellously warm. But today the sun is hidden again.

I saw the announcement of Maria Huxley's death. I am sorry, though I hardly knew her. I think I saw her only twice since the Garsington days. Evidently you haven't seen the news of Koteliansky's death. It happened on January 22. He had been very ill with a weak heart for a long while. I used to have news of him from Beatrice Campbell. I can't help thinking of him affectionately: in those early days at the Russian Law Bureau with Slatkowsky—who dyed his beard—he was very sweet. But he was, *au fond*, a real old Rabbi, laying down the law of Moses, or rather trying to drop the tables on one.

I also saw the paragraph in the newspapers about the Eastwood Council going to build a memorial to L. As far as I remember it is to consist of a recreation centre and swimming bath—and somehow it struck me as awfully funny. I am sure L. would see and enjoy the joke.

The other day I heard from Julian Morrell—Mrs. Vinogradoff now—saying she wished to publish a book of letters to Ottoline, and sending me Katherine's to her. There was one very funny one describing a row between you and L. at Higher Tregerthen. I cut a few bits out—to prevent the Philistines from blaspheming—but the rest I thought you would enjoy. I suppose she will be asking you for permission to publish L's letters to the O. I shd. let her, if I were you. She told me, incidentally, that she had three grown-up children "by my former husband"—but who he was and what happened to him I have no idea.

I'm glad you have had Ida with you. Both Mary and I liked her very much when we met her at the Kingsley Hotel: she seemed such a sweet and human person with a real sense of humour.

April 23rd. Shakespeare's birthday. I heard the cuckoo for the first time this morning. It's very strange how often that happens on Shakespeare's birthday: quite as often as not.

Your island—Padre Island—sounds lovely indeed.

On May 16, Mary and I are going off to the south of France for 3 weeks in the car. The last time I was there in the spring was in 1921, just before Katherine and I went to Switzerland. I thought it wonderful.

There goes the cuckoo again. You don't get *him* where you are! He's a very bad character, but oh how thrilling!

Mary sends her love. You know you have mine.

> Ever affectionately
> Jack

TO Else Jaffe

> El Prado, New Mexico
> Box 15
> *25 June 1955*

My dear Sister Else,

Today is a day like that one in Albuquerque with you. How good that reunion was!

It was lovely that you were so nice with Monty and Ian! Many thanks! Monty wrote enthusiastically, "Oxford and Heidelberg understood each other," and your English was so perfect, and he was very much smitten with Alfred. That was also good, this contact. Today is Nusch's birthday, and where might she be? But one never needs to worry about her. There is always so much going on here, one can hardly get it done. Angie is remodelling the kitchen, very modern, he does it gladly and sings while working! We are fine, very fine. The film, *Sons and Lovers* in Hollywood, and *Lady C.* in Paris with Adrienne Darrieux [*sic*], but one doesn't know how it will turn out, and I don't think about it.

And books they are writing about L., there is no end.

Mabel is not doing so well. She says the same thing over ten times, and since her eye operation she is very unsteady on her feet, and is bored . . . it is hard for her with her great energy, which now is failing.

We have it good in our old age, Else, whether we have earned it or not, so far heaven has done well by us. May it continue to do so! My greetings to you and yours, *molti saluti* from Angie.

Always your
Sister Frieda

I had to laugh over your understanding "Ida". As long as I was the "gracious lady" and she the "Ida" in the nursery, everything was fine, but then I was "Frieda" and she "Ida" and it didn't work. She said: "After all one often felt the 'Baroness' very strongly!"

(*Translated from the German*)

TO Barbara Barr

Box 15
El Prado, New Mexico
3 October 1955

My dear Barby,

I have just this minute finished your "Memoir" [7] and am very deeply impressed, "struck all of a heap."

It is so unsentimental and fair and somehow, subtly, you get Lawrence there on the scene, and the quality of the scene. I am so glad you have written it and it must have been good for you to write it. When you were small, I said to myself, "She will amount to more than I am." It seems to me you have come "through".

I was thinking, in your new house with the studio you ought to try and paint portraits; the two I have of Ursula are so good and are much admired. Lawrence really talks in your book.

But you must get some money for this article from that Nehls. Get Pollinger to get it for you. I was amused at the Sitwell! I heard that they are making a million and a half memorial to Lawrence at Nottingham. Mr. de Pinto [8] came to see me two

[7] Mrs. Barbara Barr's reminiscences appeared in the first volume of Edward Nehls's *D. H. Lawrence: A Composite Biography*.
[8] Vivian de Sola Pinto, who has been active in the project to honor Lawrence at the University of Nottingham, in Lawrence's day Nottingham University College. In 1951 the university published his *D. H. Lawrence, Prophet of the Midlands*.

years ago. I don't know really what they are doing. Some of that money would have come in very handy in the past! That's how it goes!

I am glad you children loved your father. When he was dead I tried to think of him with affection, but I could not. I don't think I can be fair to him. Of course he would hate me after I left him, but that he did not let me see you was not fair *to you*. I was your mother after all. If he had left me, I would have acted differently. But my leaving broke something in him. Had I stayed, *I* would have been broken; no compromise was possible. So grim is life. I am a lucky old woman and love living, every moment a gift. Now you have fun getting your new house ready and Ursula will soon be back. I hope she finds some activity she likes.

I am looking forward to your visit next year.

Make the best of your days!

Love from your mother,

Frieda

I don't believe L. said you flirted with him; he never said so to me. He would have done [so] when he was cross with you or me! Don't forget how jealous he was of you children!

TO Montague Weekley

Box 15
El Prado, New Mexico
October

My dear Monty,

I am glad you mentioned wills, because my will needs revising. I thought you had a copy of an early will where you and *Medley* [9] were trustees, both getting 500 Pounds, but I don't know if Medley is still alive; if not, the 500 for him are off. Anyhow now I have a different idea.

According to New Mexico Law A. as the husband gets *half*

[9] C. D. Medley, her attorney during the 1932 litigation to establish her as Lawrence's sole heir—to whom she was always grateful.

the property, and I wanted *to leave the other half to you three children*. You must have guessed that it is quite a valuable estate by now. I can't tell you how much, because with the stocks and bonds it fluctuates and the manuscripts you can't be sure of; but I am glad to think that I can leave you something quite worth while.

With this letter I write to Pollinger if he will be trustee; he knows more about L's work than anybody and has handled it so very satisfactorily. He deserves to go on with the job. That would be for the royalties; the rest would be divided without so much difficulty. I would also leave this house to Angie; he practically built it himself.

I think the University of New Mexico will take the upper Ranch as an L. foundation; their idea is not clear yet, but we give them the ranch if something definite comes of it.

Angelino has been very efficient at keeping the rather complicated estate together. What with the damnable income tax that takes so much, it is a chore.

Now when I have heard from Pollinger I will go to the lawyer in Santa Fe; then when I have made a will I will send you a copy. . . .

Much love, your
Mother

Thank Ian for his nice letter. Love to Vera. Barby wrote a very good sketch of L. Let me know if the amount of 3865 Pounds is correct or not.

FROM John Middleton Murry

Lower Lodge, Thelnetham
nr Diss, Norfolk, England
26 October 1955

My dear Frieda,

I begin this letter in the classical style. It is quite a long time since I heard from you: I hope you are well. I should be glad to have a letter from you.

You have been much in my mind for the last month: for I have been reading books about Lorenzo—Dr. Leavis's book,[1] in which he incidentally wipes the floor with me (but I shall bob up again); Bunny Garnett's book of reminiscences: *The Flowers of the Forest*; but chiefly Lorenzo's own books. And, of course, all the past has been flooding back on me again. Queer that the past should be more vivid than the present. Partly of course it's Lorenzo himself. Reading his books is like reliving so many epochs of our lives. Queer, too, to read a book like Leavis's, making out Lawrence to be a classic, as it were the great successor to George Eliot, putting him on the very best shelf indeed, but on the shelf: quite right in one way, but yet how wrong in another. Lorenzo is an *experience*, not a classic.

Well, well. Since I last wrote to you, I have turned 66, and I have two more grandchildren, making four. And two of them— for two are only just born—with their two mothers and fathers, and my other two children, were here together in August. It was a great patriarchal gathering. (Do you get the figures right? I have 4 children: 2 of them are married and have 2 children apiece.) Grandchildren are very satisfactory things to have about. The eldest—and I am afraid my favourite, because he was the first—is five. He is called Johnnie, but he talks more French than English, and is, by nationality, a Belgian. Anyway, he was rather in disgrace one day, because he refused to say good-bye to the children at the farmhouse with whom he plays. He gets so annoyed at having to leave them that he refuses to say the fatal good-bye. "Very well," said his mother, "I shall not say good-night to you." And I chimed in: "Neither shall I." "*Tant pis*," he replied—and after a pause—"*pour toi*." I had to rush out of the room in order to keep a straight face.

Nothing very exciting happens: which is a very good thing. I enjoy a placid life: excitements don't agree with me. Mary and I went to France in the spring, and I revisited Bandol after 40 years. It seemed so utterly changed that for a long while I could not find my way about at all—all new smart cafés and new smart villas: miles of these last. Then in July we went to Ireland for a few days to stay with the Campbells. In most ways they seem

[1] F. R. Leavis's *D. H. Lawrence: Novelist* (Alfred A. Knopf, 1955).

just the same as they used to be: and that makes it very delightful. They are the only old friends I have within reach.

We have had an incredibly fine summer here this year. Practically uninterrupted sunshine from June to mid-October. But it finished up, naturally, with the ground as hard as a rock, and it's only in the last few days, when there has been plenty of rain, that ploughing has been at all easy.

With my best love,
Jack

TO Else Jaffe

Box 15
El Prado
New Mexico
8 November 1955

Dear Sister,

The first snow on the mountains after the most beautiful autumn weather.

I wanted to sing to you on your birthday: "Always forward slowly, always forward slowly, so the —— old guard can catch up"—and now I don't know any more what the old guard was called. . . .

I hope all is well with you and your circle. I simply don't have time to grow old! Always there is so much doing! I have made a will. Tell Nusch I have bequeathed her $100 to the end of her life. Half goes to Angelino, half to the children.

We have given the upper ranch to the University of New Mexico, they will make a Lawrence memorial of it with a "scholarship" [2] and want to build houses for faculty and students to study—I will keep the little house until my death. They take care of everything, even Lawrence's little chapel. I am happy that that is arranged. Angelino helps faithfully. This was a very good year financially, but the income tax swallows so much. I never thought that I would be on such a green branch! I know Lorenzo would not begrudge it me! Monty saw Frances

---

[2] The university has established a summer fellowship, in residence, for writers.

and found her very nice. Elsa and Barby have a nice inheritance from their father. This sounds like a real business letter! I think Ida visited you! Dear Else, have a good winter and stay well. I am sending you Aldous' last book. We are going soon to Port Isabel, and perhaps we will fly to Jamaica, but only perhaps, where I would visit Millicent Rogers' son.

The trees outside my window are bare and they were so golden and beautiful! How long is such a life and how much one has experienced! And still experiences! One can indeed become very old! I read much German. A Chateaubriand, which amazed me very much, which considered the early Hitler regime to be heaven on earth. And "Letters which will not reach him". She, Heisking, is a dissatisfied one, I knew her at Uncle Oswald's. How mean they were in China! People are always horrible with each other.

Now I must dress for dinner.

> With love, your
> Sister Frieda

My greetings to Alfred. Don't take cold!
> (*Translated from the German*)

TO John Middleton Murry

> Box 15
> El Prado
> New Mexico
> *16 November 1955*

My dear Jack,

That was a feast getting your letter just as I was in a mess of bewildering packing for Port Isabel. You are a patriarch indeed! But for me you are always the old god Pan! You remember when Christianity came there was a voice heard crying: "Pan is dead." Maybe now Pan has come to life again.

So poor old Bandol had its face lifted too.

Your summer seems to have been a nice one with the sunshine and grandchildren, you sound well and happy, I somehow feel life owed it to you.

I also feel I am sitting on a green twig and can mostly chirp, but when I must read the stuff about Lawrence that they write so cleverly, I get oh, so bored. But when today for instance a bright young "lad" (an L. word) comes along and sincerely wants to understand *The Rainbow* and modestly asks questions, it's satisfactory.

I just made my Will, half for Angelino and half for the children. I also gave the ranch with L's small chapel where his ashes are to the University of New Mexico and they will build cabins for scholars and have some scholarships. It will be nice when the place comes alive again.

Also the head of Nottingham University—de Pinto—is having a "rivalry" with Eastwood where they bought L's birthplace and wanted to build a big hall (in such a small place) and the de Pinto did not think that this was suitable. Nottingham intends to have a L. library. A million and a half was mentioned!! The irony of it, when a hundred pounds would have made a world of difference in the past!

Now keep well through the winter; we may fly to Jamaica but it's only "may"!

I hope Mary is equal to all those visitors, it is a job feeding them all with all that goes with it!

I would love to see Campbell again. How elegant he could look and then with that tough looking stick and clothes in the country he looked as tough as his stick!

Well, dear Jack, "let's count our blessings"; one of those is our friendship, for me!

Yours ever,
Frieda

Best greetings to Mary.
FROM John Middleton Murry

Lower Lodge, Thelnetham
nr Diss, Norfolk, England
27 November 1955

My dear Frieda,

I've managed to get a wad of these air-mail letters at last—I don't often go near a post-office—so here goes!

Harry Moore's new book (which you had a swipe at in *The New Statesman*) [3] has just come out over here. On top of Leavis's—so there's plenty being written in the newspapers about Lorenzo just now. Some of it quite good; but mostly not.

Your saying: "So poor old Bandol has had its face lifted, too" made me laugh. That is exactly what has happened to it. Thank goodness, it's not so easy to lift the face of this village, though I have put on a few new roofs here and there. However, they say we are to have electricity by the end of next year. *Sursum corda*, which means: Lift up your hearts, but not your faces! And I'm busy making a new lawn out of part of the adjoining field, so that we can play croquet there next summer. Croquet is the great game at the Campbells', and we got into the habit of having great tussles with Gordon and Beatrice. So we thought we would like to go on, so that we can surprise them when next we go over.

The one snag about this little place is that there are too many aeroplanes. There's an American aerodrome about 5 miles away, and the beastly things come roaring over. But one gets used to them—so do the cats, the ducks, the pigs and the cows. They don't seem to give a hoot.

Tomorrow I'm going up to London with Mary—for two days. We go up twice a year, rather grudgingly. But Mary has a good look at the shops. I don't really know what I do—except sometimes see my brother; but the time seems to go quickly.

Funny you calling me Pan. Lorenzo, you remember, used Pan to kill me off in one of his stories—a queer one which I have never quite understood—all about me and Brett and a policeman in snowy Hampstead.[4] Quite a good picture of me. Of course I understood that I was well and truly killed off. But I didn't and don't understand quite what, *in the story*, I was supposed to have done that deserved death at Pan's hands.

Tell me, Frieda, for my own private satisfaction—it shall be

[3] Her article on Moore's *The Intelligent Heart* was essentially the same as the article that had appeared in *The Nation* in America. It is reprinted in this volume.

[4] "The Last Laugh."

buried afterwards—did you love me as much as I loved you in those queer days? It drove me crazy—really crazy, I think—wanting you so badly: the comfort and delight of you, and then feeling Oh God, but Lorenzo will never get over it. I mustn't, I must *not*. And I sometimes wonder what would have happened if I had not had that awful feeling of loyalty in friendship to L. Would he, could he, have accepted it? And all the while he was pitching in to me, telling me to "untwist myself". Oh Lord, if I *had* untwisted myself! And I couldn't even explain to *you* why I was behaving so crazily: but I expect you understood. But employing Pan to kill me off was a bit steep. And why did he leave *you* out of that story? All very mysterious. Explain if you can. I really want to know.

> Love, my best love, my dear.
> Jack

TO John Middleton Murry

> P.O. Box 201
> Port Isabel
> Texas
> *10 December 1955*

My dear Jack,

That is fun to make a croquet lawn. Doing things is fun! I cook and wash and iron and make my own glad rags like a young one! And thank the Lord I still can!

It is a lovely day, the water in a calm mood, all glossy and the seagulls strutting on the lawn and the Bougainvillaea blooming round the house. And the house is repainted very, very pale pink with 2 greens for the trim, and the porch glassed in. It is a comfortable house, we just got television.

I am tired of all those books on Lawrence, aren't you? Some blighter said what a blessing it was that people who had *not* known L. personally wrote about him now. I call that stupid!

Now I answer your question. I must think how it was with me. After our famous journey together, something ultimate and deeply satisfactory and new had happened to me; there it was, just an inner lovely fact, that I accepted without question for ever. I trusted you and what you would do. Of course I wanted to hear from you, but not so much. No, you did the right thing, Lawrence was already very ill. I think you averted an ugly tragedy. I don't like the Pan story and don't understand it. He really felt you as Pan and I fear envied you. That story does not make sense. Your saying "L. pitched into me" made me laugh and how he could pitch! I also owed him some loyalty and had to see him through his life span and you helped me to do it. It was tough going at times as you know. But I still believe he cared for you more than any other man or he would not have "pitched". Do you remember the sweet names he called me? "— —" was the one I hated most. When you say I was a comfort and delight that pleases me no end. . . .

A merry Christmas to you and yours and love to Mary and all the luck in the world, but the luck is already there.

Yours ever,
Frieda

TO Else Jaffe

P.O. Box 201
Port Isabel
Texas
22 January 1956

My dear Else,

Your letter made me very happy, and the picture of Julian impressed me! What a handsome, unusual boy! He will have a life! Good, I hope! So, we are in a new year; my good Hausner said to me I would probably live many years yet. That's all right with me! If one can only die decently without much bother! Like Angelino's father, who said one evening to his son: "*La mia ora è venuta*," and in the morning he was dead. I think of you so often, especially when something makes me happy, and often something does make me happy! At the beginning of February we are going to San Antonio, to a stock show, very Texan, cowboy stuff! And we will visit our General Pierce, the one whose eye was taken out. But in spite of all he still enjoys life. We have few friends here itself, but the mail is always interesting. From all the ends of the earth! Angelino is wrestling with the tax. We had a big income this year, but the tax swallows almost all. The more that comes in, the less one has!

Two Mexican women are cleaning; it sounds like a herd of elephants in the house! We have television, a new vice! One sits and gawks and gets quite dopey; but with the *kitsch*, also interesting things! Do you remember that Papa's sister Helene had a daughter, and that when Helene died Uncle Ludwig wanted our parents to take the girl, but Mama didn't want her, having three daughters herself! That is on my mind; one could no doubt have had her for a visit! I think Papa was attached to that pious sister Helene in the way he was to you.

Poor people are often much better than rich in giving help. I enjoy my quiet here, not always the thought: people are coming with whom one must be pleasant. And always sun, warmth and birds, land and sea; Padre Island, where there is a good restaurant by the water. You would like it here! Mabel is not doing well, in body and mind—but I will not forget that she visited you in Albuquerque and asks about you. This letter is quite a salad, but I did want to write to you! Much more yet—

With love,
Your sister

(*Translated from the German*)

TO Witter Bynner

Port Isabel
Texas
13 February 1956

Dear Hal,

No, we were very warm and comfortable in your guest house; I am sorry I did not answer that question. We really had a happy evening with you. You must have felt that! Poor Brett has rather a tough time by herself, with the snow and the wind and the cold.

That was a letter that cheered me, from that Helen Latham.[5]

Tomorrow we go to the San Antonio stock-show; it will be very Texan, I expect. Also see the Pierces, he had to have an eye out; he was such a talker, the general, now he has had a stroke and his words won't come out. But he wants to live.

Angie is struggling with the income tax. We had quite a good income this year, but alas the income tax swallows it nearly all, the more you have the less you get.

We are very comfortable and peaceful. I have time to read —Shakespeare again, what monsters some of his heroes are, those kings, a primitive world of men.

And those tame heroines; I am glad no man ever said to me: "Get thee to a nunnery"!

There, my fountain pen wasn't filled again and Angelino gets mad with me, that I don't fill it! He is right, but it is a bore filling them!

We have lovely weather all along, only small fires at night. We have television and stay up late (for us) at night. I hated the wrestling at first, now I like it! The young handsome ones, so quick and dancing, and the old tough ones too.

Greet Bob and Mirendi, please.

I read Aldous's last book—quite different from his other books! Have not heard from him for some time.

Angelino sends greetings. He is going for the mail, so I send my love.

Frieda

FROM John Middleton Murry

Lower Lodge, Thelnetham
nr Diss, Norfolk, England
10 May 1956

My dear Frieda,

I have just learned that you have been ill—with "a severe virus infection". It sounds truly horrible. But the same source (Univ. of New Mexico) tells me that you are "recuperating very

[5] Perhaps Barbara Latham (Mrs. Howard Cook), Taos painter.

nicely", which is a comfort. I don't at all like to think of you ill. It doesn't seem natural.

I don't seem to have any news—never do have. I've just finished a book called *Love, Freedom and Society* [6]—half of which is about Lorenzo. I think it is the best I have ever written about him: indeed I am sure it is the best I have written about him. Anyway, I'll send it to you as soon as it appears. But that won't be for a long time, since I sent it to the publisher only this morning. I hope you will like it: I think you will.

The croquet season has begun. I like playing games: but this is the only one I can manage, with my indifferent legs.

I've been reading an interesting, but horribly depressing book: *Dylan Thomas in America.* [7] D. T. was a poet with a real gift. D. T. is tragically appropriate. For he died in D. T.—*delirium tremens*—just killed himself with alcohol. So appallingly *ignoble*. Well, we may have had our failings, but that kind of disaster was inconceivable for us.

May 11. I had to break off at that point for supper: which was sardines with lemon, of which I am very fond and which always recalls a meal with Kot at the Russian Law Bureau. Since I never write anything after supper, but just sit and read in an armchair, opposite Mary in another armchair, here am I next morning. I have just finished my chores—watered my plants in the greenhouse (chiefly tomatoes and tobacco—I grow my own tobacco), started the engine which makes the electricity, opened my garden frames (full of lettuces). The spring flowers in the garden in front of me are exceptionally beautiful this year—chiefly wallflowers, forget-me-nots—and polyanthus in great profusion. But we sadly need rain. It has been what they call an "absolute drought" in East Anglia—which means no rain at all for 14 days, and it's now a week since those 14 days were up. The big horse-chestnut tree is just about to flower.

All, of course, very English—and old-fashioned English at that: the kind of place, I suppose, that Mary and I naturally make for ourselves, defying the fact that the jet-planes from the

[6] It was published in 1957, the year after her death, by Jonathan Cape.
[7] By John Malcolm Brinnin.

American air-base five miles away roar over our heads. But we are quite used to that.

Well, my dear, this is a long letter though it doesn't look so: but my writing is very small. A little of it goes a long way.

Let me have a line as soon as you feel like it. Naturally, I can't help feeling a little anxious although the news is reassuring.

> With love,
> Jack

TO John Middleton Murry

18 May 1956

Dear Jack,

It was very comforting to get your letter. I am getting quite well again.

I will tell you my tale of woe. A horrid virus attacked me, pouncing with high fever. We were driving back from Port Isabel, lost our way at "Cline's Corners" and arrived at Las Vegas instead of Santa Fe, had to go over a high mountain-path [*sic*] with ice and snow and I was nightmarishly frightened. The following night I got up, found myself sitting in a corner of the bathroom and could not get up. For half an hour I struggled, did not want to wake Angelino, who had had a hard day, but finally I did. He looked so scared at this heap of helplessness. Then a nice woman doctor came, found my high fever and bundled me into an ambulance for the hospital in Santa Fe. There was my friend Dr. Hausner. But you can't afford to be ill, too expensive.

A.[8] is in Europe; Barby [9] is with me, we have a quiet female time. I have a hunch *Love, Freedom and Society* is really good, more distance in it. I shall look forward to it. I always envy you your small handwriting, it looks so tidy. I love to hear about your chores. Lovely weather we have.

People surprised me when I was sick. Books, and my room

[8] Angelo Ravagli.
[9] Her daughter.

was like a flower shop. They even cook things and leave them on the doorstep. I did not know they felt so friendly.

Aldous is married again. He did not write to me. Maybe he wants to make a *new* start. Anyhow I am glad he is not alone, especially with his bad eyes.

Thank you for your letter, I was so glad to get it. I am almost quite well and enjoy the getting well.

Love to Mary, I see you and her sitting opposite each other in comfortable chairs in the evening.

Yours always,
F.

TO F. R. Leavis

P. O. Box 15
El Prado
New Mexico
[May 22, 1956]

Dear Mr. Leavis: [1]

I read your book. I was most interested in your reaction to Lawrence. Your defence of him is very convincing. But I think you still take that poor fish T. S. Eliot too seriously. He is like a nicely carved skeleton to me, but no flesh and blood on the skeleton. I argued with Aldous Huxley about him. . . .

As you see a connection between Lawrence and George Eliot, I read *Adam Bede* again. From the *Rainbow* on Lawrence is no longer a British writer, but a universal one. If you read again about the child Ursula's relation with her father, you will see it is not a mother and son relationship, but a father-daughter one. It happened to be mine with my father. Only instead of potatoes it was asparagus. Somewhere you mention *Anna Karenina*. I read that again soon after Lawrence and I were together. She made a mess of hers and Vronsky's marriage because she could not take the social condemnation. I decided I would not let that happen to me and my marriage. You say I was not maternal, I

---

[1] An apparently earlier draft bears the note: "I meant to send this to Leavis, but *want to send it to you*. I don't know him."

think I was, and not intellectual, but I was not dumb either and thought things out for myself. Nobody seems to have an idea of the quality of Lawrence's and my relationship, the essence of it. If in the "Captain's Doll," she insists on love, *he* is equally boring insisting on an old formula. The deep attraction was there and that was what counts. A deep attraction between two people is a sacred, mysterious thing and Lawrence's real belief and point. I never wanted a "home" or social activities, God forbid; being with Lawrence was "home" enough day by day. I wasn't bored ever.

In *Kangaroo* I think again Harriet was right in fighting his idea to lead a revolution. His task, God given, was to *write;* what would a silly little revolution in Australia have amounted to? "Not a hill of beans."

I am sorry you don't like Lawrence's poetry. You miss something you might enjoy, I believe. But I think your book will do a great deal for Lawrence and not only for him, but a better understanding for something important in life altogether.

Sincerely,
Frieda Lawrence Ravagli

TO Barbara Barr

Saturday evening
21 July 1956

My dear Barby,

It was "sure" sad to see you vanish in the red car you liked. But we must be thankful for the "cloudless" time we had together; no, not "cloudless". Brett played "Tiny" records to cheer me, then Claude [2] came, *not* so ferocious any more. Angie came at one o'clock. He has worked hard with all the stuff I did not do. He *likes* it and is good at it. Everything reminds me of you. You forgot your coat. We are sending it and the picture. Joe [3] liked it very much. Angie said: "Just right, not too old and not too young."

[2] Claude Anderson, wealthy Philadelphian who lived near Frieda.
[3] Probably Joe Glasco, whose letter on her death follows shortly.

Now *new* pictures for you. Angie said your house did not feel lived in enough. So make it nice, you will enjoy that. Hope all is well. Just a word to welcome you to your own home. Everybody sends their love.

Your mother

TO Barbara Barr [4]

4 August 1956

My dear Barby,

I was touched that you remembered my syringe. It just came. With all those needles I shall be all right. Thank you! The needles I had weren't sharp. Well, they all ask after you: you certainly were the "belle" of the season.

All dressed up, to go to the boys; Joe is giving a party, Bill not so happy about it.

Angie sent a parcel with your coat and U's moccasins. Glad to get your telegram and letter. So keep up the good work and keep well. Stokowsky came yesterday with his two little Gloria boys, still very young for his old age. Lovely weather after three days of rain. I think, when I wake in the morning, you are still around. Hope Ursula [5] will be all right on her trip to Spain and enjoy it. But shall be glad when she is back. I suppose you are busy about the house. Have you seen our Elsa? [6] Angie unhappy about the "Andrea Doria".

Betty Anderson back.

Have not been well for the last three days, but better again. Joe and Bill looked after me like two guardian angels. That's why this letter is late.

My love to you.

Greetings to Stewart [sic], from Angie to you and him.

[4] Mrs. Barr notes that the letter was mailed August 8, the day of the fatal stroke, and that Frieda had not signed it. The syringe was for the insulin Frieda was taking for diabetes during the last months.

[5] Her granddaughter, now Mrs. Alfred Alvarez.

[6] Her elder daughter, Mrs. Edward Seaman.

TO Witter Bynner [7]

El Prado
New Mexico
10 August 1956

Dear Hal,

This is your seventy-fifth birthday. How long have we known each other? It seems to me always. So on this day I want to tell you how much your friendship has meant to me. I won't be the only one who feels like this, with your rich, generous nature you have given so much to so many. Sometimes you found me a nuisance and sometimes you did not approve of me and told me so, but always your friendship was there as a support and joy.

These are my loving thanks to you on this day.

Frieda Lawrence Ravagli

FROM Angelo Ravagli to Montague Weekley, Elsa Seaman, and Barbara Barr

Box 15
El Prado
New Mexico
17 August 1956

My dear Monty, Elsa and Barby,

Your affectionate letters of sympathy for the loss of your mother and my beloved Frieda give me the strength to be able to give you a full report of what happened, by return mail. Among the avalanche of letters and telegrams that arrive daily, yours of course must have priority. . . .

My feeling is that our dearest Frieda, since the illness she had last Spring which kept her in the Sante Fe Hospital for a fortnight, had never been the same. She never fully recovered her energy and vitality. She was cured for a kind of virus which

[7] This letter was written some days earlier but postdated to coincide with a joint birthday celebration (Bynner's seventy-fifth on the tenth and Frieda's seventy-sixth on the eleventh). She had planned to give him a copy of Lawrence's book of poems *Bay* with illustrations colored by her. Angelo Ravagli brought it to Bynner after her death on her birthday, and told him her last words had been: "Don't forget Hal's book."

was never really found. Now I wonder if it was a mild stroke instead.

When I arrived home July 17th late at night, the same day that Barbara left, you can imagine how happy she was to see me back. She felt relieved of the responsibility of the household and so pleased to have Angie around again. You can imagine how pleased I was, too.

Then, one morning, she felt some kind of pain in her stomach. The night before, we had gone to a party at the boys' across the highway. She thought it was a kind of indigestion. The Doctor gave her some kind of sedative and in a day or two, she was well again.

Then, the fatal August 8th came. She went to bed earlier and I was still up when she moved from her bedroom to the glassed-in porch because the night before she had slept well there and had seen the big stars. After that I went to bed, reading a short story. At 10:00 p.m., she shouted at me, "It's late—go to sleep, blighter," and those were the last words I heard from her.

I must have just gone to sleep when suddenly, I heard a funny noise. I thought I had left the radio on. But there she was, poor thing, on the floor beside her bed, trying to get back in. I almost fainted. She was not able to speak any more. The right side was paralyzed and her mouth was twisted. It was 11:00 p.m.

With all my strength of mind, I put her back in bed and rushed to the phone. In ten minutes, the Doctor arrived. Later, more help was called and as soon as the Doctor permitted, with the help of two strong young men, Joe and Bill,[8] we brought her to her bedroom. The Doctor, a capable woman,[9] spent the night with her. The next morning, the nice Rachel Hawk came to assist her and later on that [day], we got two nurses and a hospital bed to make her more comfortable.

[8] Joe Glasco, whose letter follows, and William Goyen, the writer. Their house across the highway was on land she had given them out of friendship after the war.

[9] Dr. Martha Elizabeth Howe, who, after service as a major in the U. S. Army Medical Corps, and private practice in New York City, had moved to New Mexico in 1949.

If she really suffered, is hard to tell. The first day, she was half conscious, and half, not. Many times she understood what we were doing because she would say "thank you". However, I am convinced that on the whole, she was unconscious, and the last twelve hours, completely so.

I don't know what I would have done without the help of so many good friends. . . . I had never seen any one die before and this was a bitter experience for me.

For more details, please ask Barby to let you read Joe Glasco's letter sent to her by Air Mail yesterday. . . .

Well, my dear children and grandchildren, our loss cannot be replaced—but nobody can stop the time when it comes and when it does, we must take it graciously, as our beloved Frieda did.

Much love to all of you, grandchildren, Vera, and the fiancée of Ian, included.

P.S. Sunday I will visit Frieda's grave and put the wooden cross she wished. But later on I will lay on her grave a full length of granite stone with her name, date of birth, and death, plus her coat of arms.

Do you agree?

A. R.

FROM Joe Glasco to Barbara Barr

El Prado (Taos County)
New Mexico, U.S.A.
16 August 1956

Dear Barby:

I know what a shock it was for you to hear of Frieda's going so suddenly. Both Bill and I thought a great deal about you all through her illness. But what a blessing you were able to be here for her last summer.

I wanted now to write you about her last few days, as both Bill and I were with her constantly. The Friday before her stroke (which was Wednesday, Aug. 8, around 11 p.m.), I had a party for my mother who was here for a few days. There were about twenty people and most of them old friends of Frieda's. Mabel, Brett and Frieda were together for the last time—Spud, Becky James, Mrs. Griffin, Ruth Swayne, etc. Frieda sat at the head of a long table and was very much the Queen of the evening. She had on a dress that she had made of Italian silk (pink and blue) which Angie had brought back. She looked so charming. She was so gay and really had a very happy evening. The next day she got up early and did a little washing. Angie had gone to town and when he got back she said she had had a pain across her chest, and that it might have been her heart. Angie called the doctor and she came out (Dr. Howe). She told Frieda to stay in bed, that she thought she had strained her heart some way, but that it was not serious. Dr. Howe called Dr. Hausner in Santa Fe and they agreed on what to do. They both felt it would be wrong and bad for her to go back to the hospital in Santa Fe and it wasn't that serious. We went over several times to see her and she was very alert and gay and not at all depressed or worried. On Monday Angie had a date to go fishing. I went over and spent the day with her. We had some very nice talks between her naps. I cooked her a nice lunch which she had in bed and then a nap. Of course she insisted on taking baths and would not stay in bed. Tuesday and Wednesday we heard she was much better and didn't go over. On Wednesday (Aug. 8) night we had two guests here and Brett. As they were leaving, about 11:15, we heard the phone ringing in Brett's (as you know, we have no phone). I raced over to the house and Dr. Howe said for Bill and me to come over immediately, that Frieda had had a stroke, but not to bring Brett. We were there in two minutes and found Frieda on the front porch on the bed. Dr. Howe was there with her. She was then paralyzed on her right side and could not speak clearly. We could understand that she wished to be in her bed. We asked over and over if she was in pain of any kind and she said "no" each time. The doctor gave her injections which quickly made her rest. The doctor told us she had had a severe stroke and she was doubtful that Frieda would last the night. We did not tell Angie this as he was completely distraught and he would probably have collapsed if he had guessed how sick she was. Bill and I lay down on the sofa and waited with the doctor and Angie in the room, each of us taking turns sitting with her. By this time she was asleep, but she would occasionally wake and speak a little. At one point, Angie opened the window at the foot of her bed and he told her about the stars he could see there. She understood him and said "*Ja*". At one point during the night Dr. Howe called Angie in and told him she was very low and he went into her room alone, the doctor and Bill and I waiting outside the room. But she only fell into a deep sleep in which her breathing was very heavy and stayed that way until the next morning. It was in the early afternoon (Thurs. Aug. 9) that she became slightly conscious again and asked for water and wished to be raised a little in her bed with pillows. Dr. Howe had spent the night there by her side and had left about 8:00 a.m. We called Rachel Hawk early that morning and she came right down and sat with Frieda all that day. During this day we began searching everywhere for nurses. Dr. Howe had consulted with Dr. Hausner in Santa Fe and they agreed that she must remain at home, that the trip to the hospital was too risky and also Frieda had just the day before told Angie he must not send her there again. Late that afternoon we located a nurse in Santa Fe and Claude Anderson went to fetch her and returned about 7:30 that night. We had also found another practical nurse by this time and we then had two nurses. The one from Santa Fe stayed that night with her. Dr. Howe had given me [a] sedative for Angie and he slept some that night and I stayed there on the sofa. Frieda all during this time had trouble breathing. But she spent most of the time in a semi-coma. I went to Dr. Howe around noon and got an oxygen tank and gave her oxygen as the doctor prescribed, every twenty minutes for five minutes. This began to help Frieda a great deal. Her colour became better and she rested a little better. Her blood pressure improved. By Friday morning the doctor and nurses thought Frieda had a fair chance. But if she was to be paralyzed on her right side and without speaking, it may have been worse for her. But even knowing this, we all became very hopeful and Angie was arranging things for Frieda with this in mind. He found Mabel had a hospital bed which would crank up. We got this and brought it into the room and lifted Frieda over on to it. She was conscious during this and said "thank you". During all of Frieda's illness she always said "thank you" and "please" when she asked for something. Even when it was most difficult to speak. I gave her water at one point and she looked at me and said, "Thank you, Joe". She saw me and knew what was happening. When Angie asked her if she was in pain she always said "no". The doctor had begun feeding her intravenously on Thursday and she managed to get a lot down. Also some powdered milk. Her best time and when we were all most hopeful was Friday morning (Aug. 10). But around noon she had not gotten past this stage and remained in this state until about 2:30 p.m. when she became restless and thrashed about a lot, until she was given a sedative again. Her breathing all this time was not good, very loud and deep. Her breathing during her whole sickness was very uneven. At her worst times she would breathe fifteen seconds very deeply and then not breathe at all for fifteen seconds. The oxygen helped this and made her breathing steadier. Friday night Bill stayed with the nurse and Angie, and I went home. About 6:00 in the morning Bill called me at Brett's and said Frieda was very low and he had called Dr. Howe to come. Her pulse was weak and her breathing was very difficult and she was not conscious that morning or Friday night. Dr. Howe arrived about 6:30 a.m. and did everything in her power to save her. We all waited for that hour and then at seven-thirty she died. It was all very gentle and she didn't regain consciousness. Her pulse just became lower and lower and her breathing fainter. It was very hard for Angie. He wanted so desperately to keep her there with him.

The Hanlon Funeral Home was called and they came for Frieda. Angie picked her new dress she had made—the one she wore to the party—and also a little straw hat with the same material in a little band around it. She held the hat in one hand and a little bunch of Forget-me-nots we found by her bed (the artificial kind she loved), some that she had kept. She wore her little yellow velvet shoes and white hose that she loved. When we saw her Sunday she was completely at peace and noble and the aristocrat that she was. On Monday all day her friends came to see her then in the Chapel with all the flowers. There was no music, just Frieda and the flowers. At 4:00 in the afternoon the people all arrived that were going to the ranch and Bill and I drove Angie behind Frieda and we drove up to the ranch. Many people came up. All of her old friends, some eighty years old, walked up the steep hill to the Chapel. There were six of us who carried her from the little gate up to the chapel, and when all the people had walked up, Bill said a few words and read that beautiful poem and the Psalm [1] (see inclosed paper), and then she was buried. The weather was beautiful and a little cloudy, but the sun came out as Bill read. A little hummingbird was flying all around and finally flew into the chapel. I think it was the most beautiful funeral I have ever seen and the simplest, and I think even Frieda would have approved.

This is a long letter Barby, but I wanted to tell you all I could remember while it is fresh in my mind. Frieda was for me a great woman, I will never forget her. She has given me a great deal and I will always be grateful to her. . . .

Affectionately,
Joe Glasco

P.S. . . . Don't be too unhappy about Frieda. Seeing her there the last few weeks and days, it seems right and her life was full and complete. It was even her Birthday.

[1] Lawrence's "Song of a Man Who Has Come Through," and Psalm 121.

Essays

Katherine Mansfield Day by Day [1]

I won't write about Katherine Mansfield as a literary figure, others can do that better than I. I want to recall her as she was day by day as a woman friend and neighbour, gay and gallant and wonderful.

We were much together, but didn't talk ideas or books or art or people. I knew instinctively we had not the same taste in books or art. She was a great admirer of form and to me the form did not matter so much, it was more important to me what new substance a person had to give.

We had great times doing things together, like making pot-pourri with dried rose leaves and herbs and spices, or painting wooden boxes and having those delicious female walks and talks. She trusted me, I was older and she told me much of her life. And how she could talk. Unforgettable to me is a description of hers as she travels through France, and a French woman, with a bird perching forward on her hat, talks to her and how the bird seemed to peck at her when the French woman bent forward and said: "*Ah, ma pauvre petite.*" She had a Dickensish kind of way to give small events a funny twist, and sharp and quick she pounced on anything funny that happened and gave you a swift look, the rest of her face innocent, so that often I had a hard time not to laugh and be rude.

If I had to describe her in one word I would choose the word *exquisite*. She was exquisite in her person: soft, fine, shiny brown hair and delicately grained skin, not tall and not small and not thin nor stout, just right. When we went bathing I thought her

[1] Found among her papers, and so far as it has been possible to determine, hitherto unpublished.

425

pretty as a statuette. She was always scrupulously groomed. In the street she wore coats and skirts, very well tailored, and what Americans call a shirtwaist and a simple, slightly mannish hat. In the house or evening she wore fascinating little jackets of velvet or some unusual material and a striped skirt perhaps. I don't remember seeing her in ordinary evening dress. No moment was ever dull being with her. I learnt from her to brush my hair one hundred times every night; guiltily I remember her when I don't do so. Also I use Cuticura soap, that she introduced me to, and I am fond of its herby, not perfumy, scent. She gave me the recipe of a homemade face cream that she had from her mother, but that I lost.

If she were alive now and I would come unawares on her house, I would at once know: Katherine lives here. There would be something about the curtains or the doorknocker or some plants or fish in a bowl, that would be solely her. In one cottage she decorated her bedroom in pink and mauve with a few dark touches, and her study was white and black and yellow. She was a hard worker. "I will get up at seven and the housework must be done at ten o'clock, so that I can get some writing done in the morning," she told me; that was at the times when she had no servants. In Berkshire, where we lived about an hour's walk from each other and would dine with each other twice a week, we always tried to make a feast of our meetings. When she would say: "Frieda, those fowls were beautifully cooked and the sauce too good to be true," I swelled with pleasure. We none of us had much money, but I still have among my possessions some of her presents: heavy Russian silver buttons and a treasured book of French soldiers' songs that a French soldier had given her. One of my puddings is called Katherine Mansfield pudding. Here it is:

    3 oranges
    3 eggs
    1 cup of water
    ½ cup of sugar
    Knox's gelatine

Cut some of the outer rind of oranges, boil in cup of water with sugar. Strain, put the juice of the oranges with it, mix yolks of eggs with this till it thickens, beat white of eggs to a stiff consistency, have gelatine dissolved, mix all and put on ice.

Lunch with Mr. and Mrs. Bernard Shaw [1]

Lawrence was dead and I was in London, busy with his work. I happened to read an article where somebody wrote that Shaw had been "mean" with Lawrence. Lady Ottoline Morrell asked her friend Shaw to help Lawrence, and Shaw had only sent ten pounds. Now Shaw and Lawrence had never met and I did not think those ten pounds "mean." So I wrote to Mrs. Shaw and told her how sorry I was about that article. I also wrote her how Shaw had told a friend when he had been at a good amateur performance of Lawrence's *The Widowing of Mrs. Holroyd*, "I wish I could write dialogue like this." The friend repeated this to Lawrence. Lawrence was vastly pleased. "He ought to know about dialogue, it's very generous of him."

The Shaws asked me to lunch. I went, and going up the stairs a slim figure sprinted past me up the steps like a young hound. "Maybe this is Shaw." From their spacious apartment you could see through the big windows the boats and barges going past on the Thames. For lunch there were several people: Lady S., a feminist, and a famous bookseller and another man, I think a general. We had chicken for lunch, but Shaw, who sat beside me, only had vegetables. A footman waited on us, we had wine, but Shaw did not. On the way to the lunch in the taxi I had said to myself: "Now look out and don't make a fool of yourself for Lawrence's sake. Shaw is too clever for you."

Lawrence and Shaw were such worlds apart. Shaw and Lady S. talked about a Welsh miner who had just written a book. "Do

[1] Found among her papers, and so far as it has been possible to determine, hitherto unpublished.

428

they put Lawrence on the same level with this man?" I thought. Then Lady S. asked me: "Don't you think we all like to belong to a class, Mrs. Lawrence?" Class? after all I had married a miner's son. "No," I told her, "I would like to be a Hottentot." "I think you are an aristocrat," said Shaw to me.

Suddenly Shaw turned to me: "Is it true that you broke a plate over your husband's head?"

"Yes, it is true."

"What did you do that for?"

"Lawrence had said to me women had no souls and couldn't love. So I broke a plate over his head."

This Shaw thought over. Such a quick, violent response was alien to his make-up.

Then he asked about the ranch in New Mexico. I told them about the cabins high up among the pines, we only had horses and a buggy, and how Lawrence milked the cow Susan and looked after the chickens and split the wood for the stove and the big fireplace that he had built with the help of the Indians. How we had no civilized comforts and how wild and far away from everything the place was and how we loved it. He listened and said: "And that man wrote." I wanted to say: "Yes, but not like you," but didn't. Then they both said: "We will visit you at the ranch." But that never happened.

After lunch I told Mrs. Shaw: "I am so glad to meet you."

She opened her eyes wide: "Me, they always want to meet Shaw."

I laughed: "I also have been a writer's wife, I know."

There was such a wonderfully free atmosphere about, you were sure that nothing you said or did would shock or surprise them. If you had suddenly turned a somersault they would have taken it along with the rest. Because of this freedom Shaw and Lawrence might have liked each other, I am sorry they never met.

I am glad I had lunch with the Shaws.

Great Men, and Lies—People and Death [1]

Orage is dead. About two years ago he wanted to meet me, there was so much we knew of each other, intimate things. I had known of him through Katherine Mansfield, who had worked on the *New Age* with him. By one of those sad mistakes of life he had never met Lawrence. So we met at a friend's house, a very modern one, at dinner. One of the first things Orage said to me sitting next to me at dinner was: "You are very clever, you wear your heart on your sleeve and nobody looks for it there." So I laughed and said just what I wanted to say. We sat in a corner after dinner, talking about Lawrence and Katherine, he coming out of himself, and I. Like old, old intimates we both said nakedly much we had felt and not told before. He was a reserved man but there like it happens, seldom though, he could talk of his genuine experiences. Next morning I thought, never can I meet this man again, we have come too close, he will want to

[1] Alfred Richard Orage died November 6, 1934. In the 1920's, when he was editor of the London weekly *The New Age*, he was deeply interested in the philosophy of George Ivanovich Gurdjieff, who had established the Institute for the Harmonious Development of Man, at Fontainebleau. Orage and Dr. Maurice Nicoll, an exponent of Jung, had advocated "psychosynthesis." Frieda met Orage some time between 1930 and 1934. On October 14, 1934, he wrote her (the letter was found among her papers) about *Not I but the Wind* . . . , saying that a notice of it would shortly appear in his paper *The New English Weekly*. He added: ". . . Though it's scarcely worth your consideration, I hope you will read it and like it. It's *not* by myself, but naturally I was an active partner to it." His remarks about the Taos neighborhood indicate that he, like so many others, had visited her there. Her tribute to him is characteristic of the bases of her fondness for people. The text is from an unfinished manuscript draft.

retire into his reserve again. We have said all there is to say. "Your secrets are safe with me," I said to myself. "There is no need of our meeting again." I did not meet him again. But a friend of his had sent him my book, *Not I but the Wind*, and I had these two letters from him. I thought of him a lot and then Mabel Luhan said: "Orage is dead." I wouldn't believe it—I would not accept the loss, the terrible loss of a man with a brave voice and genuine heart. Now his *English Weekly* has come and I am furious that all his friends write so coldly about him. Have words no more fire in them to convey the grief for the loss of a man?

Ah, great men and people. The stupendous ingratitude of people to their great men puts me into a real fury tonight. There are the millions who are proud to have a radio, proud of the fact that they can afford a radio. How many, I wonder, think once of Marconi, to whom they owe their radio, not really to their own cheque-book. I know it to my sorrow now how I wasn't grateful enough to Lawrence myself. How he tried to bully me out of my false feelings for "my own good." We none of us seem to like "our own good." How well he knew that my feelings weren't my own genuine feelings, but the remains of stereotyped, inherited, conventional, ready-made feelings. When I think how at seventeen I believed in duelling and dying for your country, and if a man kissed me I would commit suicide because it would not be chaste when you weren't married. It isn't at all easy to know what you really feel. And most of us are too beastly lazy to find out how we respond genuinely to this or that. It's hard work to be a genuine human being such as we were meant to be.

A friend, a brilliant man of world fame, told me: "For ten years I thought I adored my wife and one morning I woke up and found I didn't care for her at all." Most things I have found in my life's experience were quite different from what I thought they would be. And my wishes and desires turned out to be utter strangers to my profoundest impulse for living. Our deepest impulse is buried so often under walls of old lies, they seem stone walls but are walls of cards—the least genuine breath and down they go if we will let them and not cling to our lies as precious possessions. Lawrence *was* a genuine breath, and was I grateful at the time, when he blew down my little cardhouses? Not I, at the time I clung to my little cardhouses, but now I know and am grateful. Every experience is an eye-opener, we have falsified and dramatized all the great simple experiences of our natural existence till life itself knows us no longer. We are so very falsely important. There are so many millions and millions of us today and millions that are dead and millions that will come later on. Our final needs are so few when you come down to brass tacks, everything could be so simple if we didn't complicate it all by systems and swelled head importance and ideas that are disconnected from the whole—ideas that are never thought to their final end. We can bear all that is natural, even death, even death of people we love better than ourselves. Death is natural, and life can be natural. A great man is a great man because he listens with his whole attention to the secrets of life, and then he gets his reward. Life yields him a secret. Whether it's a Marconi or a Christ or a Cézanne. There is no end to the secrets of life; and to us who are just bits of life, no more and no less. (When we *think* we are important we are sure not to be important at all. Lawrence found secrets in us human beings. We have only just begun to have a faint suspicion about the working of our inner man or woman. Under the socially emotional conception of ourselves that [is] the equivalent of the taboos in savages, something stirs its uneasy head. That uneasy head will lead the only adventure into the days to come. . . .

In Praise of Raymond Otis [1]

I lost a friend and so did many others when Raymond Otis died.

When you are an elderly woman and a friend, a much younger man in whose integrity you believe, dies, it is a loss indeed.

At once, years ago, on first meeting Ray, I responded to the good will in him; he belonged to the small army of men who are capable of conceiving a better world, because they are themselves better than most of us. Simply and unostentatiously you felt him to be good, not sanctimoniously so, but with a sense of humour and a laugh.

I remember when he had helped an acquaintance of ours, who was sent to prison; the man was older than Ray and no special friend of his. When the man was released Ray waited for him at six o'clock on a cold morning outside the prison and took him home, doing so as a matter of course.

His own character was so obviously beyond suspicion that he

---

[1] Raymond Otis died July 13, 1938. His death was the occasion of a front-page story in the Santa Fe *New Mexican* on the fourteenth, and an editorial the following day. Frieda's essay was marked "published in the *New Mexican*," but a search of the files for the following month did not turn it up. Otis was a member of the volunteer fire brigade, and the author of *Fire Brigade, Fire in the Night, Miguel of Bright Mountain*, and *Little Valley*. In the winter of 1935, when Angelo Ravagli was in France to arrange for the exhumation and cremation of Lawrence's body, Frieda was seriously ill while staying with Mabel Luhan in Taos, and was hospitalized in Albuquerque. She was staying with the Otises in Santa Fe when Ravagli returned, in April.

could fearlessly, he wasn't even aware of the fearlessness, do things that others would have been afraid to do.

Then, as a good citizen he belonged to the fire-brigade. What fun we had at his expense with that fire-brigade! When the buzzer went, he would rush for his helmet and clothes and be off, while his wife and I would laugh at his importance. And yet it was no small thing for a frail man to be ready at any hour, in any weather, to go off and risk his life.

When I had been ill and was still weak and convalescent his wife and he took me in and looked after me. Ray would bring me my breakfast himself in the morning and was so glad when I felt better. Then later in the morning he sat by my bed and read me his novel, that he had just finished. It was his novel about the young *penitente*. In it he had tried to struggle with the problems of the young American of Spanish descent, and his future. I liked that novel, it was again like Ray, sincere and generous in its conception.

Then, in the afternoons, Ray would take his wife and me for all the wonderfully varied drives round Santa Fe, Truchas and Los Alamos and Chimayo and the *pueblos;* he had thought it all out to make a contrast from day to day. And I got better and sadly feel that now I can never pay my debt of gratitude to Ray, he is beyond debts now.

Last time I saw him in Albuquerque he again was there on a campaign of good will: a scheme to bring the white Americans and Spanish Americans closer together.

Now his wife and relations and friends tell me that he died what I consider a hero's death. He was aware of his approaching death, he faced it as he had faced life, fearlessly. He talked it over with Frances and what she had better do in the future after his death. He had the reward of dying beautifully and to us he gave an example of courage, of simple, unpretentious courage. I shall always love Raymond Otis.

Frieda Lawrence Likes Texas [1]

Your paper has written pleasant things about us in Taos and I want to return the compliment, a sincere one, and tell a few things about Texas I have noticed.

I can't pretend that I know too much about the whole of Texas. I live here in the winter in a small house near Port Isabel, when the Taos winter is very cold. The house is right on the water. Of big towns in Texas I only know lovely San Antonio. So I could not write anything very big about big Texas.

One thing I observed, that here the Texans have established a new "high" in cleanliness. Other parts in the world have a reputation for cleanliness, New England for instance. But there is something grim and virtuous about it. The Dutch are clean, but there is a flat unimaginative quality about their scrubbedness. The Texas cleanliness is a gay and colorful thing. The houses, I don't mean very rich people's houses only, are spick and span and original, they are built with intelligence, they had fun building them.

I noticed that the men's shoes are always highly polished and the women's blouses fresh as daisies.

The food is kind of alive, has brains behind its serving, not dead stuff thrown at you any which way. Then they are generous, these Texans. We never buy any fish. The fishermen bring us beautiful pompano and trout and red snapper right out of the water. Grapefruit and papaya and wild duck the neighbors give us too.

[1] From the Dallas *Morning News*, February 7, 1954, Part VII, p. 7. After World War II, Frieda and Angelo Ravagli began to winter in Port Isabel, Texas, where they bought a cottage in the resort area of Laguna Vista.

I have a young painter friend, a Texan. The first time I met him in his studio, there was a beautiful, huge, blue, shimmering butterfly on the wall. It had lilac lights on its wings and later on I found that at night it was purple. "How lovely it is," I said. My friend asked: "Would you like it?" I answered: "No, you like it too." But I came home with the butterfly.

Another time I told him: "I like your shirt." "Would you like it?" He began taking it off. But this time I won. Now I don't dare admire anything any more on or about him.

The Texans' energy is as big as their hats. We went for a drive on the new highway between the Brownsville port and Port Isabel. My husband wanted to explore and went off the highway on a doubtful looking dirt road. I protested and after a mile or so we got stuck in a kind of swamp. The wheels buried themselves deeply in a nasty kind of mud. I had to jump out of the car and swallow hard not to say: "I told you so."

Then two young fishermen, one with a beer bottle in his hand, he took a swig now and then, came to our rescue. The energy, the determination, especially in the young thin one, was heartening. He walked around the car, looked at it as if he would like to lift it up in one swoop. They let some air out of the tires, shoved some wood under the wheels, then heaved and pulled and sang and ran, shoving the car to safe ground. We only stood and watched.

There is a zest in these people, as if all problems could be solved in a jiffy. It is fun to be in Texas.

D. H. Lawrence, the Failure [1]

From time to time another man sits down and writes a book or article with great gusto that D. H. Lawrence was a failure. As he sits at his desk that perhaps overlooks a campus, securely and comfortably he says to himself, "I thank my stars that I am not like that man Lawrence."

But as we are human beings, not elephants or snowbirds or submarines, it is our business to come off as much as we can as human beings and as such Lawrence was not a failure. When Mr. Ford somewhere says: "I would not give five cents for all the art in the world," it is funny, but there is a spot of failure there. Hitler may be a great mechanizer, but as a human being he seems a failure.

A child is born into the world in a special setting and most likely remains inside this setting all his life. He can't get out. That is particularly true of Europe. In America it is not so much so. A child takes this setting into its consciousness and adjusts itself to it or maybe questions it. Now the slice of time between birth and death is not so very long and the opportunities for the weaving of our life are limited. There are not so many strands to weave with.

First there is the mother and the family. Lawrence gave himself with all his loving power to his mother. He wanted to fill up the empty, sad space that life had left in her; a task too heavy for any child, it left him with a fear of women. He was born into

[1] Found among her papers, and so far as it has been possible to determine, hitherto unpublished, this seems to be a draft of a defense of Lawrence against some article or book, or some projected study, that had come to her attention, probably, because of the references to Hitler, in the Thirties.

the working class. He knew the working class with a basic knowledge, their immediate response to all that went on around them, their warmhearted generosity and their incapacity to abstract and to really think. This last was his tragedy, that they could not think or follow him; primarily he wrote for them, because he loved them. This capacity for love but not blind love, but a very seeing one was the essence of him. Also the absolute need to investigate all his relationships to their very roots. He took the responsibility of all he did very thoroughly, he thought and pondered and then came to his conclusion and stuck to it.

From his mother he got the almost puritan sense of responsibility and from his father the fun of the immediate living, quick and often violent in reaction. But besides the responsibility of his own life, he felt it was up to him to give a direction to the way humanity was going, to help make the cat jump the right way. He himself and the people he met and all he saw and sensed were the sounding board. It was personal or impersonal at the same time. He did not lay down any God Almighty rules and laws for his fellowmen but said to them as it were: here are in my books my honest-to-God experiences and my conclusions, take it or leave it, you will most likely leave it.

He had an uncanny sense of what was real and what was not. And as we all cling to our unrealities like leeches he had terrific fights with all his friends. He could not let anything phoney pass. So he was much on the warpath. Long before Hitler he had said that it is not the intellect but the blood that makes the wheels go round. But he wanted the blood of all races to function purely. And his final conclusion was that only human relations, good human relations, can save the world. Here lies the final sanity.

No man got so much out of living as Lawrence did. Nothing was dull from morning to night and all along. Though he had left his working class, he did not belong to any other, but the simplicity of a workingman's way of life was his. No servants, no luxuries, no possessions. As a very young man he had realized that they waste too much time and clutter you up. You are orderly and fresh without things, it is easy and you keep your flexibility. In the machine Lawrence saw a deadly enemy of man,

man was no longer the God in the machine but the machine had become God. Then he travelled. I doubt whether he ever thought he would find a ready-made Utopia anywhere. He loved just going to look at the world. He knew too well that a man makes his own heaven and hell. But he looked at the different places he visited with infinite gusto, getting their essence as it were through his skin. There was gusto even in his disgust. He knew how rotten Europe was, nobody better, and he hated it, but never lost his deep belief in a renewal of its oldness; he was a stepping stone from the old to the new; he chose the Phoenix for his symbol. How he loved work, work of every kind, the serious job of writing, the fun of putting a nail in, or making a chair or a mat, anything. He lived in the extreme sense of the word every moment of his forty-four years, the whole of him lived, flesh and bones and thoughts.

Does this sound like a failure? And then death looked him in the face. He looked back at him and did not flinch, though it was hard. Because it is up to man to die decently. So he faced the oncoming death like another adventure, something else he had to tackle. He tackled it to the end.

If Lawrence's life was a failure then I long for more failures like his in our day.

A Bit about D. H. Lawrence[1]

There are a few things I want to say about Lawrence because I am probably the only person who could tell them. It is not for me to interpret Lawrence, everybody must do that in his own way. These things have nothing to do with Lawrence the writer, but just with the man Lawrence, ordinary everyday things that many people may not find at all interesting and yet are typical of him. Many little things I only remembered after he was dead. For instance I can't recall that he ever broke a plate or a glass. He never put a dish too near the edge of the table that it could fall. His movements were quick and yet precise. I don't remember that he ever cut his finger or bumped himself. It infuriated him more than the occasion seemed to call for when I did these careless things. "Woman, haven't you got your wits about you?" he would say. I'd answer, "I shall be the pink of perfection by the time you've done with me, a rosy pink."

There was never anything superfluous in his life, just the necessities and a very few extras, just for the fun of it. But everything around him had to be neat. There had to be good water to drink; the place he lived in had to have charm, if ever so small; there had to be an open fireplace in one room at least, and the food had to be good. In the years of the last war we were very poor. We lived for many months on five or six dollars a

[1] Found among her papers, and so far as it has been possible to determine, hitherto unpublished, this sounds a bit as though it had been prepared for oral delivery. The reference to *The Grapes of Wrath* dates it after 1939. In 1940, at the invitation of Professor T. M. Pearce, Frieda gave a lecture at the University of New Mexico that, in a letter to him, she tentatively titled "Some More Lawrence."

week. But I think no visitor would have felt coming to our cottage that we were poor, miserable devils. There was a richness and resourcefulness about him of another sort. I was told that, after the Bible, *Robinson Crusoe* is the most widely read book. Why do we like Robinson Crusoe? Because of his resourcefulness and the fun he had.

That is why after an orgy of sympathy with such characters as Steinbeck has just written about in *Grapes of Wrath* I had a revulsion against them, because of their inefficiency. They saw their crops die year after year, the earth turn into dust under their hands, and they did not use their wits to do anything about it. It was the machine that got them down, and that wasn't their fault. But it is no wonder they were not wanted anywhere else. They expected other people to build their showerbaths for them. There is something wrong with human beings when we have to feel that way, sorry for them. Every animal has its pride and its wits, and they had none. It wasn't this spirit that made America great. Those old pioneers never felt sorry for themselves. They grimly tackled their jobs. And that is how I saw Lawrence tackle his jobs, even the job of dying.

When I first lived with him I gave myself over completely to the adventure of his spirit. That was everything. I had no axe of my own to grind. He had to share this adventure with me. Nothing that happened was insignificant. Every mortal event he had to resolve in his mind and get the hang of it. Mostly this was wonderful, but sometimes I would tire, not having his hammering energy.

All those that ever went for a walk with him remember what an experience it was. It seemed all he saw out of doors he saw for the first time, and he noticed everything, every first flower in the spring, every colour, every smell. We would gather pounds of early dandelions and make them into beer. All the wild strawberries and raspberries we gathered in their turn, and he would make a horrible bitter brew of rue and drink it and say it was good for him, and I of course had to drink it too. Also we made elderberry wine and gathered wood in the Berkshire woods.

The popular figure of a crucified failure is not the Lawrence I knew for eighteen years. It was mostly fun being with him. He travelled because he wanted to see what the world was like in other places, not because he was the hunted, haunted man running away from himself. You just had a gay time with Lawrence. After the long afternoon walks or horseback rides we would come home in the dusk, quickly light a fire and a lamp, eat and settle down to an evening by the fire. He would read or draw, or he would write letters, or go on with a book if he felt like it. Our time, our place was our own choice.

Lawrence never read any newspapers, and he didn't like phonographs. When Harry Crosby gave me a phonograph I had to play it where Lawrence couldn't hear it, or he would go on abusing it. The only time I can remember that he sent me out to get the *Daily Mail* was in Bandol when King George V was very ill. Lawrence was very disturbed and said: "They will kill him between them, those doctors and women." When the papers stated that the Prince of Wales was coming home to the King Lawrence was relieved and said: "Now the King will get better again." And he did. When I told Lawrence in astonishment, "I didn't know you cared so much about your King," he was a little embarrassed. But I never knew whether he felt sorry for George the man or George the King.

I, not being English, knew how very English Lawrence was. He longed to bring back the old gay English manliness that was England in the past. He felt a kind of atrophy creeping over the English. And especially he loved his own common people that he came from, and it was a sore grief to him that he could not reach them by his writing. They were not articulate enough. It seems as if men have lost their capacity to sense the greatness in another man. It is the same everywhere. Here in America there is a Colonel Charles Lindbergh who seems like a symbol of all that is best in America, and he stands for it. But little mingy men come up like bubbles and win the hour if not the day.

Lawrence had an absolute belief in honesty. An attempt at dishonesty made him see red. "Without honesty human intercourse becomes utterly impossible," he said. Once when we stayed at my sister's villa in Austria, a huntsman from a hunting lodge in the mountains brought down a large jar of honey. When we had the honey for tea it was full of worms. "They knew the honey had worms in it," Lawrence said. "Hadu [that was my handsome young nephew], you come with me up the mountain." And up they marched the steep mountainside with the large jug of honey. "And you know, Tante Frieda," Hadu told me afterwards, "it was terrific. We went into the cabin where the whole family was having its *Yausen* [a sundown meal], sitting around the table, and Lawrence without a word planted the jar in the middle of the table and left. The whole family sat petrified and speechless watching him." Of course people jeer at this kind of a man. Lawrence wasn't a comfortable person to be with. He had a second-sight kind of knowledge of people and what went on in them, and that was uncomfortable too. He had to be himself every minute without concessions, without compromise. He worried things out in his own soul. "You're like a dog with a bone," I would tell him. But once he had worried a question out to his own satisfaction he stuck to the result.

Once in a railway carriage a group of schoolboys got in, and when they saw Lawrence sitting in his corner, absorbed in his own thoughts, behind his red beard, they began to giggle. They first tried to suppress their giggling politely but then it got hold of them and they giggled so heartily that it caught me too. But Lawrence was quite oblivious.

The given standards he could not accept. Here was something that was Lawrence, unique and definite and clearly defined. He knew what he wanted. Just as at twenty-six he was sure to want me for his wife, in spite of all the difficulties he would have fetched me out of hell itself. Just as definitely he would never have gone to war. "Kill a man by order that has never done me any harm? No, I couldn't do it. They can kill me first. But I'll watch it that they don't." I can see his most determined face.

When he speaks of blood consciousness that so many smart ones find so ludicrous, it was no theory with him but the voice of his race, of his own English common people in him, something beyond the intellect that I had to respect whether I understood it or not, or disliked it even. It was always somehow real and genuine. He loved his fellow men often with an exasperated angry love. But it was always love. Love is really the key to Lawrence. When I said, like a woman does: "But why do you bother about other people? You have me, isn't that enough?" he replied: "Yes, it's a lot, but it isn't everything." His voice was not for me alone but for the many.

He hated the machine, believing that handling machines made people machine-like. In the sight of this machine war, perhaps he wasn't so far wrong. Men seem to have become less than machines and heroism is as dead as a dead herring.

"It is good for us to handle natural things, like water that does not come out of a tap, and wood to make one's own fire," Lawrence said.

I know that when I have seen too many people and have heard too much talk, my silent trees and fields and animals restore me wonderfully. I wish, how I wish it, that many people would take from Lawrence what I have had from him, in living. It survives his death.

A Small View of D. H. Lawrence[1]

You ask yourself after reading *D. H. Lawrence and Susan His Cow* by William York Tindall: Why did this man write this book? He must have found it such an uncongenial task. He has no enthusiasm, no sympathy for his subject. Lawrence is to him a bad writer, a bad thinker; and he thoroughly dislikes Lawrence as a man. Lawrence is no experience, no adventure for Professor Tindall. To him Lawrence has nothing to give. Maybe his motives for writing this book are the two he accuses Ursula in *Women in Love* of not having—reason and fashion. Women guided only by reason and fashion must indeed be dull.

Professor Tindall believes he is jeering at Lawrence when he dwells on Lawrence's relationship with Susan, the cow. He forgets that great nations have had their sacred bulls, their Europas, and so on. But perhaps he is like the New York slum children who have seen the milk bottle at the door but have never seen a cow. He completely ignores the fact that Lawrence reconquered the world, so to speak, with his vision; he took the old given world and tried to establish a new relationship with everything in this universe, from a human being to a caterpillar or a daisy.

As for Lawrence being a bad writer, that seems to me to be a fantastic assertion. I don't think any man writing in English has handled words more sensitively and adequately than he; even his critics admit that. As for his being a Fascist, that is bunk. He was neither a Fascist nor a Communist nor any other "ist." His

[1] This first appeared in *The Virginia Quarterly Review*, Volume 16 (Winter, 1940), pp. 127–9.

belief in the blood was a very different affair from the Nazi "Aryan" theory, for instance. It was the very opposite. It was not a theory, but a living experience with Lawrence—an experience that made him love, not hate. He wanted a new awareness of everything around us. Fortunately we have more ways of knowing than merely through the intellect, but Professor Tindall does not know this.

What I dislike about the book is the author's mean approach to his subject. "Ha-ha, my fine fellow," Professor Tindall seems to say, "I have found you out. Your ideas weren't your own, you sneaked them out of other people's books and passed them off as your own." Thus he asserts that Lawrence devoured every book in Mrs. Nutall's library—which he actually never set eyes on. It is true that Lawrence read books and enjoyed them and profited by them, evidently a different procedure from Professor Tindall's, who seems to read books only to get a sense of his own superiority from them. His book is not legitimate criticism; it is like gossip that aims to make Lawrence cheap. For example, he accuses Lawrence of snobbery and of having aristocrats for friends. But Lawrence also had friends among peasants and he treated them no differently than he treated the aristocrats.

There are so many dull, ordinary, mean people. Why not be thankful for an exceptional man instead of belittling him? Professor Tindall "missed the bus" when he wrote this book. Unless you have some understanding of your subject your book is naturally a failure. I do not like writing this, and I don't think Lawrence needs defending, but this deliberate distortion of a great man makes me cross.

Bertrand Russell's Article on Lawrence[1]

Bertrand Russell told the following story when we stayed at Garsington with Lady Ottoline Morrell: "The Christian religion was explained to a Japanese: 'Sir,' said the Japanese, 'I understand about the father and the son, but what about the honourable bird?' "

Bertie, as his friends called him, was an Honourable, and for me he was always the honourable bird and often a gay and amusing one.

Lawrence was a raw twenty-six at the time they met and his tone seems presumptuous. Russell was already well known and Lawrence was not. Lawrence thought together they could work out a scheme, a kind of reform for England. But Russell, as he tells himself, thought of what he himself could get out of Lawrence. So Lawrence was disappointed. And Lawrence had friendship enough for Russell to try and tap some other human energies in Russell. It was very obvious that Russell was a "slave to reason." There was no flow of the milk of human kindness in that group of Lytton Strachey and Bloomsburies, not even a trickle. They were too busy being witty and clever. But Russell could be kind.

Had Russell accepted some of Lawrence's concepts, as for instance Aldous Huxley understood them, he might have been a great philosopher as he is a great mathematician; their friendship might have been a wonderful thing.

[1] Russell's "Portrait from Memory" appeared in *Harper's* in February 1953. Mrs. Lawrence's reply appeared as a letter dated February 16, in the April number. The text here is that found among her papers.

As for calling Lawrence an exponent of Nazism, that is pure nonsense. You might as well call St. Augustine a Nazi. Many of the young instinctively know that Lawrence's *raison d'être* was love; considering sex is the very root of our existence, it might as well be treated seriously and "with emphasis."

I am convinced that, in some secret corner of himself, Russell has another image of a young Lawrence who was his friend and not the fantastic monster he makes him out to be.

Foreword to The First Lady Chatterley [1]

From when I first knew him, Lawrence wanted to write what he called a romantic novel, a picaresque novel. I don't quite know what that is. All his life, he wanted to write *Lady Chatterley's Lover*.

Only an Englishman or a New Englander could have written it. It is the last word in Puritanism. Other races have marriage too, but the Mediterraneans seem to have Homer's ancient pattern still of the faithful Penelope at home, but the man wanders off after Circes and Calypsos—to come home again to his Penelope when he has wandered enough; she is always there for him. The French have *l'amour*, the Americans their easy and quick divorces and so on, but only the English have this special brand of marriage. It is not the bonds of interests, or comradeship or even children, but the God-given unity of marriage. England's greatness was largely based on her profound conception of marriage, and that is part of Puritanism.

Lawrence was scared when he wrote *Lady Chatterley*. She was written in the Tuscan Hills in an umbrella pinewood. Not far from where he sat under a large umbrella pine was the sanctuary of San Eusebio. He had a large slab of stone for his bed in a small cave and a smaller slab of stone for his table and a nice little spring nearby. It was an enchanting place where Lawrence went to write every day, especially in Spring. He had to walk a little way by the olive trees to get to his umbrella pine.

[1] New York: Dial Press, 1944. Included in this publication of Lawrence's discarded first draft of *Lady Chatterley's Lover* was "A Manuscript Report by Esther Forbes."

Thyme and mint tufts grew along the path and purple anemones and wild gladioli and carpets of violets and myrtle shrubs. White, calm oxen were plowing.

There he would sit, almost motionless except for his swift writing. He would be so still that the lizards would run over him and the birds hop close around him. An occasional hunter would start at his silent figure.

The handful of peasants round us in that remote part of Tuscany gave Lawrence more unvoiced recognition than he had had anywhere we had been. He was not even very friendly, but rather aloof with them. But instinctively they felt: here is something special. They did not jeer at him and they jeer easily. They would have done anything for him.

After lunch each day, I would read what he had written in the morning, and I was struck and shocked by his ability to create with equal understanding a Sir Clifford and a gamekeeper. I could not criticize—there was an inevitability about it all.

He wrote the whole novel three times and the third version is the published one.[2] My favorite is the first draft. Lawrence said grimly after he had written the *First Lady Chatterley*, "They'll say as they said of Blake: It's mysticism, but they shan't get away with it, not this time: Blake's wasn't mysticism, neither is this. The tenderness and gentleness hadn't enough punch and fight in it, it was a bit wistful." Anyhow another mood came over him and he had to tackle the novel again. He wanted to make the contrast between the cynicism and sophistication of the modern mind and the gamekeeper's attitude sharper. To give a glimpse of the living spontaneous tenderness in a man and the other mental, fixed approach to love. *The First Lady Chatterley* he wrote as she came out of him, out of his own immediate self. In the third version he was also aware of his contemporaries' minds.

If I am not mistaken, *Lady Chatterley's Lover*, the three versions, were written in about three years from 1925 to 1928, on and off. He wanted to emphasize what he wanted to put

[2] The version of *Lady Chatterley's Lover*, first published in Florence, Italy, in 1928.

across. This idea was if you put a thing square and fair and above-board, there is no more room for unwholesome mystery. He wanted to do away with the nasty thrill of dirty stories. Words cannot be evil in themselves; it is what you put into them that makes them so. He succeeded to a great extent. It was like dynamite. The people who could not change hated it like poison, but to many it was a wholesome shock and an eye-opener.

It is an immense satisfaction that *Lady Chatterley's Lover's* first version should come out in a proper ordinary way. It seems as if the book has at last come into its own. The few missing pages of the manuscript are inconsequential. Lawrence left them blank and always intended to go back and fill them in.

It is hard for me to write about Lawrence. I feel as if the sparrows on the roof know all about him. He seems so obvious and simple. But maybe sparrows know more than complicated human beings. Maybe I who saw his life unfold hour by hour have the essence of him in my bones and marrow. But it is hard to get it out into words. The words come out like asparagus tips, but when you look at them, they don't seem as convincing as the canned article.

I will try. I believe the spring of his being was love for his fellow men, love for everything alive, and almost all creatures were more alive to him than they actually were. He seemed to infuse his own life into them. You cannot translate Lawrence into intellectual terms because he was so much more than a man with ideas, an intellectual. But he had a superb human intelligence in big and little things. It exasperated him to see how boring most people's lives were and how little they made of them, and he tried with all his might, from all angles to make them see and change. He never gave up, he did not get discouraged like most reformers. Always he took a new sprint. He was not tragic, he would never have it that humanity, even, was tragic, only very wrong, but nothing that true wisdom could not solve. It was not pity that he felt; he never insulted anybody by being sorry for them. We have to learn to take it. It is strange to think that he never got into more trouble than he did, with his absolute independence. He was attacked and abused. It made him angry, but he never felt sorry for himself. It was a spur to go on. Years after his death, I saw in Buenos Aires many of his books in a shop window as I wandered through the streets. It was a shock. "Here," I thought, "where he has never been, people buy his books." One thin, narrow man has such power all over the world. He was aware intensely of the importance of time, of the responsibility of every hour and minute. The span from the cradle to the grave is all we have to make our show, to prove ourselves. The older you get, the shorter is the time given us. The fact, "I am alive," seems more valuable every day. Lawrence knew this quite young.

He made me share what went on in him. His inner life was so powerful you had to be part of it, willy-nilly. It was hard for me to realize that nothing goes on in many people's insides—nothing at all.

For Lawrence, all creatures had their own mysterious being. Only humans seemed to have often lost theirs.

For him, a cow was not a bottle of milk on a doorstep, but a living wonder-beast, a creature to be reckoned with, as he knew to his sorrow.

Lawrence had this desire to know all the universe in its different manifestations.

He wanted to write a book, a novel, on every continent. But he only succeeded in writing European, Australian and American novels.

There was an urge in him to find new places on the earth as well as in the human soul. All races, all thoughts, all there was interested him. He had a full life, but the fullness was mostly in him. There is so much to experience and most of us experience so little. A little job, a little house, a little wife has little George and George gets older and one day he is dead and that's all. He has missed the great, vast show.

For me, Lawrence's greatest gift was this sense of a limitless universe around us, no barriers, no little social world to fidget over, no ambition to be a success. We felt we were a success in spite of the tiny bit of money we had, but we felt so rich. If a man owns a Botticelli painting and I enjoy more seeing it than the man who owns it, then that picture is more mine than his. We don't have to put things into our pockets to make them our own. Enjoying is more of possession than ownership.

In Lawrence were embodied most of the English virtues. This sounds ridiculous but it is true. Complete honesty, mentally and materially, is part of English greatness (it is unthinkable that you could bribe an English judge or member of Parliament), a sense of freedom, and pride, and above all courage. It took courage to write what he wrote in the teeth of British convention. He did not write *pour épater le bourgeois*, but just as he felt.

That he came of the common people was a thrill to me. It gave him his candour, the wholesomeness of generations of hard work and hard living behind him, nothing sloppy, and lots of guts.

He was an Englishman but never an English gentleman. He might have become one, as so many writers do, but he wouldn't.

We always lived simply, he was just a man going his own way and I tacked along.

Even such a little thing, that might have looked pretentious, as a topaz ring I offered him with the Richthofen arms on it, he would not take. He looked at it—it was nice for a little while. "No," he said, "that isn't for me."

The Lincoln story, when a senator finds Lincoln cleaning his boots and says, "But, Mr. President, gentlemen don't clean their own boots," and Lincoln replies, "Whose boots do they clean?" might have been true of Lawrence.

They called Lincoln names too. "Ape" and "baboon" and pretty names they called Lawrence. The scarecrow they make of him! But birds would never have been scared of him. Some make him a sad, mournful, sacrificial object. He wasn't often sad, but very often mad. Mostly, he was very gay and full of pep. The mournfulness lies mostly with the critics.

He could not have done the amount of work he did in the short forty-four years of his life if he had not possessed vast reserves of energy.

But the public did not get then what he had to give.

Some called him a Communist. Some others a Fascist. Neither

fits. Those concepts were too tight for his purely human outlook.

But these trends were there in his day and he had to take
notice.

Then they called him a sexual pervert. Was he?

"For men can endure to hear others praised only so long as
they can severally persuade themselves of their own ability to
equal the actions recounted: When this point is passed, envy
comes in and with it incredulity."

They never called Lawrence a professional writer—always a
genius. That made him angry. "That's my label—a genius—and
with that I am dismissed."

People seem to find it difficult to understand him. Maybe it is
that we are so used to getting our impressions in a complicated
and indirect way that it hurts us to get too naked and immediate
a contact, as in Lawrence's writing.

Once there came a letter for me and a man said in it, "You
know I would have died for you." "Those phrases!" Lawrence
scorned, "You can't die for anybody—we each have to do our
own dying and living too."

When my father died in Germany I was in England and I
wept bitterly around the cottage we were in. Lawrence said to
me sharply, "Did you expect to keep your father all your life?"
This startled me so that I left off weeping.

Of Lawrence's faults I think the chief one was quick changes
of mood and temper. He could be so furious so easily. Up and
down his barometer went at a fierce rate. He did not keep
anything to himself, but it burst forth and that was not easy to
live with.

I had my own way, but it was always broken into by his
reactions. No wonder we fought. His insistence on every trifle
was maddening. Every trifle became a problem to be solved his
way. He was never easygoing. He took all the hard, grim
way.

When I first met him, and with absolute determination he
wanted to marry me, it seemed just madness and it was—I was
older than he, I had three children and a husband and a place in

the world. And he was nobody, and poor. He took me away from it all and I had to be his wife if the skies fell, and they nearly did. The price that I had to pay was almost more than I could afford with all my strength. To lose those children, those children that I had given myself to, it was a wrench that tore me to bits. Lawrence suffered tortures too. I believe he often felt: have I really the right to take this woman from her children? Towards my first husband too, he felt strongly. Do you remember the poem "Meeting on the Mountains," where he meets a peasant with brown eyes?

But then, can I describe what it was like when we were first together? It just had to be. What others find in other ways, the oneness with all that lives and breathes, the peace of all peace, it does pass all understanding, that was between us, never to be lost completely. Love can be such a little thing with little meaning, then it can be a big one.

Everything seemed worth while, even trivial happenings; living with him was important and took on an air of magnificence.

After the first shock and surprise of this being together, as if a big wave had lifted us high on its crest to look at new horizons, it dawned on me: maybe this is a great man I am living with. I wish I knew what greatness consists of; if it were so obvious right away, it would not be great, because it's a man's uniqueness that makes him great.

We weren't soulful, Tristram and Isolde-ish. There wasn't time for tragedy. This new world of freedom and love kept us in its hold. His thoughts and impulses came up from such deep roots always more and more. I was on the alert all the time. The experience put us apart from other people that had not experienced it the same as we had. It made a barrier.

We quarreled so fiercely. But it was never mean or sneaky. We had come so close to each other, so we met each other without holding back, naked and direct.

It was ugly sometimes, this awful quarreling. We might have spared ourselves and used a little common sense, but we did not. We took it all so very seriously. Sometimes I meant to say something spiteful and he did not notice it. Then, I would say something I thought harmless and he flew into a rage. But I could always be completely myself with him. He had no preconceived, fixed idea of what a wife should be. I was I and if I was at times perplexing, then that was that.

To see him right through to the end makes me forever glad! I am grateful that I could see him back into the earth that he loved. He had made me his wife in the fullest meaning of the word, and more; he had given me his very self to keep. I cannot conceive that I would have died and he be left without me.

He died unbroken; he never lost his own wonder of life. He never did a thing he did not want to do and nothing and nobody could make him. He never wrote a word he did not mean at the time he wrote it. He never compromised with the little powers that be; if ever there lived a free, proud man, Lawrence was that man.

Foreword to D. H. Lawrence: A Composite Biography [1]

The way this book is put together is original.

You take the man you want to present, you don't say anything about him yourself, but you get his contemporaries, the people who had known him, to give their opinion. Mr. Nehls has worked hard to get all this material together. So instead of hearing one voice you hear a chorus of voices. That makes the book never monotonous or boring. But one voice is missing: the voice of the man the book is about. For that you must go to the man's work. Otherwise this book is not balanced or complete.

Nowadays a man can choose the place he wants to live in but the epoch he is born into he cannot choose. He has to take the days of his life along with his contemporaries. Superficially it seems as if Lawrence had not much in common with his day. And yet the time was ripe for what he had to say. The old standards had become weak-kneed and were no longer convincing. The age's chief product was criticism, negative criticism; but the standards were not replaced by any new approaches to living. As far as I know Lawrence is the only one who suggested in his work a new road, not the narrow old path.

The people who met Lawrence did not like him very much on the whole. I know why. He wanted to meet them on a deeper, more human level and not the conventionally accepted one. And that was bewildering. Also with his extra sense for knowing

[1] Gathered, arranged, and edited by Edward Nehls. Volume One, 1885–1919. The University of Wisconsin Press, 1957.

human beings he felt their potentiality in its entireness and he wanted them to be what they might and could be. That they resented also.

It makes me sad. They could have had a fuller life through him. But when he died I got many letters telling what a great loss the writers felt. This new generation that has passed through so many years of horror has had a lot of nonsense burnt out of it and is willing to find new paths and accepts a great deal of what Lawrence had to say.

Port Isabel, Texas
January 15, 1956

Apropos of Harry T. Moore's Book,
THE INTELLIGENT HEART[1]

Ever since I met Harry T. Moore, some time after my husband's death, he has been eager to write about Lawrence. All through these years with endless patience he has gone into the highways and by-ways to trace Lawrence's footprints, step by step. In previous books he connected Lawrence's work with its time and place, a labour of love and admiration indeed. But *The Intelligent Heart* reads almost like fiction, and a great deal is fiction to me.

Lawrence and I lived often for weeks and months in peace in the midst of a terrific turmoil and gossip that we were not aware of. So much spite against two unprententious people who lived as simply as we did. But somehow it did not matter much; we went on our way in our world. A man's new ideas are not so easy to grasp right away and it makes people hostile. There were a few like Aldous and Maria Huxley who patiently listened.

We are too near still to Lawrence to get a bird's eye view of him and his ultimate significance. The era that he was born into put a great stress on self-conscious emotions. They loomed so large, out of proportion in the scheme of things, and all the social fixtures seemed firmly fixed for eternity. Lawrence helped to change that.

[1] This first appeared as "The Bigger Heart of D. H. Lawrence" in *The New Republic*, February 28, 1955, and as "D. H. Lawrence As I Knew Him" in *The New Statesman*, August 13, 1955, with some editorial changes. The title and text used here are from a typescript dated February 4, 1955.

Now many writers tell not about human, all too human stuff, they are sick of it, but write about animals and plants and places and the sea and the sky and winds and it is a relief. Lawrence looked at the elemental part in human beings to write about. So critics, at the time he wrote, said it was nonsense, that he had no form. He was a Fascist, he was a Communist, he was pro-German, he was sex-obsessed, and all he was, was simply pro-human. Sex is such a weary word. It could mean divine urge or a nasty story, but the nasty story always gets a larger audience.

When Lawrence and I first stayed at the ugly place he was born in, I had to think of his rather frail mother, working so very hard to keep the seven people she was responsible for fed and clean and not let them go under into sordidness. I remembered how a twopenny small bunch of pansies could give her such pleasure. She was a good mother. She trained all her children to be tidy and clean and gave them standards to live by. This sounds trivial but is important for all that. But at the same time from people on the streets and buses of this mining town a strange power emanated. When you thought of the dead elegance of Lady X and the immaculate presence of the Duke of S, how much more alive these men and women on the street were!

As for the Oedipus Complex, it is not an absolute written in words of fire over all time. It was a bitter idea against the power of nature and women. This unnatural desire may occur, but is not the norm. Whether young bulls have it, I do not know, but doubt it. When you consider that in Russia the State is your mother and your whole family, then I prefer the unlikely possibility of an Oedipus Complex. Lawrence and Freud and others brought the problem of sex out into the open air and sunshine where it can flourish naturally and sanely. It does not have to hide in dark corners of shame and tragedy any more.

I had a great friend, a young Austrian doctor who had been a pupil of Freud's and had worked with him. Consequently he had been fundamentally influenced by Freud, and through him I was much impressed too. So Lawrence through this friend and me had an almost direct contact with these then new ideas.

He got most of his ideas in this living way, never so much from books, but mostly he used himself as his own guinea-pig. That is why I don't believe the story of the mystery woman who says she "gave Lawrence sex."

Lawrence was a fastidious and sensitive man, who would not go like a lamb to the slaughter with a woman who expressed herself so unfortunately. We would have heard from him about this strange and unlikely episode, mentioned in *The Intelligent Heart.*

Lawrence believed in his destiny, and his destiny included me as his wife.

I believed in his power; what he had to say he would say at any price and the price was high. If he had married another woman his work and his life would have been different. Lawrence's genius, and nobody denies his genius, has so many angles. If there is a Lord who created our universe, He did not do it only by laws and rules. Such prodigal imagination and fantasy went into this overwhelming achievement that is our globe. To Lawrence his surroundings were a mystery, a miracle through all his life.

When you think of a whale or a butterfly, of a forget-me-not or an oak tree, it is staggering to think of the endless variety that lives along with us, much too much to take in with one short lifetime.

He had, in his own way, the same uncanny understanding of living creatures as St. Francis of Assisi. When St. Francis says "my little sisters the birds", he only voiced his awareness of them in their loneliness; and when he preaches to the fishes, it is his love for them. St. Francis was a voice against the spiritual conceit of doctrines and human superiority when he put animals on a level with humans. With the accent on spirituality the animal becomes the evil principle. All that is animal must be suppressed, and God help us!

When you think of a bird in flight, handling its wings with such precision and ease, wonderful as an airplane is, the birds win. But we have come a long way from St. Francis and his little sisters the birds. Now we have chickens in cages that are fed scientifically, and they mechanically just sit and lay eggs. No air, no sun, no scratching in the dirt. Whether they cackle when they lay an egg I don't know, but I doubt it.

Lawrence had some of the awareness of the creatures and vegetation around him as St. Francis had. It is there in his writing. It gave him his special quality and made him so alive. It fascinated people and they loved to be with him. But very often they tried to turn this quality into a limited, personal, too personal relationship, and it could by the very nature of it not be personal and they were disappointed and Lawrence was angry and the feathers flew, whole clouds of feathers.

When I read Harry T. Moore's book, it seems as if it had all been strife and misery. It was not so. Lawrence could never have done the amazing amount of work in his short lifetime had it been so. There were months of quiet, peaceful living. For instance at the Berkshire cottage, Lawrence would write in the morning, while I fussed around the cottage. After lunch we would go for long walks over the fields and get mushrooms if there were any, and in the spring through the woods we found clearings where big primroses grew and pools of bluebells. In the spring we also got baskets full of dandelions and made dandelion wine. Sometimes in the middle of the night the cork of a fermenting dandelion wine bottle would go off with a terrific pop. After our afternoon exploring we came home with our loot, hungry, with muddy boots, changed into slippers and put the kettle on the fire and had tea.

In the cottage next door lived a charming brown-eyed child, Hilda Brown, who would come after school, and we would sing the songs from *The Oxford Songbook*—"All Through the Night," "The Camptown Races," and "My Wife and I Live All Alone." Then after our evening meal Lawrence would write again. I would do an embroidery or mend. It is still a mystery to me, when I think of our quiet days that flowed along so easily, how it could arouse so much speculation in people and so much spite. It seemed to have so little to do with us and our way of living.

The one time I did not believe in Lawrence's activities (he was very young then) was when he and Bertrand Russell planned to make some reform in English government. I had listened to talk on politics at my uncle Oswald Richthofen's in Berlin (he was then Minister of Foreign Affairs), and what Lawrence and Bertie discussed did not seem like politics to me.

I thought they were both off their tracks. But being brought up in the European tradition that women don't interfere in men's affairs, I held my tongue. So both being out of their elements, there was the inevitable fiasco and they blamed each other. Lawrence did not mean it when he asked Russell to leave him some money in his will; he knew that Russell wasn't a rich man.

The story of the mayor of Milan who came to breakfast in Taormina, and Lawrence threw plates at me, made me weep tears I had to laugh so hard. I had never heard it before! And we were poor and did not have so many plates!

Also *The Intelligent Heart* gives a wrong impression of my father. He slapped his young orderly, but it was no "beating." *The Prussian Officer* is a story of cruelty, and though it existed in some Germans, cruelty is a plant that grows everywhere. My father was a lovely father who wrote poems for me when I was small: how I must have all the virtues of the animals, quick as a bird and gentle as a lamb, and of course busy as a bee "and gay as a Spitz, be my little Fitz," it ended. He must have read Prescott's *Conquest of Mexico* at one time and had such names as "Fitzli-Purzli" for me, and took me to the Officers' swimming establishment and dived into the Moselle with me from the diving board (that taught me to swim), and much to the astonishment of the officers I emerged dressed in my small girl's clothes.

Because Lawrence wrote his books, the young people that read them will not be so mixed up in themselves any more. They will have something to think about and have more fun.

There is Harry T. Moore's Lawrence in *The Intelligent Heart*. But there is a Lawrence that I knew that is not there.

Appendix, Chronology,
and Index

"And the Fullness Thereof..."

Fragment No. *1. This account of the mother's childhood uses the names and technique of the memoir proper. The "small volume of reminiscences" by the mother passed, after Frieda's death, to Else Jaffe's son, Friedl, now Frederick R. Jeffrey, who lives in the United States.*

Paula's mother had lived a most happy childhood. During the First World War to console herself for the separation from her beloved daughter, the mother had written a small volume of reminiscences for Paula. It was a charming little book covered in flowery cretonne and the handwriting was clear and round and neat. In the light of the present Germany it seems incredible, more than incredible, that there could be such peace, such security and full rich life flowing as it flowed in that small town of Donaueschingen, high up in the Black Forest, at the source of the Danube. Very cold in winter with the dark pine forests around and much snow and much running water. That's where her mother was born. Fürstenberg was a small principality, the head of it the "Fürst" of Fürstenberg; he was a cultured prince who surrounded himself with the best men of the day and took part in the friendly goings-on of the town. The only communication with the outer world was the stagecoach that arrived at nine at night, heralded by the horn of the postilion. Then all the inhabitants would rush with their lanterns to the dark posthouse to get the one newspaper of the region, letters and parcels were only delivered in the morning. In the winter the coach was a sleigh. Then the dark and quiet descended on the town, only interrupted every hour by the nightwatchman's song:

> "Hört Ihr Herren und lasst Euch sagen
> Die Glocke hat ein's geschlagen,
> Bewahrt das Feuer und das Licht,
> Damit uns kein Unglück geschicht."

467

There was only one grocery store, that generously gave the children of its delicacies, dried prunes and liquorice sticks and home-made boiled candy. There was no dry goods store, only the Jew Joshua who appeared twice a year in spring and autumn with huge boxes of stuffs. Once in the early winter a pedlar came with oranges from the south Tyrol. That was the only luxury. It was a Catholic country. The small shrines with their crucifixes and madonnas were part of the landscape, and Paula's mother Anna and her beloved brother Franz would decorate with branches and flowers. Anna shivered having to go to mass at seven in the morning, on an icy winter's day.

In the winter there would be sleigh-rides to the hunting lodges of the Prince, and the children must have been treated with the greatest kindness by their elders, who arranged plays for them and other festivities. There was a schoolmaster, one Herr Fidele, who on his birthday received a velvet waistcoat from his pupils and a great sugarcone. The only other teacher was a woman who taught knitting and sewing. Also in my mother's house was the hardworking cook, who baked bread and reigned in the kitchen with great dignity. After twenty-five years of faithful service she received a gold medal and a donation from the town in a real ceremony. She died serving the family and was missed and remembered.

Fragment No. 2. *This account of trouble between the parents, and the effect on their children, seems to be based on the von Richthofen family. "Sybil" is the "Edna" of the memoirs, and the eldest of the von Richthofen sisters, Else. The extent of the fictionalization—the technique of drama-tizing scenes—is much greater, and suggests an entirely different concept of the story, presumably an earlier version than the Paula-Dario one, which is quite autobiographical. The text is that of the notebooks found at the ranch after Frieda's death, and edited by Albert Diaz.*

Things were getting worse and worse between Anne and Frederick. Like so many couples, they thought love must drop from heaven ready-made. They did not try with each other for long. [The very] fact that Frederick had a deep, serious outlook on life by nature, that he had failed, he gave in. Anne in her woman's heart and pride was hurt by his neglect. She became the unbelieving woman, the woman in revolt. He left her, he was not satisfied with her, how it hurt! She took refuge in the thought of her respectability, the lady as apart from that other world, the demi-monde. She savoured with eagerness French novels, where the *femme entretenue* was the much-beloved with the limelight on her, all the time. Anne secretly envied her the limelight. "These women get it all," she thought with a grudge. But her wounded pride took refuge in a fierce virtue, in an attitude of superior morality towards Frederick, that drove him deeper down into a scattered miserable life. She thought him immoral, so he would be.

One night Anne waited for Frederick in vain. She slept fretfully, waking up dazed and going to sleep again; at six she got up sick with rage and suspense. The strain he put on her was more than she could bear. She was so alone and near her she could hear the children get up. The despicable man, his children and hers, what a father she had given them, dear God! Contemptuously, deeply ashamed, she tried to hide her misery from the servants. But at 9 o'clock she could stand it no longer. She sent Wilhelm to look for "Herr Baron" in the town. At "eleven o'clock" he appeared himself, white, shaken, a pitiable sight. A sight that a woman never forgets or forgives, the despicable man, *her* man! Trembling inside with her contempt, she looked him up and down, jeering. "Come upstairs," she said, meeting him in the hall. He followed her, a thing without a will, into their bedroom.

"Where have you been?" she said.

"Anne," he pleaded, broken, "don't, now don't. They had invited me to the Casino of the blue dragoons and you see, later on they gambled and you know how it gets hold of me." "And now," he burst on in helpless terror, "I owe Fenningen £200; I'll blow my brains out and have done with it."

"Done with it, done with it," Anne screamed! "You blow your brains out? My children, my poor children," she cried, lashing him in her agony, the backboneless thing before her rousing her to fury.

"Anne," he said, in utter humility, "I give you my word of honour, that I will never gamble again if just this once you let me take a mortgage on the house; you must come with me and sign a document at the lawyers!"

"No," she cried, "no. That money belongs to the children. You want to take their money to pay your gambling debts with. You cur," she said, her face contracting, "blow your brains out, blow them out, that's all you're fit for!"

He could stand no more. "Stop it," he screamed, "you devil, don't you insult me any more! It would be a treat to be dead if it were only to get away from you and your biting tongue!"

Anne got scared. "I suppose I must come and sign," she looked at him contemptuously. "But I'll tell you this, from today you and I have done with each other. You can go your own grubby ways, I stay with you in your house for the children's sake," her mouth twitched, "but I'm your wife no more."

From that day, Anne and Frederick hated each other, nothing but convention and the children kept them tied together. They lived the life that is so destructive to the best in people, is murderous in its fierce hatred, always newly roused by the contact of daily life. The children vaguely feel the atmosphere of strife without understanding; there is something frightening to children in the war of the sexes. Sex, that thing not understood by children, hidden from them, yet constantly in the air, warps and tortures the life of children. Especially in the sensitive Sybil the parents' war broke something that never healed in later life.

Fragment No. 3. *The text is from the same source as the preceding fragment. "Sybil" is the "Edna" (Else von Richthofen) of a similar episode in "School" in the memoirs.*

Sybil was waking up slowly. Her delicate cameo face with the beautifully chiselled mouth wore a weary expression as she quite roused herself. The lids came down gently, slowly over her big grey eyes, she shut them again. Sunday was before her. Disgusting, hateful Sunday. Absolutely nothing to do. The whole empty day lay before her almost frightening her. She stretched herself lazily. Even the extra hour in bed did not compensate for the fact that it was Sunday. She did not feel sad, just empty. There was nothing to do but read a little, she was always reading and moon[ing] about in the garden. Even the garden she hated today. It was so hot and the flowers looked dusty and tired, the garden wall was a prison wall that held her in bondage from that big world outside where she wanted to go, where people had aims and did things. Ah, she wanted to know. This life here was trivial and dull, her parents were not cultured, home was barren! Only at school she lived! With an intense, shy feeling she thought of Fräulein Harney, the English mistress, her adored, her *Schwarm*. How beautiful and dear her eyes were, how lucky she was to adore her! Did she prefer one of the other girls though? Sybil trembled at the thought! They were just reading *The Prisoner of Chillon* with Fräulein Harney. Sybil knew every line, every word, voluptuously, intensely it sat in her brain. Yesterday on the way home from school the girls had discussed the religion of the prisoner of Chillon. Sybil still thought out her argument. School was life to Sybil, home was without stimulus. But she would have to get up now. She put her things on, slowly, wearily. She was dressed, but could not find her Sunday shoes. They were not in their place on her bootshelf. She went to the bedroom of the "children," as she called her two "smaller" sisters, which these resented. Of course there were the shoes, all muddy. That wretched Gisla had worn them on one of her escapades evidently! Sybil was in a rage. Her eyes fell on the little white wooden chest, where Gisla's dolls lived. Gisla was fiendishly untidy, but her dolls she kept scrupulously in order, she adored them. . . .

Fragment No. *4. Like some of the introductory passages that preface the memoirs, this represents her musing about the problem of doing a book about her life—at this stage, apparently in the form of a novel. Other highly fictionalized fragments were also contained in the notebooks found at the ranch after her death, and edited by Albert Diaz for* Manuscripts.

She sat at the window, her eyes fixed on the tips of the firs, their stiff top branches showing clear and dark against a metallic sky. There was something happening inside her, she felt it quite plainly. Something stirred, something urged, oh, it made her unhappy! Why couldn't she find an outlet for all this surging in her, why didn't she understand it, why had she to put up with it? This force that she did not understand, that drove her, was stronger than she was herself. It came out of her, it was she, her own self, yet she knew no more about it than some inhabitant of Southern

Nigeria. It was something outside herself yet she was tacked on to it, she was the guardian, the trustee of this unknown in her. To it she might have put the epitaph, "To the Unknown God." Yet she felt that she must be loyal to her "Unknown God," even if she *would* she *could* not leave Him in the lurch. She felt uncertain of herself. She would never, never be able to either paint or write or be a musician and yet she knew she was a "somebody," she had got something to give, something she *must* give. She had been steeped in suffering, in feeling she had dropped so many of the outer, unimportant shells that the female mind is hampered with, she was convinced that she had come to some stark human facts. Yes, she would be faithful to her Unknown God, fight with him for him. She would try to write. She smiled at one side of herself; trying to write and feeling solemn about it, Lord what a joke! Well, there it was, she had made up her mind, for better or worse; it would be for "worst" very likely. "But off I go," she said to herself and at once thought of a beautiful romantic title for her novel. . . .

Fragment No. 4A. *This, like the other fragments from the ranch notebook edited by Diaz, represents a greater degree of fictionalizing than the memoirs, though basically it deals with the same facts. This passage covers her young love for her cousin which in the memoirs appears in the chapter "Adolescence."*

And again they sat together this day. This last day. She knew it was the last evening and yet she knew it not at all. There he sat with his beautiful hands, his light brown moustache that curled back from his full upper lip and went so well with the red and brown of his fine-textured cheeks. Careless she was of tomorrow; only by an intense tightening inside her, of an eager awareness of every twitch of his eyelids, of a keen desire to be close to him, did she know something would happen. She felt so helpless. Like water trickling through her fingers, no more could she hold him, keep him; tomorrow he would be gone. But he was there now. Looking at her so tenderly, loving her; she felt it warm all over her back, like a cat being stroked and then the pain of it. He was only aware of a deep aversion against things in general; in his chest was a tightness and his teeth ground together. Gisla saw it, the even, sharp teeth. But she did not realize that he suffered her own love and the parting that hung over them swamped everything else. And now it was night and he must go. As usual she accompanied him to the garden gate where in the spring had been a scent of lilac vine in bloom, and fresh earth and now the ground was dry and hard and smelt of dust and rotting fruit. "Good-bye," she said, kissing him lightly, and as he passionately beside himself wanted to hold her, she slipped from his grasp, trying to be brave, to submit. He understood her and went. For months the sound of his long sword on the road and his even quick footfalls sounded a sad tune in her ears, driving her wild. She went to bed so changed. But she would see him once more from the bottom of the garden where the railway went, he would be passing at 10:30 and wave to her from his train. She clung to this straw as a consolation. In the morning it seemed endless till it was ten, there was all the pretence to her people, the careless everyday behaviour she shammed. She slunk out in his favourite pink frock and slowly went to the bottom of the garden, watch in hand, waiting. The rails were cut into the land that slightly rose. Between the grassy banks the train would come. There were little dry patches where some sparks from the engine had blown and burnt the grass. A few little harebells waved in the wind. She stared, she gaped, all sense of time and space suspended. The engine appeared, slowly at first, then carriages like the joints of a caterpillar, the white hankie blew out of the window, she saw the glitter of his uniform, his face a white patch; and then the train had passed slowly and was gone. It had seemed quite amiable and the space it had left between the banks did not upset her. She went indoors curiously alive. A train had passed, she still heard it click, click into the distance, why shouldn't a train pass. She was conscious of the eyes of her people on her. They did not dare offer any sympathy, but she wandered about the garden, eating an apricot or an early pear, now and then, noticing things curiously and intensely. A strange feeling haunting her as if she were looking for herself. She did not want to cry, she did not want anything, only she would not be looked at, they must leave her alone. The evening came with a bright, happy summer's moon, she stood at the window of her little bedroom overlooking the garden full of moonshine with the very black shadows of trees and the scent of a passed, hot day. The moon, she started at sight of it. "He has gone away," she said aloud. At the sound of her words she began to cry hopelessly, helplessly, with her head on the windowsill. . . .

Fragment No. 5. *The text is from the same source as the preceding three fragments. The account of Frieda's visit with her mother to Ernest Weekley's family in England, before their marriage, may be compared with "English Marriage" in the memoirs.*

And now they were crossing the channel, her mother, this man and Gisla. The sea breathed green and white in the sunshine, amazing, overwhelming in its heaving vastness; the sun melted sky and sea into a white mist of freshness. Anne was exhilarated by the salt air and the motion. She looked at Gisla, who looked such a child in her sailor dress and cap. She was afraid. The man by her side seemed so elderly, so dead. What would he make of her? She was nothing yet, but so keen on everything that came her way. Gisla was just throwing back her head laughing. Her mouth was open and showed the splendid white teeth, the salt water had curled the little hairs on her forehead; her face so freshly coloured from the wind, shone of vitality, youth and strength. Through Anne's heart shot a pang. Was it right to let this child go out to another country, to trust it to this elderly man? She looked at him and reassured herself. Yes, he was trustworthy in every way. His eyes were so reliable, dog's eyes they were, honest brown eyes. And how he worshipped the child. She felt uneasy in this new situation, a mother-in-law in a strange land.

He approached her. "Look, Mama," he said, "now you can see the cliffs of old England." There out of the white vapour rose a concrete whiteness, the Dover cliffs. Anne was impressed. Her heroic soul was impressed by this proud, impenetrable white wall. Something of the spirit of England, that England that is the envy and the despair of nations, seemed to stand there, a symbol in the white rocks. Gisla was beginning to feel queer at the thought of his parents, who were meeting them at the Dover pier. "My old people," he said, deeply moved, she could hear by the quality of his voice. He was thirty-three and loved for the first time. For the first time he wanted a woman to be his wife. His whole being was in an upheaval.

"Aren't you jealous of all my other men friends?" Gisla asked him once. "Why should I be," he had said, slightly to her bewilderment, "haven't you promised to be my wife?"

"There they are," he shouted, and on the pier in the afternoon of a sunny channel day stood arm-in-arm two old people. He, a beautiful old man looking like Michelangelo's Moses toned down by an English frockcoat, she a round, little quick old lady in a cape and bonnet with a big forehead and beautiful blue eyes. They went to meet them. The mother had only eyes for the son; yes, he was happy! It was a joy and a pang to her! He had been her own son and she had been proud of him and so far she had reigned supreme; his little flirtations had brought life to her, but they had never meant anything to him, that she knew! And now he wanted to marry: what a child he had chosen. But the father had at once succumbed to the fresh, charming creature that came to meet them. He took her arm and walked to the hotel where they would have a meal. Behind followed the two mothers and the son. The little English woman talked busily away on all sorts of things, Anne only understanding a word here and there, E. [*sic*] in a trance of bliss. Anne resented these strangers to whom her child would belong more or less. They had tea together, Mrs. — — quite at her ease, while Anne objected to the humbleness of the hotel, the rather evident middle-class atmosphere of the old lady. She was glad when it was time for the four to leave for London, while she would think over things.

At the parting Anne saw tears in Gisla's eyes: "Don't weep, you goose," she whispered to her child. Gisla laughed and all went well. In the train the old lady talked of all the family happenings, talked to her son incessantly, he hardly listening, only answering absently from time to time. The father smoked his pipe, that curious expression on his face that puzzled Gisla in the men she saw round her, something shut, you could not read them by their faces. Gisla looked out of the window. This was England! Why was it so different from other countries she had seen? Trees and fields and hedges on soft slopes wrapt in soft air. How beautiful it was, never had she seen such a sunset. Little churches and cottages peeped behind great, round trees, wooden cows in impossible green fields, how peaceful in the fading light. Something of the atmosphere of a little church, the "dim religious light" seemed to hang round the landscape. She looked up at the sky. How near it was, how close! It frightened her. She looked at her lover. Suddenly he seemed quite strange, part of this domestic closeness of things, and she quite alone, out of it; oh, and she wanted to run and get away! Like something heavy England came down on the lightness of her heart. The tears came, she stared out of the window, hard so that these people shouldn't see. The first lights of London appeared, lighting up houses, houses, and hundreds of little houses, grimy, little houses, terrifying in their endlessness. She thought of their numberless inhabitants, all being egos just like herself. She was so frightened at the thought of this infinity of beings that she wanted to get under the seat and hide from them! She laughed at her undignified thought . . . !

Fragment No. 6. *This brief fragment has been included because it contains an interesting sidelight on her nature and the trouble it sometimes caused.*

Paula's husband had looked at her in a strange way one day and said: "If people knew what you are really like, they would want to kill you." "Oh no," she cried: "Why should they, I wish nobody any harm, you know that." He did not explain. Years later an old friend told her the same thing. "No," she cried again, "I only want people to be happy and free." "Maybe that's why," his dear wife said. The two cleverest men she had known had told her this shocking thing and still she could not believe it. She did not want so much from life. She did not want diamonds, if they would come her way, she would take them, but not run after them, she did not hanker after Cadillacs or palaces or to play a role in "Society." All she wanted was a healthy small place, not in a town, decent food, a few glad rags, but above all a man, a man with courage, one that she could believe in. That would give her all else. Friends and the stars and the moon and the sun and flowers and places and wind and cold and fires. And now that she was old, but still healthy, able to do all sorts of things, she could say to herself, "I have had what I wanted, whether I have deserved it or not, dear Lord, now all I want still is to die decently and not be much trouble to others, that I die in peace. . . ."

Fragment No. 7. *Entitled "Men and Women," this brief passage is included because of the light it throws on her early attitude toward men and on the source of her opposition to Lawrence's utopian and revolutionary tendencies.*

Though Andrew had been dead for donkey's years now, she still had to argue with him, she still wanted to fight him. She was glad she had fought him in the past. He had insisted in his male arrogance that man was the master and woman had to submit to him. When a woman has a child she learns what submission is. She has to submit to forces over which she has no control. For her lifetime she has learnt that she can't be the master of her fate. It gives her a great security and her own female wisdom. She knows of the magnificence of bursting life, as it has been lived in the splendour of the past and present [and] will live in the future. Man thinks he is so much cleverer than the woman is and so he truly is, but in his own man's way he races off into most fantastic ideas and ideals, concepts, leaves the ground, soars away into heights. The woman has her own wisdom and she had better stick to it and not try to have a man's mentality. Her job is also to pull a man back from his flights and put his feet on the firm ground again. Paula had always had a great sympathy, almost pity, for men, because of their job in this world, to go ahead and face the unknown and shape it to their will. . . .

> Fragment No. 8. *This fairly extensive passage was entitled "Hollywood." Frieda Lawrence and Angelo Ravagli frequently wintered in California in the Thirties, before the war, and once visited the Carmel–Big Sur area, where Henry Miller, with whom they were friendly, lived. Chief among their "Hollywood" friends were Aldous Huxley and Dudley Nichols. This fragment appears here because it did not fit into the narrative pattern of the memoirs.*

I shall never forget the night we poured along with millions of other cars into Hollywood. After the quiet, empty roads through the desert, through Phoenix, arriving on a Saturday night about dusk in Los Angeles was a fantastic experience. In the flow of a quick running river of lights and dark cars on winding roads and not a moment's stop in the flow. At a street corner in Hollywood, Dario stops the car, *"un momento di respiro"* ("let's take a breath"), but no: pip, pip, pip goes a chorus of impatient horns behind us. Dario says the Zulus have come to Hollywood! I feel almost hysterical. After two hours search we find our Normandy Towers. At night it looks like a little Normandy village, it is like a village on the screen, real Hollywood. We stay with an old friend, though he is a young man, who works at the Foxfilm. Hollywood is charming, spread out with palm trees and pepper trees and cypresses and lawns in front of the houses in wide streets. I am thrilled by the markets—great open halls with large colourful stalls of oranges and all kinds of fruit and avocados and many vegetables. The smell when you pass them at night will always be Hollywood to me. You enter the market and take a basket and wander about and get all you want, nobody says: "Yes, madam, what can I do for you today?" No, you aren't bothered. In ten minutes you can just get all you need for a week.

The traffic on Sunset Boulevard, we are close to it, is also something "zuluesque," but Dario tackles it proudly, though my heart bounces occasionally and I watch the lights and the cars creeping out from the side of the road anxiously. You ought to have eight eyes and not two, and more people get killed every week than in the whole Ethiopian War.

We have met charming people. I think the Californian women are the most attractive women in the world. They are a mixture of naïveté and sophistication. I have an immediate contact with most of them. I am not a man, so I don't know how they strike a man, but I feel at once gay and at home with them. I have some old friends here and I meet their friends, but am agreeably surprised that nobody takes any sort of official notice of me. So many celebrities come to Hollywood that it is not impressed with them. There is the movie world, hard-working people that have their own *raison d'être*. Their world is not my world, but I am happy to get the benefit of this easy pleasant centre that they have made. It seems to me like living in Pompeii or at Marie Antoinette's *petit Trianon*. These movie stars well earn the adoration of the public because they lead a dog's life, I think. They have to get up early for the make-up, to be ready for the screen, they work all day at high pressure. Many of them have false eyelashes fixed on their lids, which sounds particularly uncomfortable. It is a great strain amusing the great public. Many go under. Nothing is more sad than to see an old superannuated movie star and he is out of it so soon! Something seems to happen, even to the most successful. Look at Greta Garbo's sad face. They know that all this they are doing is not real and I respect them for knowing it. Most people humbug themselves into believing they are living a reality, these movie stars know their movie is only a put-on show. I wouldn't be a movie star, not for a million a week. I say it's a slave's life, you have a contract and your time is no longer your own. You must come when you are wanted. Oh my beloved freedom, that **is** so precious to me!

"There is a face I call a filmface," said Paula to herself, "and it's a sad, discontented face." She had met some stars and producers of all the constellations of studios and they none of them liked their work. It was strange, she wondered why.

Was it that they were ashamed of living to entertain the big public or was it that they were the servants of the sovereign ruler, the box office? Did they know what a mushroom glory the glory of the movies was?

Of all the people Paula met there wasn't one who believed in the greatness of the movie though Paula herself believed in it as an expression of new beauty. After all photography could do so much. There was the possibility to bring in the moods of the out-of-doors to create a corresponding mood in the characters. When Paula said this she was told, "Out-of-doors photography costs too much considering the terrific amount of money that was spent." She thought it a poor excuse. "There must be something wrong here," Paula thought, "that among all these people that the rest of the world envies and admires so much, there isn't one contented happy face. . . ."

Chronology

1879, August 11. Birth of Emma Maria Frieda Johanna von Richthofen, second daughter of Friedrich von Richthofen and Anna
(née Marquier) at Metz.

1879–1897. Years covered in the memoir *And the Fullness Thereof*
. . . in the chapters "Christmas at Home," "School," "Childhood," "Adolescence," and "Grown Up," and by Fragments 1–3
and 4A in the Appendix.

1897, February 5. Ernest Weekley appointed lecturer in Modern
English at Freiburg. He taught from May to November, when
he resigned.

1898, January. Weekley appointed lecturer in French at Nottingham
University College.

1899, September. Marriage of Frieda von Richthofen and Ernest
Weekley. (There are no records of this.) The courtship, including a visit to his family in England, and the marriage, up
to the meeting with D. H. Lawrence, are covered in the memoir
chapters "English Marriage," "Octavio," and "Andrew," and by
Fragment 5 in the Appendix.

1900, June 15. Birth of Charles Montague Weekley, in Nottingham.

1902, September 13. Birth of Elsa Agnes Weekley, at 9 Goldswong
Terrace, Cranmer Street, Nottingham.

1904, October 20. Birth of Barbara Joy Weekley, at 8 Vickers
Street, Nottingham.

1912, April. Meeting of Frieda Weekley and D. H. Lawrence, followed in May by their journey to Germany together.

1914, May 28. Divorce of Frieda and Ernest Weekley.

1914, July 13. Marriage of Frieda and D. H. Lawrence.

1930, March 2. Death of Lawrence at Villa Robermond, Quartier la
Rousse, Vence.

1931, spring. Frieda and Angelo Ravagli decide to go together to the

New Mexico ranch; he is on six months' leave from the Italian army. (They first met in 1925, at Villa Bernarda in Spotorno.) That winter he is recalled to the army.

1931–1932. Difficulties over Lawrence's estate and will. Covered in the memoirs in the chapter "After Andrew's Death."

1933, spring. Frieda and Ravagli return to the New Mexico ranch. Their house is begun May 30. This, and Lawrence's death and her relationship with Ravagli, is covered in the chapter "Leaving for South America."

1933–1934, autumn to spring. Trip to Buenos Aires to visit Ravagli's brother and sister which forms the narrative framework of the memoirs through "Coming Back," the penultimate chapter.

1934, summer. A chapel is built at the New Mexico ranch to serve as a shrine for Lawrence's ashes.

1935, March 13. Cremation of Lawrence's body at the Crématoire du Cimetière Saint-Pierre, Préfecture des Bouches-du-Rhône, Marseilles. In April Ravagli brings the ashes to the United States, and they are placed in the concrete altar of the chapel. Covered in the memoirs in "Last Chapter—Friends."

1936. Lawrence's paintings sent to the United States from Italy by Ravagli's wife.

1938. Manuscripts of *Lady Chatterley's Lover* brought to the United States from Italy by Ravagli.

1938. Ernest Weekley retires from Nottingham University College.

1950, October 31. Marriage of Frieda Lawrence and Angelo Ravagli.

1954, May 7. Death of Ernest Weekley (born in 1865).

1956, August 11. Death of Frieda.

INDEX

Achievement of D. H. Lawrence,
The, 355 *n*
Adam Bede, 412
After Many a Summer Dies the
Swan, 279
Aldington, Richard, 241 *n,* 282,
329, 329 *n,* 373 *n,* 374 *n,* 375,
392, 392 *n*
"Altitude," 311
Amon, Frank, 357
Amores, 203 *n*
Anderson, Betty, 389, 414
Anderson, Claude, 356, 389, 413,
413 *n,* 419
Anna Karenina, 412
Asquith, Lady Cynthia, 186 *n,*
187 *n,* 189 *n,* 193–4, 197 *n,*
208–9, 317, 324, 357, 390
Asquith, H. H., 186 *n*
Asquith, Herbert, 186 *n,* 187 *n,*
194, 208
Augustine, Saint, 359
Austen, Jane, 323
Austin, Mary, 292, 293

Barkham, John, 389
Barnaby Rudge, 384
Barr, Stuart, 276, 278, 414
Barr, Mrs. Stuart, *see* Weekley,
Barbara
Barr, Ursula (Mrs. Alfred Al-
varez), 350, 350 *n,* 369, 370,
376, 398, 399, 414
Barrie, Sir James, 189, 189 *n*
Benrimo, Dorothy, 336, 336 *n*
Benrimo, Thomas Duncan, 288,
288 *n*

Bentley, Eric, 286–7 *n*
Benvenuto Cellini, 59
Berners, Lord, 318
Bernhardt, Sarah, 44
Bernstein, Leonard, 315
Best, Marshall, 253, 253 *n*
Betsky, Seymour, 357
Between Two Worlds, 377
Beutler, Floyd, 257, 257 *n*
Biddle, Francis, 284, 284 *n,* 319
Biddle, George, 282
Birrell, Francis, 197
Blake, William, 450
Bonheur, Gaston, 318
"Border Line, The," 223 *n,* 357,
359
Boswell, James, 325
Botticelli, 453
Brave Men, A Study of D. H.
Lawrence and Simone Weil,
241 *n*
Brett, Dorothy, 207 *n,* 222, 222 *n,*
223 *n,* 228, 231 *n,* 232, 235,
240, 250 *n,* 257, 263, 283,
293, 300, 304, 310–13, 328,
340, 343–4, 347, 349, 376–7,
384, 408, 413, 418
Brewster, Earl and Achsah, 306
Bright, Edward, 264–5
Bright, Miriam, 257, 257 *n,* 263,
265
Bright, Robert, 289, 289 *n*
Brinnin, John Malcolm, 410 *n*
Brown, Hilda, 462
Browning, Robert and Elizabeth
Barrett, 318
Buddha, 11, 12, 19

i

Burrows, Louise, 324, 327, 348
Bynner, Witter (Hal), 219 _n_, 255, 259, 272, 283–4, 329, 331, 352, 360–1, 415 _n_

"Cake," 227
Calvin, Ross, 331, 331 _n_
Campbell, Beatrice, 204 _n_, 340, 342, 355, 359, 388, 396, 401, 404–5
Campbell, Gordon, 204, 210–13, 317, 340, 342, 355, 359, 388, 396, 401, 404–5
Cannan, Gilbert, 206 _n_, 207–8, 210
Cannan, Mrs., 216
"Captain's Doll, The," 413
Carrington, Dorothy, 207, 207 _n_
Carswell, Catherine, 207, 306
Carter, Mrs. Bonham, 201
Carter, Frederick, 233, 233 _n_, 234
Century of Hero-Worship, A, 286–7, 287 _n_
Cézanne, Paul, 432
Chambers, Jessie ("Miriam" of _Sons and Lovers_), 181, 181 _n_, 183, 321, 327–8, 333, 358–9, 388, 390
Channing, Miss, 200
Chaplin, Charles, 272
"Charioteer," 267, 283
Christ, 11, 16, 19, 24, 65–7, 129–30, 225, 233, 291, 334, 338, 343, 432
"Christening, A," 186
"Christs in the Tyrol," 390
Chuangtse, 356, 359
Clarke, Mrs. Ada (Lawrence), 232, 389, 390
Communism, 46, 131, 445, 453, 460
Community Farm, 346, 346 _n_
Concha, John, 262
Condition of Man, The, 292
Confucius, 11
Conquest of Mexico, The, 463
Contes de la Bécasse, 44
Cooper, James Fenimore, 122, 308
Corke, Helen, 324, 358, 358 _n_
Coronado's Children, 9

Cottam, Betty, 3 _n_, 254, 254 _n_, 261, 263, 266
Crosby, Caresse, 390, 390 _n_
Crosby, Harry, 442
Crotch, Mrs. Gordon, 335, 335 _n_
Cunard, Nancy, 374 _n_
Cyriax, Tony ("Antonia," "Anjuta"), 177, 179–80, 182

D. H. Lawrence: A Personal Record, 181 _n_
D. H. Lawrence and Susan His Cow, 276 _n_
D. H. Lawrence, Novelist, 401, 404
D. H. Lawrence, Prophet of the Midlands, 398
D. H. Lawrence's Princess, A Memory of Jessie Chambers, 358 _n_
Dasburg, Andrew, 232, 232 _n_
Dasburg, Ida, 232, 232 _n_
David, 225, 229, 267, 360
Davidson, Bob, 316, 316 _n_
Davidson, Mrs., 324
Davies, Rhys, 230 _n_
Davis, Herbert, 141 _n_
Dax, Alice (Mrs. Henry), 246 _n_
de Berry, Dr., 317
Degen, Mabel, 299, 309, 309 _n_
Delius, Frederick, 199 _n_, 306, 306 _n_
Diaz, Albert James, 77 _n_, 468 _n_, 471 _n_, 472 _n_
Dido, 24
Dinkins, Paul, 340
Dostoevsky, Fyodor, 198, 224
Douglas, Norman, 241, 241 _n_, 317, 317 _n_, 335, 345, 373 _n_, 374–5
Dowson, Ernest, 188
Dylan Thomas in America, 410

Eisenhower, Dwight D., 349, 351
Electra, 18
Eliot, George, 149, 152, 401, 412
Eliot, T. S., 327, 354, 356–7
Emmetaz, 262, 262 _n_
Ertel, Lola Alexandrovna, 177, 179
Evans, John, 334

Fadiman, Clifton, 268
Fantasia of the Unconscious, 327
Farbmans, the, 213, 234
Farbman, Mrs., 214
Farjeon, Miss, 197
Fascism, 131, 445–6, 453, 460
Faust, 56 *n*, 59
Fechin, Tinka (Mrs. Nicolai), 254, 254 *n*, 260, 265, 308
Fergusson, Erna, 254, 254 *n*, 257, 260–1, 270
Fisher, Irene, 261
Fitzgerald, F. Scott, 12
Flowers of the Forest, The, 401
Forbes, Esther, 449 *n*
Ford, Henry, 437
Forestlovers, 149
Forster, E. M., 196, 196 *n*
"Fox, The," 215 *n*
Francis of Assisi, Saint, 461–2
Frederick the Great, 10
Frere, A. S., 256, 256 *n*, 317, 329, 346, 348, 355, 361, 369, 374 *n*, 375, 384, 387
Freud, Sigmund, 19, 89 *n*, 94, 388, 460
Frieda Lawrence Collection of D. H. Lawrence Manuscripts, The, 280 *n*, 311, 311 *n*

Gandhi, Mahatma, 12, 67
Garbo, Greta, 478
Garnett, Constance, 182, 184, 190
Garnett, David ("Bunny"), 168 *n*, 170–1, 173, 174 *n*, 175, 180, 183–4, 197, 237, 365, 365 *n*, 401
Garnett, Edward, 167 *n*
George V, 442
George, W. L., 191, 212
Gertler, Mark, 199, 199 *n*, 205–6, 207 *n*, 208, 210–13
Ghiselin, Brewster, 232, 232 *n*
Gilbert, Edward, 293 *n*
Gillett, Bobby (Mrs. Ted), 263, 263 *n*, 266
Glasco, Joe, 309, 309 *n*, 311, 413–14, 416–17
Goethe, 56 *n*, 59, 182
Golden Echo, The, 365, 365 *n*

"Goose Fair," 114 *n*, 243 *n*
Gorki, Maxim, 211
Götzsche, Arnold, 219 *n*, 220 *n*
Goyen, William, 309, 309 *n*, 311, 414, 416–17, 420–1
Grand Duke of Saxe-Weimar, 75
Grapes of Wrath, The, 440 *n*, 441
Greene, Graham, 335
Griffin, Mrs., 418
Grillo, R., 258, 258 *n*, 259, 261, 265
Gurdjieff, George Ivanovich, 430 *n*
Gusdorf, Gerson, 262, 262 *n*

Hamlin, Judge, 261
Hardy, Thomas, 308
Harris, Henrietta, 281, 281 *n*
Haskell, Muriel, 262, 262 *n*
Hausner, Eric Peter, 379, 379 *n*, 380, 407, 411, 418–19
Hawk, Bill, 275
Hawk, Harold, 261–2
Hawk, Rachel, 254, 262, 275, 419
Heseltine, Philip ("Peter Warlock"), 199, 199 *n*, 200
Higgins, Victor, 284, 284 *n*
Hilton, Enid (Mrs. Laurence Hilton), 240
Hitler, Adolf, 275–6, 279, 281, 373, 381, 437–8
Hobson, Harold, 174 *n*, 175–6, 179–80, 185
Hobson, J. A., 174 *n*
Hocking, William Henry, 367, 367 *n*, 388, 395
Hoffman, Frederick J., 355 *n*, 356
Hollywood, 477–9
Holt, Agnes, 327
Homer, 12, 449
Horgan, Paul, 254, 254 *n*, 267 *n*, 271
Hougland, Georgine, 298
Hougland, Willard, 280 *n*, 298, 307, 310, 315
Howe, Martha Elizabeth, 416 *n*, 418–20
Howland, John, 261, 263
Huckleberry Finn, 103

Hueffer, Ford Madox, 167 n, 389
Hughes, Christine, 224, 229, 250, 250 n, 253, 257, 268–9, 271, 273–4, 284, 309, 315, 322
Hugo, Victor, 154
Hunt, Robert ("Bob"), 250, 250 n, 267 n, 271, 274, 279, 283–4, 291, 300, 308, 318, 322, 326, 332, 409
Hunt, Violet, 388–90
Hutchins, Mrs., 255, 255 n
Hutchinses, the, 259, 263
Huxley, Aldous, 144 n, 288, 292, 304, 311, 329, 335 n, 370, 392 n; editing Lawrence's letters, 236–7, 240; article by, 257; at Taos party, 263; and "St. Mawr" MS., 264; critical of Virginia Woolf, 277; compliments Frieda's preface to *The First Lady Chatterley*, 289; protected by Frieda from inquiring writer, 292; eye trouble, 332; and his essay on Lawrence, 356, 359; his letters, 368; suffering from shingles, 369; his last book, 403, 409; remarried, 412; understanding of Lawrence, 447; *see also* Huxley, Aldous and Maria
Huxley, Maria, 269 n, 395, 396; Frieda's concern at not hearing from, 252; letter from, 256; no word from, 257; postcard from, 261; leaving Taos for a month, 263; and MS. of "St. Mawr," 264; stay at N.M. ranch, 287; operation, 326; death, 392–3; *see also* Huxley, Aldous and Maria
Huxley, Aldous and Maria: visit to Lawrences at Villa Mirenda, and Lawrence's comment, 226; Lawrence likes him, 233; to visit N.M. ranch, 267; in Hollywood, 270, 272, 279; planned visits, 281, 300; visit from, 324; neighbors in Hollywood, 326; Lawrences go to Los Angeles to be near them, 337, 339, 343; and hyp-

Huxley (*continued*)
notism, 348; Maria's death, 392–3; among those who listened to Lawrence, 459
Huxley, Julian, 229 n
Huxley, Juliette, 229 n

Ibsen, Henrik, 175
Ida (former nurse of Frieda's children), 346–7, 350, 383, 394, 398, 403
Iliad, 12, 25
Intelligent Heart, The, 73 n, 89 n, 113 n, 386, 386 n, 388–92, 405, 459–63
Iphigenie (Goethe), 182

Jaffe, Edgar, 41 n, 89 n, 158, 160 n, 185
Jaffe, Friedl (Frederick Jeffrey), 272, 467 n
Jaffe-Richthofen, Else, 41 n, 42 n, 62 n, 78–9, 79 n, 89 n, 141 n, 296 n, 373, 468 n; to visit in Heidelberg, 160; visit from Ravagli, 258, 317; visit from Harry T. Moore, 324, 330; visit in New Mexico, 330–1, 331 n; and MS. of *Sons and Lovers*, 335; gift of Huxley book, 403
James, Rebecca, 124 n, 125, 307, 307 n, 418
Jane Eyre, 135
Jeffers, Robinson, 269 n
"Jimmy and the Desperate Woman," 223 n
John, Augustus, 323
Johnson, Willard ("Spud," "The Spoodle"), 124 n, 124–5, 219 n, 221, 232, 232 n, 265, 300–12, 332, 418
Jonathan Swift, A Critical Biography, 366
Journal of Katherine Mansfield, The, 387
Journey with Genius, 331

Kangaroo, 413
Kieve, 270
Kiker, Henry, 257, 257 n, 300, 300 n

King, Mrs. Emily (Lawrence), 388, 388 *n*
Kiowa Ranch, 22 *n*
Kipping, Frederick Stanley, 166 *n*
Kipping, Lily, 157-8, 166 *n*
Kluge, Friedrich, 141 *n*
Knopf, Alfred A., 328
Koteliansky, Samuel Solomonovich ("Kot"), 194 *n*, 204, 220 *n*, 223, 234, 355, 359, 387-8, 396, 410

"Ladybird, The," 209 *n*, 357
Lady Chatterley, The First, 289, 289 *n*, 290-1, 298, 449-56
Lady Chatterley's Lover, 226 *n*, 229 *n*, 232-3, 240 *n*, 248, 259, 263, 265, 277, 296, 310, 313, 317-18, 337, 342, 351, 379, 389, 397
Lambert, Cecily, 215 *n*
Lane, Sir Allen, 348
Laotse, 356, 359
Laotzu, 297
Laskoffs, the, 254-5, 259, 261
Lasky, 372
"Last Laugh, The," 223 *n*
Last of the Mohicans, The, 122
Last Poems, 362
Later D. H. Lawrence, The, 276 *n*
Latham, Helen, 409, 409 *n*
Lawrence, Ada (Mrs. Clarke), 232, 389-90
Lawrence and Brett; A Friendship, 222 *n*
Lawrence, D. H.: first days with Frieda, 161 *n*, 162, 169, 171-3, 175-82, 184-5, 187, 191 *n*; and World War I, 191-215 *passim*; postwar travels, 215-32 *passim*; last illness and death, 23-5, 233-43 *passim*; plan to steal his ashes, 250-1; death in retrospect, 249, 271, 286; and Alice Dax, 264-8; and Murry and Frieda, 305-6, 340-2, 352-5, 359-64, 366, 378, 387, 405-7; trouble with immigration, 274; view of prewar Germany, 278; on American literature, 282; question of loyalty to miners, 291; re-

Lawrence, D. H. (*continued*)
ligious reformer, 292; Frieda's defense of, 277, 294-5, 333-4; Penguin editions of his works, 317; comment on his death, 320; letters to Lady Ottoline Morrell, 396
Lawrence, Emily (Mrs. King), 388, 388 *n*
Lawrence, Frieda (Frieda Lawrence Ravagli), 141 *n*, 142 *n*, 161 *n*, 276 *n*, 293-4, 294 *n*, 374 *n*, 433 *n*, 435 *n*, 476; birth of second child, Elsa, 157-9; departure with Lawrence, 163-6; comments about her, by Lawrence, 180, 186, 227, 247; Constance in *Lady Chatterley's Lover* (?), 297; Murry on, 366; last illness and death, 415-21
Lawrence, Lydia, 294 *n*
Lawrence of Arabia, A Biographical Enquiry, 395
Lawrence Center, U. of Texas, 382
Lawrence Memorial, Eastwood, 395-6
Lawrence Memorial at ranch, 280 *n*, 307, 307 *n*, 400, 402, 402 *n*, 404
Leavis, F. R., 356, 401, 404
Life and Death of Little Joe, The, 289 *n*
Life and Works of D. H. Lawrence, The, 326 *n*
Lincoln, Abraham, 453
Lindbergh, Charles, 442
Lockwood, Ward, 266, 266 *n*
Long, Haniel, 257, 257 *n*, 270
Longfellow, Henry Wadsworth, 57
Lorenzo in Taos, 238, 240, 251
Lost Girl, The ("Miss Houghton"), 182
Love, Freedom and Society, 362 *n*, 410-11
Low, Barbara, 203, 203 *n*
Lowell, Amy, 213, 213 *n*
Luhan, Mabel, 22 *n*, 124 *n*; 219 *n*, 221, 223 *n*, 228, 232, 240, 251, 257, 309, 343, 344, 384, 419,

Luhan, Mabel (*continued*) 431; two Mabels, 125–6; boasts of lovers, 227; *Lorenzo in Taos*, 240, 243, 251; house in Albuquerque, 259; goes to N.Y., 261; Taos without her, 263, 267–8; compliments Frieda's son, 273; defends Ravagli, 274; distressed for Monty at start of war, 278; poisoned foot, 281; in Hollywood, 282; operation in N.Y., 288; and Mary Austin, 292; and Brett, 300, 313; describes Taos to Lawrence, 306; in Port Isabel, 316; in *None of That*, 328; gift of ranch to Frieda, 334; eye operation, 377; and Moore, 389, 391; not well, 397, 408; and evening of Frieda's stroke, 418

Luhan, Tony, 124 *n*, 126, 236, 251, 282, 316, 334

Luna, Antonio, 253

McClintic, Guthrie, 299

McCormicks, the, 281

Mackenzie, Compton, 216, 324

Mackie, Elmyra, 255, 255 *n*, 261–2, 264

Mackie, Ted, 255, 255 *n*, 262, 264

McKinley, 282

MacLeish, Archibald, 273

Magnus, Maurice, 373 *n*

Maltzahn, "Baron," 253, 253 *n*, 257–8, 261–2, 265, 267–8

Mansfield, Katherine, 133 *n*, 300 *n*, 397; Frieda defends her, 195–6; her return, 197; her defense of Lawrence at the Café Royal, 203, 210; relations between the Murrys and the Lawrences, 204–6, 378; Gudrun in *Women in Love*, 324; friendship, 341–2, 394; anecdotes, 358, 378; Lawrence on her resemblance to Dickens, 384; *Journal*, 387; letters to Lady Ottoline Morrell, 396; Frieda's essay on, 425–6; and A. R. Orage, 430

Marbahr, Karl von, 4 *n*, 20 *n*, 52 *n*, 62 *n*, 296 *n*, 348

Marconi, 432

Marie Antoinette, 478

Marsh, Edward, 189, 189 *n*, 272, 308, 357

Marx, Karl, 242

Matson, Marcella, 5 *n*, 259

Maugham, Somerset, 356

Maupassant, Guy de, 44

Medley, C. D., 243 *n*, 399

"Meeting on the Mountains," 455

Mendel, 206–7

Merrild, Knud, 219 *n*, 256, 256 *n*, 257, 281, 314, 314 *n*

Merrivale, Lord, 113 *n*

Meynells, the, 197

Michelangelo, 475

Middleton, Richard, 188 *n*

Miller, Henry, 477 *n*

Mirabar, Tony, 124

Mirendi, 326, 332, 336, 409

Mr. Noon, 330

Mohr, Max, 233, 233 *n*

Monk, Violet, 215 *n*

Montaigne, 291, 351, 365

Montoya, Arturo, 372, 376

Montoya, Mrs., 377

Moore, Harry T., 4 *n*, 42 *n*, 73 *n*, 89 *n*, 113 *n*, 320 *n*, 355 *n*, 359, 386, 386 *n*, 388–92, 405, 459–63

Morland, Andrew, 234, 234 *n*

Morrell, Julian (Mrs. Vinogradoff), 396

Morrell, Lady Ottoline, 186 *n*, 194, 196–7, 201, 201 *n*, 210, 226, 390, 396, 428

Morris, William, 242

Mumford, Lewis, 291–2

Murry, John Middleton ("Jack"), 113 *n*, 174 *n*, 199, 203, 220 *n*, 223 *n*, 241 *n*, 242, 243 *n*, 293–4, 300–1, 338, 348, 362 *n*, 366 *n*, 377 *n*; visits Lawrences, 195, 200; the Murrys as neighbors, 201; jealousy, 204; and Katherine Mansfield, 205; against Frieda, 206; and Lawrence, 208; and *Son of Woman*, 245; misunderstood

Murry, John (*continued*)
Lawrence, 295; witness at wedding, 317; triangle with Frieda and Lawrence, 301–5, 339–41, 346–7, 352–4, 358–67, 371, 377–80, 383, 387, 394–5, 400, 403–6, 409–11; friendship, 342, 343; changed, 344; news of Koteliansky, 388
Murry, Mrs. Mary Gamble, 301 *n*, 301, 305, 340–1, 346, 352, 354, 363, 365, 371, 378–9, 381, 387, 404, 412
Mussolini, Benito, 227, 275, 277

Napoleon, 24, 33, 58
Nazism, 448
Nehls, Edward, 356, 373, 373 *n*, 398, 457, 457 *n*
Nichols, Dudley, 263, 269 *n*, 279, 300, 392
Nichols, Esta (Mrs. Dudley), 255, 255 *n*, 269 *n*, 270, 292, 300, 393
Nicoll, Maurice, 430 *n*
Nietzsche, 87, 152, 181, 198, 300
"None of That," 328
Not I But the Wind, 5 *n*, 89 *n*, 246 *n*, 252, 320 *n*, 344 *n*, 430 *n*
Nutall, Mrs. 277, 356–7, 446

Orage, Alfred Richard, 430–2, 430 *n*
Orioli, Giuseppe ("Pino"), 241, 241 *n*, 373 *n*, 374
Ortega, Joaquin, 314, 336, 336 *n*
Otis, Frances, 434
Otis, Raymond, 257, 257 *n*, 443 *n*, 433–6
Oxford Songbook, The, 462

Pansies, 232
Payne, Tessie, 265
Peace News, 302
Pearce, Helen, 289, 314, 330–1
Pearce, Thomas Matthews, 280 *n*, 312–13, 440 *n*
Perkins, Frances, 273–4
Persons and Places, 298
Peter Simple, 207–8
Pierce, General, 350, 407, 409

Pinker, James Brand, 210, 210 *n*
Pinorman, 241 *n*, 373
Pinto, Vivian de Sola, 398, 398 *n*, 404
Plato, 87
Plumed Serpent, The, 219 *n*, 224 *n*, 225 *n*, 228, 272, 352
Plutarch, 291, 359
Pollinger, Lawrence, 234 *n*, 351, 368, 398; agent handling all Lawrence's business, 234; MS. of second *Lady Chatterley*, 310; recommendation of, and news from, 315, 317–18, 327–8, 330, 335, 337; visit with, 345–6, 348; and Lawrence's letters to Koteliansky, 355, 360; and Frieda's letter to *The Times*, 367; Frieda's gift to, 391; trustee of estate, 400
Poor Relations, 216
Popejoy, Tom, 314, 314 *n*
Possessed, The, 198
Pound, Ezra, 186
Powell, Lawrence Clark, 253 *n*
Prescott, 463
Prince of Wales, 442
Prisoner of Chillon, The, 471
"Prussian Officer, The," 357, 463
Psalm 121, 421

Radford, Dollie (Mrs. Ernest), 205, 210, 212
Rainbow, The, 199 *n*, 200–1, 324, 327, 357, 362, 404, 412
Rananim, 196, 196 *n*
Ravagli, Angelo ("Angelino," "Angie"), 3 *n*, 5 *n*, 22–3 *n*, 113 *n*, 122 *n*, 244 *n*, 251 *n*, 253 *n*, 267, 269 *n*, 299, 309, 313, 326, 329, 368, 391, 397, 433 n, 435 *n*; Frieda's wish to bring him to America, 243; and N.M. ranch, 245; pottery, 270–1, 347, 349, 356; charge of immorality, 274, 275; difficulties in World War II, 276, 278, 283–4, 291–2; paintings, 282; Huxley asks help, 288; good friend and helper, 304; loss of money at fair, 319; Frieda's marriage to, 324–5,

Ravagli, Angelo (*continued*) 340; praise of, 372, 376, 382; visit in Buenos Aires, 384, 392, 394–5; Frieda's will and community-property law, 399–400, 402; death of father, 407; income tax, 408–9; in Europe, 411; return, 413–14; Frieda's last illness and death, 415 *n*, 415–17, 419–21

Ravagli, Federico, 22 *n*, 251–2 *n*, 256, 264

Ravagli, Giovacchino, 56 *n*, 70 *n*

Ravagli, Luisa (Mrs. Ferruccio Castori), 56 *n*, 70 *n*

Ravagli, Magda-Micaela, 22 *n*, 251–2 *n*, 256

Ravagli, Stefano, 22 *n*, 251–2 *n*, 256

Ravagli, Yna-Serafina Astingo, 22 *n*, 251–2 *n*

"Red Earth," 239

Red Knight, The, 265

Rees, Sir Richard, 240 *n*, 241 *n*

Religion and the Rise of Capitalism, 372

Rhodes, Eric, 253

Richthofen, Anna Marquier von ("Alti"), 147, 323, 467

Richthofen, Else von, *see* Jaffe-Richthofen, Else

Richthofen, Emil von, 41 *n*

Richthofen, Friedrich von, 42 *n*, 381, 381 *n*

Richthofen, Johanna von ("Nusch"; Frau Max Schreibershofer; Frau Emil Krug), 41 *n*, 89 *n*, 316 *n*, 382; skirt for, 144; engaged, 146; compliment from, 152; Frieda hears little from, 154; is changed, 155; letter from, 158; visit in Taos, 311, 316, 318; Gudrun in *Women in Love*, 324; financial help for, 377; birthday, 397; provision in will, 402

Richthofen, Kurt von, 62 *n*

Richthofen, Oswald von, 41 *n*, 463

Riggs, Lynn, 309, 309 *n*

Roberts, Warren, 383, 383 *n*

Robinson Crusoe, 441

"Rocking-Horse Winner, The," 310

Rogers, Millicent, 316, 316 *n*, 332, 403

Rothschild, Baron Philippe, 318, 342

Rouge et le Noir, Le, 87

Rousseau, Jean Jacques, 17

Ruell, Mrs., 321

Ruffina, 265, 265 *n*

Russell, Bertrand, 191 *n*, 192–4, 196, 213, 348, 390, 447, 447 *n*, 463

St. Mawr, 264

Santayana, George, 298

Savage, Henry, 188 *n*

Savonarola, 206

Schiller, 83, 151

Schorer, Mark, 356, 369

Schreibershofer, Max, 156

Schroer, Professor, 141 *n*

Seaman, Edward ("Teddy"), 276, 278–9

Seaman, Mrs. Edward, *see* Weekley, Elsa

Secrest, Mr., 310

Seldes, George, 240

Selected Poems by Witter Bynner, 267

Seltzer, Thomas, 220 *n*

Shakespeare, William, 12, 409

Shaw, George Bernard, 428–9

"Sick Collier, The," 186

Signature of the Sun, 331

Simms, Mrs. Albert (Ruth Hanna McCormick), 257, 257 *n*, 258

"Singing of Swans," 283

Sitwells, the, 318, 398

Smollett, Tobias, 192

Socrates, 87

Son of Woman, 245

"Song of a Man Who Has Come Through," 421 *n*

"Song of a Man Who Is Loved," 295

Sons and Lovers, 71, 167 *n*, 168 *n*, 183, 246 *n*, 259, 328, 330, 385; "Paul Morel," 170–2; Frieda's lack of belief in, 190;

Sons and Lovers (*continued*)
MS. of, 261; MS. to Mabel
Luhan, 335; movie rights, 383;
film, 397
Spectri (Ibsen), 175
Spender, Stephen, 314, 317, 355,
360
Stalin, Joseph, 349
Steinbeck, John, 441
Stendhal, 86
Stevenson, Ted, 257
Stieglitz, Alfred, 113 *n*
Stokowsky, Leopold, 414
Strachey, Lytton, 447
Stravinskys, the, 345
*Studies in Classic American Lit-
erature*, 213 *n*
Sumner, John, 290
Swayne, Ruth, 254, 254 *n*, 256,
273, 391, 418
Swift, Jonathan, 355

Taft, Robert A., 319
Tawney, B. H., 372
Tedlock, Agnes, 299, 313
Tedlock, E. W. Jr., 280 *n*, 292,
298 *n*, 313 *n*, 314 *n*, 330, 331 *n*
Thackeray, William Makepeace,
152
They That Walk in Darkness,
153
"Thimble, The," 209
Tindall, William York, 276 *n*,
321, 327, 329, 356, 445–6
Traven's Deathship, 57
Tree Grows in Brooklyn, A, 43
Trespasser, The, 167 *n*
Trilling, Diana, 369
Trinidad, 265, 265 *n*
Turner, Reginald, 234, 234 *n*
Twain, Mark, 268, 384

Undset, Sigrid, 356–7

Vaillant, Dr., 277
Vanderbilts, The (Joe and Ollie),
283, 283 *n*, 284
Venus in the Kitchen, 335
"Voltaire Be with You," 284

Waters, Frank, 281
Weber, Mariana, 146, 372
Weber, Max, 41 *n*, 372

Weekley, Barbara (Mrs. Stuart
Barr), 160–1, 161 *n*, 216 *n*;
letter from, 216; schoolgirl,
112; visits Lawrence and
Frieda, 224, 227, 229–31, 240;
last visit, 411, 416; Frieda's
concern for, 236, 251, 325,
345, 350, 368, 376, 385; defense of Frieda, 233; sketch of
DHL, 400; inheritance from
father, 403
Weekley, Elsa (Mrs. Edward
Seaman), 161 *n*; birth of, 157;
schoolgirl, 112; Frieda's concern for, 226, 230, 276, 278–9,
345, 350, 385, 414; Easter
with father, 217; father's illness and death, 369, 376; inheritance from father, 403
Weekley, Ernest, 4 *n*, 77 *n*, 78 *n*,
79 *n*, 141 *n*, 142 *n*, 474 *n*; Frieda's marriage to, 144–9, 151,
153–6, 160; reaction to her departure with D. H. Lawrence,
161–7; trouble over children,
169, 172–3, 176, 178–9, 181,
190; Frieda's later attitude towards, 321, 350–1; illness and
death, 369, 375–6, 378; Lawrence's reaction to, 455
Weekley, Geoffrey, 275
Weekley, Ian, 275, 351, 376,
383, 385, 397, 400, 417
Weekley, Julia, 350, 350 *n*, 385
Weekley, Maude, 162, 164, 164 *n*
Weekley, Montague ("Monty"),
birth and first birthday, 147–
8; development, and Frieda's
love for, 149–51, 153–8, 160,
164; after Frieda's departure,
111–12, 167, 183, 217–18;
reconciliation, 225; concern
for, 263, 279, 301, 304, 317;
thoughts on his problem, 321;
death of his father, 376, 378;
visit to Else Jaffe, 397, 402
Weekley, Vera (Mrs. Montague),
272, 276, 278, 325, 345–6,
350, 385, 400, 417
Wells, Dan, 257, 257 *n*
Wells, H. G., 306
West, Anthony, 357

White Peacock, The, 188 *n*

Wicroff, Mr., 111

"Widowing of Mrs. Holroyd, The," 428

Wilhelm, Kaiser, 73–4

Williams, Tennessee, 300

"Wintry Peacock," 114 *n*, 243 *n*

Women in Love ("The Sisters"), 183, 201 *n*, 203 *n*, 207 *n*, 210, 223, 327, 343, 348, 390, 445

Woolf, Virginia, 277

Yorke, Dorothy (Arabella), 213, 213 *n*

You Touched Me, 300

Zangwill, Israel, 153

Zarathustra, 152

Zeitlin, Jake, 253, 253 *n*, 256, 261, 264

Zimmerman, James, 307, 307 *n*

A Note on the Type

THE TEXT of this book is set in *Monticello*, a Linotype revival of the original Binny & Ronaldson Roman No. 1, cut by Archibald Binny and cast in 1796 by that Philadelphia type foundry. The face was named Monticello in honor of its use in the monumental fifty-volume *Papers of Thomas Jefferson*, published by Princeton University Press. Monticello is a transitional type design, embodying certain features of Bulmer and Baskerville, but it is a distinguished face in its own right.

Typography and binding design by
GEORGE SALTER